Merry Christmas John "O"

Love

Mom and Dad

19/2002

*f*P

OTHER BOOKS BY GEORGE F. WILL

WITH A HAPPY EYE BUT...

———— ✦ ————

America and the World
1997–2002

GEORGE F. WILL

THE FREE PRESS

NEW YORK · LONDON · TORONTO · SYDNEY · SINGAPORE

*f*P

THE FREE PRESS
A Division of Simon & Schuster, Inc.
1230 Avenue of the Americas
New York, NY 10020

THE FREE PRESS and colophon are trademarks
of Simon & Schuster, Inc.

For information regarding special discounts for bulk
purchases, please contact Simon & Schuster Special Sales at
1-800-456-6798 or business@simonandschuster.com.

Designed by Dana Sloan

Manufactured in the United States of America
10   9   8   7   6   5   4   3   2   1

Library of Congress Cataloging-in-Publication Data
Will, George F.
    With a happy eye but—America and the world,
    1997–2002 / George F. Will.
        p. cm.
    Includes bibliographical references and index.
    1. United States—Politics and government—1993–2001.
    2. United States—Politics and government—2001–3.
    3. United States—Foreign relations 2001–5. 4. World
    politics—1989– I. Title

    E885.W55 2002
    973.929—dc21
                                        2002072206
ISBN 0-684-83821-4

To Katherine Will Jorgenson
With love and admiration from her brother

Credits and Permissions

Acknowledgments

The process of preparing this, the seventh, collection of my columns and other writings forcefully reminded me that life is unfair, and that I greatly benefit from that fact. There cannot be a writer anywhere who has better—more professional and agreeable—assistants than I have in Mary Longnecker and Seth Meehan. Georgetown University continues to be an unfailingly reliable source of smart and diligent young helpers, such as Tom Johnson, Heath Carter and Matt Sullivan.

Bill Rosen of The Free Press is an editor, so he is supposed to be disagreeable to a writer. He is not. He is instructive, and a friend. Amazing. Alan Shearer, Jim Hill and the others at the Washington Post Writers Group—go ahead, try to sneak a factual mistake past Chris White—are gifted at making me seem more gifted than I am. So are *Newsweek*'s editor Mark Whittaker and She Who Must Be Obeyed—Pam Hamer.

It is not fair that I have constant access to so much of the world's finite supply of talent. But life is unfair.

Contents

THE WORLD 67

JUSTICE AND INJUSTICE 115

WITH A
HAPPY EYE
BUT...

Introduction

We can only
do what it seems to us we were made for, look at
this world with a happy eye
but from a sober perspective.

—W. H. AUDEN,
"The Horatians"

What? Look at the world with a happy eye, even after 9/11/01? Yes, indeed, *especially* after the terrorism that abruptly rang down the curtain on a remarkably carefree, and remarkably uncharacteristic, era in modern American history.

Who are the "we" who supposedly are "made for" a happy stance toward life? Auden intended the pronoun's antecedent to be humanity generally. And maybe humanity is so made. That depends on a philosophical, even theological judgment as to whether all of humanity has a common Maker, as well as an opinion on His disposition. Be that as it may, for the portion of humanity privileged to be Americans, looking upon the world cheerfully is simply doing what comes naturally. And the reasons why Americans should be of good cheer were underscored by the nature of our nation's enemies, who announced themselves at 8:48 A.M. Eastern Daylight Savings Time on the eleventh day of the second September of this millennium.

When the first hijacked aircraft, traveling much faster than commercial aircraft are authorized to fly in that space, came screaming low over the Hudson River and into the South Tower of the World Trade Center, the country was paid a huge, if unwitting, compliment. To the perpetrators of this mass murder, the United States is a provocation. It is because it is, as the sixteenth president said, a nation dedicated to a proposition: that all men are created equal. And that proposition is a distillate of the rich cultural inheritance of Western civilization, with its due regard for individual autonomy and rights, and a society of duties and disciplines that incubate respect for rights and competence in the exercise of autonomy.

The scream of the incoming aircraft was a howl of negation. As such, it was remarkably sterile. The terrorists' critique of Western society lacked the analytic rigor of Marxism, and consequently it lacked the brio that Marxism briefly acquired—until events proved uncooperative—from its doctrine of historical inevitability. History was supposed to have an inner logic. The unfolding of that logic—the "march of events"—could be accelerated or retarded a bit by this or that political program, but the outcome was predetermined. The terrorism was neither logical nor deterministic but reflexive, a wild recoil from what America is. Terrorism does not articulate or advance an alternative vision of human community remotely capable of coping with the world of applied reason that the West has made, a world the vast majority of people desire once they have glimpsed its possibilities.

It is a sobering responsibility for America to be the clearest expression of this vision. However, it is safe to say that on 9/10/01 many Americans did not look upon their circumstances, or those of their nation, from a sober perspective. It is not even clear what counted as sobriety during the years covered by the columns and other materials in this collection.

In the last years of the last century, and through the first twenty months of this one, looking upon the world with a happy eye was easy for Americans. Indeed, their challenge was to avoid giddiness about their good fortune in living in such times. The nation was not merely at peace, it was feeling less threatened from abroad than at any time since the 1920s. And Americans were almost startled—somewhat as in the 1920s, come to think about it—by their own prodigies of wealth creation.

Certainly sobriety was utterly absent during the mass irrationality and exhibitionism in the week following the death of Princess Diana, an episode that historians will, I suspect, find deeply symptomatic of the temper of the times before the eruption of terrorism. Auden once wrote that

> *Our intellectual marines,*
> *Landing in little magazines,*
> *Capture a trend.*

Columnists try to be trend capturers, and this columnist wonders whether the Diana death hysteria tapped, among other things, a hitherto unsuspected hunger for a poetic dimension of life, a dimension sometimes scanted by that of the West's commercial civilization.

Money, according to Ralph Waldo Emerson, a very American thinker, represents the prose of life. In the years covered in this collection Americans were preoccupied even more than usual with how money is made—and lost. If one were to pick a Person of the Era, politically speaking, he would be the unelected head of the Federal Reserve Board, an institution the arcane workings of which few Americans understand. Think about that. These pretty much happy years have been presided over by a man, Alan Greenspan, who, even when he is mildly happy—which is about as happy as central bankers ever are—has a demeanor about as cheerful as Woodrow Wilson's must have been when he learned of the sinking of the *Lusitania*.

So the prose of life has been much with us. "Poets," noted a pretty good

one, G. K. Chesterton, "have been mysteriously silent on the subject of cheese."
He was, of course, being droll. That silence of the poets is not mysterious.
Cheese does not summon poetic thoughts. Still, money and other prosaic things
are the normal preoccupations of journalists, as Chesterton, a *very* good one,
knew. And even when, as in the 1920s and again seven decades later, politics is
especially prosaic, that does not preclude a vigorous enjoyment of civic life.

In his book *The Good Citizen: A History of American Civic Life,* Michael
Schudson of the University of California, San Diego, notes that in 1922 the
Lincoln Memorial was dedicated. In 1924 the nation's two defining original
documents, the Constitution and the Declaration of Independence, which
had been kept in a State Department vault, were put on display in the Library
of Congress. In 1935 the Supreme Court, which held its first Washington
meetings in the basement of the Capitol and since 1860 had met in the old
Senate chamber, at last got its own home, the temple-like building across the
street from the Capitol. President Franklin Roosevelt laid the foundation stone
of the Jefferson Memorial in 1939.

Schudson believes that these attractions of patriotic pilgrimages are less
monuments than shrines. They serve America's civil religion. As is the quin-
tessentially American extravaganza that the sculptor Gutzon Borglum, with
the blessing of President Calvin Coolidge, began carving on Mount Rushmore in 1927, at about the time Henry Ford built Greenfield Village and John
D. Rockefeller, Jr., launched the restoration of Colonial Williamsburg. Notice
the melding, beginning in the 1920s, of two complimentary streams of American reverence—for political heroes, and for the quotidian of small-town life.

In the years leading up to 9/11/01, politics—presidential sex, presidential
DNA on a little blue dress, presidential impeachment, a presidential election
with dueling supreme courts (those of the United States and Florida)—became, to say no more, peculiar. When Joseph Lieberman became the first Jew
nominated to run on a national ticket, he exclaimed, "Only in America!" Oh?
This was 132 years after Britain's Conservative Party, not then a deep lagoon
of advanced thinking, produced a Jewish prime minister and 44 years after
Catholic Dublin elected a Jewish mayor.

Until 9/11/01 it seemed that the only presidential election in the years
covered by this collection would be long remembered not for what it started
but for the way it ended—with an electoral train wreck. As the 1932 election
approached, President Herbert Hoover, who was about to be swept from office by a tidal wave of discontent, received a telegram from an angry voter:
"Vote for Roosevelt and make it unanimous." Boring unanimity was not
America's problem in November 2000. Ten months later Americans were
fused into incandescent unity by the heat of burning jet fuel.

Of course, the fact that a presidential election evenly divided the nation
did not mean that the nation was bitterly divided. Fifty years ago, scorching ar-

guments boiled around names such as Julius and Ethel Rosenberg, Alger Hiss, Joseph McCarthy, and Douglas MacArthur. Thirty-five years ago, American politics was roiled by disputes about whether African-Americans should have the *right* to enter restaurants and voting booths. Thirty years ago domestic tranquillity was a casualty as the nation fought a ground war of attrition on the mainland of Asia with a conscript army, for ill-defined purposes. In 1981 a president who considered the Soviet Union "the focus of evil in the modern world" replaced a president whose secretary of state (Cyrus Vance) thought that Jimmy Carter and Leonid Brezhnev "have similar dreams and aspirations about the most fundamental issues."

Those were years of serious political differences. But at the dawn of the first decade of the twenty-first century the great political question seemed to be, When will there again be a great political question? Then terrorism gave us a surfeit of enormously consequential questions, ranging from where and how to wage war to how much liberty must be curtailed in the interest of security. It was exhilarating. And it reminded Americans, who were an avid audience for Steven Spielberg's *Saving Private Ryan* and *Band of Brothers,* and who made Tom Brokaw's celebration of *The Greatest Generation* a best-seller, why people can be nostalgic for war.

In January 1946 Charles de Gaulle, fresh from his heroic role as France's liberator and disdaining the banal normality of peacetime administration, abruptly resigned as president of France's provisional government. Having fought for *la grandeur de la France,* he told a colleague, with characteristic hauteur, that he did not deign to "worry about the macaroni ration." Well. A recently published list of prudential maxims (e.g., "Never give your wife an anniversary present that needs to be plugged in"; "Never order barbecue in a place where all the chairs match"; "Never buy a Rolex from someone out of breath") should have included this one: Never wish for an era of scintillating politics.

This isn't—yet—one. But that's nothing new: William Henry Harrison's 1840 presidential campaign caught the public's attention by distributing pocket handkerchiefs printed with a picture of his purported birthplace, a log cabin. Actually, he was born on Virginia's splendid Berkeley Plantation. So when Americans lament the high nonsense quotient in contemporary campaigns, they should remember the words of Dwight Eisenhower: "Things are more like they are now than they ever were before."

Yet different, too. Peacetime politics has become less central to the nation's life than at any time since, yes, those 1920s. But Chris DeMuth, head of the American Enterprise Institute, Washington's most intellectually high-powered think tank, believes that the marginalization of politics can be said to have begun eighteen decades ago.

In 1820 John Dalton, a British chemist and physicist, published a paper,

"Memoir on Oil, and the Gases Obtained from it by Heat," which presaged the basic science that would result in the modern oil and petrochemical industries. During a lecture in April 1820, Hans Christian Ørsted, a Danish physicist, noticed that a magnetic needle aligns itself perpendicularly with a wire carrying an electric current. Within a week of learning of this evidence of a relationship between electricity and magnetism, André-Marie Ampère, a French physicist, prepared the first of his papers on the theory of electromagnetism, from which came (via Michael Faraday) machines that generated electrical energy from physical motion, and motion from electrical energy.

"The events of 1820," says DeMuth, "mark the beginning of the modern age—the age when science and industry have displaced politics as the driving force of social and economic development." In America today, and even in many European nations, where giving politics precedence over economics is considered the cardinal virtue, politics is an increasingly secondary phenomenon. This is so because political argument is primarily confined to the question of what portion of the wealth created by industrial applications of science should be distributed through government, and to whom.

The authors of 9/11/01 are having none of that. They would radically revise, and enlarge the stakes of, political argument. They would enlarge politics by melding it with religion as a regulator of all of life. What they are up against, recoiling from, is exemplified by two of the most consequential facts of our era, calculated by Dale W. Jorgenson of Harvard's John F. Kennedy School of Government: the first logic chip, created in 1971, had 2,300 transistors, whereas the Pentium 4, released late in 2000, had 42 million. And between 1974 and 1996 the prices of memory chips decreased by a factor of 27,270. Terrorism is a futile damper of this inferno of social change.

It is a remarkably prosperous inferno. In an age when two of every three poor American families have microwave ovens and three out of four have VCRs attached to their color televisions, the pervasiveness of affluence is changing the political categories by which we classify citizens. James Twitchell of the University of Florida, author of *Lead Us into Temptation: The Triumph of American Materialism*, says, "One of the reasons terms like Yuppie, Baby Boomer, and Gen-X have elbowed aside such older designations as 'upper middle class' is that we no longer understand social class as well as we do lifestyle, or what marketing firms call 'consumption communities.'"

And class matters less and less. In 1875 the British elite lived on average seventeen years longer than the population as a whole. Today that difference is one year.

On a number of other domestic matters the news has been good. And certain explanations of the good news have become apparent to everyone except those who report the news. (An actual *New York Times* headline: "Crime Keeps on Falling, but Prisons Keep on Filling." *But?*) Journalists deal in news and believe that the phrase "bad news" is redundant and "good news" oxy-moronic. They go through life looking upon the world much as Job did after he lost his camels and acquired boils. Americans have never been like that, and were never less so than in the years immediately prior to 9/11/01. In those years per capita beef consumption hit a per capita high, the number of weight-loss centers declined sharply, and the magazine *Eating Well* ceased publication. Americans were not tempted by asceticism. They were looking at this world less with a happy eye than with a glazed look of surfeit.

Americans are legatees of the Enlightenment faith in mankind's ability to bend the recalcitrant world to reason. Their experience doing just that has confirmed their native optimism. Before breaking fascism and then commu-nism, they put a bridle and snaffle on nature itself. Did they have a problem getting across, and getting the most out of, the Great American Desert (as maps used to identify the expanse west of Missouri)? They did, so they built railroads across it and irrigated it. Did they have a problem controlling floods and producing power? They did, so they did things such as build the Hoover Dam, which required first moving the Colorado River. San Francisco's Golden Gate? Piece of cake. Americans threw a bridge across it.

For Americans, the word "problem" in politics, as in mathematics, implies a solution waiting to be found. In this, Americans are looking on the world with too happy an eye. Society, and hence politics, is not as tidy as mathemat-ics. Lots of problems do not have solutions, at least not neat and complete and permanent ones. And some solutions create their own problems, world with-out end, amen.

So what next? Remember the rule: There are knowns, unknowns, and unknown unknowns. Collections such as this necessarily have a retrospective cast. Granted, the recent past is inevitably pregnant with the future, even an unimagined future, as was 9/10/01. This much-chastened columnist knows he does not know what the future will look like. One Catholic priest, asked how one might come to understand the Church's teaching on Heaven and Hell, answered succinctly, "Die." If you want to know what comes next, live.

Live with due sobriety. But live while looking around with a happy eye. Americans did so after 4/15/61 (the firing on Fort Sumter). Eighty years later they did so after 12/7/41. And they have resumed doing so sixty years later, soon after 9/11/01.

February 25, 2002

OVERTURE

To the "Gallant Girls" (Just Kidding) of National Cathedral School

Headmistress, reverend clergy, faculty, distinguished guests, proud parents, and, especially, members of the Class of 1999:

Eighteen years ago I used my column briefly to alert the world to the birth of a daughter. With the want of foresight for which columnists are rightly ridiculed, I, whose previous parenting experience had been exhausting, which is to say had been with boys, made a prophecy about raising this girl.

I said, "For a dozen or so years Victoria, I assume, will be quiet and delicate and inclined to sit for hours reading Louisa May Alcott and making doilies. She will be dressed in blue velvet dresses decorated with small yellow flowers. . . . But as soon as she takes an interest in popular music or popular boys she will be sent to school at a thick-walled convent on a high mountain overlooking an inaccessible valley in a remote region of Portugal."

Well, we live and learn. In fact, the happiest adults live *to* learn—live *for* the delight of learning's astonishments, with which the world is prodigal. My hope is that through learning you will cultivate your capacity for astonishment. That is the gist of my remarks today, which I can distill into three rules:

First, go through life with, as it were, a crick in your necks from looking backwards, at the path by which we come to the present. That path is littered with astonishments, and learning about them is delightful.

The second rule is: Happiness is a talent, one that involves *never* being bored. Boredom is a sin because, as a character in a Saul Bellow novel says, "Boredom is the shriek of unused capacities."

The third rule is: The process of learning is so rich in the delights of astonishment, you should get right at it, this summer, this afternoon. Do not waste a minute. After all, you are going to have to spend six hundred hours brushing your teeth.

Now, my remarks today constitute a rare occasion, one on which a parent can slip a word in edgewise in the presence of our remarkably, sometimes alarmingly, opinionated and articulate daughters, among whom reticence is not cultivated. To know our daughters, and to recall that just a generation ago young women were said to need something called "assertiveness training," is to appreciate the astonishing velocity of social change in our time.

You, Class of 1999, are of the first generation that can take for granted opportunities that previous generations of women had to take by storm. Consider this:

In 1955, Adlai Stevenson was the epitome of progressive thinking. He had been the Democrats' presidential nominee in 1952 and would be again in 1956. In 1955 he kept in rhetorical trim by giving the commencement address at Smith College.

Addressing those he called the "gallant girls" of Smith, Stevenson said they had "a unique opportunity to influence us, man and boy." He urged them "to restore valid, meaningful purpose to life in your home" and to address the "crisis in the humble role of housewife." He said the gallant girls could do all this "in the living room with a baby in your lap, or in the kitchen with a can opener in your hands." And, he said, "Maybe you can even practice your saving arts on that unsuspecting man while he's watching television!"

Well.

If a speaker spoke like that to today's young women, they would use a can opener to open his skull to see what was in it where a brain was supposed to be. Nowadays, only the reckless refer to women graduates as "girls."

Last November I wrote a column about young women, including some of you, playing field hockey in Florida. The New York *Post* gave the column a cheeky headline: "Chicks with Sticks."

"Chicks"? Gracious. Such retrograde language.

Evolving linguistic standards are somewhat interesting, but really are not worth dwelling on, considering how rich the human story is in more interesting changes. Let me mention a random few.

———

SOME SCHOLARS suspect that Henry VIII may have died partly from scurvy, produced by a deficiency of vitamin C, the result of a scarcity of citrus fruit. Which means that twentieth-century commoners live far better than sixteenth-century royalty. Astonishing, when you think about it.

Speaking of royalty, congratulations to many of you: you *are* royalty. Sort of. Granted, you are royalty at some remove, but still, many of us here today almost certainly are descended from Charlemagne.

Really. Do the math.

Assuming there are 3.5 generations to a century, there have been about forty-two generations since Charlemagne's birth. If we were to assume there was no intermarriage among each of your ancestors, your ancestors alive twelve centuries ago would have numbered two to the 42nd power, or more than 4 trillion. But there were at most 80 million people in Charlemagne's Europe. So there had to have been lots of intermarrying. So many of those who lived in Charlemagne's Europe, including Charlemagne, must be related to many of us here today. Astonishing.

In 1610 Galileo discovered moons around Jupiter. From that discovery he correctly inferred something astonishing—and damaging to mankind's self-esteem: we are not the center of the universe.

Then, in 1755, the Lisbon earthquake astonished people into doubting the divinely ordained orderliness of the universe.

On the astonishingly prolific day of February 12, 1809, the day Lincoln was born, so was Charles Darwin. Darwin came to argue that the human race is continuous with the primordial slime from which it emerged.

That was said to make it difficult to believe in God—until thoughtful people asked this: What is *more* difficult to believe, that there is something providential in the human story, or that primordial slime evolved randomly into the author of Hamlet?

Speaking of Shakespeare, there is astonishing news: we all use the English language the way he did. Sort of. For most people, most of the time, about 50 percent of their talk involves the recycling of about 100 words. And although Shakespeare's plays contain 29,066 different words, 40 words make up 40 percent of the texts of his plays.

James Joyce's *Ulysses* contains almost the same number of different words: 28,899. But just 135 words make up half the text.

Ah, but what Shakespeare and Joyce produced when they mixed in the other words is magical, astonishing.

Even mundane matters are pregnant with surprising delights. Do you know the role played by the bicycle in the emancipation of women? At the end of the last century, when the bicycle became a symbol of modernity, bike riding became one reason why trousers became acceptable for women—and corsets became dispensable. Astonishing, is it not, how even the history of everyday life is full of startling caroms of cause and effect?

Now, you may think that all the really cosmic astonishments are behind us. If you think that, you must not have noticed the news eleven days ago: astronomers using the Hubble space telescope have determined that the universe is expanding at a rate that dates the beginning of everything—the Big Bang—at 12 billion years ago.

Into what is the universe expanding? What caused the Big Bang? Big questions; answers to come. It seems there are a few astonishments yet in store for us.

Meanwhile, there are comparable astonishments wherever there is a child, or an adult blessed with a childlike capacity for wonder.

G. K. Chesterton once said: A seven-year-old is astonished when told that Tommy opened the door and found a dragon. But a three-year-old is astonished when told that Tommy opened the door.

The three-year-old is rightly astonished. Opening a door—the operation of the human hand; the operation of human volition—is itself astonishing.

So, Class of 1999, when you get to college, get to work on the myriad as-tonishments of learning. Time is scarce.

If, after all, you spend—and you should—even two minutes a day brush-ing your teeth, in the next 50 years you will spend 600 hours brushing. If you spend—and you should—15 minutes a day during baseball season reading box scores, over the next 50 years you will spend 2,187 hours reading them. That is the equivalent of 55 weeks—more than a year—of eight-hour workdays.

Now, a final thought for you, the gallant *women* of NCS.

We parents know that you often regard us, your parents, as faintly ridicu-lous. There was a medieval pope who, once a year, paraded through the streets of Rome wearing a ludicrous hat, in order to discourage excessive veneration of him. We parents do not need to do that. The excesses of the Class of 1999 do *not* include excessive veneration for parents. In your eyes, parents are al-ways, as it were, wearing ludicrous hats. But mind how you judge us: you are implicated in what we are.

It is a biological fact that adults produce children; it is a social, even spiri-tual fact that children produce adults: most of us do not become truly grown-up until we have helped children grow up. Thus do the generations form a braided cord.

Victoria Will, for one, has good reason to understand this.

Seven and a half years ago, when Victoria had just turned eleven, Mari and I told her we were going to have a baby. Victoria, calculating with the speed of a mainframe computer, *instantly* burst into tears and exclaimed, "Now you won't cry when I go away to college!"

Well.

The baby became David, now nearly seven, and his inclusion in the hu-man comedy has increased by one the large number of those here today who will feel desolation when Victoria and the rest of you go to college.

Three months from now, when you are outward bound, we who love you in a way that you cannot imagine, a way that you will not know until you experience the astonishments of parenthood—we who love you will have aching holes in our lives.

This is painful. It also is as it must be.

There is in life a lot of taking leave, a lot of letting go. But even though we, your parents, have had some practice at it, that does not make it easier.

So when you are off at college, learning the sort of things college students learn—from the cause of the War of Jenkins' Ear to the cure for a hangover—take time to write us letters.

I see puzzled looks. Of course: some of you may not know what letters *are*. Let me explain.

It is astonishing but true that once upon a time, long, long ago, before cell phones and e-mail and cyberspace chat rooms, primitive peoples who had an urge to communicate produced, by hand, artifacts—they were called "letters"—that recipients could actually hold in their hands, to keep and bind into bundles with red ribbons and cherish. The way we, your parents, have held and cherished you.

So when you are away, occasionally record your astonishments in letters. Letters will not substitute for your delightful presence. However, they will be a welcome token thereof.

But there I go again, sounding as dated as Adlai Stevenson did at the Smith College Commencement in 1955. I had better subside before completing my disgrace in the upward-rolled eyes of my daughter.

It has been good of you, Class of 1999, to let me slip these words in edgewise. Now, remember: Live with a crick in your neck from looking back in history; cultivate the immunity to boredom that learning confers; and brush your teeth at warp speed, so you can get on to the next astonishment.

Thank you.

June 6, 1999

Chicks with Sticks

WELLINGTON, FLORIDA—It is 7:15 A.M. and even the sun seems sluggish as it struggles to rise. However, the day already resounds with the sound of swarms of people living the strenuous life, a sound that suggests the shape of America's future.

Like the clackety-clack of hundreds of castanets, the sound reverberates from hard plastic balls hit hard by curved sticks. The sticks are where America soon will be—in the hands of field hockey players. These young women will use those sticks—actually, they will use attributes honed while wielding the sticks—to smash to smithereens whatever remains of the "glass ceiling" limiting the rise of women in the professions.

The annual field hockey festival drew 165 teams of 16 players, 127 of the teams composed of young women under age nineteen. So for four days this town had the world's highest concentration of ponytails and a maddeningly incessant use of the word "like." As in this ecstatic exclamation overheard in a vendor's tent: "Oh like wow here's a pair of like shorts from Ireland, which is like my favorite place!"

Young women outgrow that inexplicable, insufferable verbal tic, but they will forever have what field hockey gives: confidence, discipline, controlled aggression. Which are all they need to consolidate their supremacy.

High school games of twenty-five-minute halves are played by teams of eleven (wearing mouth and shin guards; this is not for shrinking violets) on fields 100 yards long and 60 yards wide. The object is to hit the ball into a net. The rules are not recondite, but in enforcement they are—perhaps this is what deep thinkers at serious quarterlies call a "gender difference"—inscrutable. For example, how do you determine—and why is it wrong—when "a player moves or interposes herself or her stick, keeping an opponent from attempting to play the ball"?

However, the rules are enforced by referees who brook no demurrals and hence receive none. Besides, young women—this *is* a gender difference—have a sense of honor and proportion, so they play on where young men would protest or pout.

In the 1972–73 school year, 3,770,621 boys and 817,073 girls participated in interscholastic sports. In 1996–97: boys, 3,706,225; girls, 2,472,043. Women now make up 37 percent of college athletes, and women's participation in intercollegiate sports is increasing much faster than men's. It is difficult to prove but as difficult to doubt a connection between those numbers and this fact: more than half the students in law and medical schools may soon be women.

Washington, which thinks it hung the moon and causes social as well as oceanic tides, believes it authored women's athletic progress—that Title IX (1972) did it. That rule, forbidding sex discrimination by federally assisted educational institutions, did indeed help ignite the explosive growth of women's sports opportunities (and the contraction of men's, as many schools have canceled some men's programs to produce numerical equality of participation). However, Title IX reflected as well as influenced the emancipation of women.

The book that got Western philosophy going is basically about education, and in *The Republic* Plato had much to say about athletics ("gymnastics") as a means of stimulating the spirited side of human nature while bringing it under the sway of reason in the form of rules. He was not altogether sound on the question of the equality of women, but he got the social utility of sports right.

Concerning which, the Duke of Wellington never said the battle of Waterloo was won on the playing fields of Eton, but something of the sort could be said about the advancing ascendancy of American women. It is being won on places like the twenty-two hockey fields recently laid out here on polo fields just west of Palm Beach.

Team sports are not quite (as many Pattonesque football coaches imagine) the moral equivalent of war. However, they are artfully contrived challenges that administer stress, demand both collective efforts and individual strivings for distinction, and reward grace under pressure. Add those social virtues to women's intrinsic superiority (a big topic; suffice it to say they have a higher ratio of philosophical inclinations to animal propensities), and men will live at the mercy of women's magnanimity.

After one game when Victoria Will, now 18, was 15, she clattered into the house like Achilles in cleats. To the question "How did the game go?" she replied jauntily, "We kicked butt." Such spiritedness, which presumably will undergo refinement, gives some older women the vapors. But where the vapors are concerned, Victoria's stick-wielding generation believes it is better to give than receive.

December 6, 1998

Marines, Rough and Polished

MARINE CORPS RECRUIT DEPOT, SAN DIEGO—The 9 P.M. darkness resounds with shouted cadences of freshly minted marines marching to meet family and friends at the end of the twelve-week basic training. Up Interstate 5, at Camp Pendleton, seasoned marines, many of whom passed through this depot, are getting gear together for possible flights to the Persian Gulf.

New marines may not yet understand what America's experienced servicemen and -women know: occasional crises are fleeting reminders to civilians of the reasons for having military services. The rest of the time, many Americans think of the services only when worrying about why they are so, well, *different*—so disconcertingly military.

It is said that the past is another country. Increasingly, America's military is, too, because the services—the marines especially—are rigorous inculcators of values and lingering echoes of a receding American past, before rigor went out of fashion.

There is indeed a widening gap between the civilian and military cultures. And as more and more military jobs become more technical, a culture gap is opening within the services, a gap between those whose jobs are just jobs and those who are warriors. In a survey of army personnel, 32 percent of men and 55 percent of women did not agree that the army's primary focus should be on war fighting.

There should be a gap between civilian and military cultures, especially in a democracy. That widening gap should be narrowed somewhat, but not by permeating the military with the civilian culture's values.

Nowadays much is said about the need to "close" the gap and "reconnect" those cultures. Former Navy Secretary John Dalton says, "As American society changes, the Naval service changes with it. That's not bad. That's the way it's supposed to be." Senator John McCain—no one has more standing to speak on the subject than this Annapolis graduate, aviator, and heroic Vietnam War POW—says, "It's a fundamental principle that armed services can truly serve a democracy only if they are a reflection of that society and are impacted by the same social trends."

To which one must respectfully respond: Not really.

Senior marines here, whose mission is to make marines, know that the phrase "volunteer military" is a misnomer. America has a *recruited* military. Recruiting one Marine often involves more than twelve arduous months of interviews with the prospect and his or her parents, and approximately five hundred telephone calls.

After which, and after intensive preinduction mental and physical preparation, about 14 percent of recruits will fail to make it to "the crucible." That is the arduous new eleventh week of basic training, when stress, fatigue, and hunger test the recruits' assimilation of the first ten weeks of Marine training in values as well as war fighting.

Drill instructors always have been wrathful Old Testament gods to recruits, but now they also are, in too many cases, essentially the first fathers in the recruits' lives. So, "reflect" society? Basic training must correct the consequences of contemporary society's defects. Basic training administers a crash course in honorable behavior—instruction that should be performed, throughout childhood and adolescence, by families, schools, and religious institutions.

Reflect society? Remember George Orwell's unminced words: "We sleep safely in our beds because rough men stand ready in the night to visit violence on those who would do us harm."

Rough, yes, but also polished, disciplined professionals, who became that by shedding, under the scalding rinse of basic training, much of what contemporary society inculcates: materialism, sullen resentment of hierarchy, the language of victimization spoken by grievance groups, the litigiousness of rights-based politics, and the celebration of "self-expression," however unworthy the self being expressed.

Some worriers about the gap between civilian and military cultures worry especially about this: that the young marines who are marching this night to meet their parents (who in some cases will not recognize the slimmed, hardened, and upright versions of the children they knew three months ago) have, regarding civilian society, a sense of moral superiority. However, instead of trying to disabuse the young marines of the pride they have earned, civilian society, if it thinks the gap between it and its military is too wide, might try moving toward the military.

John Hillen of the Council on Foreign Relations says that those who regret the gap between the military and civilian cultures should remember that civilian society senses nothing amiss in a magazine article headlined "The Ten Commandments: What They Mean Now." Make the military "reflect" society, and you may revive the army's accommodationist slogan of a few years ago: "The Army Wants to Join You!"

Good grief. Don't sleep too soundly.

November 22, 1998

A Summons to Gratitude

Popular culture can be a political barometer, and there is a storm warning for President Clinton in the public's response to the movie *Saving Private Ryan.* Viewers leave theaters shaken, sometimes in tears, with their patriotism enriched by a quickened sense of the pain that bought our contemporary pleasures. The movie is about bravery, sacrifice, and, above all, leadership. The warmth of the public's embrace of this shattering movie is a measure of the depth of the nation's yearning for honor as it tastes the bitter dregs of Clinton's presidency.

The movie's maker, Steven Spielberg, is famously enthusiastic about Clinton. Spielberg misunderstands either the message of his movie or the nature of his recent house guest.

The rush to designate *Private Ryan* as the greatest war movie is, in part, proof that hyperbole is today's lingua franca. Still, the movie's strong claim to high regard begins with the stunning verisimilitude of the opening twenty-five-minute depiction of the fighting on Omaha Beach. Because the scene is so protracted and portrays the butcher's bill of mid-twentieth-century munitions, it packs more emotional wallop than the opening and closing scenes (Antietam and the attack on Fort Wagner in South Carolina, respectively) of an even better war movie, *Glory.*

Private Ryan has set a standard of realism by which all subsequent war movies will be measured. Art is catching up with journalism.

In September 1862 two men worked their way across some dark and bloody ground in northern Maryland. They were armed with devices of profound importance for the future of war, and hence of politics: cameras. They had been sent by Mathew Brady, in whose Manhattan studio there soon opened an exhibit called "The Dead of Antietam." *The New York Times* reported, "The dead of the battle-field come up to us very rarely, even in dreams. . . . Mr. Brady has done something to bring home to us the terrible reality and earnestness of war. If he has not brought bodies and laid them in door-yards and along streets, he has done something very like it."

But the civilian world would not soon look war in the face. In World

War I, no photo of a corpse appeared in a British, French, or German newspaper. It was not until 1943 that *Life* magazine created controversy and a new era in journalism (and, in time, in the game of nations) when it published a photograph of three dead Americans on a New Guinea beach. By the time of Vietnam, graphic journalism was ascendant in a wired world. There is an element of postmodernist irony in the fact that, three decades later, Americans are said to be at long last learning about "the reality of war"—at the movies.

Indeed, they are thought to be learning about it for the first—and last—time. Many people seem to see *Private Ryan* as a retrospective on war, which is thought to be something of which we have seen the last. However, history proves that a great nation is always living in war years or interwar years. Hence it is well to wonder whether American society can still furnish forth the sort of men who clawed their way ashore through a storm of steel in Normandy.

That is a question addressed by Major General Josiah Bunting III, superintendent of the Virginia Military Institute, in his new book, *An Education for Our Time*. It is suitable summer reading for anyone interested in the deeper implications of *Private Ryan*.

Bunting, whose book is a scintillating blueprint for a morally serious college, recalls the ending of the movie adaptation of James Michener's Korean War novel, *The Bridges at Toko-ri*. An admiral muses about the death of a friend, a marine officer, a pilot, a veteran of World War II. The friend had died in a strange war whose purposes were not obvious. The admiral wonders: Where do we get such men as these?

Bunting writes that such men often come from colleges, which had better understand the nation's unending need for them:

> Not a few are killed. It is the cost of doing business if you are a powerful democracy in the twentieth and twenty-first centuries. Surely in our national future crouch hundreds of wars, waiting silently for men, and now—barbarous to think—for women to join them. We are . . . no farther advanced than in our ancient furies. For every Shiloh and Saratoga, there will be a dozen Khe Sanhs and Kuwaits. Our students should be ready for them.

Today almost no military history is taught on campuses, which are nurseries of hostility toward the same armed forces that preserve the freedom to live a life of ingratitude. *Private Ryan* is, among other things, a summons to gratitude for what Bunting calls "the allegiance of that generation of military and naval officers who remained with the colors from 1918 to 1941, disregarded, ill-paid, unpromoted, allegiant to a cause only because it was right. But prepared to serve for that reason alone."

The men who fought World War II were drawn from a vast reservoir of American decency. Their sense of duty impelled them into the ranks of those who (in the words of a Stephen Spender poem) "left the vivid air signed with their honor." When next we need their like, we will find some of them among those who have recoiled from the indecent example of today's commander in chief. That recoil will be his positive legacy. All of it.

Fortunately, America has enjoyed a holiday from history, internationally, while enduring this dangerously frivolous president. But in Iraq and elsewhere, cold-eyed men have taken the measure of his littleness, and of America's deepening dilemma of his vanished authority. Soon the holiday will be history. And, sooner or later, so will the notion that war is a subject only for historians and moviemakers. It is time to remember Trotsky's mordant words: "You may not be interested in war, but war is interested in you."

August 17, 1998

In Praise of Fierce Patriotism

Decoration Day, as it was called when Americans still vividly remembered what it was they were supposed to be remembering, used to be May 30, no matter what, never mind the pleasures, commercial and recreational, of a three-day weekend. An upstate New York town with a militarily resonant name—Waterloo—began the tradition in 1866, and in 1868 May 30 was designated "for the purpose of strewing with flowers or otherwise decorating the graves of comrades who died in defense of their country during the late rebellion." Walter Berns, who is eighty-two and grew up in Chicago, remembers Memorial Day (as it was renamed after World War I) parades up Michigan Avenue still featuring a few Civil War veterans, national heirlooms as fragile as porcelains.

Berns, a former professor of political philosophy and still very much a philosopher, at the American Enterprise Institute, has just published a profound book, *Making Patriots,* a timely mediation on a paradox: for Americans, patriotism is especially vigorous—and peculiarly problematic.

For Spartans, patriotism was not problematic: even the gods were the city's gods. But with the coming of Christianity, with its distinction between what should be rendered to Caesar and what to God, patriotism became complex, and especially so after the Reformation's multiplication of Christian denominations. When Martin Luther stood before the authorities and said *"Ich kann nicht anders"*—"I cannot do otherwise"—he asserted the primacy of individual judgment, which made the claims of patriotism conditional.

However, patriotism, although now conditioned by other loyalties, still was, as it had been for Spartans, parochial: It was entirely about a particular people and their traditions. Then came something new: America.

In a nation founded on "self-evident principles," principles purportedly of universal validity, patriotism involved more than looking inward and backward. Berns notes that in our creedal nation, the first nation not based on tradition, a word frequently heard in other nations' backward-looking patriotisms— "fatherland"—has no place. Our Founding Fathers are revered primarily for their creed, which was their greatest deed.

But the creed contains a problem for patriotism. The creed says we are endowed by our creator with rights, not duties, and that we grudgingly and conditionally surrender limited powers to government only to escape the "inconveniences" (John Locke's carefully chosen word) of the state of nature. So we become citizens out of self-interest. Of what kind of patriotism are such people capable?

The answer—fierce patriotism—is written in row upon row of stone markers in military cemeteries. Alexander Hamilton, one of General Washington's aides during the Revolutionary War, wrote (in *The Federalist,* no. 8) that "the industrious habits of the people of the present day, absorbed in the pursuits of gain and devoted to the improvements of agriculture and commerce," do not make for good soldiers. Hamilton was wrong.

What Lincoln called "the silent artillery of time" has done its work, reducing to mental rubble our understanding of the origin of Memorial Day in the decoration of the graves of a war that killed 620,000 Americans, about 1.8 percent of the population in 1865. Two of Lincoln's greatest speeches, his First Inaugural and his Gettysburg Address, invoke soldiers' graves. The former concluded by invoking "the mystic chords of memory, stretching from every battlefield, and patriot grave, to every living heart and hearthstone." The latter was delivered at the dedication of a military cemetery.

Human beings are biological facts, patriots are social artifacts, and much has changed since John Jay said (in *The Federalist,* no. 2) that Americans were "a people descended from the same ancestors, speaking the same language, professing the same religion." Now we are more "diverse."

But even then we were more diverse than Jay's words suggested. Aside from 757,000 slaves (in a total American population of 3.9 million), there were, for example, enough Americans who spoke only German that Congress seriously considered printing laws in German as well as English.

And again, in our nation, patriotism is creedal, not ancestral. Many ardent patriots who have recently arrived here know, better than some people with many ancestors buried here, precisely why they are patriotic.

In 1991 Florida, in a fit of the modern spirit of "nonjudgmentalism" and "multiculturalism" and all that, enacted a statute requiring public schools to teach that no culture "is intrinsically superior or inferior to another." Well. As Berns says, this told Florida's immigrant communities something they knew to be preposterous—that they might as well have stayed in Cuba or Haiti or wherever.

To them, especially: Happy Decoration Day.

May 27, 2001

The Unabomber and
American Squeamishness

David Gelernter, professor of computer science, fresh from vacation, sorting through mail in his Yale office, thought the package was someone's dissertation. When he pulled the wrapping cord, smoke billowed out with a hiss and a strange smell. Then the package sent by the Unabomber emitted "a terrific flash," and Gelernter was blown into a long—it will never end—journey of pain, involving many surgeries, a cornea transplant, therapy, diminished capacities, lost time.

Yet such is this extraordinary man's undamaged mind and strengthened spirit that he was also catapulted into soaring self-discovery and social insight, one result of which is his short, exhilarating book *Drawing Life: Surviving the Unabomber.* Alternately droll and furious, ebullient and acidic, it stands against one of the sins of the age, self-pity.

"When I looked down at my right hand I saw the bones sticking out in all directions and the skin crumpled like paper." His blood pressure measured zero. That was in 1993, when for many months his undamaged eye could see "the lines of surgical staples holding my chest closed, the regions on my legs where layers of skin had been sliced off to provide raw materials for chest grafts."

In 1997 his reassembled body contains a spirit impatient with a society in which the word "judgmental" has only pejorative connotations—as though a nonjudgmental society could have justice. A student of America on the eve of the Second World War, he cites a 1937 *Life* magazine story on a foiled bank robbery: "The picture at right shows the two dead bandits lying in the street where the police dropped them." *Life* called it the "neatest trap of the year." This was, Gelernter says, good news: "For violent criminals this long-ago society bristled with contempt. . . . It was judgmental."

America then was, he says, the world's least passive country. Today we even sentence criminals with words tinged with "a certain wistful sadness," the tone of voice of a society uneasy about being judgmental. And a newsmagazine's cover on the capture of the suspected Unabomber carried the headline "Mad Genius." There was no evidence to support either the adjective or the noun, but the idea of madness is, as Gelernter says, exculpatory. The phrase, say, "evil fool" would have been judgmental.

A society that is, as Gelernter says, "too squeamish to call evil by its right name" is a society in which *People* magazine anoints the Unabomber one of the most fascinating people of 1996. Which suggests not just how much we have changed but also why we have changed since 1936, when the *Londoner's Guide to New York* said, "One may walk the streets for years without seeing anything more criminal than the solicitation of alms or the manifestations of inebriation."

Being a target of the Unabomber brought Gelernter into contact with the media, which filled him with "disgust and dark amusement." He was stunned by "the assumption in the news industry that a person wants to be addressed and treated as a 'victim.'" The fact that American society's admonition has changed from "count your blessings" to "nurse your grievances" helps explain the passing of the America depicted in *Life* magazine at the beginning of 1957: "Americans greeted 1957 with high-decibel revelry and effervescent optimism. The old year that was ticking away had been a very good one. . . . The year to come looked just as good or even better."

But in a society looked upon as a victimization machine, individuals are not actors, they are acted upon, and self-pity sits on their chests like a pile of bricks. Of course, people do get acted upon in life—few as shatteringly as Gelernter has been—but that is no excuse for thinking of people as passive clay.

Part of Gelernter's therapy has been immersion in the spirit of prewar America, in which the guidebook for the 1939 World's Fair said, "The pedestrian finds it pleasant to stroll at the Fair, where the walks are of bituminous asphalt." Gelernter marvels: "*Asphalt,* the rubbery-hot smell and black sheen of it when you lay the stuff down: progress, the triumphant vanquishing of discouragement and mud."

He believes that America's intellectuals are merchants of discouragement, teachers of passivity, justifiers of self-pity. However, his experience has left him, on balance, confident about the mass of Americans: "If you insert into this weird slot machine of modern life one evil act, a thousand acts of kindness tumble out." Echoing the psalmist, he says, "Life is a stubborn return from sorrow again and again." His is the voice of an angry, happy man.

September 18, 1997

The Unabomber's Sanity

The surrealism surrounding the Sacramento trial of the Unabomber begins with this idea: Even if Theodore Kaczynski is guilty of the cold-blooded and cowardly acts of assembling and mailing bombs that killed three people and maimed at least twenty-two over seventeen years, he should not be sentenced to death because that would distress David Kaczynski, who hastened the capture of his brother.

After reading the Unabomber's "manifesto," a long denunciation of technology, David notified authorities that he suspected that his brother, for many years reclusive and estranged from his family, might be the author. But this service should not earn David any consideration concerning the disposition of the case. He had a civic duty to do what he could to curtail the career of a serial killer. That he did that duty—only after protracted agonizing—confers on him no right to influence the moral calibrations of the criminal justice system.

During David's collaboration with the FBI before Theodore was arrested, David believes he received from the FBI what *Newsweek* calls "assurances that the government would reward his cooperation by sparing his brother's life." But even if he was encouraged to think that he had "assurances," the FBI was still seeking a fugitive and was entitled to use guile while avoiding what would have been, in effect, an absurdly premature plea bargain.

Theodore's lawyers wanted to argue that he is too insane to formulate an intent to kill. Defense lawyers have their duties, but who actually *believes* that the man who meticulously assembled sophisticated killing devices, while frustrating one of America's most ambitious manhunts, did not and could not intend to kill?

Kaczynski, who offered to plead guilty in exchange for immunity from a death sentence, inconveniently insists he is sane. This causes some people to assert that his refusal to save his life by pleading insanity proves his insanity. Similar reasoning works to make the most atrocious crimes the least punishable: "Only someone insane could do terrible things." (If so, the Nuremberg trials were indefensible.)

Various "experts" have come forth to wring recondite conclusions from obvious facts: Kaczynski was eccentric, unhygienic, antisocial—not to mention "abnormally" given to blowing people up—and therefore . . . But nothing follows from those facts, and they do not trump two serviceable rules that can help prevent a meltdown of the criminal justice system as a means of assigning blame and affirming moral judgments.

One is that a person is responsible for his actions unless they are a pure reflex or the result of a delusional state utterly beyond rational control. The other is that if someone says, with clarity and without evident delusion, that he believes himself sane, he is.

Consider an actual expert. James Q. Wilson, one of the nation's foremost scholars of crime, has a lively interest in this case, for two reasons. His most recent book, *Moral Judgment,* concerns the "abuse of excuses" in the criminal justice system. And the Unabomber mentions him (blandly) in the manifesto.

Wilson believes that the writing of the closely reasoned manifesto demonstrated sanity while establishing—indeed proclaiming—a political motive for murder. The Unabomber's protracted, seventeen-year premeditation powerfully justifies the presupposition that he knew the nature and quality of his actions. Could he tell right from wrong? Clearly he thought, as terrorists do, that he was in the right and was righting wrongs. And his secretiveness demonstrated that he knew, while disdaining, society's standards of right and wrong.

The subjects of crime and punishment instructively demarcate differences between liberals and conservatives. The former are inclined to regard man as disposed by nature to spontaneous sociability. And they are inclined to locate the causes of crime in irrational and correctable social arrangements or, more recently, in psychological or biological processes, the autonomous nature of which diminishes or altogether erases the criminals' responsibilities.

Liberals are disposed to favor punishment only when it is drained of retributive elements and when it is justified as therapeutic for the offender and society. Conservatives resist assaults on the concept of responsibility, assaults arising from this non sequitur: All behavior is in some sense caused, therefore causation attenuates—often to the vanishing point—responsibility.

Would executing Kaczynski deter others like him? Perhaps not, but so what? One purpose of punishment is to civilize the wholesome—wholesome because it buttresses civilization—desire for vengeance against the vicious. Unless the Unabomber is executed, his final victim will be society's confidence in assigning responsibility and its serenity in expressing retributive anger.

January 8, 1998

The Black Lung Disease of the Intelligentsia

Too much of a good thing, said Mae West, is wonderful. But that is not true if the good thing is tolerance. Too much of that is both a cause and a consequence of a culture in which "judgmental" has become an epithet. Tolerance is a virtue only when it is difficult—when it involves keeping strong beliefs on a short leash. Tolerance that reflects the absence of strong beliefs is a symptom of a distinctively contemporary form of decadence: the comfortable disbelief in the propriety or importance of ever making emphatic judgments about behavior.

These thoughts are occasioned by the release last week of more entries from the journals of Theodore Kaczynski, the Unabomber, who can savor the pleasures of writing as he lives the rest of his life in a prison cell not less commodious than his mountain shack. But why should the man who killed three and maimed at least twenty-two have the rest of his life?

Of one victim, prosecutors wrote, "The bomb so badly destroyed Gil Murray's body that his family"—Murray, 46, had two children—"was allowed only to see and touch his feet and legs, below the knees, as a final farewell." Kaczynski wrote that he had "no regret" about killing Murray, even though the target of that bomb was a different forestry official. He had seventeen years of premeditated murder and attempted murder, seventeen years of evading capture and honing his killing devices, incorporating razor blades and other slicing metal, for effects such as this one described by prosecutors: "Thomas opened the package; the ensuing blast drove shrapnel into his body, leaving a gaping hole in his head, opening his body and piercing his organs with nails. He died at age 50 on the floor of his own home, his wife at his side trying in vain to aid and comfort him."

At his trial Kaczynski refused to plead insanity and resisted his lawyers' portrayal of him as mentally disturbed. His journal entries are redundant evidence that he was correct. Individuals are responsible for their actions unless (in James Q. Wilson's formulation) "those actions are caused by a pure reflex or a delusional state utterly beyond rational control."

But there is a burgeoning intellectual industry devoted to multiplying the number of behaviors that are said to be beyond rational control. Anthony Daniels, a British physician, writes in *The Wall Street Journal,* "Young people who haven't a clue when World War II took place or who fought it are perfectly *au fait* with neurochemistry. They know they would stop shoplifting or mugging if only someone would balance their brain amines for them." Oddly, the "irresistible" (perhaps rising from an "addiction") urge to steal or be violent rarely erupts when there is a policeman nearby. And as Daniels says, medical or neuropsychological explanations of behavior in terms of factors beyond the reach of consciousness are somehow never invoked to explain attractive traits or good deeds. It seems that we, not our hormonal balance or biochemical mechanisms, are fully responsible for our good points.

Society increasingly flinches from judgments commensurate with the worst crimes. That is one reason, in the estimate of John DiIulio, the Princeton political scientist and criminologist, there are walking around in American society about 500,000 murderers who have not been caught or who have served time and been released. The ratio of persons murdered to persons executed from 1977 to 1996 was about 1,000 to 1. David Gelernter, the Yale professor of computer science who was one of Kaczynski's victims, says Di-Iulio's statistics "show an approach to murder so casual as to be depraved." Not executing Kaczynski shows the same thing.

Granted, his plea bargain was struck as his trial was on the verge of becoming a shambles. Judicial debacles are unamazing in a country in which the selecting of the jury for the O. J. Simpson trial took almost as long as the Founders took to write the Constitution. Still, the case of the coldly rational and savage Kaczynski, whose journal says he killed for pleasure (the pleasure of revenge against the modern world), refutes familiar arguments against capital punishment.

The point of executing murderers, writes Gelernter in *Commentary* magazine, is not vengeance, or we would let the grieving parties decide the killer's fate. Rather, capital punishment is a "communal proclamation" of virtuous intolerance: it says that murder is intolerable. "The community certifies births and deaths, creates marriages, educates children, fights invaders. In laws, deeds, and ceremonies it lays down the boundary lines of civilized life, lines that are constantly getting scuffed and needing renewal."

But here's the rub: "An execution forces the community to assume forever the burden of moral certainty; it is a form of absolute speech that allows no waffling or equivocation. Deliberate murder, the community announces, is absolutely evil and absolutely intolerable, period." So critics are exactly wrong when they say capital punishment reflects surrender to emotions (such as grief and rage). Quite the contrary, it represents modern society's overcoming its impulses, such as sentimentalism, squeamishness, and, most of all, the restful flight from being "judgmental." Gelernter understands why it is that although the American community supports capital punishment, the intelligentsia does not.

It is not because the intellectuals, having finer sensibilities, abhor killing more than other people do. Most people, Gelernter notes, could not kill a dog. Rather, the crucial factor is that "the death penalty represents absolute speech from a position of moral certainty, and doubt is the black-lung disease of the intelligentsia—an occupational hazard now inflicted on the culture as a whole."

"Excellent," purred Kaczynski in his journal when a newspaper described a victim "blown to bits." When a secretary opened a bomb intended for her boss, Kaczynski wrote that the "bomb drove fragments of wood into her flesh. But no indication that she was permanently disabled. Frustrating that I can't seem to make a lethal bomb." Not as frustrating as the inability of the community to act with moral certainty—to be appropriately judgmental—toward this cold-blooded killer.

May 11, 1998

Minibars and Family Values
in Vegas

L AS VEGAS, NEVADA—In a city not known for nuances, former Mayor Jan
Jones called a visitor's attention to a portentous one. A hotel going up on
the Strip will, she says, have minibars in the rooms. If your reaction is "So
what?" you are not in a Las Vegas frame of mind.

Thousands of American hotels have minibars in their rooms, but most Las
Vegas hotels do not because they do not want guests loitering in their rooms, they
want them in the casinos. Jones, whose successor in City Hall is a lawyer for Mafia
figures—viva Las Vegas!—says minibars in the rooms are evidence that the city
wants to be known for more than what it primly calls "the gaming industry."

Think of minibars as signs of family values. Seriously. This city wants to
become a family vacation destination. Already it is coining money off things—
rooms, entertainment—that, once upon a time, it almost, or actually, gave
away to attract gamblers. About half of revenues on the Strip, home of eleven
of the world's twelve largest hotels (the largest is in Thailand), come from noncasino sources, and noncasino revenues are growing nearly four times faster
than casino revenues.

The city itself—an American improbability, "a cruise ship on a sea of
sand" says *National Geographic*'s William Newcott—is growing faster than anything other than a cactus should be expected to grow in a desert (annual rain-
fall: four inches). More than 75,000 people move in every year, requiring a
new school to open every month.

New Las Vegans are drawn here because residency is, Jones says proudly, a
good deal. Gambling taxes generate so much revenue that there is no income
tax, and the average newcomer household pays $1,889 in sales and other taxes
annually while receiving $6,102 in government services.

This city, where caviar is served on a golf course, has an urgent and
poignant hope to become more like a normal city—like, say, St. Louis. (Like
many cities, St. Louis has become a bit like Las Vegas: a riverboat casino sits
next to the Gateway Arch.) But even Jones has a hard time getting the hang of
normality. She stresses the fact that the city now has a big NASCAR race and
the National Finals Rodeo, and Garth Brooks and Bob Dylan are coming, so
is the Broadway musical *Chicago,* and Jones thinks the city might land an NBA
franchise in five years, and . . .

Yes, but what about normality outside of entertainment? You know,
things like other businesses. Having no inventory tax, Nevada has lots of ware-
houses, but it still has not substantially diversified its economic base: hotels,

gambling, and recreation directly provide about one-third of all jobs and indirectly generate many more.

For tens of millions of Americans, increasingly incited by their governments, which run lotteries and tax casinos, gambling is a regular part of weekly recreation. The spread of gambling across the nation, instead of hurting Las Vegas, has helped it in two ways. It has removed the stigma from gambling, and hence from this city, and has made a visit to this city as desirable for gamblers as a visit to Yankee Stadium is for baseball fans. By the end of this year, the city will have 122,000 hotel and motel rooms (New York City has a piddling 62,500), and the hotel occupancy rate is a gaudy 90 percent.

Nevada is a monument to "entrepreneurial federalism." In its first fling at that, it exploited other states' resistance to liberal divorce laws. No state could beat Nevada in the competition to have the shortest residency requirement or the longest list of easy-to-prove grounds for divorce. In 1931, the year construction of Hoover Dam down the road began, the legislature let loose a force more powerful than the Colorado River: casino gambling.

Over lunch in one of the restaurants in the new $1.9 billion Bellagio Hotel, Jones, who is practically a native by Nevada standards, says she came here in 1981 because her family, based in California, owned four Las Vegas supermarkets. The markets had forty-eight slot machines. The markets were losing money as markets—on food and soft drinks and paper towels and such. But they were making a lot of money on the slots.

And there you have the great constant in a city that is almost a caricature of America's whirl of change. Jones says that ten years from now Las Vegas will be as changed as it is now from ten years ago. No doubt, but its heartbeat will still be gambling, which will still be called gaming.

July 1, 1999

The Anthropology of Latte Towns

A harbinger of politics as consumption was the discovery that faded blue jeans could be pricier than unfaded ones. This signaled "status inversion," whereby you ascend in estimation (your peers' and your own) by descending in lifestyle, dress, and manners.

Today people sip designer water that costs more than gasoline as they drive thirsty sport utility vehicles (time was, "sport" and "utility" had opposite connotations) to Fresh Fields, where, David Brooks writes, their sense of seriousness and superiority can be sustained by buying commodities for "middle-aged hypochondriacs, like whole grains." For fun there are Ben & Jerry's ice cream cones with attitudes.

How, Brooks asks, did "the quintessential bourgeois activity, shopping," become a bundle of "quintessential bohemian activities: art, philosophy, social action"? His answer in his book *Bobos in Paradise: The New Upper Class and How They Got There* is that Marx got two things wrong.

Marx said classes inevitably conflict and are defined by their means of production. However, the bohemian and the bourgeois classes have melded, producing Bobos—the bohemian bourgeoisie, defined by consumption. In an America swimming in discretionary income, consumption is an assertion of Bobo cultural values.

Bobos are generally affluent (more than 9 million household incomes exceed $100,000) and many live in what Brooks calls "Latte Towns," where there may not be many artists and intellectuals but many people want to drink coffee like one. Often these are university and high-tech towns (e.g., Boulder, Colorado, or Burlington, Vermont, home of Ben & Jerry's) where the aspiration is for life to resemble an extended hobby or an unending graduate school. Work should be playful, but play should be earnest and self-improving (see "sport utility," above). In Latte Towns, lots of children are named Dylan and Joplin.

Such towns have magazines to help anxious consumers protect their status and self-esteem by making exquisitely nuanced decisions about the simplest things. Such magazines feature articles such as "Where to Get the Best Bread." Imagine the status subtraction for having the second best.

The purpose of such perfectionism in consumption is, Brooks says, for people to show that they are "smart enough to spend the very most." There is a chain of clothing stores with a perfect Bobo name, "Anthropologie," where, Brooks says, "the feel of the store says 'A Year in Provence,' while the prices say six years out of Medical School."

The ostentation of intellectual consumption is characteristic of the new upper class of Bobos. Ralph Lauren ads cater to this: the wooden motorboat near the green light at the end of the dock, Long Island before Levittown. History has been called the graveyard of aristocracies, and in America the graves of those the Bobos supplanted were dug by admissions officers at Ivy League universities.

In the 1950s they interred the WASP establishment, replacing an elite of blood with one of brains. A society of accomplishment displaced one of pedigree. Brooks says the average (by SAT scores) Harvard freshman in 1952 would have been in the bottom 10 percent of freshmen of 1960. In 1960 just ten of Princeton's sixty-two football players were from prep schools. Three decades earlier, every player was.

In its power to set tastes and manners, the Bobo elite makes America today as hierarchical as in the 1950s. Bobos, says Brooks, are "epistemologically modest," claiming to be too short on certitude to be "judgmental." Except, of course, about some things, such as smoking, which is considered more sinful than breaking at least five commandments. And Bobos favor the indoctrination of children, who, Brooks notes, are more "awash in moral instruction" than Victorian children were. Today's three R's—pumped into them by television and teachers—are racial sensitivity, recycling, and reproduction.

Today, Brooks says, to calculate a person's status, multiply his net worth by his antimaterialist attitudes. The 1960s countercultural radicalism has, he says, been reconciled with bourgeois consumption. But Brooks's thesis—that 1960s radicalism has been gentrified—takes too seriously the 1960s radicals' own self-flattering estimate of their seriousness.

A few years ago some long-of-tooth radicals had a conniption when Nike used the Beatles refrain "You say you want a revolution" in a sneaker ad. They said consumerism was "co-opting" their cause. But their cause was always a style—an alternative consumption pattern—tarted up as politics.

What hath their revolution wrought? A brochure, "The Feng Shui of Ironing," that comes with Rowenta irons. It explains that "a wrinkle is actually 'tension' in the fabric. Releasing the tension by removing the wrinkle improves the flow of ch'i." Right on, Rowenta.

April 9, 2000

Et Tu, Brooks Brothers?

Yes, yes, we have been told. Philosophers tell us that change is life's only constant. Poets tell us that the center cannot hold, and all that is beautiful drifts away like the waters. Scientists say even the continents are adrift.

But Brooks Brothers, the clothier founded in Manhattan in 1818, was supposed to be the still point of the turning world. For generations it has defined conservatism in men's dress—blue and gray natural-shoulder suits, blue and white oxford cloth shirts with button-down collars, striped ties.

So why in recent years have the clothier's display windows become a silent pandemonium of scandalizing colors? What are those lavender dress shirts—about the coral-colored ones, let us not even speak—doing in Brooks Brothers stores, even the flagship store that opened in 1915 at the corner of Forty-fourth and Madison Avenue?

Selling, that's what those lavender and coral shirts are doing. So says Brooks Brothers' believable CEO, Joseph Gromek, who, it is heartening to note, is not wearing one of them this day. He says that when such shirts are worn under gray or navy suits "they calm down a lot." File that under "faint praise."

An informal poll of sales personnel in half a dozen Brooks Brothers stores found some insistence that the colorful shirts are a drug on the market. However, these salesmen—they were all men, and old enough to remember the days before male peacockery—may have been allowing their wishes to color their thoughts. ("Europeans" and "Women trying to change their husbands" were the acerbic answers these disapproving men gave to the question, Who buys those shirts?)

Brooks Brothers, which went through a rocky patch in the 1980s, is now coining money: in the most recent half-year reporting period, operating profits were up 118.3 percent over the corresponding period last year. Evidently Brooks Brothers is solving a problem that politicians always face: how to appeal to a wider electorate without alienating their base.

Brooks Brothers' base consists of hidebound mossbacks who hate change—in short, people who are the backbone of this republic. But a few years ago the average age of the clothier's customers was in the fifties, so the problem was to get other people into the store. (Time was, Brooks Brothers on Madison Avenue closed on Saturdays because "outsiders" shopped then.) Now youth has come knocking at the door, but youth often does not know how to dress up—or down.

Dress up? They are a lost generation, sartorially. They attend college classes looking like derelicts—or like their high school and even their college teachers. (The following proposition resists proof but is irresistibly plausible: Today's slovenly standards in education are not unrelated to the disorder and indifference to standards communicated by many teachers' appearances.) Then they enter the business world and have no clue how to cope (a hint: not jeans) with that deplorable innovation called "casual Fridays."

In 1955, when William F. Buckley, a Brooks Brothers customer, founded *National Review* (not far from that cultural epicenter, Forty-fourth and Madison), he said the magazine "stands athwart history, yelling 'Stop!'" For an iconic institution such as Brooks Brothers, there is a duty to stand athwart fashion fads and say, as insistently as commercial imperatives will permit, "Not so fast."

Brooks Brothers' patrons are used to slings and arrows. In *Guys and Dolls*, which opened on Broadway in 1950, a gangster disparages his doll's interest in a "breakfast-eating, Brooks Brothers type." Sloan Wilson's *The Man in the Gray Flannel Suit* featured a Brooks Brothers man. That novel, a critique of postwar "conformity," came a decade before America began to experience the fruits of aggressive nonconformity to what were disparaged as "bourgeois values." In 1970, after the 1960s had done their worst against good taste, a fashion Bolshevik declared, "Button-downs were the ultimate symbol of uptightness."

Well, the world turns and the counterrevolution against the 1960s and all its works continues. Uptightness does not seem like such a sin, now that we live surrounded by cultural unraveling. Brooks Brothers' best-selling item is the button-down shirt (more than half a million a year), and half the shirts Brooks Brothers sells are blue.

Such data put a spring in the step of those few, those happy few for whom it shall forever be the 1950s, with a Sinatra song always in the air as they stride briskly toward martinis beneath the clock at the Biltmore Hotel, which was— nothing lasts—a very short walk from Forty-fourth and Madison.

December 28, 1997

Secrecy and the Mother of Stupidity

Governmental secrecy breeds stupidity, in government decision making and in the thinking of some citizens. Secrecy helped produce Oliver Stone, the paranoiac whose 1991 movie *JFK* found a mass audience for the notion that the assassination of President Kennedy was the work of a vast right-wing con- spiracy. This caused Congress to create the Assassination Records Review Board in the hope that openness would set the country free from dark suspi- cions.

Last week the board completed its work, having made public 4 million pages of previously secret documents. They do nothing to contradict the con- clusion that Kennedy was killed by Lee Harvey Oswald, acting alone, and they will not open minds as closed as clams. But as the board said, secrecy itself causes conspiracy theories to ferment, leading the public "to believe that the government had something to hide." Secrecy made Joe McCarthy and his mirror images, those on the left who believe America is a conspiracy orga- nized against their civil liberties. Often government hides the truth from itself, with results expensive or dangerous, or both.

Obviously some governmental secrecy is necessary, in the interest of na- tional security or to guard certain deliberative processes in domestic matters. However, most secrecy is not necessary, and an iron law of institutions guar- antees that the ratio of unnecessary to necessary secrecy increases steadily. It does so because bureaucracies steeped in the culture of secrecy come to regard secrets as property to be hoarded and bartered in dealings with rival bureau- cracies that are doing the same thing. Bureaucracies use secrecy to increase what Max Weber called "the superiority of the professionally informed." Bureaucracies, Weber noted, relish superiority relative to poorly informed publics and parliaments.

Daniel Patrick Moynihan so argues in his latest book, *Secrecy: The American Experience*. The culture of secrecy began when much else (a serious federal income tax; the Soviet Union) did, in 1917, during the hysteria attendant upon a new phenomenon, world war. War has been the engine of the growth of much of the modern age, from big government to big science, and it brought secrecy in its train.

Secrecy and an attendant mentality. So the governor of Iowa decreed an English-only policy for all public and telephonic conversations. (Gracious, what might get said in German?) A society at ease with secrecy will be susceptible to epidemics of suspicion. Hence this official justification for the wartime internment of West Coast Americans of Japanese extraction: "The very fact that no sabotage has taken place to date is a disturbing and confirming indication that such action will be taken."

In the 1940s U.S. military code breakers read 2,900 messages between Moscow and its agents in the United States. Thanks to which the U.S. government had ample proof of the espionage of Alger Hiss and the Rosenbergs. But the proof was kept secret, and not just from the public. President Truman, too, was not informed, and hence he was unable to make his rhetoric and actions about communism and security more congruent with the truth. Truman was kept ill informed by the decision of an excellent man who greatly admired his fellow Missourian: General Omar Bradley, chairman of the Joint Chiefs of Staff. Bradley's decision was nothing personal, it was merely a bureaucratic reflex—the military hoarding its property.

Moynihan is most exercised about the radical overestimation of Soviet economic might and the comparable underestimation of ethnic tensions and other factors that led to the Soviet Union's largely unanticipated mortality. The problem, Moynihan says, is that the government took Soviet economic statistics too seriously, and the secrecy of government analyses shielded them from the scrutiny of dissenters. Only occasionally did independent evidence of the senses reaffirm reality, as with General George Lee Butler's first trip to Moscow, in December 1988.

As one of the senior officers involved in drafting U.S. war-fighting strategy against the Soviet Union, Butler studied that nation in great detail. He was convinced that America's adversary was a mighty garrison state of waxing strength. Then he landed at Sheremetyevo Airport near Moscow and thought the dilapidated runway was an open field. As he was driven into Moscow on similarly ragged roads, past crumbling buildings, the gearshift in his car broke off in his driver's hand. By the time he headed home, Butler had a much better understanding of the Soviet Union than he had acquired from government deliberations enveloped in secrecy.

Moynihan may blame too much on secrecy. Perhaps there was, among U.S. policy elites, a predisposition to believe in the efficacy of a command economy. Some analysts of a sharply different mentality—e.g., Nicholas Eberstadt of the American Enterprise Institute and G. Warren Nutter, an economist of the University of Chicago school—got things right.

In a long, trenchant introduction to Moynihan's book, Richard Gid Powers, a historian at City University of New York, says that the damage secrecy has done to the political culture exceeds even that done to policy. (We did, after all, win the Cold War.) Powers notes what he calls "postmodern secrecy mongering": "Balzac said that the fundamental principle of popular writing is that behind every great fortune lies a great crime. Postmodern popular culture holds that behind every great political career lies a great scandal—a formula that provides the catharsis of discrediting the powerful, thereby vicariously empowering everyone else."

Moynihan, who knows how to couch an argument in terms congenial to an era unenthralled with government, says secrecy is a form of government regulation. But whereas most regulation limits what the public can do, secrecy limits what it can know. Which is why, he says, it is for losers.

October 12, 1998

The Triumph of "Perceptions"

Someone—someone with a prepostmodern turn of mind—once said that the trouble with facts is that there are so many of them. Today the problem seems to be that there are so few of them. This thought is brought on by several matters recently in the news, starting with a new wrinkle in an entertaining contretemps about memories from the remarkable infancy, or perhaps the later childhood, of Senator Robert Torricelli, New Jersey's freshman Democrat.

Seven weeks ago Torricelli, who serves on the committee investigating campaign irregularities, gave a tug to the nation's heartstrings when he advertised his sensitivity about insensitivity toward Asian-Americans. Sensitivity mongering has special éclat when coupled with a boast of victimhood, and Torricelli managed this coupling. He remembered how pained he was by unflattering Italian-American stereotypes that he recalls being fostered by Senator Estes Kefauver's televised hearings into organized crime. Torricelli's *cri du coeur* was a three-hankie performance: "It is among the first memories I have of government of the United States, and probably the first hearing of the United

States Senate I ever witnessed. It was only on a flickering television screen, but I will never forget it, and even if I tried, my family would never allow me."

"Among"? "Probably"? "Witnessed"? He was five days old when Kefauver's hearings ended in 1951. When a journalist asked Torricelli about his prodigiously early interest in public affairs, Torricelli upbraided the journalist for missing the larger point, about "insensitivity."

You might think that, having been caught perpetrating such a whopper, Torricelli would have slunk off to wherever such people slink. Think again. The very traits that cause people to tell such tales make them impervious to embarrassment, so last week Torricelli blew on the cooling embers of the controversy by writing a letter to *The Wall Street Journal*. In it he continued his lamentation about the sorry state of journalism as evidenced by people writing about something as "trivial" as the question of whether his melodramatic memory was real or fictitious, or whether his emotional trauma occurred when he was five days old or perhaps when he saw "footage from the hearings as an older child." That last is apparently now his story and he's sticking to it, for now.

Torricelli could save himself a lot of bother by simply invoking the Reich Rule of Epistemology. It is that any proposition is true—or true enough, or as true as anything gets—if it comports with one's feelings about, or "perceptions" of, something. Former labor secretary Robert Reich was recently found (by journalist Jonathan Rauch) to have fabricated events recounted in his book *Locked in the Cabinet,* which is loosely—*very* loosely—called a "memoir." For example, Reich recounts being bombarded by rude questions hurled at him through dense cigar smoke ("my eyes water. I feel dizzy") at an all-male ("There isn't a lady in the room") lunch of the National Association of Manufacturers.

But it was a breakfast; at least a third of those attending were women; NAM rules forbid smoking; the transcript records no questions remotely like those Reich recounts. Asked about this, Reich breezily noted this—what? disclaimer?—in his book: "I claim no higher truth than my own perceptions. This is how I lived it."

A few decades ago, the word "existential"—a European import as popular as the Volkswagen beetle—was an all-purpose license to assert almost anything. Any proposition, however much at variance with boring evidence, could be said to express the "existential reality" of the speaker's experience. Today there is another equal-opportunity epistemology: Anyone has a right to postmodernism's protection against standards of accuracy.

Postmodernism is the degenerate egalitarianism of the intelligentsia. It launches a non sequitur from a truism. The truism is that because our knowledge of facts is conditioned in complex ways by the contexts in which facts are encountered, the acquisition of knowledge is not simple, immediate, and infallible. The non sequitur: Therefore all assertions are equally indeterminate—and equally respectable. All ascriptions of truth are arbitrary, so there are no standards of intellectual conscientiousness. So whoever has power shall decree the truth.

In a ceremony in Boston last Saturday, on the seventieth anniversary of the execution of Sacco and Vanzetti, Mayor Thomas Menino accepted a design for a memorial to the two men who were convicted of murder in what was called "an American Dreyfus case," one tinged with passions aroused by the men's anarchist politics and immigrant backgrounds. Menino says, "Our acceptance of this work of art is a statement by the city that these men did not receive a fair trial." Actually, it is a statement that they were innocent.

It is arguable that both were. And it is arguable that both were guilty. Or that one was innocent, the other not. Certainty about this case, always elusive, is by now probably unattainable. So political pressures prevail. And given the watery postmodernism of the age, why not? After all, there are no reliable facts, only "perceptions."

A California community college has scheduled a three-day September seminar to teach that the assassination of President Kennedy was the result of a conspiracy. One scheduled speaker thinks the conspiracy was organized by Israel. Another speaker, the elected head of the board of trustees of the community college district, reportedly has said, and subsequently has denied saying, that Lee Harvey Oswald worked for the Anti-Defamation League of B'nai Brith. Such theories are not markedly more vicious and imbecilic than those of the movie *JFK*, perpetrated by the intellectual sociopath Oliver Stone. Such people can justify any intellectual licentiousness by claiming no higher truth than their own perceptions.

Torricelli says that people who dwell on his "trivial" fabrication are neglecting the momentous story of "the deterioration of the political process." Actually, his notion of what is trivial is part of that story.

September 1, 1997

Rodney King Revisited

Latasha Harlins, a fifteen-year-old African-American, put a $1.79 plastic container of orange juice in her backpack and, with $2 in her hand, approached the cash register of the Empire Liquor Market Deli in South-Central Los Angeles. The deli, one of 3,300 L.A. convenience stores owned by Korean-Americans (including one that had been robbed by Rodney King), had been burgled more than thirty times, frequently robbed (most recently, seven days earlier), and was constantly plagued by shoplifters. Soon Ja Du, 49, was at the cash register. Another spark was about to fall on the dry tinder of the nation's second largest city in March 1991.

Du, who lived far from South-Central and feared blacks, shrieked that Harlins was trying to steal the juice and grabbed Harlins's sweater. Harlins put the juice on the counter and knocked Du down with three punches. Du threw a chair at her and grabbed a revolver from under the counter. Harlins turned her back and began walking out. Du braced herself on the counter and, holding the gun with two hands, killed Harlins with a single shot in the back of the head. All this, occurring thirteen days after the videotaped beating of Rodney King by LAPD officers was recorded by the store's security camera.

Although the jury found the killing intentional, and convicted Du of voluntary manslaughter, the judge ruled that there had been no premeditation and essentially blamed Harlins. The judge said that Du had merely acted "inappropriately" in "overreaction." For shooting an unarmed girl in the back of the head, Du was sentenced to probation (the judge worried about the absence of a Korean translator in prison) and four hundred hours of community service, fined $500, and ordered to pay the cost of Harlins's funeral. (Two years earlier a postal worker had been sentenced to six months in jail for shooting a dog to death.) Du was sentenced five months before riots—which often targeted Korean-owned businesses—erupted in response to a suburban jury's almost complete exoneration of the four police officers charged with criminal conduct in the beating of Rodney King.

Episode by appalling, infuriating, heartbreaking episode, the story of a city stumbling into a nightmare—fifty-four dead in the worst rioting since the New York draft riots of 1863—is told in Lou Cannon's new book, *Official Negligence: How Rodney King and the Riots Changed Los Angeles and the LAPD*, a dazzling demonstration of the reporter's craft. Journalism has been called a first rough draft of history, but Cannon's precise dissection of the events of 1992, their antecedents, and their reverberations is not apt to be bettered by historians.

At 12:45 A.M. on March 3, 1991, Laurence Powell and other officers confronted King after a 7.8-mile chase at speeds of up to 115 mph. King's body looked "buffed out" (shaped by lifting weights in prison), and he was gibbering and glistening with sweat, like someone "dusted" (high on PCP). Two hours earlier Powell, who was responsible for training other officers, had been asked at a roll call to demonstrate the correct use of the metal baton. He failed and should have been summarily assigned to desk duty until proficient. Instead, it was he who landed the first and most damaging of all the blows on King, when King charged at him.

That three-second charge was in the first thirteen seconds of the eighty-one seconds of mayhem that were videotaped by a private citizen. But the television station to which the citizen gave the tape deleted those thirteen seconds on the ground that they were not quite of broadcast quality. The truncated tape was broadcast thousands of times. Then the jury in the officers' trial saw the full tape, including King's charge.

One strand of Cannon's elegantly braided narrative is a history of the LAPD from its creation in the aftermath of racial disorders—the mass lynching of Chinese in 1871. He traces the LAPD's decline from the proud cadre celebrated on *Dragnet* to the eve of the riots, when it was an understaffed, underfunded, badly trained, execrably led force driving cars with 100,000 miles on their odometers and radios that did not work. Cannon tells how abandonment of the "choke hold" for resistant suspects forced a reliance on bone-breaking batons and how the injuries to arresting officers and persons arrested increased.

Cannon argues that the beating of King was neither racial nor unambiguously illegal; that it was judicial malpractice to move the trial of the officers to a mostly white suburban community within the L.A. media market; that the LAPD was negligent about preparing for disorders; that the riots were fanned by the police decision to abandon the intersection of Florence and Normandie, where hovering helicopters were filming savagery much worse and less justified than what the officers had done to King after verbal commands, a "swarm" by four officers, and two jolts of 50,000 volts from a Taser stun gun failed to subdue him.

Damian Williams, one of those at the intersection who used a brick and a claw hammer to fracture Reginald Denny's skull in ninety-one places, pulled down the pants of another unconscious victim and spray-painted his genitals black while a mob laughed. Williams, who was acquitted of the most serious charges, argued that he had been intoxicated by the riot—a fact that a rational society would think deepened, not attenuated, his guilt.

One of the ugliest facets of the multilayered scandal of misgovernment that Cannon recounts was the second, federal trial of the police officers. It was double jeopardy and was, Cannon argues, a purely political trial ordered to serve the election-year needs of President Bush. Fear, says Cannon, was the thirteenth juror as the other twelve deliberated—if deliberation was possible under the siege of a bomb scare and demonstrators vowing that the jury's choice was convictions or chaos.

The moral of Cannon's riveting story, which the cumulative effect of his meticulous reporting makes it unnecessary for him to stipulate, is: Much of the real drama of democracy is local, where incompetent government is literally lethal. Because Cannon has written, we have been warned.

February 16, 1998

Victimhood as an Equal Opportunity Condition

I t is generally wrong to assume that any government policy, however preposterous it has become, has hit bottom. In today's government, the bottom is a downward-moving target.

The New Republic calls a new wrinkle in affirmative action from the Small Business Administration "the reductio ad absurdum of victimhood politics." But a late entry in the absurdity sweepstakes is a theory discussed at the Commission on Civil Rights.

The new nuance in the SBA's racial spoils system concerns set-asides for federal contractors deemed "socially and economically disadvantaged." Since 1987 the presumption has been that contractors are "socially disadvantaged" if they are black, Hispanic, Native Americans, Asian Pacific Americans, or Subcontinent Asian Americans. Now the golden door to the advantageous status of "disadvantaged," and to set-asides, has been opened wider.

One "distinguishing feature" that the SBA will now assume to have contributed to social disadvantage will be "long-term residence in an environment isolated from the mainstream of American society, or other similar causes not common to individuals who are not socially disadvantaged." That isolated environment criterion makes members of Congress or the Harvard faculty eligible for "socially disadvantaged" status if they decide to moonlight as contractors.

Furthermore, set-asides shall be available for those who have had "personal experiences of social disadvantage" that have been "substantial, chronic and longstanding." Furthermore, when parceling out set-asides the SBA will consider "education, employment and business history to see if the totality of circumstances shows disadvantage in entering into or advancing in the business world."

Recently the Civil Rights Commission discussed "ability grouping" of students on the basis of aptitudes. Why is this considered a problem, let alone a federal civil rights matter? An answer was supplied by Commissioner Yvonne Lee, a Clinton appointee, who began by noting that "within the Asian-American community you do see an overrepresentation of Asian-Americans in certain so-called honor groupings or advanced classes."

That, she said, "discriminates against the students" by preventing them from "being exposed to other courses of studies." She said the discrimination problem of "ability grouping" does not involve only "students who are stuck at the bottom rung. It also affects students who get labeled as whiz kids and they get stuck in the upper rank and never get exposed to other opportunities."

Commissioner Robert George, a Princeton professor of government, was politely nonplussed. He asked if Lee really was saying "that ability grouping is inherently discriminatory" and is particularly discriminatory against Asian-Americans because, by grouping them at the top of certain categories, "it deprives them of other opportunities."

Lee, who runs a San Francisco public relations firm, said yes, she believes "Asian-Americans are overrepresented in middle management, technical, professional ranks because throughout their educational ladder they've been shifted toward that area because they were thought to be smart in math and all the technical areas." Thus "they were shielded away from other social studies and other courses." Ability grouping put them "in a certain track," thereby denying them "the opportunity to be exposed to other aspects of education." Asian-Americans "are being hurt in later years when you see the other aspects of development that they did not have in their social interaction."

Getting "stuck in the upper rank" is a "civil rights problem" that millions of young Americans are studying diligently in the hope of acquiring. But Commissioner Lee sees people through contemporary liberalism's lens—as members of grievance groups who are essentially passive and who need to have their consciousnesses raised. She thinks they are victims who are "shifted" here and "put" there, allowing themselves to be stigmatized as "whiz kids." And they are improperly concentrated ("overrepresented") in the academic and vocational areas they choose to be in.

The implicit premise, central to the logic of contemporary liberalism, is that their choices result from social pressures and stereotypes and other facets of victimhood, and therefore are not really free choices. Therefore their choices need not be respected and can be considered ripe for remedial government action.

Thus is the government, locked in the logic of group preferences, drawn toward the receding bottom of a bankrupt policy. Its descent is rationalized by a new social science, victimology.

September 14, 1997

The Census and Tiger Woods

An enormous number of people—perhaps you—are descended, albeit very indirectly, from Charlemagne. And an enormous number are descended from Charlemagne's groom. Trace your pedigree back far enough, and you may find that you are an omelet of surprising ingredients.

Booker T. Washington, Frederick Douglass, Jesse Owens, and Roy Campanella each had a white parent. Martin Luther King (who had an Irish grandmother and some Indian ancestry), W. E. B. Du Bois, and Malcolm X all had some Caucasian ancestry. The NAACP estimates that 70 percent of those who identify themselves as African-American are of mixed racial heritage. And then there is Tiger Woods, who calls himself "Cablinasian"—Caucasian, black, Indian, Asian. Bear such things in mind as the Office of Management and Budget decides whether to make a small but consequential change in the census form.

The 1790 census classified Americans into five categories: white males sixteen years and older, white males less than sixteen years, white females, other white persons, and slaves. In 1860 Chinese and American Indian were added as distinct races. Today the census offered five major categories: white, black, Asian/Pacific Islander, American Indian/Native Alaskan, and other.

Now there is a rapidly spreading belief that the "other" category is unsatisfactory, because it does not contribute to an accurate snapshot of the population, and it offends sensibilities: Why should a child of a white-black marriage be required to identify with one parent, or as an "other"? So OMB is considering adding a sixth category: "multiracial."

This would serve the accuracy of the census in a nation experiencing a rapid surge in interracial marriages, which increased about 550 percent between 1960 and 1990. The number of children in interracial families rose from 500,000 in 1970 to 2 million in 1990. Between 1960 and 1990 the percentage of African-American marriages involving a white spouse more than tripled, from 1.7 percent to 6 percent. Sixty-five percent of Japanese-Americans marry someone of another race.

The multiracial category would serve civic health by undermining the obsession with race and ethnicity that fuels identity politics. Such politics proceed on the assumption that individuals are defined by their membership in this or that racial or ethnic group, often a group that cultivates its sense of solidarity by nurturing its grievances. The multiracial category is opposed by many who have a stake in today's racial spoils system and thus favor maintaining the categories that help Balkanize America.

It is estimated—probably too conservatively—that 10 percent of blacks would check a "multiracial" box on the census form. As more and more people accurately identify themselves as "multiracial," the artificial clarity of identity politics will blur. The more blurring, the better, because it will impede application of the principle of categorical representation—the principle that people of a particular group can be understood, empathized with, and represented by only members of that group.

Today some native Hawaiians want out of the Asian/Pacific Islander category, and some Indians and native Alaskans do not want the native Hawaiians included in their category. Some Creoles, Americans of Middle Eastern descent (there are 2 million of them), and others want their own categories. Such elbow-throwing prickliness is one consequence of government making membership in distinct grievance groups advantageous.

Race and ethnicity are not fixed, easily definable scientific categories. The law once regarded the Irish "race" as nonwhite. Today, ethnicity and race can, to some degree, be matters of choice. Many Hispanics regard "Hispanicity" as an attribute of race; others are more inclined to identify themselves as Hispanic when it is not presented as a racial category.

OMB's decision will follow last week's report from the Commission on Immigration Reform, which recommends a "new Americanization movement" emphasizing the melding of individuals rather than the accommodation of groups. It argues that national unity should be built upon a shared belief in constitutional values and that the nation "admits immigrants as individuals" and must "emphasize the rights of individuals over those of groups."

Today the government concocts "race-conscious remedies" such as racial preferences for conditions it disapproves. This encourages Americans to aggregate into groups jockeying for social space. Perhaps it would be best to promote the desegregation of Americans by abolishing the existing five census categories, rather than adding a sixth.

However, the "multiracial" category could speed the dilution of racial consciousness. One criticism of this category is that "multiracial" does not denote a protected class under the law and therefore gathering data about those who think of themselves as "multiracial" serves no statutory purpose. To which the sensible response is: Good.

October 5, 1997

Making Uniforms into Billboards

Major League Baseball is considering selling advertising on players' uniforms. The ads might be small patches on the sleeves.
—A NEWS ITEM

L OS ANGELES—The outlook wasn't brilliant for the Jiffy Lube Giants this day. They trailed the Burger King Dodgers 4–3 with but one inning left to play.

Dodgers pitcher Kevin "Chevy Trucks: Like a Rock" Brown (during the seventh inning stretch, which was brought to the fans at Microsoft Dodger

Stadium by Frito-Lay; General Motors bought the naming rights to Brown) toed the big "S" on the chocolate-brown Snickers pitcher's mound and glared toward the red Papa John's Pizza home plate, where the recently renamed Barry "Tylenol" Bonds menacingly waved his black Twizzlers Licorice bat with the bright yellow M&M's sweet spot on the barrel.

The Dodgers' How Do You Spell Relief? R-O-L-A-I-D-S bullpen was busy as the Giants' runners took their leads from the pink Victoria's Secret first base, the purple Eunice and Ralph's Bar, Grill, Bowling Alley, Truck Stop, Massage Parlor, and Pawn Shop second base, and the sea blue Santa Monica Condominiums: If You Lived Here You Would Be Home by Now third base. The Giants' coach in the Hertz coaching box at third peered toward his manager in the Motel 6 visiting team dugout, then ran through his signals to Bonds, tugging the Toyota bill of his Dr Pepper cap, brushing the Maxwell House patch on his left sleeve, the Visa card logo on his right hip pocket, the MCI script on his left thigh, his Southwest Airlines belt.

Brown touched the Starbucks resin bag, ground the pilsner yellow Coors Light ball into the Citibank logo in the pocket of his bright green TruGreen-ChemLawn glove and . . .

———

HAS IT come to this? Not yet. And the people pondering the advertising-on-uniforms question say not to worry. A word to the wise: Worry.

Those thinking about putting advertising on uniforms say it is unthinkable that baseball could become like stock car racing, where drivers, wearing jumpsuits plastered from shoulder to ankle with advertisements, drive cars that are rolling billboards and at the end of a race pop out of their cars holding particular products—say, a sponsor's soft drink. But the way to prevent a slide down a slippery slope is to stay off the slope.

Some will say: Lighten up—we are already slaloming swiftly down the slope. Ads on uniforms would just be additional bits of ballpark signage, as would putting one small—say, two-inch-square—logo on one sleeve (the "R" of the uniform manufacturer, Russell Athletic, already is on the other).

Let us be clear. Baseball, like any business, should be unsleeping in pursuit of profits. "Soaring revenue" is the second-most beautiful phrase (second to "Opening Day") in the American language. America would be a better, holier place if the Fortune 500 list of biggest businesses were Major League Baseball and 499 also-rans.

Ballpark signage is as traditional as players' spitting. (The origin of the term "bullpen" is lost in history's mists, but some say it was born when pitchers warmed up along fences adorned with Bull Durham tobacco signs.) Corporations make sensible advertising decisions by buying naming rights to ballparks, thereby helping themselves, their communities, and baseball. (Why is a ballpark bearing the name of a business offensive to fastidious fans who get misty-eyed thinking of old ballparks named for businessmen: Crosley Field, Ebbets Field, Wrigley Field, Shibe Park, Griffith Stadium, Comiskey Park, or Navin Field, which then became Briggs Stadium before becoming Tiger Stadium?) If businesses want to sponsor (and they do) pregame lineup announcements, calls to the bullpen, seventh-inning stretches—good.

But advertisements on uniforms cross a line—a fine line, but one worth drawing—between advertising so strategically placed so that large numbers of people are apt to see it (say, on the scoreboard) and advertising so unavoidable it is assaultive. Advertising on players, the necessary focus of fans' attention, obscures the fact that within the cheerful swirl of commerce at a ballpark, there is a baseball game—dignified competition in a zone of its own, within the white lines.

Furthermore, baseball, unique among American sports, is in its second century of traditions that are still more often cherished than traduced. Those traditions, which include some teams' uniforms (Yankees, Red Sox, Cardinals, among others), are a marketable asset. So baseball has a *business* interest in conserving the aura of being a bit more than a mere business. So leave the sleeves alone.

April 8, 1999

Oh, Swell. New York Wins Again.

Only in America. In a year in which presidential politics is a Horatio Alger story, proving that a Yale-educated son of a president can grow up to run for president against a Harvard-educated son of a senator, the national pastime is proving that two teams from New York, each with a payroll the size of the GDP of a medium-sized Third World nation, can get to the World Series. Is this a great country or what?

Listen up, New York. Not that you, in your self-absorption, give a damn, but this is how the rest of us feel about your October party: A wit who disliked both Thomas Carlyle and Mrs. Carlyle said that it was good of God to arrange for the two of them to marry so that only two people instead of four would be made miserable. For America west of the Hudson, the best thing about a subway Series is that it *guarantees* that millions of New York baseball fans—the followers of whichever team loses—are going to be depressed.

A subway Series is particularly galling to us geezers who were growing up embittered when, from 1949 through 1953, the Yankees won all five Series. In 1949, 1952, and 1953 they played the Dodgers. In 1951 they played the Giants, who played in the Polo Grounds, just across the Harlem River from Yankee Stadium. (In 1951 all *three* New York teams finished first: the Dodgers and Giants tied, and the Giants won the playoff on Bobby Thomson's home run.) What happened in 1950 that prevented every game of five consecutive Series being played in New York? This happened.

The Philadelphia Phillies, who had been in only one World Series (in 1915, which they lost), suffered a September swoon, shrinking their nine-game lead over the Dodgers, and they were limping. The Phillies lost seven of nine; the Dodgers won twelve of fifteen and trailed the Phillies by just two with two games to play, in Brooklyn. The Phillies lost the first. If they lost the last one, they would face a three-game playoff against the sizzling Dodgers.

The score was 1–1 in the bottom of the ninth when Cal Abrams reached second with no one out. Robin Roberts pitched to Duke Snider, who scorched a single to center fielder Richie Ashburn, like Roberts and Snider a future Hall of Famer. Ashburn could run like a whippet and played shallow. He fielded Snider's hit on the first bounce. The Dodgers' third-base coach waved Abrams around third. Abrams was out by a country mile. The Phillies won in the tenth. But had Abrams been held at third, with Jackie Robinson, Carl Furillo, and Gil Hodges due up, the Dodgers probably would have won and probably would have whomped the sagging Phillies in the playoff. In the Series, the Yankees swept the Phillies.

But for that third-base coach's mistake (for which he was fired), no Series game after 1948 and before 1954 would have been played outside a circle with a seven-mile radius. In 1954 the Indians beat the Yankees by winning an American League record 111 games (in a 154-game season). If 103 wins (the 1954 Yankees total) had, as 103 almost always do, sufficed to earn a place in the Series, the Yankees would have been in six straight. Make that ten straight: they were in the 1955, 1956, 1957, and 1958 Series. They were also there in 1960, 1961, 1962, 1963, and 1964.

In the twentieth century's ninety-five Series, more than half—forty-nine—included at least one New York team, and thirteen featured two. Thirty-three Series were won by New York teams—twenty-five by the Yankees. So now a new century begins and . . . yet again both Series teams are from New York. As has been said, history isn't one damn thing after another; it's the same damn thing over and over.

This year Payroll Number 1 (the Yankees' $114 million) battles Payroll Number 3 (the Mets' $99.8 million). Somehow Payroll Number 2 (the Dodgers' $105 million) managed to miss the postseason. The Yankees and Mets would not be where they are if the people running them did not have tremendous baseball acumen. But they also have huge advantages in local broadcast revenues. There is something amiss in baseball when so much is predictable just by counting the number of television sets in each team's market.

A few weeks ago this column dealt with a report (submitted to Baseball Commissioner Bud Selig by Yale president Richard Levin, former senator George Mitchell, former Federal Reserve Board chairman Paul Volcker, and this columnist) concerning Major League Baseball's revenue disparities and competitive balance. The report documented that today's gargantuan revenue disparities produce ludicrous payroll disparities and competitive imbalance. The report noted that in the five seasons since the 1994 strike, there had been 158 postseason games, *all* won by teams in the top two payroll quartiles. And all World Series games had been won by teams in the *top* quartile.

Critics of the report noted this year's successes of the A's (the twenty-third largest payroll), White Sox (twenty-fourth), and Giants (eighteenth). Well. Their combined postseason record this year: three wins, nine losses. Depending on whether this year's Series goes four, five, six, or seven games, the teams in the top two quartiles will have won between 185 and 188 postseason games since 1994, those in the bottom two quartiles only 3.

Now, one does not want to be a wet blanket at baseball's movable feast, the World Series. Both the Yankees and Mets are gallant competitors, blending youth and age and featuring at least four probable future Hall of Famers (Mike Piazza, Derek Jeter, Roger Clemens, Joe Torre, and perhaps John Franco, Bernie Williams, and Mariano Rivera, too). Arguably, the Yankee dynasty is, on balance, beneficial to baseball. If there's no Goliath, there is no way for Davids to prove their pluck. And the trains (yes, children, there were such things) that took the Yankees to Saint Louis created a reason to buy a ticket to see the Browns (yes, children, there was such a team). Besides, the two best teams are supposed to get to the Series, and this year they seem to have.

One more thing: a subway Series encourages New Yorkers to vent their native rudeness on each other rather than on the rest of us.

October 30, 2000

Americans voted with their remote controls and gave the subway Series the lowest television ratings in World Series history.

Nykesha Sales Misses the Point

Has New England lost its once formidable mind? Evidently, given the goings-on at the University of Connecticut, and with a senator from Vermont.

Nykesha Sales, a senior on U. Conn.'s women's basketball team, was one point shy of the school record when she suffered a season-ending injury. Her coach is just a man, but a Nineties Man—caring and sensitive. He felt her pain and got Villanova's coach to agree that at the beginning of the game Villanova would stand around while Sales hobbled to the basket for an uncontested layup. U. Conn. would give Villanova an uncontested layup and the game would continue, with everyone feeling noble. The person whose record Sales broke said she could think of no reason why this was improper.

Here is why. Part of the beauty and much of the moral seriousness of sport derives from the severe justice of strenuous play in a circumscribed universe of rules that protect the integrity of competition. Records are worth recording—and worth striving to surpass—because they serve as benchmarks of excellence achieved *under the pressure of competition.*

Some people say that what may be the most revered record in American sports—Joe DiMaggio's fifty-six-game hitting streak in 1941—was facilitated by one or more sympathetic rulings by which official scorers turned what should have been errors into DiMaggio hits. But if so, at least those were not public travesties proudly staged, as by U. Conn.

Going into the last day of the 1941 season, Ted Williams was batting .3995. If he had sat out that Sunday's doubleheader, his average would have been rounded up to .400. Not wanting to back into glory, he played, went six for eight, finishing at .406. That was sportsmanship and respect for the game.

On the last day of the 1910 season, the detested Ty Cobb was not playing, and he led the well-liked Napoleon Lajoie for the batting title. Lajoie would need a hit in almost every at bat in that day's doubleheader against the Browns. The Browns manager told a rookie third baseman to play far back, lest he get hurt by Lajoie line drives. Lajoie went eight for nine, including six bunts toward third. Baseball's government (back then, it had one) counted Lajoie's eight hits but fiddled enough arithmetic to declare Cobb the winner over Lajoie, .384944 to .384084.

What did the government—the commissioner—of the Big East Conference do about U. Conn.'s antics? Feminists, who are not having much fun in this year of Their Man and Monica, probably did not enjoy it when the commissioner justified the Sales charade by trying to sound sensitive about gender differences. He said "men compete" but "women break down, get emotional."

Actually, such is the progress on the gender front that men are acting foolishly, too. A male judge (who does not play golf, let alone high-pressure professional golf—seventy-two holes in four days) recently issued a judicial fiat requiring the professional golf tour to allow a male golfer who has trouble walking long distances to ride in a cart. Another victory for compassion, "compensatory opportunity" (an early name for affirmative action) and the entitlement mentality: everyone is entitled to what they want, no matter what must be made a mockery of. So the mere fact that you physically cannot do something athletic is no impediment to (sort of) doing it.

And the mere fact that your favorite lake is little does not mean it cannot be a Great Lake. Congress has passed a bill containing a provision by Senator Patrick Leahy, Democrat of Vermont, declaring that there shall henceforth be six Great Lakes. Leahy's office offers many rationalizations, ranging from the fact that Lake Champlain is geologically similar to the real Great Lakes to the fact that an important Revolutionary War battle occurred on it.

The real reason is, of course, money—more money will leak into Vermont from government programs if Lake Champlain is elevated, by legislative fiat, to the glory of Lake Ontario, the smallest Great Lake, which is fifteen times larger than Lake Champlain. Never mind the unassailable principle that any piddling puddle you can see across is not a Great Lake.

Lincoln, who lived when facts were still stubborn things, asked: If I call a tail a leg, how many legs does a dog have? Five? No, four, because calling a tail a leg doesn't make it a leg. That is why Lake Champlain is not a real Great Lake and Ms. Sales scored 2,176, not 2,178, real points in her career.

March 5, 1998

1951 Diminished

Say it ain't so.

Actually, don't bother. It is so, and it illustrates the role of rules, written and unwritten, in making sport something worth caring about.

Last week, *The Wall Street Journal*'s Joshua Harris Prager turned an almost fifty-year-old rumor into a dispiriting fact. Prager's exemplary journalistic sleuthing demonstrated that baseball's most storied comeback, which culminated in baseball's most famous moment, was assisted by cheating. And the moment—Bobby Thomson's 1951 home run off Ralph Branca to give the New York Giants a bottom-of-the-ninth, come-from-behind victory over the Brooklyn Dodgers in the final game of a three-game playoff—may have been so assisted. On Sunday, Thomson admitted he took pilfered information—but not on that fateful pitch.

On August 11 the Giants were thirteen and a half games behind the Dodgers. But Giants manager Leo Durocher, never a martyr to any code of sportsmanship, had recently installed a method for stealing the finger signs by which opposing teams' catchers called for particular pitches. A man with a telescope in the Giants' centerfield clubhouse would signal by buzzer to the Giants' bullpen. There a player could relay information to the batter—say, tossing a ball in the air if a curveball was coming, doing nothing on a fastball. By August 27 the Giants had won sixteen games in a row—thirteen of them at home.

Although the Giants played brilliantly even without the illicit home field advantage—they won fourteen of their last eighteen road games—the cheating had to help. It is axiomatic: Hitting is timing, pitching is upsetting timing. Hitting a fast-moving round ball with a round bat is not a piece of cake even when you know what the pitcher intends. But knowing is a huge advantage. However, not all ways of knowing constitute cheating.

In 1961 baseball outlawed recourse to any "mechanical device" to penetrate an opponent's secrecy. Nowadays Major League Baseball notifies teams not to use "electronic equipment" to communicate during a game with any on-field personnel, including those in the dugout or clubhouse. All clubs videotape batters and pitchers, and many players consult the tape of their previous at-bats during games. But the monitors are supposed to be "well away from" the dugout.

However, acute observation, unassisted by technology, is a legitimate aspect of competition. Anything an opponent's carelessness leaves exposed to the naked eye—say, a pitcher revealing his pitch selection by holding his glove at one level when throwing a fastball and at another when throwing a breaking ball—is fair game.

Which is why pitchers and catchers are apt to change the sequence of signs when an opposition runner reaches second base, from which he can see the catcher's signs. Some players consider that a base runner at second stealing signs is akin to a player peeking at an opponent's cards in a card game: It diminishes the accomplishment of winning. Some pitchers are inclined to retaliate against a batter they think is getting signals from a runner on second.

Wes Westrum was the Giants' first-base coach on April 30, 1961, when Willie Mays hit four home runs in a nine-inning game. On all four pitches that Mays hit out, Westrum—a former catcher; catchers are baseball's best empiricists—decoded the pitcher's behavior and signaled to Mays the kind of pitch that was coming.

Mickey Mantle could hit a home run when he was so hung over he had trouble finding second base. (Yes, that happened.) Imagine when Mantle knew what pitch was coming. Which he did when Yankee pitcher Bob Turley, sitting in the dugout, deciphered the opposing pitcher's moves. Turley whistled to signal fastballs, staying silent on breaking balls.

There is no written rule, but it is part of baseball's rich common law that batters shall not glance back to see where the catcher is setting up because that reveals the intended pitch location. A catcher may give a peeking batter a polite warning. If the batter is a recidivist, the catcher then may set up outside but call for a pitch inside. When the batter leans out toward where he thinks the pitch is going, his ribs receive a lesson about respecting the common law.

Sport is a moral undertaking because it requires of participants, and it schools spectators in the appreciation of, noble things: courage, grace under pressure, sportsmanship. Sport should be the triumph of character, openly tested, not of technology, surreptitiously employed. The importance of protecting the integrity of competition from the threat of advantages obtained illicitly is underscored by the sense of melancholy, of loss, that baseball fans now feel about the no longer quite so luminous season of 1951.

February 8, 2001

Fifty-one Two-Bit Solutions

Treasury Secretary Robert Rubin clearly needs a vacation. He frets that if, as seems likely, states are given the right to choose images for the backs of quarters, Congress must forbid "frivolous or inappropriate designs." Why? Lest anything that scandalizes Washington's gravity and banality should appear where an eagle now adorns our most-used coin? Quick, before Congress spoils the fun, here are fifty-one suggestions:

Alabama: Harper Lee. She wrote only one novel, but what a novel: *To Kill a Mockingbird*. Alaska: Secretary of State William H. Seward, who bought it for two cents an acre. Arizona: Carl Hayden, sheriff in Arizona Territory, then U.S. senator for forty-one years (1927–1969) and father of the maker of modern Arizona, the Central Arizona Project. Arkansas: Sam Walton, founder of Wal-Mart. California: Forget the movie *Chinatown;* honor the man—William Mulholland—who brought water to southern California. Colorado: From the only state into which no river flows comes the life giver of the West, the Colorado River. Connecticut: Samuel Colt, whose product also helped settle the West.

Delaware: John Dickinson, one of those talented pamphleteers who kindled the Revolution and later a luminary of the Constitutional Convention. The District of Columbia: American royalty—Duke Ellington. Florida: The Florida panther, endangered emblem of America's original wildness. Georgia: Flannery O'Connor, Milledgeville's gift to American fiction. Hawaii: The U.S.S. *Arizona,* lest we forget. Idaho: Perhaps it is time to forgive and remember a son of Hailey, unlikely birthplace of a pioneer of literary modernism, Ezra Pound. Illinois: Born in Germany, John Peter Altgeld exemplified moral equilibrium under pressure as governor in the 1890s, in the era of the Pullman strike and the Haymarket riots. Indiana: Eugene V. Debs was a pioneer of generous-spirited radicalism and labor's rights. Iowa: A man whose reputation does not do justice to his merits—the engineer, humanitarian, and president from West Branch, Herbert Hoover. Kansas: Phog Allen built KU's basketball greatness as coach for thirty-nine seasons. Kentucky: One of the greatest statesmen never to be president, Henry Clay (see Washington, below).

Louisiana: Louis Armstrong, a founding father of American music. Maine: Margaret Chase Smith, who helped rescue anticommunism from Joe McCarthy. Maryland: Democracy needs the leavening raucousness of an H. L. Mencken. Massachusetts: As president he had a hard act to follow (George Washington) and to precede (Thomas Jefferson), but John Adams was among the wisest of the Founders. Michigan: A pair, each indispensable—Henry Ford and Walter Reuther. Minnesota: In 1926 a poet expressed her era's yearning for magic: "Everything today has been heavy and brown. Bring me a Unicorn to ride about the town." In 1927, in thirty-three hours between Long Island and Paris, Charles Lindbergh electrified his era. Later he married that poet, Anne Morrow. Mississippi: William Faulkner has had ample honors; Eudora Welty, a writer's writer, has not. Missouri: Huck lighting out for the territories and away from the boneheads who today want to censor him. Montana: Norman MacLean, whose *A River Runs Through It* is a hymn to the state. Nebraska: O Willa Cather of Red Cloud, who did justice to those who pioneered the prairies.

Nevada: Bugsy Siegel or Wayne Newton. Just kidding. Seriously, Frank T. Crowe, who supervised the building of Hoover Dam. New Hampshire: Robert ("I'd as soon write free verse as play tennis with the net down") Frost, who knew that "happiness makes up in height for what it lacks in length." New Jersey: Great poets can find the stuff of poetry anywhere. William Carlos Williams found it in Paterson. New Mexico: An American original, whose canvases are as stunning as this state—Georgia O'Keeffe. New York: Let's not let facts discombobulate the charming myth of Cooperstown's Abner Doubleday, who had nothing to do with inventing baseball. North Carolina: Wilmington's Michael Jordan. North Dakota: Lewis and Clark, who passed through what became Bismarck. Ohio: Folks there disliked Sherwood Anderson's fictional Winesburg, but it became a literary landmark.

Oklahoma: Jim Thorpe, one of America's first sports superstars. Oregon: The symbol of Beaverton's Nike corporation is everywhere else, so the "swoosh" might as well be on the quarter. Pennsylvania: Joe Paterno, Penn State's football coach, has proven that "student athlete" is not necessarily an oxymoron. Rhode Island: Turbulent Anne Hutchinson was expelled from Puritan Massachusetts—a good sign—and became founding mother of the smallest state. South Carolina: General James Longstreet's shilly-shallying around Gettysburg helped preserve the Union, whose coinage he can now adorn. South Dakota: Mount Rushmore, an agreeable example of American excess.

Tennessee: James Polk, who brought the nation to the Pacific, is perhaps the president with the highest ratio of real importance to historical reputation. Texas: Nolan Ryan—5,714 Ks—played baseball like a gunslinger. Utah: Brigham Young, whose westward trek still takes one's breath away, was a Moses who made it all the way to his promised land. Vermont: Born on the Fourth of July, 1872, in Plymouth Notch, the thirtieth president presided over a 45 percent increase in America's ice cream production. How many presidents deserve as much of the nation's gratitude as Calvin Coolidge does? Virginia: Stonewall Jackson, who, had he not been killed at Chancellorsville, would have been at Gettysburg and . . . (see South Carolina, above). Washington: Senator Henry M. "Scoop" Jackson (see Kentucky, above). West Virginia: Senator Robert Byrd should be his state's choice for the quarter because his rapacity in Washington accounts for torrents of money that have flowed into the state. Wisconsin: Frank Lloyd Wright, whose genius had a midwestern tang. Wyoming: Out where women shared the harshness of frontier life, women's suffrage came early, and so did the first elected woman to be inaugurated as a governor, Nellie Tayloe Ross (January 5, 1925).

If you do not like this list, make your own. The only requirement is that it contain something Washington would consider frivolous and inappropriate.

August 18, 1997

Santa and His 214,200 Reindeer

"We shall soon be having Christmas at our throats," says a character who is not the least bit like his creator, the novelist P. G. Wodehouse, who was preternaturally cheerful through all his ninety-four years. Today the nation begins its annual recovery from its collision with Christmas, vowing to shape up and sin no more, right after the next cup of eggnog.

And there you sit, stunned reader, knee-deep in the remnants of gift wrappings, somewhere in the drifts of which are buried the batteries and two or three tiny and indispensable plastic parts for a toy. Feeling put-upon? Consider how Santa is feeling this morning.

With the help of calculations from a science newsletter published by the National Association of Scholars, you can appreciate what Santa accomplished last night. Actually, he did it in thirty-one hours, thanks to the many time zones and the Earth's rotation, and assuming that he has the good sense to work from east to west.

If we count as children all people under eighteen, there are 2 billion of them. The newsletter assumes, unconvincingly, that Santa does not deliver to

Muslim, Hindu, Jewish, and Buddhist children—as though they don't see Santa at their local Neiman-Marcus and demand to board the gravy train. But if the newsletter is correct (and if civil rights laws do not get Santa prosecuted for having a "disparate impact" on various protected classes of people), Santa's constituency is just 15 percent of the world's children, or 378 million.

Assuming, on the basis of world census figures, 3.5 children per household, Santa must visit 91.8 million homes, or 822.6 households per second. That gives him one one-thousandth of a second to tether the reindeer to the chimney, or perhaps the satellite dish, get down the chimney, distribute the loot, scarf down the Oreos and milk (or perhaps Stilton and port in the tonier precincts), and get moving again on his journey of (assuming an urban-rural mix of Santa's target audience and a distance of 0.78 miles between households) 75.5 million miles.

So his sleigh is moving 650 miles per second, which is three thousand times the speed of sound—a hop, skip, and a jump ahead of the fastest thing made by man, the Ulysses space probe, which putters along at 27.4 miles per second. A conventional reindeer, on a good day and steroids, can hit fifteen miles per hour.

However, the newsletter judiciously notes that although no flying, sound-barrier-busting reindeer have been found, there are 300,000 species of living organisms yet to be classified. Granted, most are insects and germs, but even if 299,999 are insects and germs, we cannot rule out the possibility of a species of remarkable reindeer, even a species with a total population of just eight. (Or 214,200. See below.)

Santa's postulated reindeer certainly earn whatever they eat. They haul a sleigh that is heavier than fruitcake.

The newsletter suggests assuming that each child gets only, say, a medium-size Lego set weighing two pounds. David Maseng Will, age five, who weighs his Christmas take on a truck scale, says the newsletter should be better briefed on the modern child's expectations. But even on the weird assumption, the sleigh leaves the North Pole carrying 321,300 tons, not counting Santa, who, were he a she, would be delicately described as "full-figured."

The newsletter insists that a normal, walking-around reindeer can pull three hundred pounds, tops. That is about what Santa probably weighs at the peak of an enlarging season of candy canes and pfeffernuesse cookies. However, the calculation assumes that Santa's unconventional reindeer can pull ten times more than the conventional sort. Even so, Santa needs not eight but 214,200 reindeer. And that herd increases the weight on your roof to 353,430 tons, which the newsletter says "is four times the weight of the *Queen Elizabeth* (the ship, not the person)."

Trouble is, air resistance from 353,430 tons traveling 650 miles per second generates terrific heat, so the two lead reindeer, who won't be that for long, each absorb 14.3 quintillion joules of energy per second. They instantly burst into flame, as then do the two behind them, and then the next two, and so on. Santa runs through 214,200 reindeer in 4.26 thousandths of a second.

Not that he notices. He is disoriented by deafening sonic booms and by experiencing centrifugal forces 17,500 times the force of gravity. Even if he weighs only 250 pounds, he is slammed into the back of his sleigh with 4,315,015 pounds of force.

The newsletter concludes that Santa is dead but it cannot explain who put the lump of coal in its stocking.

December 25, 1997

NASA and the Meaning, if Any, of Life

The Department of Transportation deals with the movement of things, which is important. The Department of Agriculture deals with food, which is vital. However, the National Aeronautics and Space Administration deals with the origin, nature, and meaning, if any, of the universe. Attention should be paid.

Space lost its hold on America's imagination after the last lunar expedition in 1972. But the really exciting research had just begun, with the 1965 discovery that the universe is permeated with background radiation that confirmed that a Big Bang had indeed set what are now distant galaxies flying apart.

A famous aphorism holds that the most incomprehensible thing about the universe is that it is comprehensible. It is remarkably so because of advances in particle physics and mathematics. And because of magnificent telescopes, such as the Hubble, which is now eleven years old and due to cease functioning in 2010. Operating above the filter of Earth's atmosphere, it "sees" the past by capturing for analysis light emitted from events perhaps—we cannot be sure how fast the universe is expanding—12 billion years ago.

Astronomy is history, and NASA's Next Generation Space Telescope, coming late in this decade, will see even nearer the Big Bang of 13 billion to 15 billion years ago. That was when, in a trillionth of a trillionth of a trillionth of a second, the Big Bang inflated from a microscopic speck to all that now can be seen by NASA's wondrous instruments.

Mankind is being put in its place, but where is that? Mankind felt demoted by Copernicus's news that this cooled cinder, Earth, is not the center of the universe. Now Martin Rees, Britain's Astronomer Royal, in his new book, *Our Cosmic Habitat,* adds insult to injury: "particle chauvinism" must go. All the atoms that make us are, it is truly said, stardust. But Rees puts it more prosaically: they are nuclear waste from the fuel that makes stars shine.

So is life a cosmic fluke or a cosmic imperative? Because *everything* is a reverberation from the Big Bang, what is the difference between fluke and imperative?

Rees says our universe is "biophilic"—friendly to life—in that molecules of water and atoms of carbon, which are necessary for life, would not have resulted from a Big Bang with even a slightly different recipe. That recipe was cooked in the universe's first one-hundredth of a second, when its temperature was a hundred thousand million degrees Centigrade. A biophilic universe is like Goldilocks' porridge, not too hot and not too cold—just right.

Here cosmology is pressed into the service of natural theology, which rests on probability—actually, on the stupendous improbability of the emergence from chaos of complexity and then consciousness. Natural theology says: A watch implies a watchmaker and what happened in the universe–the distillation of the post–Big Bang cosmic soup into particles, then atoms, then, about a billion years ago, the first multicellular organisms that led, on Earth, to an oxygen-rich atmosphere and eventually to us—implies a Creator with a design so precise.

Perhaps. But not necessarily, unless you stipulate that no consequential accident is an accident. "Biological evolution," says Rees, "is sensitive to accidents—climatic changes, asteroid impacts, epidemics and so forth—so that, if Earth's history were to be rerun, its biosphere would end up quite different." There is a lot of stuff in the universe—the estimated number of stars is 10 followed by twenty-two zeros. But as to whether there are other planets with life like Earth's, Rees says the chance of two similar ecologies is less than the chance of two randomly typing monkeys producing the same Shakespearean play.

"Eternity," says Woody Allen, "is very long, especially toward the end." The end of our universe—long after our sun has died, 5 billion years from now—is certain to be disagreeable.

In his book on the universe's infancy *(The First Three Minutes),* Steven Weinberg concludes that "there is not much of comfort" in cosmology. It indicates that Earth, "a tiny part of an overwhelmingly hostile universe," is headed for "extinction of endless cold or intolerable heat," either an unending expansion or a fiery collapse backward—a Big Crunch.

Yet research such as NASA's is its own consolation. "The effort to understand the universe is," says Weinberg, "one of the very few things that lifts human life a little above the level of farce, and gives it some of the grace of tragedy." Not a negligible mission for NASA.

February 22, 2002

1997: Year of Living Dangerously

It was largely a year of contentment—by the standards of this blood-soaked and ideologically intoxicated century, a year of serenity. Yet it also was a year of living lachrymosely. Not since the 1920s has there been a year in which politics mattered less. And the memory of man runneth not to a year when there was an episode of disproportion comparable to the planetwide vapors occasioned by one of the year's uncountably numerous automobile accidents, this one in Paris. At year's end, surely there were many millions of people who had participated in the great global crying three months earlier and who were wondering, perhaps a bit sheepishly, "What was that all about?"

The biggest news, an event that really was momentous, was of a sort that seemed barely discernible as an event. That is because it actually was a con-catenation of trillions of events—all the choices and exertions by billions of people around the world, but most remarkably in America, that drove the cur-rent process of rapid and sustained wealth creation, for which there simply is no historical precedent. This republic, born of religious impulses and disci-plines that proved conducive to commerce (thrift, industriousness, deferral of gratifications), was, in the eighth year of the century's tenth decade, pleased by its productivity but queasy about the continued coarsening of its culture. And some Americans were uneasy about the possibility that America's first great scold had been prescient: *"Religion brought forth Prosperity, and the daughter destroyed the mother. . . . There is danger lest the enchantments of this world make them forget their errand into the wilderness."* Thus spoke Cotton Mather.

So prodigiously did economic growth generate revenues for the govern-ment, the political class could hardly avoid balancing the budget. But it did avoid it. While preening about producing—well, promising, for the year 2002—the first balanced budget since 1969, the political class proved itself more united by class interests than divided by ideology: it generated a geyser of domestic spending increases that prevented the economy from balancing the budget right now. Republicans ran a Congress that increased appropriations for all the Cabinet-level departments that Republicans so recently were promising to abolish, and for the Legal Services Corporation and the Corporation for Pub-lic Broadcasting and . . . and so ended the noisy pretense of Infantile Republi-canism, the idea that there was afoot a challenge to the post–New Deal, or at least the post–Great Society, configuration of the central government.

Seventy people fled the country or took the Fifth Amendment to avoid talking about the president's innovative campaign finance practices, which he said were beyond reproach and proof that reforms are urgently needed. Re-formers said there is "too much" money in politics. Ted Turner promised $1 billion to the United Nations. The movie *Titanic* cost more ($200 million) than the president's 1996 campaign. Edith Haisman, the oldest survivor of the *Titanic,* died at 100. So did Frank Shomo, 108, the last survivor of the Johnstown flood of May 31, 1889, when he was 100 days old.

The world was made safe from land mines and chemical weapons—it says so, on pieces of paper. Perhaps Saddam Hussein, who demonstrated that U.N. inspectors are in Iraq at his sufferance, has not read those pieces of paper.

In Iowa a fertility specialist counted to seven and declared that the treatment of Mrs. McCaughey had achieved an unexpected degree of "success." In Boca Raton, Florida, an umpire asked if the twelve-year-old catcher was wearing a protective cup. "I'm a girl," said Melissa Raglin. That's no excuse. Rules are rules, said some baseball bureaucrats. The president of the local chapter of the National Organization for Women sniffed, "Harassment." A friend of Timothy McVeigh's testified, "If you don't consider what happened in Oklahoma City, Tim is a good person."

A gadget named Sojourner gave the world a close-up glimpse of Mars—in the nick of time, given that evidence from the Hubble telescope suggested that a galaxy racing toward our galaxy at 300,000 miles an hour may produce an obliterating collision in just 5 billion years. Thirty-nine adherents of Heaven's Gate decided not to wait. A sheep named Dolly was a marvel. So was a golfer named Tiger.

Alberta Martin, 90, the last living widow of a Confederate veteran, was 21 when she married her husband, who was then 81 and promptly fathered a child. Daisy Anderson, one of two known surviving widows of Union veterans, was 21 when she married an ex-slave, then 79, who had enlisted after the Emancipation Proclamation. Alberta and Daisy met this year at Gettysburg, at the burial of a casualty from July 1–3, 1863—no one knows from which side—whose remains were found last year, protruding from the hallowed ground.

Time's scythe took from us perhaps the best ballplayer never to play in the major league—the first baseman for the Homestead Grays, Buck Leonard, who was known as "the black Lou Gehrig" because a racially blinkered nation did not yet know how to think of Gehrig as the white Buck Leonard. For connoisseurs of sinewy prose and savory journalism, no death diminished the public stock of pleasure more than that of columnist Murray Kempton, who crafted sentences like this (concerning an Eisenhower campaign stop in 1956):

> *In Miami, he had walked carefully by the harsher realities, speaking some twenty feet from an airport drinking fountain labeled "Colored" and saying that the condition it represented was more amenable to solution by the hearts of men than by laws, and complimenting Florida as "typical today of what is best in America," a verdict which might seem to some contingent on finding out what happened to the Negro snatched from the Wildwood jail Sunday.*

In 1997 America was in many ways a much better place than it was when that sentence was written, but it did not have any better craftsman than Kempton.

December 29, 1997

1998: Not in Good Taste

"Tasteless," said the ombudsman for women's issues in Hannover, Germany, speaking not of the food but of the restaurant that serves its "sushi a la Jungfrau [virgin]," spread over naked women with caviar stuffed in their navels. But if *real* tastelessness is your taste . . .

What Eve or an apple or a serpent did to Adam (whichever did it, we know it wasn't *his* fault), the intern's thong underwear did to Bill Clinton. The worst political year since 1968 began with the First Victim assuring the nation that her sweetie pie was a victim of the Vast Right-Wing Conspiracy. By the end of the year the VRWC included even most moderate Republicans, a species about as fierce as fireflies. Scientists examining light from distant stars concluded that the universe has been expanding steadily since the Big Bang and will expand forever. Good. Maybe someday there will be someplace far enough away that there will not be even a whiff of the Clintons' fragrance.

So mesmerizing was the spectacle of Clinton's self-immolation, many may have missed the little sigh that signaled the end of the "Republican Revolution." Four years after the cymbal-crash elections of 1994, Republican control of Congress had produced . . . oh, never mind. In California, the Republican gubernatorial candidate gave a speech on education reform while standing beneath a sign proclaiming DAN LUNGREN—CALIFORNIA'S NEXT GOVENOR.

Virtuecrats were not on sabbatical in 1998. They were on crusade against smoking, the theory being: although there are almost as many ex-smokers as smokers in America, smokers are not responsible for their actions. And although government gains monetarily from smoking (cigarettes are the world's most heavily taxed consumer good, and many smokers die before collecting their Medicare and Social Security entitlements), governments should sue tobacco companies to "recoup" the costs of smoking. Result? Lawyers' fees of $8.2 billion. In Chicago, a son, 51, sued his mother for calling him names. What did she call him, "litigious"?

Responding to, and fomenting, the latest health fright, your government, unsleeping in its nannyness, proposed that airlines establish peanut-free seating areas. And some schools, where the curriculum probably is toxic, banned peanut butter. In a small upstate New York community a public-school teacher with tenure was fired for incompetence, slovenliness, disobedience, and physically abusing students. And the firing required only three years, twenty hearings, $200,000 in legal fees, and an undisclosed payment to the teacher.

Mark Twain said he would like to live in Manchester, England, because the transition to death would be unnoticeable. The pope visited Cuba, the Castroite bleakness of which has earned its author his destination in the next life. Something resembling peace came to Ireland. When India conducted a nuclear test, the United States warned Pakistan: Do not respond. Pakistan said: Please speak up—we can't hear you over the noise of our nuclear test. The United States warned Serbia not to do in Kosovo what it had done in Bosnia. Then the United States warned Serbia not to do it again. Once too often Iraq tormented Uncle Sam, who, eschewing pinprick attacks, inflicted a knitting-needle attack.

Echoes of wars: In Spotsylvania, Virginia, the National Park Service improved signs to help the flocks of tourists find where Stonewall Jackson's arm is buried. The nation showed its gratitude to the World War II generation with *Saving Private Ryan* and Viagra. Those who were inconsolable about the end of *Seinfeld* somehow found the strength to go on. In London, fifteen thousand spectators were projected for the march commemorating the first anniversary of the death of Princess Diana. Three hundred showed up.

Death, as it must to all, came to W. E. Diemer, 93. In 1928, as a young accountant at the Fleer Chewing Gum Company in Philadelphia, he was messing around with a recipe and the only food coloring handy (it was pink) when—eureka!—he invented bubble gum. When Daisy Anderson was 21, she married a 79-year-old veteran—*there* is a soldier we should all salute—and her death at 97 leaves just two remaining widows of Civil War veterans. Three Westerners wearing white hats rode off into the sunset: Roy Rogers, Gene Autry, and Barry Goldwater. Ol' Blue Eyes, gone to the Recording Studio in the Sky, should be careful not to step on Carl Perkins's blue suede shoes.

Chet Hoff, 107, who was the oldest former major leaguer, remembered striking out Ty Cobb in 1911. When the cab taking Dick Sisler to Ebbets Field for the last game of the 1950 season stopped at a traffic light, a priest recognized the ballplayer and offered him a rose, which he said was blessed. Sisler said, "Father, I'm not a Catholic." The priest said, "Take it anyway. Maybe it will bring you good luck." In the top of the tenth Sisler touched the rose in his uniform pocket, then homered. His Phillies—yes, the *Phillies*—won the pennant. Now, *that's* a miracle. The sports number of 1998 was 136—home runs by just two guys. In Massachusetts (of course!) they call it "nonresult-oriented competition": no keeping score in soccer games for those ten or younger. "It's dumb and stupid," says a ten-year-old fascist. "It's fun to win." The government will come after him when it is finished with Microsoft.

The year sagged to a close with a Kentucky woman, a former Santa Claus, suing Wal-Mart for sex discrimination. She was replaced by a man when a boy pinched her breast (why isn't he being sued for impersonating a president?) and exclaimed, "Mom, Santa Claus is a woman!" Wal-Mart's lawyer says, "Santa Claus is a man. He has a beard. He is married to Mrs. Claus." Why isn't that lawyer being sued for the indelicate utterance of the obvious? In South Africa, archaeologists unearthed the skeleton of the earliest (so far discovered) upright-walking predecessor of *Homo sapiens.* The skeleton was face down, almost as though the creature had seen 1998 coming.

December 28, 1998

1999: Satisfactory, Sort Of

Nineteen ninety-nine was a suitable exclamation point for a century that would like to be remembered more for its wealth than for its wars. America's prodigious wealth creation threatened to deprive Americans of the delights of complaining, at least other than as Gilbert and Sullivan did:

> *Oh don't the days seem lank and long*
> *When all goes right and nothing goes wrong.*
> *And isn't your life extremely flat*
> *With nothing whatever to grumble at!*

Some baseball fans grumbled: a Los Angeles TV sports anchor said, "Dodgers and Angels highlights at eleven. Please watch anyway." And there was war.

In Kosovo—actually, *over* Kosovo—NATO practiced a kind of warfare made possible by modern technologies and perhaps made necessary by modern sensibilities. It was a war waged on the principle that there are values important enough to fight, meaning kill, for, even if they are not important enough to die for.

Kosovo was a small, mostly Muslim entity, brutalized by a mostly Orthodox nation of which Kosovo was (and is) legally a part. As the year ends, Chechnya is a small, mostly Muslim entity being brutalized by a mostly . . . oh, never mind. At the year-end, Albanians in Kosovo are conducting ethnic cleansing against Serbs in Kosovo.

Hillary Clinton visited the Balkans and said scenes of ethnic cleansing reminded her of—the Holocaust? No, silly, she's a baby boomer, so the scenes reminded her of a *movie* about the Holocaust *(Schindler's List)*. When she decided to make of herself a gift to New York, Pat Moynihan, whose Senate seat she aspires to fill (well, occupy), tartly said she would bring to the job "Illinois/Arkansas enthusiasm."

The author of the autobiography *Monica's Story* said, "I like to be able to reach up on my bookshelf for one of Shakespeare's plays, and I would like to think that people will do that with this book." The majestic constitutional machinery of impeachment seemed simply too large to employ against someone as small as Bill Clinton. Elsewhere, the annals of romance were enriched: Romeo and Juliet, Abélard and Héloïse, John McCain and the national media.

The Republican-controlled Congress, which convened five years ago vowing death to four Cabinet departments, especially Education, this year appropriated for Education $320 million more than Clinton requested. When marines in North Carolina were ordered to fly forty-two jets out of the path of Hurricane Bonnie, only twenty-one were fit to fly. The sclerotic government, fierce protector of the public education system, called Microsoft a dangerous monopoly and lectured it on the importance of innovation.

Friends of high art were in high dudgeon when Mayor Rudolph Giuliani opposed a museum exhibition that included a portrait of the Virgin Mary splattered with elephant dung. Would the dudgeon have been as high if Giuliani had acted, as surely he would have, against similar treatment of a portrait of Martin Luther King?

Some 2.5-million-year-old skeletal remains of a creature who used tools—sharp stones, to cut meat—were discovered in Ethiopia. They may come from the earliest known human ancestor. Scientists discovered an ancient coastline 550 feet below the Black Sea, evidence of a catastrophic flood about 7,500 years ago, perhaps when Noah set sail. The Associated Press: "Israel has marked a new spot where it says Jesus fed a multitude of 4,000 with just a handful of fish and loaves." *Israel* says that?

In the publishing fiasco of the year, Edmund Morris wrote an unintelligible novel about himself and called it a memoir of Ronald Reagan. Three books about Harry Potter of the Hogwarts School of Witchcraft and Wizardry were numbers one, two, and three on the best-seller list, and exasperated children were snapping at their parents, "Please turn off the TV, we're trying to read."

Crayola renamed its "Indian red" crayon "chestnut." Next target for the sensitivity police: the Oldsquaw duck. A Department of Agriculture diversity enforcer was indignant about lack of diversity on the Florida Tomato Committee.

Even though no notice is posted forbidding the sin, a spokesman for New York City's Parks Department justified the $1,000 ticket issued to a man whose two daughters, 9 and 11, and a friend, 11, were caught climbing a tree in Central Park: "If we listed every rule, we'd have more signs than trees." More from the annals of crime: "I don't think we'll be tape-measuring," said a sheriff's spokesman concerning the Manatee County, Florida, ordinance forbidding women to expose more than 75 percent of their breasts in public, or anyone to expose more than two-thirds of his or her buttocks. Russian mobsters rented a casino for a bash to celebrate Al Capone's hundredth birthday. Sergei Khrushchev, Nikita's son, 63, became an American citizen.

The best players in the history of hockey (Wayne Gretzky) and basketball (Michael Jordan) retired, and the best columnist (Meg Greenfield) died. Bessie Cohen, dead at 107, was 19 when she survived the Triangle Shirtwaist fire that killed 146 of her coworkers in Manhattan in 1911. Prince Rostislav Romanov, a London banker and great-nephew of Tsar Nicholas II, died at 60. In 1993 his DNA helped establish that human remains found in a wood near Ekaterinburg were those of the murdered tsar and his family.

In the last month of the last year of the last century before medicine becomes *really* modern, scientists completed mapping virtually an entire human chromosome. Soon the $3 billion Human Genome Project, the most important scientific undertaking ever, will have mapped all twenty-three chromosomes. The 3 billion bits of information will lead to a revolution in the prevention, diagnosis, and treatment of diseases.

In 1999 health was helped by heeding warning labels like this on a Swedish chain saw: DO NOT ATTEMPT TO STOP CHAIN WITH YOUR HANDS.

December 20, 1999

2000: The Most Interesting Year of the Millennium, So Far

The Florida peninsula, the last part of the continental United States to emerge from the ocean, has been called a geological afterthought. This year caused many Americans to curse geology and wish that the afterthought had gone unthought. A wit says that before November 7 Al Gore argued that his opponent was a nitwit and after November 7 he argued that his voters were nitwits. George W. Bush warned people not to "misunderestimate" him, but the thirty-six-day election day showed that Gore did. The baseball team Bush used to own a bit of gave shortstop Alex Rodriguez a ten-year contract worth a *minimum* of $252 million, enough to buy the Twins and the Expos and have about $72 million in change left.

When Chicago named a street Hugh Hefner Way, an incensed man got a street in his Chicago suburb temporarily named Alan Greenspan Way. Call the behavior police: a Washington gala celebrating the thirty-fifth anniversary of Medicare featured 102-year-old Mark Powell, who said he smokes five or six cigars a day. The government, toiling to make this a more perfect union, decided to protect us from the menace of . . . Microsoft. But the government knows heroism when it sees it and honored the 131 agents who in a predawn raid managed to subdue six-year-old Elián González. Speaking of bravery, Hillary Clinton vowed that as senator she would not vote to confirm any Supreme Court nominee "who would vote to overturn *Brown v. Board of Education*."

In New Orleans, Al Davis withdrew his daughter from her public school and enrolled her in a private school. Davis is superintendent of New Orleans' public schools. In Canton, Ohio, a mother put her six-year-old, who had a doctor's appointment, into the bath so he would not notice when the school bus stopped at his house. But when the bus came he ran naked to the window. His school ruled him guilty of sexual harassment of the children on the bus. Bowdoin College's catalog described a women's studies course that asks, "Is Beethoven's Ninth Symphony a marvel of abstract architecture, culminating in a gender-free hymn to human solidarity, or does it model the processes of rape?" The faculty at Ohio's Bowling Green State University vetoed a professor's planned course on political correctness. Kathleen Dixon, director of women's studies at the university, explained, "We forbid any course that says we restrict free speech."

At Camp David, Israel's Prime Minister Ehud Barak offered Yasser Arafat unprecedented concessions, and the result was (redundant) evidence for the axiom that no good deed goes unpunished. A referendum in mighty Denmark told the European Union's single-currency bullies to buzz off. Taiwanese voters gave the U.S. State Department heartburn: they had the temerity to elect a president who thinks his nation actually is a nation and should be treated as what it actually is—independent. Saddam Hussein spent another year in what Secretary of State Madeleine Albright contentedly calls a "box." Trouble is, he is in there building weapons of mass destruction.

Feminists in several nations worked to ban male urinals because urinating standing up is an assertion of aggressive masculinity. The Serbian people replaced Slobodan Milošević with a professor who translated into Serbian the world's best recipe for good government, *The Federalist Papers*. The United States tiptoed into the chaos of Colombia's interminable civil war, in the name of—really—fighting drugs. (America's biggest drug pusher is government, shoveling Ritalin into public-school pupils—especially boys, to cure their boyishness.) Americans are still at daggers drawn over the Confederate flag, but 310 years after the Battle of the Boyne, America's president had a bright idea, captured in this *Los Angeles Times* headline: "Clinton Tells Northern Ireland to Resolve Issues." Why didn't anyone think of that before?

Thirty-seven years after a bomb killed four little African-American girls in a Birmingham church, two men, 61 and 69, were arrested for the crime. There was carnage among the dot-coms, but it was a good year—these things are relative—for the Soprano family. It was a bad year for Firestone and the end of the road for Oldsmobile. Professional wrestling's popularity, a television program about voting people off a deserted island, and adults playing on little silver scooters were evidence of the infantilization of America. Torrid sales of the fourth novel about the boys and girls at Hogwarts School for Witchcraft and Wizardry suggested that America's children are less childish than America's adults. O. J. Simpson got into a traffic altercation, probably while searching for the real killers.

It is said that not until about 1910 did the average visit to a doctor do more good than harm. Around that time, Oliver Wendell Holmes said, "I firmly believe that if the whole *materia medica* could be sunk to the bottom of the sea, it would be all the better for mankind and all the worse for the fishes." Medicine has advanced, but historians may say that the age of modern medicine dawned with the decoding of the human genome, which was nearly completed this year. In sub-Saharan Africa the AIDS pandemic raged.

Death came at 100 to Josef Felder, the last of the ninety-four members of the Reichstag who on March 23, 1933, voted against ceding the Parliament's powers to Hitler. Colonel Thomas Ferebee, dead at 81, was a 26-year-old major on August 6, 1945, when he pushed the lever that released a new kind of bomb from the B-29 *Enola Gay*. Clyde Sukeforth, Brooklyn Dodgers scout, coach, and manager, died at 98. He introduced a promising infielder to club president Branch Rickey: "Mr. Rickey, here is Jack Roosevelt Robinson." In the bottom of the ninth inning of the 1951 Dodgers–Giants playoff game, Sukeforth answered the Polo Grounds bullpen phone and recommended that Ralph Branca rather than Carl Erskine pitch to Bobby Thomson. Oh, well.

December 25, 2000

2001: Ring the Bells Backward

On the morning of September 11, commuters heading for World Trade Center offices read *New York Times* front-page headlines about the arrest of a person charged with hijacking an airliner from Canada to Cuba thirty years ago and about rumored smuggling of nuclear materials in Central Asia. And about attempts to regulate displays of bare midriffs and cleavage in a New Jersey high school. Northern Virginia commuters driving past the Pentagon carried *Washington Posts* with a front-page headline about—you may remember this short-lived creature—the budget surplus. September 10 had been a slow news day.

Year 2001 began just after dueling supreme courts, Florida's and the nation's, settled one of the strangest presidential elections. The president inaugurated on January 20 would, conventional wisdom said, be unable to lead. On September 20, he spoke to a joint session of Congress, and conventional wisdom changed.

Year 2001 ended with perhaps the most remarkable demonstration of military might in American, if not world, history: less than three months after the most lethal terrorism in human experience, a regime complicit in the attacks was annihilated by U.S. power projected 8,000 miles. Some U.S. munitions were delivered by planes that took off in Missouri; others were guided to targets by special forces operating on horseback against cave dwellers.

September 11 caused the demotion of some worries. After the attacks, when F-16s began patrolling over Washington and New York, the Environmental Protection Agency stopped complaining that F-16 reconnaissance flights over Iraq were venting gases that threaten the earth's ozone layer. Planned Parenthood of New York City responded to September 11 by offering free abortions at certain locations.

An American corporation cloned a human embryo, rekindling anxieties voiced two centuries ago by Charles Lamb: "Can we ring the bells backward? Can we unlearn the arts that pretend to civilize, and then burn the world? There is a march of science; but who shall beat the drums for its retreat?"

An Oxford University newsletter said that between 1968 and 1970 Bill Clinton "followed the B.Phil. course." "Followed"? What a delicate way of saying he failed to get a degree. Oxford's Balliol College alumni notes included this from Nick Tee, a 1968 graduate: "I legally became Nicola Dian Capron Tee last year." A New Jersey court ruled that "gender dysphoria"—dissatisfaction with one's gender—is a protected handicap under state law protecting the disabled. A health plan for city employees was expanded to cover sex-change operations. In San Francisco, of course.

A Utah brewery advertised its Polygamy Porter with the slogan "Why have just one?" An English grocer became the "Metric Martyr," convicted of the crime of selling bananas measured in pounds and ounces, in violation of EU regulations. A Bavarian who made a rude gesture at a traffic camera was convicted of the crime of rudeness toward the police. School officials in West Annapolis, Maryland, adopted this zero-tolerance policy about sexual harassment: playing tag violates the "no touching" decree.

When Enron's share price was $84, the company's market capitalization was $70 billion. Then, suddenly, the share price was 25 cents. But American entrepreneurship produced contact lenses that turn the wearer's eyes the color of his favorite NFL team, such as the 49ers' red and gold. The University of

Illinois offered this history course: "Oprah Winfrey: The Tycoon." To finance a house, a New York couple tried to sell to a corporation, by Internet auction, the naming rights to their baby. No takers. His name is plain Zane.

Lithuania's newest theme park is Stalin's World, for those nostalgic for the good old gulag days. It is surrounded by barbed wire and watchtowers. Inside are concentration camp barracks and statues of Lenin, Stalin, and other builders of socialism. Admission costs $1.40.

In a year when America was yanked back into the maelstrom of history, many obituaries evoked some of the stony paths to the present. Such as that of Rex T. Barber, 84, who was one of the P-38 pilots who on April 18, 1943, using information from cracked Japanese codes, shot down Admiral Yamamoto, who made December 7 a day that would one day be a companion to September 11 in America's memory. Montana's Mike Mansfield, 98, became Senate majority leader. Fibbing about his age to recruiters, he was in the Navy at 14, just before the Yanks went "over there."

Gerhart Riegner, 90, was the World Jewish Congress official who in August 1942 alerted the world to Nazi genocide plans. Emilie Schindler, 93, was the wife of Oskar, who had a List. Murray Aronoff, 75, was a crew member of the steamship *Exodus* carrying 4,500 Jewish refugees to Palestine. He led an unsuccessful four-hour fight against British troops—"They had sidearms, machine guns and tear gas, and we had canned food and potatoes and rocks"— who boarded the ship, turning it back to Europe as part of a policy to balance the Arab and Jewish populations in Palestine. Most of its passengers later made it to Palestine.

Rose Freedman, 107, was the last survivor of the Triangle Shirtwaist fire that killed 146 in Manhattan in 1911 and spurred worker-safety legislation. Michel Navratil, 92, was the last male survivor of the *Titanic* in 1912. Percy Goring, 106, was the last known British survivor of the disastrous 1915 Gallipoli campaign that almost destroyed the career of its young architect, Winston Churchill. American Fred Roberts, dead at 105, experienced chemical warfare—mustard gas—as a doughboy in France eighty-three years ago. Gerard Zinser, 82, was the last survivor of John Kennedy's *PT 109* crew.

Finally, the nation lost two of its most distinguished women. No American has written better short stories than Eudora Welty, 92, of Jackson, Mississippi. The nation's capital lost a leader who understood the kinship of the words "city," "citizen," and "civility." Katharine Graham was 84.

December 24, 2001

THE WORLD

War Beyond the World
of Westphalia

It was a portent. At the Washington National Cathedral service three days after the September 11 attacks, the congregation, including the president, did not sing the fifth verse of the "Battle Hymn of the Republic" as it often has been sung in recent years. Many tender spirits have considered the hymn too bellicose—the grapes of wrath and the fateful lightning of a terrible swift sword—so the verse has been sung, "As He died to make men holy, let us live to make men free." At the cathedral, the verse was sung as it was written in 1862, when there was a lot of dying being done: "As He died to make men holy, let us die to make men free."

The Bush administration is telling the country that there is some dying to be done. "What this war is about is our way of life," Defense Secretary Donald Rumsfeld says, "and our way of life is worth losing lives for."

If the nation is to think clearly about war, it must ration its use of two recurring words: "justice" and "tragedy." The goal is not to "bring terrorists to justice," which suggests bringing them into sedate judicial settings—lawyers, courtrooms, due process, all preceded by punctilious readings of Miranda rights. Rather, the goal is destruction of enemies.

And what America suffered at the hands of its enemies was not a "tragedy." That word is freighted with connotations of blind forces (the San Francisco earthquake) or of inevitable misfortune arising from a deeply rooted flaw or vice (the stuff of ancient Greek tragedies). What erupted on September 11 is a war of aggression. Hence the suitability of the swift response from NATO, a defensive alliance.

Here are two of history's recent oddities. NATO was created to counter the Soviet Union, but in nearly fifty-three years the only invasion of a NATO member's territory occurred in the South Atlantic, when Argentina attacked the Falkland Islands. And when, on September 12, NATO for the first time invoked Article 5, which stipulates that an attack upon one NATO nation shall be considered an attack on all member nations, the attack in question did not come from an identifiable nation.

Some may think we have been rudely shoved beyond the world first codified by the Peace of Westphalia in 1648, the world of nation-states exercising a monopoly on the use of force. There has been much chatter about new forces—"globalization," nations "pooling" their sovereignty—making nations into entities of reduced importance. But events are demonstrating the vitality and utility of nations.

Nations govern territory and can be held accountable for what tolerated groups do when enjoying sanctuary in that territory. In combating nations that support terrorists, the pertinent nations are few, and they can be given incentives—offers they can't refuse—to police their portions of the planet.

Such policing was supposed to have been completed long ago. However, as John Keegan, the eminent British military journalist and historian, wrote six months ago, there has been regression:

> *The Clausewitzian analysis is breaking down. It is true that war is an extension of policy—but only when waged by stable states. War is escaping from state control, into the hands of bandits and anarchists. The great work of disarming tribes, sects, warlords and criminals—a principal achievement of monarchs of the 17th century and empires in the 19th—threatens to need doing all over again. Not many military establishments possess the skills, equipment and cultural ruthlessness necessary for the task."*

However, U.S. spending on counterterrorism skills and equipment has doubled in the past five years. And U.S. military history does not tell of a culture deficient in ruthlessness.

The civilian culture will take its cues from the top of the political order and the president's national security staff—two former defense secretaries (Dick Cheney and Rumsfeld), a former general victorious in a complex coalition war, who is also a former chairman of the Joint Chiefs (Colin Powell); a Russia specialist who served on the National Security Council as the Soviet Union crumbled (Condoleezza Rice)—is the most experienced since the George Marshall–Dean Acheson team of the late 1940s and early 1950s.

They will have to sup with some unsavory people, such as Russia's President Vladimir Putin, the butcher of Chechnya, who has had bitter but useful experience with Afghanistan. But as Winston Churchill said during the Second World War, if Hitler invaded Hell, he, Churchill, would find something favorable to say about the Devil.

September 23, 2001

The Relevance of General Sherman

I fear the world will jump to the wrong conclusion that because I am in Atlanta the work is done. Far from it. We must kill three hundred thousand I have told you of so often, and the further they run the harder for us to get them.

—GENERAL WILLIAM TECUMSEH SHERMAN, 1864

America's Civil War provides many analogies by which we measure—and sometimes misunderstand—today's military developments and American ways of waging war.

Because facets of the Afghanistan operations—real-time intelligence, stealthy aircraft, precision munitions—are so modern, we miss the fact that the war requires an American tradition of warmaking that has a nineteenth-century pedigree. And the bloody uprisings by fanatical Taliban and Al Qaeda prisoners underscore the pertinence of Sherman's understanding of how to define victory over an intensely motivated enemy.

When military operations in Afghanistan began, just four weeks after September 11 and three weeks after General Tommy Franks was told to begin planning attacks, some critics were quick to say that the operations had not begun quickly enough. Then they said the tempo of operations was too torpid. Critics compared Franks—and Colin Powell, ever mindful of allies' sensibilities—to General George McClellan. Those were fighting words, because McClellan was a reluctant fighter.

One of President Lincoln's commanders, McClellan was notoriously reluctant to close with Confederate forces, the strength of which he consistently overestimated. This drove Lincoln to distraction, and to sarcasm about hoping to "borrow" the army if McClellan was not using it.

Sherman, an energetic user of the army, believed its principal use against the Confederacy was not to occupy territory but to destroy enemy personnel. His reason for believing this has contemporary resonance during a war against fanatics, many of whom come from the privileged strata of corrupt and exploitative societies.

Long before secession, Sherman despised the South for its caste and class systems. In 1843, when stationed in South Carolina, he wrote, "This state, their aristocracy . . . their patriarchal chivalry and glory—all trash. No people in America are so poor in reality, no people so poorly provided with the comforts of life."

So why did the Confederate army, composed mostly of poor whites, fight for a social system beneficial only to a tiny landed minority? Partly because of the élan of its martial elite, those whom Sherman called "young bloods" who were "brave, fine riders, bold to rashness and dangerous in every sense."

Sherman, writes professor Victor Davis Hanson in his book *The Soul of Battle*, considered the Confederacy "a motley conglomeration of distrustful factions." Sherman thought the really dangerous faction—dangerous during the war, and potentially afterward—consisted of what Hanson calls "young zealots, men between 18 and 40 who often formed the cavalry of the South and were led by rabid knights like Nathan Bedford Forrest, Joseph Wheeler and Jeb Stuart. These fanatics embodied the martial spirit of an apartheid culture and would never surrender unless both the South and its army were in ruins, and the lives of their families at stake. Most in the cavalry corps were the children of the wealthy, excellent horsemen, full of youthful vigor and insolence."

The South, although militarily weak, "fielded," Hanson says, "individual warriors who were among the most gallant and deadly in the entire history of warfare." Hence what Sherman called "the awful fact": Victory required "that the present class of men who rule the South must be killed outright."

Donald Rumsfeld says his preference is for Al Qaeda fighters to surrender rather than fight to the death: "It ends it faster. It's less expensive." General Richard Myers, chairman of the Joint Chiefs, says, "This is not a war of extermination." Such statements are perhaps obligatory and even sincere.

However, is surrender really less expensive in the long run? It is a reasonable surmise that a reformed terrorist is a very rare terrorist and that the rate of recidivism will be high among terrorists who are forced to surrender but continue to believe they are doing God's will when they commit mass murder of infidels. So, as far as is consistent with the rules of war and the husbanding of the lives of U.S. military personnel, U.S. strategy should maximize fatalities among the enemy, rather than expedite the quickest possible cessation of hostilities.

Many Americans will vehemently reject any analogy between Confederate and Al Qaeda elites. But Sherman might have felt vindicated by a postwar letter from one former Confederate general to another, D. H. Hill to Jubal Early: "Why has the South become so toadyish & sycophantic? I think it is because the best and noblest were killed off during the war."

December 27, 2001

The Healthy Aspect of War

War is unhealthy because of its violence, but also because of diseases spread by mass movements of men, often weary and sick, through disordered societies. Diseases arising from camp life, social disruption, and unhygienic field hospitals have killed far more soldiers than has battle.

But modern war has driven dramatic improvements in public health, from Florence Nightingale's professionalization of nursing during the Crimean War to advances in surgery and control of infectious diseases. Because of today's war against terrorists, tomorrow's Americans will live better and longer.

That is the cheerful implication of the otherwise ominous fact that President Bush's budget asks Congress to more than quadruple spending—from $1.4 billion to $5.9 billion—on bioterrorism research. Last week Defense Secretary Donald Rumsfeld was unspecific in saying "it is likely" terrorist attacks "will grow vastly more deadly" than those of September 11. But budgets often make government's thinking clear, and the bioterrorism money may imply Rumsfeld's meaning.

Dr. Anthony Fauci, director of the National Institute of Allergy and Infectious Diseases at the National Institutes of Health, says this infusion of money will accelerate our understanding of the biology and pathogenesis of microbes that can be used in attacks, and the biology of the microbes' hosts: human beings and their immune systems. One result should be more effective vaccines with less toxicity.

Consider smallpox, one of the diseases at the top of the grim list of bioterrorist threats. The last U.S. case of smallpox was in 1949, but general vaccination of children continued until 1972. However, among every million people vaccinated, one or two died, so the vaccine was killing more than was the disease. Military vaccinations continued until the early 1990s but now are restricted to special operations troops who might go places where bioweapons might be found.

The last recorded case of naturally occurring smallpox was in 1977 in Somalia. In 1979 the World Health Organization declared the world free of this scourge. But, says Fauci, it is "nonsense" to assert that the only remaining smallpox stocks are securely held in Russia and at the Centers for Disease Control in Atlanta. He says the Soviet Union made "vats and vats" of smallpox, some of which could have fallen into terrorists' hands.

Now imagine something far more frightening than twenty hijackers flying planes into buildings. Imagine twenty fanatics willingly infected with smallpox and infiltrated into America. From history and from a contemporary experiment, we have two appalling pictures of what might happen.

The picture from history is presented by historian Elizabeth Fenn's book

Pox Americana: The Great Smallpox Epidemic of 1775–82, published a few weeks after September 11. Her subject is a war-driven epidemic—notice that it coincided with the American Revolution—that killed 130,000 and maimed many more, from Massachusetts to Mexico.

In 1775 the crucial determinant of vulnerability to smallpox was prior exposure to it. In England's congested cities, exposure was constant, so most adults were immune. Not so in thinly populated America. Before Washington was driven to inoculate his forces, immunity was concentrated among the affluent, such as John and Abigail Adams, who could afford inoculation. Washington's army was composed largely of poor men, so the British army was at first much less susceptible than Washington's. And Fenn says there is strong evidence that the British waged biological warfare, attempting to spread the disease in American ranks.

Fenn's history, with its stomach-turning descriptions of the disease's ravages, is particularly terrifying because America today, with urban congestion and no smallpox vaccination, is even more vulnerable to an epidemic than America was two centuries ago, when travel was not able to spread the opportunistic microbes across the continent in five hours.

Less than three months before September 11, some national security specialists tried thinking the unthinkable. An exercise named Dark Winter postulated a smallpox attack in Oklahoma City. Smallpox has a twelve-day incubation period during which infected people have no symptoms. For a few days following that, before definitive signs of the disease, the person is highly infective. So it can be spread widely before its existence is known. Dark Winter concluded that in just three months the attack would have caused a million deaths in twenty-five states.

The exercise indicated that the health care system lacks vaccines and other elements of a "surge capacity" to cope with mass casualties, and the political system lacks adequate plans for allocating care, imposing quarantines, controlling panic, and so on. The president's proposed $5.9 billion is a bargain. It will improve public safety immediately and public health eventually.

February 7, 2002

Next, Weapons of Mass Disruption?

Americans have received their marching orders. They have been told to stiffen their sinews, summon up their blood—and go to the mall. And a movie. This summons to normality is akin to Henry V's rallying cry when sacking Harfleur. However, energetic everydayness, even lightheartedness, is suddenly a serious duty. Just as there is at all times a moral obligation to be intelligent, there is today an obligation to be cheerful.

It would be irrational for Americans to begin acting as though terrorists are capable of making daily life hazardous for Americans generally. Acting that way would cripple the country's social and economic vigor, its defining assets. And an even more important reason for not allowing current problems to knock America off its normally jaunty stride is that the nation's equilibrium may soon be tested by even bigger problems.

When in 1820 the argument about the admission of Missouri to the Union as a slave state aggravated sectional animosities, Thomas Jefferson called the crisis a "fire bell in the night," awakening the nation to the possibility of worse to come. Last week's fire bell was anthrax, a small sample of what can be called the terrorism of substances, biological and chemical. There have been hearings, reports, and books on these subjects, but complacent democracies are educated primarily by events, not exhortations—the British did not bring Churchill to power until Hitler approached the English Channel ports.

What might be the next alarm bell to ring? Of course, a truck bomb would intensify national nervousness by making things that are ubiquitous—trucks—seem ominous. And high explosives directed against, say, Hoover Dam would not only complicate life in the Southwest, it would underscore the unsettling message that even big things can be pulverized. However, it is time to think about attacks using things not solid and directed against things not as solid as skyscrapers or dams.

Consider cyberterrorism, assaults that can be undertaken from anywhere on the planet against anything dependent on or directed by flows of information. Call this soft terrorism. Although it can put lives in jeopardy, it can do its silent, stealthy work without tearing flesh or pulverizing structures. It can be a weapon of mass disruption rather than mass destruction, as was explained by the President's Commission on Critical Infrastructure Protection in its 1997 report on potential cyberattacks against the "system of systems" that is modern America.

"Life is good in America," the report says, "because things work. When we flip the switch, the lights come on. When we turn the tap, clean water flows." Now suppose a sudden and drastic shrinkage of life's "taken for granted" quotient. The report notes that terrorist attacks have usually been against single targets: individuals, crowds, buildings. But today's networked world of complexity and interconnectedness has vast new vulnerabilities with a radius larger than that of any imaginable bomb blast. Terrorists using computers might be able to disrupt information and communications systems and, by doing so, attack banking and financial systems, energy (electricity, oil, gas), and the systems for the physical distribution of America's economic output.

Hijacked aircraft and powdered anthrax—such terrorist tools are crude and scarce compared with computers, which are everywhere and inexpensive. Wielded with sufficient cunning, they can spread the demoralizing helplessness that is terrorism's most important intended by-product. Computers as weapons, even more than intercontinental ballistic missiles, render irrelevant the physical geography—the two broad oceans and two peaceful neighbors—that once was the basis of America's sense of safety.

A threat is a capability joined with a hostile intent. In early summer 1997 the U.S. military conducted a threat-assessment exercise, code-named Eligible Receiver, to test the vulnerabilities of "borderless cyber geography." The results confirmed that in a software-driven world, an enemy need not invade the territory, or the air over the territory, of a country in order to control or damage that country's resources.

The attack tools are on sale everywhere: computers, modems, software, telephones. The attacks can shut down services or deliver harmful instructions to systems. And a cyberattack may not be discovered promptly. The report says, "Computer intrusions do not announce their presence the way a bomb does."

Already "subnational" groups—terrorists, organized crime—are taking advantage of legal and widely available "strong encryption" software that makes their communications invulnerable to surveillance. How invulnerable? John Keegan, the British military analyst, quotes William Crowell, former deputy director of the largest U.S. intelligence agency, the National Security Agency: "If all the personal computers in the world were put to work on a single [strongly encrypted] message, it would still take an estimated 12 million times the age of the universe to break a single message."

Now suppose a state or group or state-supported group used similar cybermarvels to attack, say, U.S. banking and financial systems or the production and distribution of electric power. Americans know how impotent, and infuriated, they feel when a thunderstorm knocks out their electrical power for even a few hours. The freezer defrosts, the Palm handheld cannot be recharged, *SportsCenter* is missed. War is hell. And speaking of war:

It would be interesting to know how many of the thousands of foreign students who have earned advanced degrees in computer science (and nuclear engineering, while we are at it) at American universities have come from, and returned to, the Middle East. If we are supposed to stiffen our sinews and summon up our blood for a battle, it would be well to remember that the siege of Harfleur, for which Shakespeare's Henry V exhorted the stiffening and summoning, was won in 1415 by the skill of English archers skilled with longbows, the high technology of the day.

October 29, 2001

Scary Scenarios from a Decorous Cassandra

Former senator Sam Nunn, the Georgia Democrat, is among the best presidents this nation never had. As was the case with another such, Senator Henry Jackson, the Washington Democrat, Nunn's most conspicuous service—stressing security threats that people would rather not think about—was an impediment to his presidential aspirations.

Recently Nunn, a decorous Cassandra, addressed a small meeting of military and other specialists on the subject of new security threats. He presented a quiz in which he sketched eight frightening scenarios and asked his listeners to decide which were fact and which were fiction.

1. A region declares itself a state independent of the fragmenting Soviet Union and asserts ownership of nuclear weapons on its territory, requiring nuclear commanders to swear allegiance to the new state. Russian troops sent to retrieve thousands of tactical nuclear weapons are thwarted by the new state's militia. Only Russia has the unlock codes needed to launch strategic nuclear missiles, but the locking devices are built in the new state, which could replace the old ones.

2. A cadre of political and military figures—the defense minister, the chief of the General Staff, a senior intelligence official, and some extreme nationalist politicians—topple the regime of a heavily armed nuclear state, placing the president under arrest. The plotters declare a nuclear alert for all forces. The military retains control of launch codes, but the military splinters, breaking and confusing the nuclear chain of command until the coup collapses.

3. Blips on Russian radar sites suggest one or more missiles being launched from the Norwegian Sea, where U.S. and U.K. submarines operate with ballistic missiles capable of hitting Moscow in fifteen minutes. In Russia's doctrine, the main option is to launch retaliatory forces no later than ten minutes after an attack is detected. Russia's General Staff orders missile commanders to begin launch preparations. Two minutes before deadline, Russia's warning center informs the government that the flight path of whatever has been detected involves no threat. Days later, the Russians find a misplaced U.S. notification of a satellite launch.

4. A computer hacker calling himself "Phantom Dialer" gains access to various computer networks worldwide, including those of universities,

corporations, banks, federal agencies, and military facilities, including top secret weapons research sites. FBI agents find Phantom Dialer in Portland, Oregon. He is brain-damaged by viral hepatitis, with fingers gnarled from typing on a computer twenty hours a day. He lives in a room filthy with rotting food and dog feces. The FBI flinches from prosecuting him and instead keeps the story quiet.

5. Two hackers penetrate computer systems worldwide, including systems at a U.S. Air Force laboratory and the South Korean nuclear agency.

6. After Desert Storm, Libya, convinced it cannot compete with sophisticated U.S. weaponry, cultivates twenty-five computer whizzes. Their mission is to be able, by 2000, to disrupt U.S. telecommunications, energy, finance, transportation, and emergency services.

7. A criminal organization spirits tactical nuclear weapons out of Russia and sells them to terrorists supported by Libya and Iran. At Russia's Ministry of Atomic Energy, disgruntled personnel, having gone unpaid for months, sell weapons-grade fissile materials to a criminal organization.

8. Two nations with extreme religious and historical animosities (including three recent wars and a simmering war over disputed territory) acquire nuclear weapons, but not enough of them to deter a disarming nuclear first strike, and neither has a sophisticated warning system. As terrorism increases, the military leader of one of the nations tells his prime minister that they must launch a preemptive strike or lose their weapons.

Nunn says scenarios 1 through 5 have occurred, 6 and 7 are imaginary, and 8 may be unfolding on the Indian subcontinent. "The world," he says, "has never before had an empire collapse still containing over 30,000 nuclear weapons, tons of chemical and biological weapons, thousands of missiles, and scientists who know how to make these weapons, but don't know how to feed their families."

Nunn's suggestions include: a joint U.S.-Russian missile warning system (which could lead to missile defense cooperation); joining with Russia to provide missile launch warning to both India and Pakistan; helping Russia solve any Year 2000 computer problem affecting its missiles, nuclear arsenal, or nuclear power plants; joint law enforcement efforts targeted at terrorism; and working with Russia to safeguard and eliminate our weapons-grade plutonium and highly enriched uranium stockpiles.

We live, Nunn says, in an era of "big challenges and little ideas." He is too polite to say: little leadership, too. However, his insistent voice is a reproach to others who are not doing their duty to describe the world as an increasingly dangerous place.

June 21, 1998

Arms Control by F-16

When Israel's foreign minister, Shimon Peres, accompanied by Ambassador David Ivry, recently visited the Oval Office, President Bush remarked that Israel certainly has the right ambassador for the moment. He said this because Ivry has shown that he understands how preventive action is pertinent to the problem of weapons of mass destruction in dangerous hands. Bush's remark, pregnant with implications, revealed that the president as well as the vice president remembers and admires a bold Israeli action for which Israel was roundly condemned twenty years ago.

On the afternoon of June 7, 1981, Jordan's King Hussein, yachting in the Gulf of Aqaba, saw eight low-flying Israeli F-16s roar eastward. He called military headquarters in Amman for information but got none. The aircraft had flown below Jordanian radar. So far, so good for Ivry's mission, code-named Opera.

Ivry, a short, balding grandfatherly figure with a gray mustache, was then commander of Israel's air force, which had acquired some of the seventy-five F-16s ordered by Iran from the United States but not delivered because of the 1979 revolution that toppled the shah. The F-16s were to be tested to their limits when Israel learned that Iraq was about to receive a shipment of enriched uranium for its reactor near Baghdad—enough uranium to build four or five Hiroshima-size bombs.

The reactor was six hundred miles from Israel. Ensuring that the F-16s had the range to return to base required the dangerous expedient of topping off the fuel tanks on the runway while the engines were running. Measures were taken to reduce the air drag of the planes' communications pods and munitions racks.

Prime Minister Menachem Begin ordered the attack to occur before the uranium arrived and the reactor went "hot," at which point bombing would have scattered radioactive waste over Baghdad. The raid was scheduled for a Sunday, to minimize casualties. It was executed perfectly. Aren't we glad. Now.

The raid probably was not Israel's first preemptive act against Iraq's attempts to acquire nuclear weapons. In April 1979 unidentified saboteurs blew up reactor parts at a French port, parts awaiting shipment to Iraq. In August 1980 an Egyptian-born nuclear physicist important to Iraq's nuclear program was killed in his Paris hotel room.

The U.S. State Department said Israel's destruction of the reactor jeopardized the "peace process" of the day, said relations with Israel were being "reassessed," canceled meetings with Israeli officials, and suspended deliveries of military equipment, including F-16s, pending a decision about whether Israel had violated the restriction that weapons obtained from America could be used only for defensive purposes. *The New York Times* said Israel had embraced "the code of terror" and that the raid was "inexcusable and short-sighted aggression." The *Times* added this remarkable thought:

> *Even assuming that Iraq was hellbent to divert enriched uranium for the manufacture of nuclear weapons, it would have been working toward a capacity that Israel itself acquired long ago. Contrary to its official assertion, therefore, Israel was not in "mortal danger" of being outgunned. It faced a potential danger of losing its Middle East nuclear monopoly, of being deterred one day from the use of atomic weapons in war.*

The *Times* was sarcastic about fear of Saddam Hussein ("even assuming . . . hellbent") and sanguine about his acquiring nuclear weapons, which would deter Israel from using such weapons. But ten years later Americans had reason to be thankful for Israel's muscular unilateralism in 1981.

Today on Ivry's embassy office wall there is a large black-and-white photograph taken by satellite ten years after the raid, at the time of the Gulf War. It shows the wreckage of the huge reactor complex, which is still surrounded by a high, thick wall that was supposed to protect it. Trees are growing where the reactor dome had been.

The picture has this handwritten inscription: "For Gen. David Ivry, with thanks and appreciation for the outstanding job he did on the Iraqi nuclear program in 1981—which made our job much easier in Desert Storm." The author of the inscription signed it "Dick Cheney, Sec. of Defense 1989–93."

Were it not for Israel's raid, Iraq probably would have had nuclear weapons in 1991 and there would have been no Desert Storm. The fact that Bush and Cheney are keenly appreciative of what Ivry and Israel's air force accomplished is welcome evidence of two things: In spite of the secretary of state's coalition fetish, the administration understands the role of robust unilateralism. And neither lawyers citing "international law" nor diplomats invoking "world opinion" will prevent America from acting as Israel did, preemptively in self-defense.

November 1, 2001

The End of Human Nature, Not History

When in 1988 Gorbachev declared competition the essence of socialism, Francis Fukuyama said, "We've reached the end of history." In 1989, the year of the fall of the Wall, Fukuyama published, in *The National Interest* quarterly, "The End of History?" Widely read, fiercely debated, and frequently misunderstood, it had remarkable fecundity as the catalyst of serious thought about political choices after the death of communism.

Since then, Gorbachev has appeared in a Pizza Hut ad, and Fukuyama's thesis—call it melancholy triumphalism—has seemed confirmed. It is that the exhaustion of ideological alternatives to bourgeois liberalism—rights-based, pluralist, market societies—presages the unification of mankind in agreement on the fundamental aims of life.

History, he argues, is directional, progressive, and approaching its destination. However, the agreed-upon aims of life are banal: constitutionalism and consumerism, a world made safe by tamed governments, and publics sedated by material satiation.

This tranquillity will be purchased by the trivialization of man, who will be reduced to the material appetites of his animal nature. Yeats, in perhaps this century's most quoted couplet, said:

> *The best lack all conviction, while the worst*
> *Are full of passionate intensity.*

However, throughout history the best, too, have usually had passionate intensity, without which bravery and other forms of nobility are unlikely.

Ten years on, Fukuyama, now with George Mason University, has published, again in *The National Interest*, "Second Thoughts." He affirms the premise of his earlier argument. However, he retracts, for ominous reasons, his conclusion about the human project approaching finality.

His premise is that two motors drive history. One is economic, meaning applied science—from steam power to computer chips—which increasingly punishes societies that do not maximize, through markets, the dispersal of decision making. History's second motor is what Hegel called the individual's "struggle for recognition," meaning equal dignity as a moral agent, which liberal democracies affirm with a panoply of rights.

In the 1990s U.S. foreign policy looks like Fukuyama's premises transmuted into policy through what he calls "three interlocking propositions constituting a 'democratic syllogism.'" The propositions are:

First, liberal democracies rarely fight one another.

Second, the correlation between a certain level of economic development and democracy strongly suggests that economic development is the most efficacious promoter of democracy. Above "a level of $6,000 per capita GDP in 1992 parity purchasing power," says Fukuyama, "there is not a single historical instance of a democratic country reverting to authoritarianism. Spain, Portugal, Greece, Taiwan and South Korea all made their transitions to democracy at or near this magical figure."

Third, the best way to promote growth is globalization—integrating nations into international trade and capital markets. Fukuyama says the "evolutionary logic" of history, imparted by "the integrating forces of economic modernization," is not refuted by the persistence of premodern nationalisms and ethnic conflicts in Rwanda, Somalia, and the Balkans or the cultural resistance of Islamic theocracies.

In 1999, even more clearly than in 1989, only democracy legitimizes a regime, and supposed alternatives to market arrangements, principally the "Asian development model" exemplified by Japan's state-directed development, seem discredited.

Yet, says Fukuyama, his "end of history" thesis was wrong. It assumed that human nature is a known constant. But to assume that, there would have to be an "end of science," and particularly of biology, the source of the new neuropharmacology and perhaps soon much else.

Just with the widespread use of Ritalin and Prozac, "a major revolution in the control of social behavior has been launched in the past decade without fanfare or significant debate." And that major revolution is minor compared with the potential alterations that may be made possible by manipulations of the structure of DNA.

Our understandings of political justice and general principles of morality reflect our understanding of human nature. Hence all bets about the destination of directional history are off when that nature becomes malleable—something given not by God or evolutionary inheritance but by human artifice. This artifice can produce new motors of history, with unknowable potentials for good and evil.

In a sense, Fukuyama's thesis—that human history is no longer driven by passionate differences—is not vulnerable to what science does: it will not really be refuted if human nature is abolished and post–human history begins.

Meanwhile, his thesis is largely unscathed by a decade's events: Liberal market democracy still is the only alternative for peoples wishing to participate in modernity, as all peoples seem to wish to do as soon as their societies become porous to today's information technologies.

So far, so good. The trouble is, a decade, even one as eventful as that since 1989, is but a blink in the human story.

June 17, 1999

New Consequences
for Old Ideas

In China and Kosovo, two of this century's durable arguments are resonating loudly. As a result, two thinkers not often thought of nowadays—Hannah Arendt and Robert Lansing—are again pertinent to U.S. foreign policy.

President Clinton and President Jiang Zemin delicately exchanged theories about the prerequisites of a nation's progress. Obliquely referring to the suppression ("resolute measures") of the 1989 Tiananmen Square demonstration for democracy, China's president said the suppression was necessary for "stability," which sustained China's progress. Clinton suggested that freedom is a necessary condition for stability, because tyranny is self-destabilizing.

Clinton is right. As was Hannah Arendt, when she changed her mind.

In 1951 Arendt, who had come here from Hitler's Germany, published *The Origins of Totalitarianism,* the bleak thesis of which was that a modern state, imposing an ideology by means of such modern instruments of social control as bureaucracy and mass communication, could achieve a goal that had eluded all other regimes in history: permanence. Under a sufficiently ruthless state, the citizenry's consciousness would be conscripted, and all dynamics of change from within would be neutralized. As George Orwell said, imagine a boot in your face—forever.

In 1956 Arendt rejoiced that her theory was slain by a fact—the Hungarian Revolution, when the streets of Budapest were full of defiant people, their unconscripted consciousnesses shaking the regime. Arendt saw in this a spontaneity that was "an ultimate affirmation that human nature is unchangeable," that no state succeeds in "interrupting all channels of communication," and that "the ability of people to distinguish between truth and lies on the elementary factual level remains unimpaired; oppression, therefore, is felt for what it is and freedom is demanded."

In the forty-two years since then, the proliferation of information technologies has made hopeless the tyrant's task—that of monopolizing information in order to hermetically seal a captive population against outside influences. Change is the only modern constant, and even despotic states exert decreasing control over it.

When Clinton returns from immense China, which is bursting out from under its government, he will confront the resonance of his secretary of state's words about little Kosovo. And Woodrow Wilson's words.

Madeleine Albright has said, "We are not going to stand by and watch the Serbian authorities do in Kosovo what they can no longer get away with doing in Bosnia." However, Robert Lansing, Wilson's secretary of state, said in 1918 that "certain phrases" of Wilson's "have not been thought out."

Such as "self-determination," the subject of six of his famous fourteen points. When Wilson used the phrase, Lansing wondered, "What unit has he in mind? Does he mean a race, a territorial area or a community?"

Wilson spoke of self-determination with reference to "limited self-government for the peoples of Austria-Hungary" and "for other nationalities under Turkish rule." Thus "peoples" were casually equated with "nationalities," and self-determination for each was declared by Wilson to be a universal right, "an imperative principle of action." So saying, he sowed dragon's teeth.

When Wilson spoke, a German corporal recovering from a gas attack was planning a political career, and in 1938, as he prepared to dismember Czechoslovakia in the name of the self-determination of the ethnic Germans of the Sudetenland, Hitler said, "At last, nearly twenty years after the declarations of President Wilson, the right of self-determination for these three and a half million must be enforced."

Kosovo is a province of Serbia. Ninety percent of Kosovo's 2.2 million inhabitants are ethnic Albanians. They are a "people" increasingly reluctant to live within a nation that oppresses them. U.S. policy has two prongs. It advocates greater autonomy for the province but not independence—not full self-determination. And it says that oppression within Serbia is not just Serbia's business.

The "undigested" phrase "self-determination," said Lansing, "is simply loaded with dynamite" and "will, I fear, cost thousands of lives. . . . What a calamity that the phrase was ever uttered!" People have gone right on uttering it. FDR and Churchill in the Atlantic Charter of 1941 affirmed the rights of "peoples," and the U.N. Charter endorses the self-determination of "peoples."

Toward China, U.S. policy attempts to promote the long-term stability of a free society by judiciously enmeshing China in the world in ways that weaken the government's ability to impose the brittle stability of tyranny. Toward Kosovo, U.S. policy attempts to dampen the force of the detonation of American-made political dynamite. In both places, old American ideas and arguments are having new consequences.

July 2, 1998

Disintegration

As the president of the world's most powerful nation visits the world's most populous nation, note that the future is being defined by disintegrative forces, worldwide.

In Europe in 1500 there were approximately five hundred political entities. By the beginning of the nineteenth century there were a few dozen. The unifications of Italy and Germany further reduced the number. By 1920 Europe had twenty-three states with 18,000 kilometers of borders. But by 1994 it had fifty states and 40,000 kilometers of borders. In the four decades after 1945, U.N. membership tripled.

These figures lead Pascal Boniface, a French scholar, to say we live in "the secessionist age," in which secession—Kosovo is just the instance *du jour*—is the principal threat to peace. Writing on "The Proliferation of States" in *The Washington Quarterly,* Boniface argues that whereas war used to be the hammer that pounded nations—including this one—together, now war often is an instrument for dismantlement.

The disintegration of the Soviet Union and Yugoslavia, and the divorce of the Czech Republic from Slovakia, exemplify various forms of contemporary fissuring. Boniface sees the potential for further fracturing of nations almost everywhere, from Yemen to Iraq (which "seems to be living under a stay of execution, with a Sunni area around Baghdad, a Shi'i zone in the south, and a Kurdish one in the north"). In Indonesia, some of the 180 million people from five hundred tribal groups spread over 18,000 islands are apt to aspire to constitute the next Hong Kong or Singapore—a small, independent economic prodigy.

Indian Sikhs on the border with Pakistan seek an independent Khalistan. There is Gurkha secessionism in the Himalayan foothills and Islamic separatism in Kashmir.

Much splintering is ascribed to the recrudescence, in the post–Cold War thaw, of religious and ethnic impulses. Marx and others wrongly argued that such impulses were preindustrial forces that had lost their salience and been supplanted by economic motives in the industrial era. But if Boniface is right, it may be time to revive respect for economic interpretations of historic changes.

He argues that one reason for the proliferation of nations is the pursuit of prosperity through miniaturization. "Prosperity has dethroned power as the primary concern of states." So "when a cultural or ethnic group decides that it is the principal generator of wealth in a larger nation or federation, a secessionist movement is just a press release away."

As "the arms race has given way to a prosperity race," the Lombard League has risen in the north of Italy to express resentment of unity with the backward south. Mexico's north resents the south. (Novelist Carlos Fuentes reports hearing people say, "In Mexico there are 90 million people. If we were only 30 million, we would already be a First World Country.") In Spain, regional nationalism is strongest in the Basque and Catalan regions, the two wealthiest. South Korea's ardor for reunification of the peninsula has cooled since Germany counted the costs of its reunification.

America's march to true nationhood was halting, in part because of economic rivalries among regions. In his new book, *A History of the American People,* Paul Johnson notes that the word "nation," which some Southerners found objectionable, does not appear in the Declaration of Independence or the Constitution, and even Chief Justice John Marshall, the supreme nationalizer, used the word gingerly: "America has chosen to be, in many respects and for many purposes, a nation."

Early in the nineteenth century, during debates on the building of the National Road, Senator William Smith of—where else?—South Carolina objected to "this insidious word," which was, he said, inimical to "the origins and theory of our government" as a confederation of sovereign states. It took roads—and canals, railroads, the postal service, and especially the New Deal's redistribution of wealth toward the South—to provide the economic prerequisite of national unity.

Which China should note, given the huge and growing disparities between its booming coastal and lagging interior regions. "What makes China susceptible to fracturing is economic diversification," writes Boniface. "The rich in China are no more likely to want to support the poor than the rich anywhere else."

Boniface believes that era of territorial acquisition by conquest has been followed by an era of territorial "unloading"—"a rush to become smaller in the hope of being able to pass through the eye of the needle leading toward greater wealth." In light of the worldwide waxing of centrifugal forces, America's unique combination of vast size and equitably distributed prosperity makes American preeminence seem even more likely to be prolonged.

June 25, 1998

Language and the Logic of Events

Political language can infuse its own logic into events. President Clinton says Serbian atrocities in Kosovo constitute "genocide." If so, then what can realistically be said to remain of the premise on which NATO went to war?

The premise was that the appropriate conclusion of this crisis would leave Serbia diminished and chastened but retaining sovereignty, albeit radically circumscribed, over Kosovo. However, genocide surely justifies the survivors' complete emancipation from their tormentors.

Serbia's atrocities are not genocide—a campaign to exterminate an entire category of people—but they are patent war crimes. They are intended to terrorize a people into flight. Their unintended consequence probably will be to get NATO into the nation-creation business.

In the whirl of war, events can, in a week, drain serious statesmen's political formulations of plausibility. After a week of Serbia's bloody rush to create new facts on the ground in Kosovo, it is no longer pertinent to say (as Defense Secretary William Cohen did at the beginning of the war) that the bombing could end if Milošević "embraces the principles of Rambouillet" or, as Henry Kissinger does in an essay written for this week's *Newsweek,* that a plausible settlement would involve "the withdrawal of Serbian forces introduced [into Kosovo] after the beginning of negotiations at Rambouillet."

Those futile talks in France in February involved a quest for the status quo 1989, before Serbia revoked Kosovo's autonomy. But because of the campaign of terror that Serbia vastly intensified in Kosovo last week, last month is ancient history. And the phrase "too clever by half" perfectly describes such a plan for fine-tuning the appropriate presence of war criminals among their victims.

A distressing, but perhaps sensible, oddity of the war's first week was that NATO's tactics implied a goal superior to NATO's stated goal. The stated goal was to prevent atrocities. But the tactic of concentrating air attacks on what most threatened airplanes—Serbia's air defenses—implied that NATO's overriding goal was to minimize NATO casualties, even if that would have the clear consequence of allowing the Serbian war criminals additional days to inflict casualties on Kosovars.

Economizing NATO lives is not a contemptible goal. Indeed, it is not optional. Such economizing, as well as minimizing the likelihood of captured pilots, reflects more than the humanity of the democracies. It also reflects a hardheaded assessment by NATO's leaders of the fragility of such public support as the war against Serbia enjoys.

Still, this calculation is a sobering reminder of the narrow parameters within which NATO nations—not least the United States—operate when combating rulers who do not share the democracies' civilized aversion to casualties, including casualties inflicted by war's inevitable collateral damage on the other side's civilians. Thus this war began with NATO announcing what it would *not* do: use ground combat troops.

This in spite of a general truth that is of particular pertinence to NATO's stated goal in this war: Wars are generally won by men with rifles occupying the contested ground. Men with rifles and pistols are sufficient for ethnic cleansing and are not targets that $45 million combat aircraft are designed to thwart.

When NATO says its objective is to "degrade" Serbia's capacity for ethnic cleansing in Kosovo, it sets a goal so muzzy and modest that success can be declared at any point. (Saddam Hussein had essentially won the post–Gulf War when U.S. policy was defined down to "reducing" his capacity to threaten his neighbors.) NATO may now be resolved to be a regional policeman, but a policeman of a peculiar kind—one that will not walk the beat but will fly over it.

Events are in the saddle, riding NATO. If NATO makes Serbia so weak that Kosovo is safe, Kosovars will feel that secession is safe. What could then become unsafe is Europe between Germany and Russia. Ten to 15 percent of the 170 million people who live there are ethnic minorities within their nations. For example, according to professor P. Edward Haley of Claremont McKenna College, writing in the *Los Angeles Times,* 25 million non-Russians live in the Russian federation and 40 percent of ethnic Albanians live outside Albania.

If by its action in Kosovo NATO seems to affirm the principle of ethnic self-determination, or if the drama being played out there emboldens armed ethnic minorities to assert a right to self-determination, then NATO, which has expanded eastward and probably is not done expanding, could learn that a policeman's lot is not a happy one.

March 30, 1999

Kosovo and America's Identity

History, which lurches along its zigzag path by fits and starts, has had a particularly twitchy period since the bombing in the former Yugoslavia began March 24. The world is different now, but not as different as some summations suggest.

NATO, formally defined as a defensive alliance for the protection of the territorial integrity of its members, has waged a war for, effectively, the dismemberment of a nonmember state that had not attacked or threatened a NATO member. NATO has waged war to affirm certain values, and the war crimes tribunal for the former Yugoslavia, acting in the name of those values, has indicted, for attacking citizens in his nation, a serving, elected president of a non-NATO nation.

It is emphatically not true that what has been affirmed is the principle that "the international community" will "not tolerate" barbarism. Sudan may be counterexample A, but there are many other counterexamples, too.

Rather, what has been established is that the North Atlantic community—which, unlike the "international community," is not a fiction—has again proved itself to be more than a geographical expression. It has shared values, political institutions for expressing them, military institutions for defending them, and the will to do so—with two huge limits on its will.

One limit is that it believes the defense of these values is important enough to kill for but not important enough to be killed for. Some say the defining characteristic of this war was that it was not a war of national interests, as traditionally defined in terms of territorial security or aggrandizement. That is indeed an important characteristic: The generally liberal-to-left governments now in power in most NATO nations could be comfortable only with war waged for reasons untainted by calculations of merely national interests.

The war was, in a way, symbolized by the twenty-four Apache helicopters that were deployed with much fanfare but never saw action because the battlefield environment was deemed too hazardous. The war was waged for eleven weeks without a single NATO combat casualty. To achieve this, tactics were adopted that obviously increased the perils of Kosovars under the hammer of Serbian forces and of civilians in the downward paths of NATO's ordnance. Those tactics included purchasing alliance unity by a pledge not to use ground forces, relying exclusively on airpower operating from high altitudes, and dramatically expanding, after a month, the list of eligible targets.

The second limitation on NATO's will is that it will act in defense of its values only in its own backyard. There is a pleasant irony in this.

The "progressive" elements in America who finally found, in Kosovo's sufferings, a cause worth waging war for are often the same elements who decry "Eurocentrism" in the teaching of history and literature and in the interpretation of what it means to be an American. But this was not just a war in Europe. It was a war also about Europe—about what Europe means at the end of the century. Hence it was also a war about America's identity.

For Europe, and for Americans, who participate in Europe's dramas, this seventy-five-year century—what it has lacked in length it has made up for in intensity—began in June 1914 in the Balkans, where a spark (an assassination) lit the fuse (Austria's desire to punish Serbia) that ignited the guns of August. The century ended in 1989, when one remaining consequence of the First

World War—Soviet communism and its footprint in central Europe—crumbled with the Berlin Wall.

Europe has spent the subsequent ten years gingerly tiptoeing toward "pooled" sovereignty. Eventually, its advocates say, this must mean federalism, symbolized by the euro, the common currency. All this is being undertaken to make the continent safe, at long last, for its system of nation-states.

There is under way an acceleration of the Americanization of Europe, and not just, or even primarily, in the sense that America provides the great precedent of a federal union spanning a continent. The war has intensified the rhetorical Americanization of Europe. It is now speaking, and hence thinking, as Americans began doing in their Declaration of Independence, as custodians of values with universal validity.

NATO nations are not claiming a manifest destiny to colonize the world with their values. But they will police their back yard with a new boldness. This, many "progressives" will be disconcerted to learn, reflects a robust patriotism and cultural confidence that is not bashful about claiming moral superiority in the hierarchy of nations.

June 11, 1999

Russia's Long Crawl Up from Communism

As the tragedy of the Russian submarine *Kursk* unfolded, Vladimir Putin's government responded with mendacity, lying about many things and suggesting that some other nation's submarine had collided with the *Kursk*. Which is to say, the government behaved like what it is, a cabal run by a third-generation apparatchik: Putin, whose grandfather was in Lenin's and then Stalin's personal security details and whose father was a Communist Party functionary, was a KGB careerist before converting—if you think as the Clinton-Gore administration evidently does—to democracy.

The nature of Putin's government is pertinent to America's presidential choice. Al Gore, much more than George W. Bush, adheres to the anachronistic idea that Russia must be treated as a great power—witness Gore's quest for Russia's permission for America to defend itself against ballistic missiles and his passion to preserve the twenty-eight-year-old ABM treaty. Gore should read in *The National Interest* quarterly Zbigniew Brzezinski's essay "Living With Russia," which argues that "there is no solid foundation" for Russia's claim to global status.

Russia's domestic conditions are "bordering on social catastrophe"—ruined agriculture, collapsing infrastructure, and steady deindustrialization of the imploding economy. In 1999 direct foreign investment in China was $43 billion, in Poland $8 billion, in Russia $2 billion to $3 billion. Sixty percent of recent births are not fully healthy, 20 percent of first-graders are diagnosed with some mental retardation. Since 1990 male life expectancy has declined five years, to around sixty.

Russia's demographic crisis—its population dropped from 151 million to 146 million in the 1990s—exacerbates its geographic crisis. To the east are 1.2 billion Chinese with an economy that is four times larger than Russia's and is lengthening its lead. To the west are 375 million Europeans with a surging economy ten times the size of Russia's. To the south are nine Muslim states with combined populations of about 295 million Muslims (not counting Turkey's 65 million) seething about Russian brutality against Chechnya. By 2025 the population of the nine may be 450 million (plus Turkey's 85 million).

Nevertheless, Brzezinski's basis for "longer-term optimism"—*very* longer term—is that Russia's dilemmas are so dire, it has no realistic choice but to join a "Vancouver to Vladivostok" West. But for the foreseeable future, Russia's government justifies pessimism.

Unlike in the formerly Communist countries of Eastern Europe, there are, Brzezinski says, no former dissidents in Russia's government. It consists, "with no exception," of the sort of people—"former apparatchiki, criminalized oligarchs, and the KGB and military leadership"—who could be governing the Soviet Union if it still existed. Unlike Germany and Japan after losing a war, Russia after losing the Cold War was not occupied and reformed. And even though Putin's office has a portrait of the Westernizing Peter the Great, Russia's "renunciation of the Soviet past has been perfunctory"—the corpse of Lenin, founder of the gulag, is still honored in central Moscow.

Brzezinski contrasts Russia's stagnation today with Turkey's rapid modernization after the disintegration of the Ottoman Empire in 1918–22. The slow decline of that inefficiently repressive empire allowed the development of a cadre of intellectuals and military officers—the Young Turks—eager to westernize. Turkey quickly adopted the Swiss civil code, the Italian penal code, and the German commercial code. Russia's progress, says Brzezinski, will be delayed until "Russia's past imperial and global status will have become a distant memory rather than an entitlement."

Putin's talk of a Russia "which commands respect" as "a great, powerful and mighty state" is delusional. Alexander Lebed, a former general and current politician (who, granted, has an ax to grind), claims there are fewer than ten thousand combat-ready troops. Last year the Associated Press reported that fuel is so scarce that military pilots average twenty-five hours of flying a year, compared with the Western air forces' minimum of about two hundred hours.

The *Los Angeles Times* reports that Putin says the submarine fleet may be cut to ten and that last summer "the Baltic Fleet owed so much money to the Kaliningrad bread factory that the plant refused to supply any more bread." An indicative indignity occurred in 1995, when a submarine was stripped of its missiles and used to transport potatoes to Siberia.

The submarine *Kursk* was named for the city that had been supplying it with food and other supplies. That city's name is also attached to the great 1943 battle—history's largest tank battle—that guaranteed the survival, for a while, of the Soviet regime. The Putin government's response to the *Kursk* submarine's tragedy demonstrates how long and arduous is the crawl up from communism.

September 3, 2000

Italy's Fifty-ninth Postwar Try

Italians have selected a new government, and politically fastidious people throughout the North Atlantic community are saying the Italians did not do it quite right. It is Italy's fifty-ninth government since the Second World War. Silvio Berlusconi, 64, the richest Italian, will be prime minister. Before Italians voted two Sundays ago, they were hectored by editorial harrumphing from European newspapers, urging them not to do what they then blithely did in choosing Berlusconi. You will not be astonished to learn that he is a conservative.

Berlusconi has frequently been indicted on serious charges, including tax evasion and bribing judges. But his three convictions were subsequently dismissed. His more than $12.8 billion worth of holdings (banks, real estate, Italy's largest publishing house, and much more) do indeed pose colossal conflicts of interest that must be dealt with. He controls the three largest commercial television networks, with 80 percent of the commercial television audience. But people fretting about Berlusconi's control of some media are notably less worried about the leftist tilt of Italian state television.

Much of the European intelligentsia's dislike of Berlusconi is ideological. Eleven of the fifteen nations in the European Union have left-of-center governments, and the EU itself is a nascent superstate, the repository of collectivist impulses that have been seeking new means of expression since the collapse of socialism.

A self-made, unapologetic entrepreneur, Berlusconi represents the wealth-creating private sector against the wealth-distributing public sector. (As does

George W. Bush, the first president with an M.B.A.) He favors tax cuts and re-form of Italy's baroque electoral and sclerotic regulatory systems. Most unfor-givable, in the eyes of his despisers, is his affection for the United States: "I am on whatever side America is on . . . I can never forget how Americans saved us after the war." He means U.S.—actually CIA—assistance to Italy's democratic forces when Communists came close to a takeover in 1948.

Americans are awash in war nostalgia—Tom Brokaw's book *The Greatest Generation,* the movies' *Saving Private Ryan* and *Pearl Harbor.* For Americans, World War II connotes emotional clarity and military and political heroism. For Italians, memories of the war and postwar struggles are more mixed and burdensome. A small and dwindling quantity of Mussolini nostalgia taints, very slightly, a fringe of Berlusconi's coalition.

Mussolini's dictatorship was much nastier than is suggested by the charac-terization of it as tyranny tempered by anarchy. But fascism has long since stopped being a fighting faith. And even when it was one, Italians were a ter-rible disappointment to Il Duce. Governed so often by conquerors, Italians have always had minimal respect for the state.

Yes, there is some xenophobia and other extremism in Berlusconi's coali-tion. Some supporters favor separatism for northern Italy. But national unity is still something of a novelty. Less than two centuries ago "Italy" was still a ge-ographical, not a political, expression. Many Berlusconi supporters robustly—and sensibly—dislike the busybodies of Brussels who run the European Union, but some use disgraceful rhetoric, as when one important ally de-nounced "European technocrats and pedophiles" and called the departing prime minister "a Nazi dwarf." But before being too condescending about Italian rhetorical excesses, remember that Al Gore suggested that George W. Bush is sympathetic to slavery. (He said Bush's Supreme Court nominees would have views akin to those held in days when blacks "were considered three-fifths of a human being.")

Italian political culture has long had an operatic streak. A fourteenth-century ruler, not content with the title "Nicholas, the severe and merciful, tribune of liberty, peace and justice, liberator of the holy Roman republic," embellished it: "Nicholas, severe and merciful, deliverer of Rome, defender of Italy, friend of mankind, and of liberty, peace and justice, tribune august." Berlusconi is in that tradition of self-dramatization. He is what another media baron, William Randolph Hearst, wanted to be—Citizen Kane, but with a happy final reel.

Will Italy's Citizen Kane find happiness? Berlusconi says, "There's nobody on the world stage who can possibly claim to be a match for me." In a—what? testimonial?—that sets something of a record for damning with faint praise, a member of Berlusconi's 1994 government says, "He's a megalomaniac, yes, but he's not Kim Il Sung." So there.

Berlusconi, elegantly tailored and smooth as marble, is a gaudy self-creation, another Italian work of art. It was characteristic of Dutch, not of Italian, painters to celebrate serene domesticity in pictures of kitchens. Italians prefer style and spectacle. In his book *The Italians,* the late Luigi Barzini marveled at the discrepancy between Italians' dazzling cultural achievements over the centuries and the mediocre quality of their political history. Italian political culture, Barzini said, has made "all revolutions irresistible but superficial, and all new regimes unstable."

"Italians," Barzini wrote, "have always excelled in all activities in which the appearance is predominant: architecture, decoration, landscape gardening, the figurative arts, pageantry, fireworks, ceremonies, opera, and now industrial design, stage jewelry, fashions, and the cinema." Practicality has been another matter. Italian medieval armor was gorgeous. It also was too light for combat, for which German armor was preferred.

The Italian peninsula was the incubator of modernity. Italians—Leonardo, Galileo, Machiavelli, Columbus, and many others—transformed mankind's sense of politics, society, and the universe. But Italians, painters and connoisseurs of so many beautiful pictures, often produce a politics more picturesque than practical. Berlusconi is certainly the former. How well he succeeds in being the latter will determine how soon Italy has its sixtieth postwar government.

May 28, 2001

Cheddar Man and the Abolition of Britain

"All right," said the [Cheshire] Cat; and this time it vanished quite slowly, beginning with the end of the tail, and ending with the grin, which remained some time after the rest of it had gone.

—LEWIS CARROLL, *Alice's Adventures in Wonderland*

LONDON—About Prime Minister Tony Blair, architect of the "New Labour" and apostle of the "Third Way" (American-style capitalism blended with European statism), the question is, What is there besides his grin? The Third Way is thin gruel, its mantra of "modernization" as watery as Bill Clinton's 1992 celebration of "change." Blair's government, preoccupied with the politics of presentation, has a remarkably high ratio of rhetoric to real programs. However, it is advancing, or allowing to advance, the most radical agenda in the nation's history. How else to describe the dissolution of the nation and the submersion of its component parts in the gray leviathan called "Europe"?

Blairism is the radicalism of purposeful inertness. It is part cause and part effect of both centrifugal and centripetal forces. After not quite three centuries as a unified entity, bits of Britain, a composite nation, are spinning outward ("devolution," via legislatures in Scotland, Wales, and Northern Ireland). But all are being tugged toward a new center, Brussels, the cold bureaucratic heart of "Europe," as that becomes a political as well as a geographic category.

Blair's political profile is not just blurry at the edges, it is blur straight through. Blairism consists of embracing conservatism but calling it something else—deploring Thatcherism while preserving its consequences, such as deregulation, privatization, and democratization of the trade unions. Blair's most specific campaign promise—to reform, and particularly to end the waiting lists in, the sclerotic National Health Service (with three-quarters of a million employees, one of Europe's largest employers)—remains spectacularly unfulfilled. Although in 1997 Labour gave the Tories their worst shellacking of the twentieth century, winning a 179-seat majority, a recent poll put the Tories just three points behind.

The politics of pure presentation ("spin" and "focus groups" are recent American imports into Britain's political lexicon) works only until it is recognized as such. But there is a brain behind Blairism. It belongs to Gordon Brown, chancellor of the Exchequer. He is a Scot (that matters) who approvingly quotes Alan Greenspan. Even when throwing red meat to "Old Labour" class warriors (he lambasted Oxford for being a haven of private-school toffs when it turned down a state-school graduate who was accepted at Harvard), he does so in a Thatcherite vocabulary stressing the meritocracy and efficiency necessary for an entrepreneurial society.

Brown is making sure that the most important issue in British politics does not come to a boil before the next election, which must occur no later than 2002 and will probably be next year. The issue is whether to scrap the national currency and join the euro currency, with all that implies for surrendering control of monetary policy and then (inevitably) fiscal policy, and sliding ever deeper into "harmonization" with (meaning subordination to) the emerging European superstate.

Brown is cleverly kicking this issue down the road by making much of the five "conditions" that must be met before Britain joins the euro. But all five are economic, which means that political principles (such as sovereignty and self-government) are irrelevant. Thus does materialism supplant political morality as *Homo economicus* has (*pace* Aristotle) eclipsed *Homo politicus*.

And all five conditions are so vague, and are tied to such fudgeable data, that they can be declared met whenever Brown desires. Which will probably be after the next election, if Labour wins it.

Many Europhiles are English intellectuals of the sort George Orwell despised because they despised their nation: "England is perhaps the only great country whose intellectuals are ashamed of their nationality." (Orwell did not live to see America in the 1960s and 1970s.) Trust intellectuals to use a 1,222-page tract to advance their politics. It is Norman Davies's *The Isles,* a slapdash, padded, trendy, and tendentious history of Britain from Cheddar Man to Tony Blair.

Shortly after the last ice age, a man was buried in Cheddar Gorge in what is now England. His body was discovered in 1903, and in 1996 samples of his DNA were compared with DNA samples from some villagers in that area. A close match was found with a forty-two-year-old teacher in Cheddar Village, who is thus a direct descendant of the man from the Middle Stone Age. And—here is Davies's political point—Cheddar Man lived before nature had separated the British Isles from the European landmass. Therefore he was "a Continental," so why make a fuss about Britain's going (back) into Europe?

Also, the Plantagenet kings spent more time (because they had more territory) in France than in Britain. And the pedigree of the term "Great Britain" runs only to 1707 (the unification of the English and Scottish crowns) and that of "the United Kingdom" only to 1801 (the dissolution of the Irish Parliament). And so on, all of this selective mining of British history culminating in a crashing non sequitur: contingencies produced Britain; therefore, its dissolution is a matter of moral indifference and probably desirable.

The moral of the story supposedly is that the British nation is a result of geologic caprice and (relatively recent) political improvisations that are less durable than the cultural and ethnic differences now recrudescent. Identity politics has come to Britain.

What is vanishing, and not slowly, is the nation to which the United States traces much of its political and cultural DNA. Unless this disappearance is resisted and reversed, soon all that will linger, like the Cheshire Cat's grin, will be a mocking memory of the nationhood that was the political incarnation of a people who (as has been said), relative to their numbers, contributed more to civilization than any other people since the ancient Greeks and Romans.

July 10, 2000

The European Union's Lawlessness

A political drama of recent decades has been Europe's progress, ideological and institutional, in transforming "Europe" from a geographical expression into a political category. Now the European Union has committed the arrogant and lawless folly of declaring, in effect, that Austria's new government, produced by recent elections, is illegitimate. This declaration underscores why many thoughtful people question whether Europe's progress toward political unity is really progress.

Joerg Haider, 50, is a trim, glossy, well-tailored, telegenic, and articulate politician. He is also frequently adolescent and reptilian, in a "populist" sort of way. As is common with populists, he taps into unpleasantness latent in the public. George Wallace did, as did some of his late-nineteenth-century American progenitors, such as Mary E. Lease, who, in rhetoric of a sort familiar at the time, called President Grover Cleveland "the agent of Jewish bankers and British gold."

Haider gives voice to anti-immigrant sentiments shared by those who resent the fact that 10 percent of Austria's residents are immigrants, many from the Balkans, where recent events set the stage for the EU's decision to isolate Austria. One Balkan event was an eruption of tribalism that recalled Europe in the 1930s and 1940s. The other was NATO's decision to disregard the niceties of sovereignty in order to stop Serbia's government from exercising a free and brutal hand in a province of Serbia.

European anxiety about Austrian extremism of the right is understandable. It was in Vienna, then the polyglot capital of the Austro-Hungarian Empire, a bouillabaisse of peoples and nations, that the Austrian Hitler acquired his anti-Semitism. But before a stable, temperate democracy such as Austria is assaulted, even diplomatically, for a choice it has made in conformity to democratic due process, that choice should pose a clear and present danger to the parties doing the assaulting.

What threat does the participation of Haider's party in a coalition government in one of Europe's less weighty nations pose to prosperous, pacific, bourgeois Europe?

From Mussolini through Franco and Perón, there have been many flavors of fascism. And Haider's cocktail of tribalism and wounded national pride (the reason for his warm words about Waffen-SS soldiers and aspects of Third Reich policies) perhaps deserves to be classified as a watery residue of what ceased being a fighting faith in Europe fifty-five years ago. He is a recidivist in stirring the ashes of the 1940s. He has contemptibly called the concentration camps "punishment camps," and on Sunday he endorsed reparations for ethnic Germans expelled from Czechoslovakia at the end of the war. But those ashes are stone cold, and Haider increasingly resembles a witless teenager trying to annoy adults with his naughtiness.

On what *principle* did the EU act? Defense of the rule of law? No Austrian or other law has been broken by Haider. He poses no threat to Austria's regime of rights. And as for the muzzy charge that he is an affront to the EU's values, three questions: Where are they codified? If Haider had a Communist past or expressed selective admiration for the Soviet Union, would he draw the EU's censure? (Surely not.) And if punishing Austria, in an act of capricious bullying, for the normal and nonthreatening operation of its electoral system expresses the EU's values, what makes those values admirable?

To say that Austria has a right to accommodate Haider's Freedom Party and the 27 percent of the electorate who recently supported it is not to make a fetish of majoritarianism. The U.S. constitutional system certainly does not. The essence of constitutionalism in a democracy is not merely to shape and condition the nature of majorities but also to stipulate that certain things are impermissible, no matter how large and fervent a majority might want them.

The purpose of a Bill of Rights, the Supreme Court has said, is "to withdraw certain subjects from the vicissitudes of political controversy, to place them beyond the reach of majorities." Which is what the First Amendment does by saying "Congress shall make no law" doing this or that (abridging freedom of speech, establishing religion, etc.) no matter what Congress's constituents desire.

But no Austrian or European bill of rights or other law justifies turning the understandable recoil against Haider—a recoil part moral and part aesthetic—into a diplomatic onslaught that will enlarge Haider. This onslaught is an extralegal, and therefore antilegal, exercise in moral exhibitionism. Europeans have far more to fear from such unprincipled and unconstrained authoritarianism by the EU than from Haider's repellent but impotent exhibitionism.

February 10, 2000

Denmark and Goliath

In this election season, the world's attention should be on . . . Denmark. No vote this year involves larger stakes—national identity; self-governance—than those at issue in Denmark's September 28 referendum on adopting the euro, the European Union's single currency.

Proponents of the euro are relying, as usual, on two arguments. One is patently false, the other tellingly spurious.

The falsehood is that this is "just about money." Actually, it is another giant step toward creation of a European superstate, a Leviathan requiring surrender of nations' sovereignties, leaching away the prerogatives of national legislatures. Cultural homogenization—"harmonization," in the EU's prettified patois—would follow. Monetary union entails a unitary state, not a Europe of democratic nations. As William Blackstone understood more than two centuries ago, "The coining of money is in all states the act of the sovereign power."

Pro-euro forces stress that the value of Denmark's krone is linked to the currency of Germany, which uses the euro. Anti-euro forces respond that Denmark retains the right to delink from Germany and that the linkage proves that adopting the euro must serve a political rather than an economic agenda.

Last summer, when Denmark's prime minister, Poul Nyrup Rasmussen, who is pro-euro, said Denmark could always choose to withdraw later, the Italian president of the European Commission, Romano Prodi, retorted that euro membership is "by definition permanent." All the "opt-out provisions" and "reserved powers," devices used to entice reluctant nations into the EU's web, are apt to be eventually declared inoperative.

The spurious argument is the last resort of intellectually bankrupt political causes: inevitability. Danes, say those advocating replacement of their thousand-year-old currency with the twenty-one-month-old euro, "have no choice." But Denmark, like Britain, is flourishing outside the euro, which is sinking in value. And an economic panel, called the Three Wise Men, has concluded that any economic benefits of joining the euro would be "slight and uncertain." So much for the euro proponents' scaremongering about rejection triggering high interest rates and capital flight.

Recent polls showing anti-euro leads of five to eleven points suggest Danes may make the choice they supposedly do not have. In Denmark, as elsewhere, proponents of the euro include most elites of business and labor, all Danish broadcasting, and forty-six of forty-eight newspapers (one is neutral). EU single-currency propaganda is directed even to primary school pupils.

But speaking by telephone from Copenhagen, Holger Nielsen, the anti-euro chairman of the Socialist People's Party, says laconically, "We have no money but good arguments." Actually they have some money, some of it sent from Britain by a saving remnant of Thatcherites. Jens-Peter Bonde, an anti-euro member of the European Parliament, says, "This is David and Goliath, but don't forget who won."

Democracy will win if the euro loses on September 28. Indeed, Denmark's disinclination to bow to Brussels has already strengthened the embattled ideal of a Europe of self-governing nations.

Seven months ago the other fourteen members of the EU, in a spasm of autocratic high-mindedness, imposed feckless sanctions on Austria to express disapproval of an outcome of Austria's democratic process.

Austria's sin against the (unwritten, unannounced) EU standards of political hygiene was to include the right-wing Freedom Party in its governing coalition. The party won 27 percent of the vote in last October's national elections. The party's offenses include unwelcoming policies regarding immigration, unsavory comments by its leader, Joerg Haider (who is not in the government), about Austria's Nazi past—and, perhaps most intolerable to the EU, skepticism about the EU's virtues.

Danes disliked the European Union's extralegal bullying of a small nation, so the EU, knowing the issue was helping Danish opponents of the euro, appointed a panel to rationalize removing the sanctions. Which it did last week, reporting that Austria's treatment of immigrants is superior to that of many other EU members and that Freedom Party ministers have been admirable, especially concerning restitution for Jewish property stolen during the war.

The sanctions were farcical—limits on political, military, and cultural interactions—and at an EU summit in Portugal, the usual group photograph was not taken, so some fastidious leaders could avoid being photographed with Austria's duly elected chancellor, Wolfgang Schuessel, who is not from the Freedom Party. These sanctions that were born of EU arrogance were jettisoned cynically in an attempt to manipulate Danish opinion.

Rather than being reassured, Danes should note that the EU, instead of repenting its presumptuousness, contemplates yet another bureaucracy, this one to "monitor and evaluate" the member nations' fidelity to "European values," as bureaucrats shall define them. By firmly saying "no" to the euro, Denmark can slow the continent's slide into "harmonization"—a bleak harmony unenlivened by democracy and national diversities.

September 21, 2000

The Currency of Cultural Blandness

The age of chivalry is gone. That of sophists, economists, and calculators has succeeded and the glory of Europe is extinguished forever.

—EDMUND BURKE

To see the banknotes of Europe's new common currency is to see Europe's future. They are not pretty.

Their design is studiously, indeed ideologically, abstract. Gone are the colorful, celebratory currencies of the twelve participating European Union nations (Britain, Denmark, and Sweden are not adopting the euro) with their pictures of national heroes of statecraft and culture, and of arts that express national narratives. With the euro, Europe says goodbye to all that.

The windows, gateways, and bridges depicted on euro banknotes have one thing in common: They do not exist. The currency could come from anywhere. Or nowhere, which is what "utopia" means.

Tuesday's introduction of the euro marks a momentous milestone on the march to turn "Europe" from a geographical into a political denotation. Enthusiasts say the march leads to a sunny upland of a perpetual peace produced by the subordination of politics to economics. And they say it will put an end to attempts to forge continental unity by beating plowshares into swords for Roman legions, Napoleonic marshals, or German armies.

Critics say that even if the common currency "works" economically, the unjustifiable cost will be cultural blandness and the attenuation of democracy. That, they say, is an unavoidable consequence of subordinating politics to economics—reversing the five-century fight to give representative national parliaments control over public finance.

It will not "work," even understanding that narrowly as producing economic efficiency. America's continental monetary policy works because when Michigan slumps, Texas may beckon. There will be no such labor mobility between, say, Greece and Ireland. But economic efficiency is not really the point of subordinating politics to economics. Politics is the point.

The common currency serves the political objective of changing Europe's civic discourse by supplanting political reasoning with economic calculation. The euro is an instrument for producing a European superstate, which requires erasing from the nations' populations their national identities, which means their distinctive memories. Here we go again, yet another European campaign against "false consciousness," this time meaning patriotism.

Under the euro, nations cede fundamental attributes of sovereignty—control of monetary (and hence, effectively, fiscal) policy to the European Central Bank in Frankfurt. This advances the integration of Europe's nations into a continental federation, under which nations will be as "sovereign" as Louisiana and Idaho are.

In addition to a currency, the EU has a parliament, a supreme court, and a passport, and it is working toward a military and a criminal justice system. It has a flag no one salutes and an anthem no one knows.

Three weeks ago the fifteen heads of the EU members' governments agreed to a convention, modeled on the one that met in Philadelphia in 1787, to draft a constitution. However, Europe lacks some things that America had then, including a common language and a shared political culture embodied in common political institutions. And a James Madison and a George Washington.

As London's *Daily Telegraph* says, the question of "a Europe of states versus a state of Europe" is rapidly being resolved in favor of the latter. But "European democracy implies a European demos, which does not exist." And the EU's cultural—hence political—incoherence will increase when it adds 13 more nations, some of which will have as much in common with other members as Minnesota has with Paraguay.

Who wants the euro and the superstate it implies? The EU's disparate publics do not, but two elites do. One is a commercial elite that believes the business of Europe is business—never mind freedom, democracy, justice, culture, different national characters—and that a common currency will expedite it a bit. The other elite consists of the sort of intellectuals Europe always has a surplus of—those eager to remake mankind in order to make it worthy of the shimmering future the intellectuals are dreaming up.

What can justify Europe's turning its future over to economic calculators? Europe's past does, say euro enthusiasts—the Somme, the Holocaust, and the blood-soaked centuries that preceded those defining events of the last century. So their enthusiasm is cultural despair in drag.

The euro is part of the EU's campaign for the dissolution of nations and the dilution of particular cultures. "To attempt to be religious without practicing a specific religion," said Santayana, "is as possible as attempting to speak without a specific language." The euro is part of Europe's attempt to be great without being anything in particular. Call it euro-utopianism.

December 30, 2001

The Rape of Nanking Remembered

Something beautiful, an act of justice, is occurring in America today concerning something ugly that happened long ago and far away. The story speaks well of the author of the just act, and of the constituencies of conscience that leaven this nation of immigrants.

The rape of Nanking, a city of 1 million, by the Japanese army was perhaps the most appalling single episode of barbarism in a century replete with horrors. Yet it had been largely forgotten until Iris Chang made it her subject.

Her book *The Rape of Nanking: The Forgotten Holocaust of World War II* is refuting its subtitle. Already a best-seller in its fifteenth printing, it has stimulated seminars and conferences at Harvard, Yale, Princeton, and many other places, and is assisting those honorable Japanese who are combating their country's officially enforced amnesia regarding what the Imperial Army did in December 1937 and January 1938.

Japanese soldiers murdered tens of thousands of surrendered Chinese soldiers and almost certainly more than 300,000 noncombatants. (Civilian deaths at Hiroshima and Nagasaki totaled 210,000. Britain and France suffered a combined total of 169,000 civilian deaths from 1939 to 1945.) The Nanking killing continued for seven weeks in front of international witnesses, without any attempt at concealment and with the sadism of recreational murder.

Chinese were used for bayonet practice and beheading contests. People were roasted alive, hung by their tongues from hooks, mutilated, drowned in icy ponds, buried up to their waists and then torn apart by German shepherds, buried up to their necks and run over by horses or tanks. In addition to pandemic rape by Japanese soldiers even of young children, some of them tied to beds or posts for days, fathers were forced to rape their daughters, sons their mothers.

In 1996 interest in Nanking's calamity was quickened by Chang's research, which led her to the descendants and diaries of John Rabe, the "Oskar Schindler of China." Rabe, who died in 1950, was a German businessman who lived in China from 1908 through 1938. A committed Nazi and leader of local Nazi activities, he nevertheless was one of a handful of foreigners who, at great risk to themselves in the welter of random violence, organized the "safety zone" that saved thousand of lives.

Chang, 29, who now lives with her husband in California's Silicon Valley, grew up in Urbana, Illinois, and graduated from the University of Illinois, where her father is a physics professor and her mother is a microbiologist. Both parents were born in China—her father near Nanking, eleven months before the rape—and they first stimulated her interest in the historians' neglect of Nanking's martyrdom.

Cold War politics contributed to the neglect: both China and the United States were solicitous of Japanese opinion, so too little was done to build a historical record by encouraging survivors to speak. And Japan compounded its crime by censorship. A certain, shall we say, understatement is customary in a country whose emperor, announcing surrender in August 1945, referred to the atomic bombing of Hiroshima and Nagasaki as developments "not necessarily to Japan's advantage." But something more sinister than cultural reticence explains resistance to candor about Nanking by portions of official Japan.

Senior politicians and officials have referred to the rape as "a lie," "a fabrication," and "just a part of war." Although Nanking fell with only slight Chinese army resistance, Japan's Ministry of Education rewrote one textbook to say, "The battle in Nanking was extremely severe. After Nanking fell, it was reported that the Japanese army killed and wounded many Chinese soldiers and civilians, thus drawing international criticism." The Japanese distributor of the film *The Last Emperor* cut the scene depicting Nanking's fate.

Fortunately, fresh interest in the untold history of the Second World War in Asia, and particularly China's suffering, was an indirect consequence of the Tiananmen Square massacre, which energized communities of Chinese origin around the world. Chang's book, the fruit of her training at the Johns Hopkins writing seminars, acquired early momentum from brisk sales in cities with large Chinese populations—San Francisco and Los Angeles, of course, but also Washington, Houston, Vancouver, and Toronto. Sales quickly reached the critical mass that triggers self-sustaining word-of-mouth advertising among readers, reviewers, and booksellers.

Justice delayed is not necessarily justice denied. Indeed, delayed justice can be especially luminous when rendered at a historical distance, leaving a truthful impress on mankind's memory. Elie Wiesel, Auschwitz survivor and Nobel laureate, says that to forget a holocaust is to kill twice. Because of Chang's book, the second rape of Nanking is ending.

February 19, 1998

Arafat, Castro, and the Liberal Mind

Although the Niagara of words from people connected with, or commenting on, the visits of Yasser Arafat to the United States and of Pope John Paul II to Cuba was bound to contain some nonsense, the quantity of it has been astonishing. But useful, because it illuminates the liberal mentality.

The Holocaust Memorial Museum extended (then scotched, then re-extended) an invitation to Arafat to visit. The invitation came at the behest of several of the State Department's makers of Middle East policy who "felt strongly," *The Washington Post* reports, that a visit "could mark a psychological breakthrough for skeptical Jews and help Arafat understand the fears of an adversary." Skeptical Jews presumably doubt the peaceful intentions of Arafat, whose vocation is the killing of Jews; whose Palestinian Liberation Organization is committed to the destruction of the Jewish nation created in the aftermath of the Holocaust; who funds the dissemination of the idea that the

Holocaust is a Zionist fiction. Imagine the State Department mind that thinks Arafat needs "help" to understand the Holocaust.

The idea that Arafat's visit to a museum would be a "breakthrough" illuminates three defining assumptions in the liberal mind: Harmony is the natural condition of mankind. Conflict is the result of misunderstandings or "psychological" problems, meaning irrationalities, that can be dispelled by "dialogue." And foreign policy, like all government, should be therapeutic. (Hence the national "conversation" on race. And the academic discipline of "conflict resolution.")

The liberal assumption undergirding the "peace process" is that constant territorial and other concessions by Israel will so improve the regional "atmosphere" (a synonym for "psychology") that Israel's final borders will not matter much. State Department liberals cannot understand what Prime Minister Binyamin Netanyahu understands: for Arafat, an Israeli withdrawal to the 1967 borders would be an "interim solution." Israel's destruction is his final solution.

The pope's visit to Cuba illuminates the liberal mentality's inability to disapprove of a Communist as heartily as it disapproves of Joe Camel. Exhibit A is this *Washington Post* headline: "Castro and the Pope: Opponents with Shared Values/While Differing on Religion, Both Embrace Altruism and Reject Unbridled Capitalism." So *that* is Cuba's system—not communism but capitalism-on-a-bridle, a New Deal with a Latin beat.

The New York Times says the pope's criticism of "savage capitalism" is among his views that "match" Castro's. Even considering the source, that is a remarkably tendentious gloss on the pope's meditations on the challenge of preventing the mutually dependent dynamisms of capitalism and democracy from degenerating into callous majoritarianism and desensitizing self-indulgence.

The "shared values" analyses arise from liberalism's approval of "diversity," disapproval of cultural "chauvinism" (a.k.a. "ethnocentrism"), discomfort with "intolerance" (other than of Joe Camel), and penchant for discerning the moral equivalence of diametrically opposed systems. Still, must *Time* magazine refer to the pope and Castro as "two giants of the 20th century"? The pope, a spark that lit the fuse in Eastern Europe, is perhaps the most consequential man of the century's second half. Castro's giant achievement—it is remarkable—is to have prevented his captive population of 11 million from participating in the greatest years of wealth creation and freedom expansion in history.

Perhaps it amounts to breaking a butterfly on a wheel, but consider *Time*, again: "Both are absolute rulers of their realms. . . . Each plays a dominant role on the world stage, imposing his system of belief upon millions through brilliant intellect and sheer force of will."

Vatican City, Cuba, whatever. Castro's "force of will" would be nothing without his police; his "brilliance" makes him an intellectually buffoonish inhabitant of the ludicrous little cul-de-sac called Marxism. Even in Cuba, there are few Marxists, other than those trying to impose Marxism.

The pope, who in two decades has been seen by more people than anyone in history, does not *impose* "his system" on any of the 981,465,000 communicants who freely confess his faith. Living in an age when religion is no longer a necessary legitimizer of political and social arrangements, he has made his religion the most powerful delegitimizer of the sort of arrangements that keep Castro's boots on 11 million necks.

Two giants? Hardly. An unfortunate island's unhappiness was deepened for decades because Castro seized power on January 1, 1959. The world changed profoundly and for the better because of the event announced by a puff of white smoke over the 108 acres of Vatican City on October 16, 1978.

January 21, 1998

The Hijacking of the Holocaust

Without an intellectual anchor, cultural institutions are carried along by prevailing intellectual winds, which blow from the left. Familiar exhibits of this process are universities, where various subjects are enveloped in fogs of politics and abstractions.

But now the U.S. Holocaust Memorial Museum, and the problematic academic field of "Holocaust studies," are illustrating this process. The Holocaust is being exploited by academic entrepreneurs and factions with political agendas, all working to blur what the museum exists to insist upon: the distinctiveness of the calamity that befell European Jewry.

The museum's mission is solemn and circumscribed: the commemoration and study of the Holocaust in all its particularity. But the museum and the academic discipline—if such it can be—of Holocaust studies are becoming besotted with a repellent silliness about this most serious matter.

John Roth, philosophy professor at Claremont McKenna College and designated director of the museum's Center for Advanced Holocaust Studies, apologizes for a 1988 essay he says "created the impression" that he considered Israel's treatment of the Palestinians in Israel comparable to the Nazis' treatment of Jews. Here is what he said on the fiftieth anniversary of the Nazis' 1938 Kristallnacht pogrom: "Kristallnacht happened because a political state decided to be rid of people unwanted within its borders. It seems increasingly clear that Israel would prefer to rid itself of Palestinians if it could do so. . . . As much as any other people today, [the Palestinians] are being forced into a tragic part too much like the one played by the European Jews fifty years ago."

Roth did rather more than just "create the impression" he now regrets. He is not wicked; he loves Israel, where he has taught. However, his careless writings reflect slovenly thinking of a drearily familiar kind. It is the thinking of someone who has been too much marinated in the flaccid leftist consensus of the campuses, where reckless rhetoric enhances prestige.

He exploited the Holocaust for vulgar rhetorical effect when the 1980 election of Ronald Reagan moved him to remember "how forty years ago economic turmoil had conspired with Nazi nationalism and militarism . . . to send the world reeling into catastrophe that virtually annihilated the Jews of Europe." Then, after coyly denying "clear parallels" between America in the 1980s and Germany in the 1930s, he slyly implied parallels: "Still, it is not entirely mistaken to contemplate our postelection state with fear and trembling."

In an interview with USA Today during the 1988 campaign, he complained that the candidates were not addressing the problems of the poor and asserted a similarity to Nazi persecutions: In Nazi Germany, he reportedly said, educated professionals allowed themselves to ignore what was happening to the Jews.

Roth might belong at the museum. Its director of education, Joan Ringelheim, has said "women and minorities, the working class and the poor, prior to and after the Holocaust, have often lived in conditions similar in kind (although not always in degree) to those in the Holocaust." Oh, not always.

Comparing Nazi misogyny and the exploitation of Jewish women by Jewish men, Ringelheim has stressed the extent to which "the sexism of Nazi ideology and the sexism of the Jewish community met in a tragic and involuntary alliance." So the Holocaust was a serious episode of sexual harassment.

Holocaust studies generate many jargon-soggy analyses from others, such as this: "The manichean biologism of the Hitlerian cosmology is neither fluid nor primarily transcendental, though it does premise its empirical behavior on putative ontic truths, racial struggle being the immanent locus of adversarial transempirical actualities." Still, better such opacity than another scholar's assertion that the Holocaust was an environmental problem: "thousands of pounds of human ash dumped into lakes and rivers."

The Holocaust is being hijacked, turned into an empty flask to be filled up with academic obscurantism and trendy political advocacy masquerading as scholarship. In the process, writes Gabriel Schoenfeld ("Auschwitz and the Professors" in the June issue of Commentary), the hijackers submerge the Holocaust into the muddiness of proliferating "victim studies." This, Schoenfeld says, traduces the museum's core mission of understanding and memorializing the Jews' tragedy "in all its uniqueness and specificity."

Schoenfeld recalls that in 1981 Robert Alter, professor of Hebrew and Comparative Literature at Berkeley, cautioned that a "topic or event, however momentous, is not an academic discipline." As the Holocaust becomes "academicized" (Alter's word) it becomes trivialized, reduced to just another instance of injustice.

The museum should be, as it is, a research center, and certainly the Holocaust is a suitable subject for academic courses. But nowadays every intellectual enterprise is conditioned by its context—today's faddish, politicized, ax-grinding academic culture. That culture is seeping into the museum, diluting its noble gravity and single-mindedness.

June 18, 1998

Germany: Unending Self-Examination

The grainy, often badly focused black-and-white photographs from the eastern front are of Jews and others being tormented, humiliated, shot, and hanged, of corpses in mass graves—the workaday world of genocide. Such has been this century's dark side, these photographs might have scant power to shock but for the significance of their amateurishness: Eighty percent of the photos in the exhibit were taken by ordinary soldiers in the German army, and most record actions by the regular army, not the SS, the Waffen-SS, or the Einsatzgruppen killing squads.

Consider the remarkable reaction to the presentation of history by the Hamburg Institute for Social Research in the photographic exhibit "The German Army and Genocide." That the army on the eastern front was immediately, deeply and constantly involved in genocide and other war crimes is, says Dr. Bernd Greiner of the institute, not news to historians. But many Germans have clung to the conviction that Nazi criminality was the work of a lunatic fringe and corrupted members of elites, such as doctors and lawyers. Did not the Nuremberg war crimes tribunal give the army a moral acquittal?

No. The tribunal said the army, filled by conscription, would not be categorized, as the SS was, as a criminal organization. But the tribunal also said the army had abandoned the rules of warfare and was implicated in genocide.

The photo exhibit, seen so far by a million people in Germany and Austria, makes graphic the wide sweep of possible complicity in murder: every family had at least a father, son, uncle, cousin, or nephew in the army. And the conflagration of soul-searching begun by the exhibit has been fueled by two publishing events.

Shortly after the exhibit opened in 1995, Victor Klemperer's wartime diaries were published. Klemperer, a Jewish academic married to a non-Jew, managed by luck and stealth to survive the war, during which he wrote that by early 1942, drawing upon common gossip, he could describe the hierarchy of concentration camps, including killing camps in eastern Poland. (He cited Treblinka by name.) A fourteen-part television series has been made from the diaries. The publisher, which, Greiner says, expected to sell five thousand copies of the diary, has sold half a million.

Germany's unending self-examination was further agitated by the 1996 publication of Daniel Goldhagen's *Hitler's Willing Executioners: Ordinary Germans and the Holocaust*. Goldhagen's thesis is that German society was saturated by an "eliminationist anti-Semitism," which produced a high degree of voluntary participation in genocide. Goldhagen's idea—that Hitler merely unleashed a cultural latency and fulfilled the sick logic of Germany's history—was extreme. However, it acquired extra resonance in the context of the exhibit of photographs taken, in a matter-of-fact manner, by ordinary men doing extraordinary evil.

The exhibit has been seen in thirty-four German and Austrian cities (after the 1938 Anschluss, many Austrians were drafted), and fifty more have requested it. It was scheduled to open this month at the Cooper Union in Manhattan, but that has been delayed indefinitely, pending an expert panel's review of each of the approximately one thousand photographs.

The review was occasioned by a Polish historian's demonstration that eight to twelve photographs taken in three Ukrainian villages are of victims of Stalin's NKVD. Even this did not help the German army's reputation: in one village the NKVD killed six hundred suspected collaborators; then, three weeks later, the German army arrived, forced Jews to disinter the six hundred, and shortly thereafter participated in murdering two hundred of the Jews.

The exhibit has catalyzed the cleaning out of some dark recesses of Germany's mental attic. Several dozen people have come to the exhibit bearing family albums containing photos like those in the exhibit: photos of soldiers cutting the beards off Jewish men, photos of bodies hanging from streetlamps. Some of these photos are displayed in albums, like photos of family vacations. In Austria a visitor to the exhibit identified the soldiers in a gruesome photograph: He had been in their unit.

The exhibit has been cathartic, revealing something still boiling beneath the crust of Germany's normality. Greiner says, "We, the originators of the exhibit, were expropriated of our product. The public took over." Which is proof of Germany's healthy, fact-facing vigor, even fifty-four years on.

In America, where approximately one thousand World War II veterans die each day, a different kind of catharsis is occurring. The cultural mechanisms of mass memory—movies (e.g., *Saving Private Ryan*), books (e.g., Tom Brokaw's *The Greatest Generation*), the drive to build a World War II memorial on the Mall here—attest that the attic of our national memory is an inspiring place to pass some time.

December 19, 1999

July 10, 1941, in Jedwabne

Sixty years ago, on July 10, 1941, half the Polish town of Jedwabne murdered the other half. Of 1,600 Jews, about a dozen survived. Why did the murderers do it? Professor Jan Gross of New York University may not fully realize that he has found the answer.

It is in his astonishing little book (173 pages of text), just published by Princeton University Press. The title, *Neighbors,* is an ice dagger to the heart, but only after the book has been read. The word "neighbor" connotes moral sympathy ("neighborly") as well as physical proximity. But not on July 10, 1941, in Jedwabne.

Gross says, "This is a rather typical book about the Holocaust" because it does not offer "closure"—"I could not say to myself when I got to the last page, 'Well, I understand now.'" Perhaps he is flinching from the awful answer his book supplies.

On June 22, 1941, Germany attacked the Soviet Union, which was occupying the part of Poland containing Jedwabne. On June 23 a small detachment of Germans entered the town. There were almost immediately some isolated atrocities by Poles against Jews—one man stoned to death with bricks, another knifed and his eyes and tongue cut out. German policy encouraged pogroms by local populations, and there were some ghastly ones near Jedwabne. One of the first questions asked of the Germans occupying the town was, Is it permitted to kill the Jews?

After the carnival of killing, the Germans reportedly thought the Poles "had gone overboard" and said to them, "Was eight hours not enough for you to do with the Jews as you please?" But the murderers were not socially marginal people. At a town meeting—democracy, really—Jedwabne's leaders met with the Germans. Gross quotes a witness: "When the Germans proposed to leave one Jewish family from each profession, local carpenter Bronisław Szleziński, who was present, answered: We have enough of our own craftsmen, we have to destroy all the Jews, none should stay alive. Mayor Karolak and everybody else agreed with his words."

The mayor coordinated the killing, but otherwise, Gross says, "people were free to improvise." Peasants from nearby villages got word of the planned pogrom and came to town as to a fair. A Pole recalls that "the Jewish population became a toy in the hands of the Poles." The Holocaust has been called a manifestation of modernity because of its industrialization of murder. But in Jedwabne hooks and wooden clubs were used. A head was hacked off and kicked around. To escape the killers, women fled to a pond and drowned their babies, then themselves. But most were burned alive in a barn while the town was searched for the surviving sick and children. A witness: "As for the little children, they roped a few together by their legs and carried them on their backs, then put them on pitchforks and threw them onto smoldering coals."

Gross estimates that half the town's men participated, and because the killings were concentrated in a space no larger than a sports stadium, everyone "in possession of a sense of sight, smell, or hearing either participated in or witnessed the tormented deaths." A murderer in uniform can resemble a cog in a machine, but the last faces seen by Jedwabne's Jews were the familiar faces of neighbors. It was, Gross says, "mass murder in a double sense—on account of both the number of victims and the number of perpetrators."

The Germans' involvement was confined to photographing events and, in one instance, offering the sort of advice professionals offer amateurs. A witness recalls that when Poles with thick clubs were battering six Jews, a watching German said, "Do not kill at once. Slowly, let them suffer."

In 1996 Daniel Goldhagen's book *Hitler's Willing Executioners: Ordinary Germans and the Holocaust* argued that German society was saturated by an "eliminationist anti-Semitism" that produced a high degree of voluntary participation in genocide. His premise—that Hitler merely unleashed a cultural latency and fulfilled the sick logic of German history—reduces Hitler's role to that of mere catalyst. Goldhagen did stress the powerful role of Third Reich propaganda. But, then, what of the Poles of Jedwabne, who were not Germans and who did their uncoerced murdering after just two weeks of German occupation, before being conditioned by propaganda?

Christopher Browning, author of *Ordinary Men,* a study of middle-aged German conscripts who became consenting participants in mass-murder police battalions in Poland, argued that cruelties inflicted by the Khmer Rouge against fellow Cambodians and by Chinese against Chinese during Mao Zedong's Cultural Revolution cannot be explained by Goldhagen's model: centuries of conditioning by a single idea. Neither can Jedwabne be explained by

Easter sermons characterizing Jews as God killers, or by medieval myths about ritual murders of children by Jews, or by lust for plunder.

Gross's book accords with Browning's admonition that explanation must involve "those universal aspects of human nature that transcend the cognition and culture of ordinary Germans." Or ordinary Poles. At bottom, the explanation is not in this or that national history but in humanity as it quickly becomes when severed from social restraints.

Gross quotes, but does not sufficiently dwell on, philosopher Eric Voegelin's thoughts about "the simple man, who is a decent man as long as the society as a whole is in order, but who then goes wild, without knowing what he is doing, when disorder arises somewhere and the society is no longer holding together." Political philosophies that celebrate atomistic individualism need to be reread in the light cast by the crematoria of Auschwitz.

The Holocaust, writes Gross, is "a foundational event of modern sensibility, forever afterward to be an essential consideration in reflections about the human condition." So, again: Why in Jedwabne did neighbors murder their neighbors? Because it was permitted. Because they could.

July 9, 2001

Israel at Fifty

It has been said that mankind hopes vaguely but dreads precisely. Surely that is especially true of Jews, various of whose religious observances commemorate calamities or narrow deliverances from calamities. Hence the necessity of a Jewish state.

Jews made up 10 percent of the population of the Roman Empire. If today they were the same proportion of the world's population that they were then, they would number 200 million. They number 13 million. The world was a much more dangerous place for Jews before they had a national home, even though that home is in a rough neighborhood. The problem of stateless Jews is no more. The long, rescuing arm of Israel can reach even into Chechnya.

History became pregnant with Israel when Zionism was energized by Theodor Herzl, reacting to the anti-Semitism swirling around the 1894 Dreyfus trial in France. But in a sense, Israel is a lingering echo of the French Revolution's idea that a people find true fulfillment only through revived nations. Zionism is an especially defensible nationalism. Having had a uniquely hazardous history, Jews deserve a common future.

The lash of events as well as the Zionist idea brought Jews to Palestine, where in the 1930s Jews asked newcomers, *"Kommen Sie aus Überzeugung oder kommen Sie aus Deutschland?"* (Do you come from conviction or from Germany?) When Israel was founded, by a declaration of independence fifty years ago May 14, on one-sixth of 1 percent of the 7.5 million square miles of land of what is too casually called "the Arab world," it was already engulfed in war.

It has experienced at least four wars (1948, 1956, 1967, 1973). Five if you count the 1969–70 "war of attrition." Six if you count the continuing conflict with terrorist organizations, including the PLO, Israel's interlocutor in a peculiar "peace process" in which the PLO remains committed to Israel's destruction.

If peace is understood, as it should be, as more than the mere absence of clashing armies, Israel has never known a moment of it. There are few forms of cant more deserving of disdain than the recurring American injunction—from a powerful nation insulated by two broad oceans and two friendly neighbors—that Israel should "take risks for peace." Israelis take a risk boarding a bus.

In three weeks in 1973, Israel's casualties, as a percentage of its population, were larger than U.S. casualties in eight years of war in Vietnam. Yet although no nation ever had a better excuse for becoming a garrison state, Israel remains a vigorous democracy. Sometimes it is almost alarmingly vigorous: the saying is, "two Israelis can make three factions."

It is still the only democracy, the only salient of American values, in a still inhospitable region. As Binyamin Netanyahu has said, there still is no Syrian Lech Wałesa or Palestinian Andrei Sakharov. And there is no reason to believe that when the Palestinians have fully achieved their second state (historically and ethnically, Jordan is Palestinian), the twenty-second Arab state, it will be the first Arab democracy.

The 1967 war, the six days that shook the world, erupted on June 5, when Israel, surrounded by more than 370,000 troops, 2,000 tanks, and 600 fighter and bomber aircraft, launched preemptive air strikes. Israel told Jordan that if it did not attack, Israel would not cross the 1949 armistice line. Jordan, perhaps moved by Egypt's disinformation (Nasser said Israel's air force had been destroyed), attacked and lost the West Bank. In the aftermath of that war a wit said: Imagine, the Japanese have the great trading nation, the Jews the great warrior nation.

Before 1967, Israel was the sentimentalists' delight—Mozart among the orange groves, Athens reborn. On June 5, Sparta stood up. Since then, the premise of every "peace process" has been that Israel, by yielding something tangible—land—for something intangible—a better "atmosphere"—would produce a Middle Eastern atmosphere so peaceful that land would be irrelevant to Israel's security.

When Israel balks at betting its life on this hypothesis, critics say Israel is being provocative. Actually, Israel's very being is provocative to its armed enemies. Hence Israel's existential anxiety. When President Richard Nixon suggested a

U.S. security guarantee, Prime Minister Golda Meir replied, "By the time you get here, we won't be here." A poem by Stephen Crane says:

> *A man said to the universe:*
> *"Sir, I exist!"*
> *"However," replied the universe,*
> *"The fact has not created in me*
> *A sense of obligation."*

That is understood in Israel, which knows that the fiftieth anniversary of its nationhood is also the sixtieth anniversary of the sacrifice of a small nation for the convenience of large nations, at Munich.

May 7, 1998

JUSTICE AND INJUSTICE

"Do Not Iron Clothes on Body"

All of us have seen them, those words of warning or instruction that appear on products we buy: "Do not eat this sled." "For best results do not apply this floor wax to your teeth." "This antifreeze is not intended for pouring on breakfast cereal." We hardly notice them, let alone consider what they say about the times in which we live. The sled, wax, and antifreeze warnings are apocryphal. But you could not know that. After all, *The American Enterprise Magazine* offers these from real life:

On a bag of Fritos: "You could be a winner! No purchase necessary. Details inside." On a bread pudding: "Product will be hot after heating." On a bar of Dial soap: "Use like regular soap." On a hotel shower cap: "Fits one head." On a package of Nytol sleeping aid: "May cause drowsiness." On a string of Christmas lights: "For indoor or outdoor use only." On the packaging of a Rowenta iron: "Do not iron clothes on body."

The warning about a product's being hot after heating may be a response to the famous case wherein a woman successfully sued McDonald's because she was burned when she spilled—she was a passenger in a stationary car at the time, with the cup between her legs—the hot McDonald's coffee she had just bought. (If the coffee had been cool, a complaint about that could have been packaged as a lawsuit.) But try to picture in your mind the event involving two or more heads that the manufacturer of the shower cap was worried about.

Give up? Well, then, answer this: If there are people who press their pants while in their pants, are they the sort of people whose behavior will be changed by a warning on the packaging the iron comes in? If there are people who have done that once, are there any who have done it twice? If not, does that demonstrate that even the dimmest among us has a learning curve that actually curves?

Such questions are stirred by the great toothbrush litigation just getting under way in Chicago. What Charles Dickens did with *Jarndyce v. Jarndyce* in *Bleak House* as an index of cultural conditions, perhaps some modern novelist will do with *Trimarco v. Colgate Palmolive et al.*

The "et al."s include some other manufacturers of toothbrushes and the American Dental Association. All are to be hauled before the bar of justice by Mark Trimarco, speaking for himself and—this is a class-action suit—"all others similarly situated." The others are suffering from what Trimarco's complaint calls "a disease known as 'toothbrush abrasion.'" Abrasion a disease? The plaintiff's materials also call it "an injury." And "a distinct clinical entity caused by toothbrushes of the following bristle types: firm, medium and soft, both natural and synthetic."

The complaint says people suffering from this self-inflicted injury are consumers who were not "informed or warned about the danger of toothbrush abrasion." And: "It was the duty of the defendant manufacturers to furnish a product, i.e., toothbrush, which was in reasonably safe condition when put to a use in a manner that was reasonably foreseeable considering the nature and intended function of the product."

But the toothbrushes "were unsafe and unreasonably dangerous for their intended use in that the packaging contained no warning as to the risks of toothbrush abrasion or instructions on how to brush to avoid toothbrush abrasion." The American Dental Association is a defendant because it gave its seal of approval to the toothbrushes.

The complaint charges negligence because the manufacturers knew or should have known about the disease/injury/clinical entity since "at least 1949" but continued to manufacture toothbrushes that were "likely" to cause abrasion. *Likely?* If the result is "likely," you would think that the class of plaintiffs would be a majority of all who brush their teeth.

If toothbrushes are, as charged, "unreasonably dangerous" because of the absence of warnings and instructions, try to imagine the words that, if printed on toothbrush packages, would immunize manufacturers against such a complaint: "Warning: In brushing, too much is too much." "Instructions: Hold brush in hand. Insert the end with the bristles into your mouth. Move brush up and down. Stop before you wear out your teeth." Or perhaps: "Look, this toothbrush is not normally a dangerous implement, but neither is it intended for ninnies who can't figure out how to brush their teeth without doing them irreparable harm."

This suit is just part of a great American growth industry: litigation that expresses the belief that everyone has an entitlement to compensation for any unpleasantness; litigation that displaces responsibility from individuals to corporations with money. This industry was, of course, up and running before the tobacco litigation, but that taught lawyers just how lucrative it could be to blame individuals' foolishness on, say, Joe Camel.

Now many cities are suing gun manufacturers for the "costs"—the numbers are guesses—of shootings. In a new wrinkle in tort law—a move that would make a trial lawyer blush, if that were possible—individuals who have been shot are suing groups of manufacturers without claiming to have been injured by a product made by any of the targeted manufacturers.

If you—your teeth are suddenly feeling a bit abraded, are they not?—want to climb aboard the latest gravy train pulling out of the station, log on to www.toothbrushlawsuit.com. You will be greeted warmly: "Welcome to the Toothbrush Lawsuit Web Site." Illinois residents can dial 1-877-SOREGUMS. From the Web site you will learn that the disease is "progressive." That means not that Al Gore likes it, but that it gets worse if you keep making it worse. You also will learn that toothbrush abrasion "is most prevalent in those with good oral hygiene, i.e., people who brush their teeth." And "there are studies that show that people who do not brush their teeth, never develop" symptoms of toothbrush abrasion. Consider yourself warned.

May 10, 1999

Microgovernment and the Law of Litigation

MADISON, WISCONSIN—Scott Southworth is a mild-mannered twenty-six-year-old from the small Wisconsin town of New Lisbon. However, his lapel pin—two tiny feet, symbol of the right-to-life movement—announces that he is a Christian conservative not bashful about announcing his convictions in an uncongenial setting.

He is a graduate of the University of Wisconsin, a museum of liberalism, and of its law school, where he learned the joys of litigation. Now he is inflicting his legal learning on his alma mater. And he is illustrating the temptation of judicial activism for conservatives.

While a student, he was annoyed that portions of the mandatory student fee he paid were distributed to many organizations—for example, those promoting homosexual and liberal causes—whose agendas appall him. So he sued, and his case, successful so far, seems headed for the Supreme Court.

His cause is just but raises a question: Do conservatives really want government—meaning, inescapably, courts—delivering so much justice?

A federal court has said he has a First Amendment right not to pay fees used to subsidize ideologies offensive to his religious and personal beliefs. The court enjoined the university from collecting from any student any portion of the fee that subsidizes anything offensive to that student.

This is a recipe for an administrative nightmare and an incentive for universities to withdraw from funding any group potentially offensive to anyone. Which pleases Southworth.

He says government has a right to speak for itself, as when the Wisconsin Legislature denounced the KKK. However, he says government does not have a right to force people to fund offensive speech by others. A federal court siding with him has enunciated a broad new First Amendment right of conscience. When Southworth is asked if, because of that right, the National

Endowment for the Arts might be declared unconstitutional, he says, with quiet relish, "Give me time."

Conservative protests about the uses of student fees are roiling many universities, which respond that academic freedom, properly understood, requires respecting their broad discretion to create a stimulating learning environment. This requires "diversity," hence the wholesome cacophony of subsidized advocacy.

Conservatives rejoin, often correctly, that they are turning to courts only because they have been provoked. The problem that they say requires judicial remedy is that of universities defining diversity in ways unfriendly to conservatives.

In 1995 conservatives rejoiced when the Supreme Court said the University of Virginia could not refuse to subsidize a Christian magazine devoted to proselytizing. The Court said the university's policy of not subsidizing religious or political activities constituted unconstitutional discrimination based on the content of speech. Southworth, an honest man who hews to principles more clear than prudent, favors that decision only if Virginia students who are affronted by evangelism, or Christianity, or religion generally, can be exempt from an appropriate portion of the mandatory fees.

But can a conservative be content to have courts controlling universities and other institutions of civil society, permeating their internal operations with government supervision? The unjust treatment of conservatives does not justify their participation in today's reflexive recourse to litigation rather than persuasion—politics—to improve their lot. What litigation like Southworth's advances is what Jonathan Rauch of *National Journal* calls "microgovernment."

Remember Casey Martin, the professional golfer who has a circulatory disorder that makes him incapable of walking eighteen holes? The Professional Golfers' Association said he could not compete riding in a cart because walking is an essential part of golf. Martin got a court to overrule the PGA, holding that, under the Americans with Disabilities Act, Martin has a right to ride.

It is, Rauch says, an interesting question whether walking is part of golf, but a more interesting question is why government should answer such questions. Such government derogates society's self-governance through nongovernmental institutions, such as the PGA.

Microgovernment's aim, Rauch says, is to use the lever of litigation to pry open every aspect of life so government can fine-tune fairness. Government increasingly polices behavior, monitoring workplace jokes to prevent a sexually "hostile environment" and ordering colleges to set up as many interviews for female as for male athletes. A jury applying the government's rules fined the producers of *Melrose Place* $5 million for their unfairness in not allowing an actress to play a seductress after she became pregnant.

Southworth's suit should awaken universities from their dogmatic slumbers about "diversity" and the affronts they inflict in its name. But the suit is an incitement to microgovernment, which produces, cumulatively, very big government indeed.

October 22, 1998

Hate Crimes: The Criminal Law as Moral Pork Barrel

Matthew Shepard, a gay student at the University of Wyoming, was beaten and left lashed to a fence near Laramie through a cold high plains night. He has died. His assailants should die: Wyoming has capital punishment for first-degree murder. Now, imagine the trouble they would be in if Wyoming were one of the twenty-one states with laws against "hate crimes" based on sexual orientation.

President Clinton has rushed to re-endorse broadening federal hate crime laws to cover crimes motivated by the victim's sexual orientation, disability, or gender. Currently, federal hate crimes include only those based on race, color, religion, and national origin.

Congress continually uses the criminal law as a moral pork barrel, for indignation gestures. Compassion is today's supreme political value, so politics is a sentiment competition. It is less about changing society than striking poses: theatrical empathy trumps considerations of mere practicality. But the multiplication of hate crime categories—statutes stipulating that some crime victims are especially important—is an imprudent extension of identity politics.

In their book *Hate Crimes: Criminal Law & Identity Politics,* James B. Jacobs and Kimberly Potter define such politics as individuals relating to one another as members of competing groups defined by race, gender, religion, sexual orientation, disability, and so on. In such politics, it is strategically advantageous to be recognized as victimized or otherwise disadvantaged.

Hate crime laws are, Jacobs and Potter argue, "morale-building legislation" because they confer such recognition. But does the competition for special government-conferred status for particular groups advance the aim of hate crime laws: a more tolerant society?

Such laws mandate enhanced penalties for crimes committed as a result of, or at least when accompanied by (can juries be counted on to distinguish causation from correlation?), particular government-disapproved states of mind. Granted, law has the expressive function of stigmatizing particular conduct. However, should government plunge deeper into stigmatizing thoughts and attitudes? The consequence will be more and more crimes presented by prosecutors as especially wicked because the defendants had odious (but not illegal) frames of mind.

Should we saddle juries with the task of detecting an expanding number of impermissible motives for acts already proscribed? Should jurors decide:

Is the utterance of a racial or ethnic slur during an assault conclusive evidence that the assault is a "hate crime" and thus more odious than the same assault absent the slur? Does a black (white) mugger presumptively choose his white (black) victim because of his race? Are rapes invariably hate crimes because rapists pick their victims because of gender?

Was the 1989 Central Park "wilding"—the near-fatal rape and beating of a white jogger by a gang of black and Hispanic youths—a hate crime? No, the youths did not suffer enhanced penalties, because they also assaulted Hispanics that evening. They got more lenient treatment because of the catholicity of their barbarism.

For the flavor of the future under broad hate crimes laws, consider an Ohio prosecutor's questions when trying to prove a white man's racist motive for having a dispute with a black person at a campground. The prosecutor asked about the white man's relations with his black neighbor: "And you lived next door . . . for nine years and you don't even know her first name? Never had dinner with her? Never gone out and had a beer with her? You don't associate with her, do you? All these black people that you have described that are your friends, I want you to give me one person, just one, who was really a good friend of yours."

Before passing laws that will make such inquisitorial questioning routine in millions of cases involving violent—and nonviolent—behavior, consider that, according to the FBI, in 1996 there were just twelve murders classified as hate crimes. And the many thousands of reported hate incidents include a small fraction of 1 percent of all crimes. Most are vandalism (e.g., graffiti) or intimidation (e.g., verbal abuse).

Now, some motives for seemingly similar deeds *are* so much worse than others that they make some deeds different not only in degree of odiousness but in kind: painting "Beat Michigan" on a bridge is not quite the same offense as painting "Burn Jews" on a synagogue.

However, surely the criminal law can take cognizance of such distinctions without codifying an ever-more-elaborate structure of identity politics. And surely Shepard's assailants would deserve no less severity if he were not gay and their motive had been, as it may partly have been (how *do* we disentangle motives?), pure sadism.

October 15, 1998

Punishing States of Mind

Meet federal Judge Whittaker J. Stang, who is old, dyspeptic, and too good to be true: "I like my clerks smart, young and pretty. And if anybody doesn't like it, they can sue me for sexual harassment, age discrimination, and—I don't know—brains discrimination, how's that? Can they sue me for intelligence discrimination yet? . . . Take note! I've hired black ones five or ten times at least. They were also smart, young and pretty."

Stang is one of many tangy characters in Richard Dooling's *Brain Storm,* a hilarious novel about hate. Set in the near future, it is a serious novel of ideas, including Dooling's idea that laws mandating enhanced penalties for "hate crimes" create, in effect, thought crimes.

Joe Watson ("Like many lawyers, Watson originally went to law school because he had been unsettled by the prospect of graduation from college") has an expensive wife and a bland but remunerative job at an establishment law firm. Then Stang assigns him to defend a racist lowlife who killed a deaf black man he found in bed with his—the lowlife's—wife. Watson loses his wife, temporarily, and his job, permanently, because, rather than plead his client guilty, he throws himself into the task of overthrowing the idea of "hate crimes."

In real life, the first U.S. laws criminalizing hatred made it illegal to use hateful speech or commit symbolic acts expressing hatred. These were declared unconstitutional because they were not "content neutral": if you painted a peace symbol on a synagogue, you got a mild sentence for vandalism; if you painted a swastika, you got ten years for a hate crime. So instead of directly banning hateful speech and acts, legislatures enhanced the penalties for acts that seemed motivated by hate or that seemed to have occurred because of the victim's status or the perpetrator's hatefulness.

This distinction without a difference is, a Dooling character says, a bonanza for lawyers: "Hate could mean more business for them than crack cocaine. After all, hate is everywhere, and it's free!" But proving intent to do something is hard enough without having to prove it was done with a bad attitude. Imagine the potential for abuse when the law invites prosecutors to prove to juries that a particular motive—a proscribed hatred of a group accorded special government protection—caused the killer to pull the trigger.

Brain Storm is a crash course in neuroscience and the possible behavioral implications of neurological disorders. One of Dooling's characters is a scientist who says that believing in free will is akin to believing in leprechauns. The mind, she says, is "a symphony orchestra with no conductor"—hundreds of billions of neurons cooperating to produce consciousness, and we have no idea how. But new brain-scanning technologies can produce, in effect, pictures of, say, rage or contentment: the glucose uptake, oxygen consumption, blood flow, and electrical or magnetic activities correlated with particular states of mind. So is it unreasonable to postulate genetic, biological, environmental, or medical causes of violence—causes that can be removed?

The trouble is, the law holds us responsible for controlling our minds, which, presumably, control our bodies. Unfortunately, government increasingly wants to inventory and furnish our minds.

Today government, although hard pressed to provide basic services, has ever more ambitious plans for fine-tuning citizens' minds. Joe Camel has been killed and Budweiser's frogs and lizards will soon find themselves in the government's gun sights as part of its metastasizing campaign against socially undesirable desires (and not only those of "kids"). Political hygienists bent on "campaign finance reform" are hot to gut the First Amendment to protect the (supposedly) gullible public from overdosing on "too much" political speech. To protect that fragile flower, womanhood (the law enshrines that stereotype), from "hostile work environments" (whatever annoys a particular woman on a particular day), a federal judge has held that use of gender-based terms such as "foreman" or "draftsman" could constitute sexual harassment. Government has found that classified ads for homes with an "ocean view" and with "family rooms" discriminate against the blind and singles, respectively.

So pay attention when Dooling says, "The day is fast approaching when all speech will be regulated in the interest of civil rights and the prosecution of hate criminals who commit gender crimes through the hostile and abusive use of illegal words." And read *Brain Storm* for a subtle, entertaining depiction of the tangle that results when government undertakes to punish not only crimes but states of mind.

June 6, 1998

"Bigotry" and the Boy Scouts

New Jersey's Supreme Court has unanimously issued a ruling that deserves to be reviewed by the U.S. Supreme Court, which four years ago issued a unanimous ruling that may be incompatible with the New Jersey ruling that the Boy Scouts cannot discriminate against homosexuals. The controversy, with wide ramifications for American freedom, is not about whether the Scouts' policy is right but whether the Scouts have a right to it.

James Dale, now 29, became a Scout at age eight, earned Eagle Scout status, and was an assistant scoutmaster in New Jersey when Scout officials saw a newspaper photo of him as a leader of a gay rights group at Rutgers University. The Scouts promptly expelled him, saying that homosexuality is incompatible with the Scout obligation to be "morally straight" and "clean."

Dismissing the Scouts' position (with which many religious denominations and various other groups agree) as "bigotry," New Jersey's chief justice, writing for the court, said the Scouts are (like a restaurant, which is open to the general public) a "public accommodation" and therefore covered by New Jersey's statute forbidding discrimination on the basis of sexual orientation. Another justice, the court's leading liberal, argued, with more length (forty-four pages) than legal relevance, that "decades of social science data" have refuted the "myth" that homosexuals are "inherently immoral."

The Scouts will take to the U.S. Supreme Court the argument that their constitutional (First Amendment) right of "expressive association" trumps New Jersey's statute. Addressing that argument, the New Jersey court said that the Scouts, with 5.8 million members nationwide, are not "selective" enough to qualify as "distinctively private."

In 1984 the U.S. Supreme Court ruled 7–0 (Justices Warren Burger and Harry Blackmun, both Minnesotans, had been Jaycees, so they recused themselves) that Minnesota Jaycees were required to admit women. This was because of a state statute forbidding denial, on the basis of sex, of "full and equal enjoyment" of a "place of public accommodation."

But the Court limited the sweep of that ruling by noting that organizations make themselves "available to the public" in various ways. The Court rejected the Jaycees' "expressive association" defense but stressed that the Jaycees are a primarily commercial organization whose "unselective criteria" (only age and sex) were not importantly related to the organization's message.

However, the Scouts, unlike the Jaycees, are a creedal organization with an explicitly moral mission, albeit one that conflicts with the moral philosophies of seven New Jersey justices. So the Scouts' "expressive association" claim is stronger than the Jaycees' was.

Furthermore, in 1995 the Court unanimously held that organizers of Boston's Saint Patrick's Day parade had a First Amendment right to exclude from the parade a group of Irish-American gays, lesbians, and bisexuals. The group had been formed for the purpose of participating in the parade to express pride in their Irishness and their sexual orientation, and to express solidarity with similar people who had tried to march in New York's parade.

The Court held that a parade is not mere motion, it is inherently expressive and that the First Amendment protects a speaker's (in this case, the parade's) "autonomy" in choosing the content of his message. The Court rejected the claim that the parade lacks "genuine selectivity" and therefore lacks an "expressive purpose."

Notice that the New Jersey justices have objected precisely to the fact that the Scouts *are* genuinely selective. By objecting to the Scouts' selection criteria, the justices have conceded the Scouts' expressive purpose.

The New Jersey court's ruling that the Boy Scouts' convictions about sexual morality cannot be tolerated has, of course, been praised by liberals as a blow for toleration. The court's ruling that the Boy Scouts must be made to bow to the state's orthodoxy on sexual morality has, of course, been praised by liberals for advancing diversity. The court's ruling that the Boy Scouts' convictions do not deserve respect has, of course, been praised by liberals as a luminous example of showing respect for others.

In several other states with statutes forbidding discrimination on the basis of sexual orientation, challenges to the Scouts' right to exclude homosexuals have failed. But now New Jersey's judicial authoritarianism has advanced, by the means preferred by contemporary liberalism (litigation rather than legislation; judicial fiat rather than democratic persuasion), the liberal agenda of breaking more and more institutions to the saddle of the state.

The legal reasoning (leave aside the moral exhibitionism) of the New Jersey justices—two of whom, including the chief justice, were appointed by Republican Governor Christine Todd Whitman, who applauded the decision—is ripe for review.

August 15, 1999

Privacy and the Boy Scouts

In this litigious republic, litigation often is politics carried on by other means, and, like politics, litigation sometimes makes strange bedfellows, as in a case to be argued before the Supreme Court next month and to be decided by early summer. The question at issue is: Should New Jersey Boy Scout organizations be permitted to exclude gay men from being scoutmasters?

New Jersey says this violates the state's antidiscrimination law. But the Scouts have acquired an unlikely ally, an organization of gays and lesbians that says the Scouts' policy is not right but the Scouts have a right to it.

Gays and Lesbians for Individual Liberty has filed a friend-of-the-court brief prepared by the Institute for Justice, a merry band of libertarian lawyers in Washington, D.C. GLIL argues that defeating the New Jersey Scouts would be a Pyrrhic victory for gays and lesbians, who have, historically and still, a large stake in society respecting what the Scouts are asserting, the First Amendment right of freedom of association.

Last year New Jersey's Supreme Court unanimously ruled that the Scouts' policy is "bigotry" and that the Scouts are, like a restaurant that is open to the general public, a "public accommodation" and therefore covered by the state's statute that forbids discrimination on the basis of sexual orientation. The court argued that the Scouts, with 5.8 million members nationwide, are not selective enough to be considered "distinctively private."

The Scouts appealed to the Supreme Court, citing their right of "expressive association," which the Court has defined as "freedom to engage in association for the advancement of beliefs and ideas." In its brief GLIL vigorously deplores the Scouts' creed, which is that homosexuality is incompatible with the Scout obligation to be "morally straight" and "clean." But GLIL agrees that the Scouts are a creedal organization with an explicitly moral mission. And citing much history—for example, until the late 1970s the IRS denied tax-exempt status to organizations that "promoted" homosexuality—the GLIL brief argues that gays have suffered "when freedom of association has not been respected and governments have been allowed to trample on the rights of citizens to freely gather together."

The GLIL brief says the New Jersey decision is pernicious because "it places the government in the intolerable position of second-guessing a private organization's interpretation of its own rules and articulation of its own message." Furthermore, the New Jersey ruling is perverse because it says the right of expressive association belongs only to organizations that have messages more forcefully stated than is the Scouts' disapproval of homosexuality. The New Jersey court parsed the Scout oath about being "straight" and "clean" and said the oath does not forbid homosexual conduct. Furthermore, the court said the Scouts did not produce sufficient evidence that the organization wants to communicate disapproval of homosexuality. This is an incentive for the Scouts to increase their antigay emphasis.

The law has recently taken an interesting carom regarding gays and the First Amendment. In 1995 the Supreme Court held that the University of Virginia had impermissibly practiced viewpoint discrimination when it refused to give funds from the student activities fees to a newspaper expressing religious (and antigay) views. Two years later, in the first federal appellate case applying to a gay organization the principle affirmed in the University of Virginia case, a circuit court held that the University of South Alabama violated freedom of speech and association when it denied student fee funding to a gay student group.

GLIL argues that the inclusion of gays in all facets of life is profoundly desirable because it sends "a message of tolerance and acceptance." But when a private association is involved, the First Amendment requires that "this message must be sent through private choice and must not be communicated due to government coercion." As the Supreme Court has said, freedom of association "plainly presupposes a freedom not to associate." When the Court affirmed the right of Minnesota to require the Jaycees to admit women, it stressed that the Jaycees were not a creedal organization using the exclusion to convey a specific message about females.

The GLIL, warning against "creeping infringement" of freedom of association, notes that gay organizations often seek and administer "gay environments," including clubs, retreats, vacations, and professional and alumni organizations. America needs a livelier understanding of the arithmetic of rights that GLIL understands: Multiplying rights, such as the right of a gay to be a scoutmaster, can mean a net subtraction from freedom.

March 26, 2000

In June, the Supreme Court ruled, 5–4, in favor of the Scout's understanding of their right of freedom of association.

The Privacy of the Unencumbered Self

Following the U.S. Supreme Court's logic to a conclusion that the Court itself flinched from reaching twelve years ago, Georgia's Supreme Court last week struck down that state's antisodomy law. The court said the law violates the state constitution's privacy right.

Often, what a court does is less consequential than the reasons it gives for doing it. Indeed, often the reason a court gives for doing something *is* what it does. In privacy-rights cases running back to 1972, courts are teaching Americans to misunderstand themselves—literally, their selves.

In 1986 the U.S. Supreme Court narrowly (5–4) affirmed the constitutionality of Georgia's law that criminalized sodomy. The 1986 case, involving a homosexual, established that consenting adults had no constitutional right to engage in homosexual conduct. (Last week's case involved heterosexual sodomy.) One justice in the 1986 majority, Lewis Powell, later said he regretted his vote. That was understandable, given the evolution of the Court's rationale for the privacy right from 1961 to 1972.

In 1961 the Court dismissed on technical grounds a challenge to a Connecticut law banning the use of contraceptives. However, two justices dissented, arguing that enforcement of a ban on the *use* of contraceptives would require government intrusion into the zone of privacy necessary for healthy marital intimacy. So the privacy right was defined and justified in terms of society's stake in a valued *relationship,* not merely in terms of an individual's right to choose. The right was not—not yet—linked to a government stance of neutrality among various choices people might make.

Four years later the Court overturned Connecticut's law, but still not because privacy protects individual autonomy in sexual lives; rather, because privacy serves "a relationship," the institution of marriage, which is "an association that promotes a way of life" about which society is not neutral. The Court could have reasoned directly from this decision to its 1986 decision about Georgia's antisodomy law—if there had not been two intervening decisions.

In 1972 it overturned a law that banned not the use but the distribution of contraceptives. Because use was not the issue, neither was intrusive enforcement that would injure the institution of marriage by bringing government into bedrooms. Nevertheless, the Court overturned the law, arguing that it violated privacy simply because it unjustifiably interfered with individual choices. The stage was set for the 1973 judicial earthquake *Roe v. Wade.*

The radicalism of that decision, which established a broad constitutional privacy right to abortion, stemmed from this fact: the Court severed the justification for the privacy right from any contribution that right makes to the socially valued relationship of marriage. Instead, the Court said, the privacy right "is broad enough to encompass a woman's decision" to terminate a pregnancy. Mere deciding, not marriage, was what mattered. One justice, using the language from the 1972 decision, stressed "the right of the *individual* [the court's italics], married or single" to enjoy "freedom of personal choice," without inhibition by husbands or parents.

The court had arrived at what Harvard's Michael Sandel, in his book *Democracy's Discontent,* says is a privacy right defined in terms of a "voluntarist conception of the person." Henceforth, government would strive to protect individuals' autonomy in making certain important choices while remaining neutral about the content of those choices. Which is why in 1986 the Court seemed inconsistent in upholding Georgia's ban on consensual adult sodomy.

It was too late for the Court to say that homosexual activity is outside the zone of protected privacy because it has "no connection" with "family, marriage or procreation." Since 1972 the privacy right in sexual contexts has had no necessary connection with those social relationships.

Upholding Georgia's proscription of sodomy, the Court in 1986 insisted, correctly but awkwardly, that moral neutrality is not a constitutional necessity of law because "law . . . is constantly based on notions of morality, and if all laws representing essentially moral choices are to be invalidated . . . the courts will be very busy indeed." This is true, but the Court was locking the barn door after selling the horse.

The Court had put its prestige behind the idea that individuals should be thought of as freely choosing selves "unencumbered" (Sandel's word) by social roles or relationships that society values. Is it merely coincidental that, as the Court has been embedding this "voluntarist" image of the individual into constitutional law and the country's consciousness, marriage has been increasingly treated as just another choice, to be casually made—and unmade? Society's neutrality has resulted in no-fault divorces.

Sandel is a liberal but is uneasy with the reasoning that courts use to give liberals some victories. He would overturn Georgia's law and broadly affirm gay rights by recurring to pre-1972 reasoning about privacy. He would have the law regard homosexuals, like everyone else, not simply as sovereign choosers, "unencumbered" by social roles, but as "situated selves," defined by engagement in roles and relationships society wants to encourage. Sandel would ground the elemental gay right (to intimacy protected from intrusive government) in society's stake in encouraging homosexual unions that are (to borrow language from the 1965 decision) "intimate to the degree of being sacred . . . a harmony in living . . . a bilateral loyalty" in an association for a "noble purpose."

Some thoughtful critics will say courts should not employ such language to give society's imprimatur to homosexual intimacies. And these critics will insist that such assigning of social values should generally be done not by courts but by political, representative institutions. However, Sandel and his critics can agree that much damage is done when we define human beings not as social beings—not in terms of morally serious roles (citizen, marriage partner, parent, etc.)—but only with reference to the watery idea of a single, morally empty capacity of "choice." Politics becomes empty; citizenship, too.

The moral of the story is: When a court does the right thing for the wrong reason, it does the wrong thing.

December 7, 1998

Prison, Procreation, and FedEx

Six days before September 11 purged much of the silliness from public life, the Ninth U.S. Circuit Court of Appeals, famously imaginative and frequently reversed, outdid itself. Rummaging around in the U.S. Constitution, it discovered that male inmates in prisons have a "fundamental" right to procreate by artificial insemination.

However, female prisoners do not have the corresponding right. And the Ninth Circuit Court is uncharacteristically reticent about whether males can exercise this right only with an actual spouse or also with a significant other. It is unclear why, as a matter of constitutional law, as the Ninth Circuit Court imagines it, that difference should make any difference.

William Gerber, 41, resides in a California prison, where, as a "third strike" felon, he is serving a life sentence for his third conviction, this time for making terrorist threats, using narcotics, negligently discharging a gun, and illegally possessing a gun as an ex-felon. Chafing at the way imprisonment interferes with his social life, two years ago he sued, charging a violation of his civil right to send some of his semen to a Chicago sperm bank that would impregnate his wife.

In early September, a three-judge panel of the Ninth Circuit Court ruled, 2–1, that Gerber is correct: James Madison and the others in Philadelphia 214 years ago did indeed provide just such a right. Joined by Stephen Reinhardt, another judge who provides the U.S. Supreme Court with steady work reversing Ninth Circuit Court rulings, Judge Myron Bright explained how "the right to procreate survives incarceration."

California regulations—which Bright, remarkably, given his penchant for activism, has not rewritten—forbid conjugal visits for prisoners serving life sentences. But, Bright notes, the Supreme Court has several times affirmed the "fundamental" nature of the right to procreate—at least, Bright judiciously adds, "outside the prison context." But he says that context is constitutionally irrelevant because no "legitimate penological objectives" are served by not recognizing Gerber's procreative right.

In 1942 the Supreme Court struck down Oklahoma's Habitual Criminal Sterilization Act, saying that prisoners have a constitutional right to retain their procreative abilities for use after incarceration. Bright says that ruling, by stressing the "fundamental" nature of the procreative right, "lends support" to the notion that prisoners retain "some form" of such right in prison.

Although the San Francisco–based Ninth Circuit Court is a factory for manufacturing novel rights, Bright inexplicably accepts that prisoners have no constitutional right—given his jurisprudence, why ever not?—to conjugal visits. Neither is there, he says, a constitutional right for women inmates to be impregnated. "We cannot," he says, "ignore the biological differences between men and women."

However, prison authorities understandably worry that women prisoners will now claim that the Constitution's guarantee of equal protection of the law will confer upon them the right to be inseminated, which will create substantial burdens for prison administration. And when that claim is made, as surely it will be, Bright surely will say that niggling administrative matters cannot interfere with the enjoyment of "fundamental rights." He already says "it is simply impermissible to restrict the constitutional rights of one group because of fear that another group will assert its constitutionally protected rights as well."

Dissenting, Judge Barry Silverman, who has a dry sense of humor—and needs it, given the *Through the Looking Glass* logic of many of his Ninth Circuit Court colleagues—wrote, "This is a seminal case in more ways than one" because "the majority simply does not accept the fact that there are certain downsides"—a delicious choice of words—"to being confined in prison." One of them is "the interference with a normal family life."

Yes, he says, the Constitution's proscription of "cruel and unusual punishments" protects prisoners from measures such as forced sterilization. However, that hardly establishes "a constitutional right to procreate from prison via FedEx."

Silverman does not subscribe to the jest that inmates retain only two rights in prison: the right to serve their time and the right not to be exposed to secondhand smoke. However, Silverman quotes Wisconsin's Supreme Court: "Incarceration, by its very nature, deprives a convicted individual of the fundamental right to be free from physical restraint, which in turn encompasses and restricts other fundamental rights, such as the right to procreate."

Before Gerber gets his heart set on fatherhood, he should consider this: in the five terms from 1996 through 2000, the U.S. Supreme Court reviewed ninety rulings of the Ninth Circuit Court and reversed seventy-seven of them.

Now, will a post–September 11 sobriety restrain the Ninth Circuit Court's silliness? Don't be silly.

November 8, 2001

Stem Cells and Human Flourishing

Americans know this is not the decision that the science community needs to go forward full force.

—Representative Richard Gephardt

President George W. Bush's stem cell decision, both the substance of it and the manner of his making it, has changed American politics profoundly. It is now clearer than ever that America's two parties represent a cultural cleavage much deeper and more dramatic than the traditional, indeed banal, party divisions about taxes and spending and the like. The parties represent different sensibilities—different stances toward nature, including human nature. Let it

never again be said that contemporary politics is uninteresting. It is indicative
that Bush, who has been parsimonious of presidential rhetoric, used his first
nationally televised address—his first postinaugural claim on the nation's attention—to discuss (in the words of Leon Kass) "the human future."

Bush's decision has been characterized, even by his aides, as a "compromise." However, Kass, the scientist and philosopher who is Bush's choice to
head a commission on biomedical ethics, suggests that "solution" is a more apposite description. Bush did not try to split the unsplittable difference about
the use, including the production, of embryos—unquestionably living entities, unquestionably of the human species—as resources for research. Rather,
Bush said cells will be used only "where the life-and-death decision has
already been made." This has been widely mischaracterized as a "middle
course." Midway between what and what? Actually, it is strict fidelity to his
campaign promise that there would be no federal funding for research "that
involves destroying living human embryos."

Bush's decision is that such destruction is wrong but that it is acceptable to
seek benefits from the sixty or so "lines" of stem cells that have resulted from
such wrongs. Is this coherent? It is if you hold, reasonably, that one can materially participate in a wrong by accepting a benefit from it if, but only if, three
conditions obtain: one must not cooperate with the wrong, one must not enable the wrong, and one must not provide inducements for the wrong.

Bush's position is so measured and principled that his critics are in danger
of embracing extremism. All extremists share an attribute: They elevate a single value over all others. Indeed, the defining attribute of fanaticism is an insistence on acting as though one consideration—liberty, equality, fraternity,
whatever—trumps all others. See the statement by Richard Gephardt, above.

Extremists are, in the phrase of the nineteenth-century historian Jacob
Burckhardt, "terrible simplifiers." Gephardt's statement suggests that questions
surrounding embryonic stem cell research, and implicitly all questions of
biomedical ethics, are actually quite simple. Gephardt's statement, which may
be becoming part of the Democratic Party's catechism, expresses the "science
über alles" school of thought. And "science" really is shorthand for anything that
conduces to the material well-being of those wielding the power of choice.
This categorical imperative to go "full force," sometimes called the "technological imperative," is often confused with compassion.

Kass's voice is different:

*Because we belong to the nature we study and seek to control, our power over
nature eventually means power also over ourselves. We are not only agents
but also and increasingly patients of our scientific project for the mastery of nature. Our self-conception, if not also our very being, lies upon the table science—biology, medicine, psychology—has prepared. How shall we treat this*

patient? What standards of health and human flourishing shall guide our self-manipulations?

In making his decision about embryonic stem cell research, Bush, who throughout his public life has been the object of unrelenting condescension from his critics, sought counsel from an array of remarkably learned thinkers, and crafted a solution so rigorous and sophisticated that the condescenders still do not fathom it. And he has leavened the nation's thinking by asking Kass to organize what are certain to be increasingly complex and momentous debates about biomedical ethics.

At the dawn of the atomic age, Albert Einstein said that the world had more to fear from bad politics than from bad physics. At this dawning of a new age of biomedical possibilities, both enticing and ominous, good politics has prevailed. That is, the nation's foremost political person has begun the task of defining humane circumscriptions of biological sciences that can be badly used.

By opting for prudence—for respect, awe, and gratitude for life's mysteriousness—against the "full force" scientific project, Bush has understood this Kass axiom: "We stand most upright when we gladly bow our heads."

August 14, 2001

Peter Singer Comes to Princeton

PRINCETON, NEW JERSEY—The university's motto, "Dei Sub Numine Viget," does not say, as some Princetonians insist, God went to Princeton. It says, "Under God's Power She Flourishes." As the academic year commences, Peter Singer comes to campus to teach that truly ethical behavior will not flourish until humanity abandons the fallacy, as he sees it, of the sanctity of life.

He comes trailing clouds of controversy because he argues, without recourse to euphemism or other semantic sleights of hand, the moral justification of some homicides, including infanticide and euthanasia. He rejects the particular moral order that supposes that human beings are extraordinarily precious because God made them so. He also rejects secular philosophies that depict human beings as possessing a unique and exalted dignity that sharply distinguishes them from, and justifies their tyranny over, other species of animals.

The appointment of the fifty-three-year-old Australian philosopher to a tenured professorship of bioethics was unanimously recommended by a Princeton search committee and approved by President Harold Shapiro, who chairs the National Bioethics Advisory Commission.

Princeton's position is that Singer's copious publications are serious scholarship; that he has helped to shape worldwide debates concerning animal rights and the ethical dilemmas posed by new medical technologies that blur the boundaries between life and death; that universities do not endorse views by permitting the teaching of them; that Singer's views can be rationally defended; that intellectual diversity is a good thing; and that (in Shapiro's words) Singer is challenging long-established ways of thinking.

Critics of the appointment argue that 150 years ago slavery was defended no less rationally, given certain premises, than Singer defends his views, and the slavery proponents had premises not more repellent than Singer's. Critics note that a university's passion for intellectual diversity is today much more apt to encompass advocacy of infanticide than of protection for the unborn. They argue that a great university exists not only to provoke students to think about difficult matters, which Singer certainly will do, but also to transmit, down the generations, sustaining precepts of our civilization, some of which Singer wishes to extirpate. And they argue that the derivative prestige that Singer's views will gain from his Princeton connection will weaken respect for life and for the rights of the severely handicapped.

The critics are mostly correct. However, their worries about Singer's potential influence on students and public policy are excessive. He will be, on balance, a useful stimulant at Princeton. And he will be particularly useful to his most adamant critics. He appalls the right-to-life movement, but actually he is the abortion-rights movement's worst nightmare. The logic of moral reasoning often is that he who says A must say B. Singer and other prochoice people say A. But he then says: A entails B, and B includes infanticide.

Singer subscribes to utilitarianism, which holds that there is a single goal for human conduct: satisfaction of preferences and avoidance of suffering. Hence the foundation of morals is the obligation to maximize the satisfaction of preferences and minimize the thwarting of them. Like Jeremy Bentham (1748–1832), the founding father of utilitarianism, Singer believes that push-pin is as good as poetry—that one pleasure is as good as another. And Singer, the principal progenitor of the animal-rights movement, says the pleasures and sufferings of other species are not necessarily of a moral significance inferior to those of humans. To say otherwise, he says, is specieism.

Regarding humans, he says that assigning intrinsic moral significance to birth is arbitrary and logically indefensible. Birth is morally insignificant because a newborn, like a fetus, is incapable of regarding itself as a distinct entity with a life of its own to lead. Because there are, he says, degrees of personhood, the intrinsic moral significance of the taking of the life of an individual

gradually increases, like the physical being of the individual, from near noth-
ingness in infancy.

With muscular candor, Singer faces biological facts: he does not deny that
killing a fetus or a baby involves killing a human being. He has contempt for
mincing, flinching language. (In an example of that, Kate Michelman, the
abortion-rights advocate, has spoken of an aborted fetus undergoing "demise.") Singer says infanticide is not necessarily more morally important than
abortion, which is morally negligible. In fact, some infanticide is not even as
important as, say, killing a happy cat. (A cat can be self-conscious and thus has
a degree of personhood. Hence his use of the political category "tyranny" to
describe *Homo sapiens'* treatment of animals.) Killing an infant is never killing
a person and is morally permissible in at least two kinds of situations.

One is when a handicapped baby faces a life in which suffering will pre-
dominate. Singer has cited Down syndrome and spina bifida babies. However,
he, like most people, is not well informed about Down syndrome citizens,
some of whom are taxpayers who read the sports pages on the way to work.
And spina bifida can involve a wide range of affliction. Singer's response to
these facts is that sparing a Down or spina bifida baby's life should be based on
a utilitarian calculation with reference to the baby's projected quality of life
and the impact of the baby's life on others, all of which will depend on the
severity of the disability.

Another situation when infanticide is justified is when parents with a
handicapped baby—Singer's example is a hemophiliac—will, if relieved of the
burden of the baby, have another baby that will be happier than the handicapped baby would be and will bring the parents more happiness. By one form
of utilitarian calculation, concerning which Singer is agnostic, the arithmetic
is easy: the total amount of happiness would be increased.

Actually, the logic of his position is that until a baby is capable of self-aware-
ness, there is no controlling reason not to kill it to serve any preference of the
parents. Indeed, he has proposed (but is rethinking) a one-month postnatal period for legal discretionary infanticide. During the Senate debate on partial-birth
abortion—in which procedure all of a baby except the top of the skull is delivered from the birth canal, then the skull is collapsed—two prochoice senators
were asked: Suppose the baby slips all the way out before the doctor can kill it.
Then does it have a right to life? Both senators said no, it was still the mother's
choice. Told of what the senators said, Singer says briskly: They're right.

Singer's vocation is the important one of thinking about various choices
forced upon us by modern medicine. What care is owed to anencephalic babies (born, essentially, without brains but with some brain-stem functions) or
to persons in a persistent vegetative state? What is the moral importance of the
distinction between allowing nature to take its course with the terminally ill
and intervening to accelerate the course of nature?

But proximity, even familial attachment—these are moral irrelevancies in Singer's analysis of one's obligations to others. Should one spend a sum to ease the suffering of a family member or send the same sum to ease the sufferings of ten Sudanese? Singer is consistent: In the Sudan the money will better serve the world's total amount of happiness. To his credit, he does not practice what he preaches. He told a *New Yorker* magazine interviewer that money he spends on nursing care for his mother, who has Alzheimer's disease, at least does provide employment for a number of people who find something worthwhile in what they're doing.

Thus were debutante parties rationalized during the Depression. *The New Yorker's* interviewer calls Singer's rationalization a noble sentiment. However, utilitarianism has no place for nobility, which presupposes the upward pull of a thoughtfulness that is higher than the low, common calculations of pain and pleasure or of satisfying preferences and avoiding suffering.

Singer may fancy himself the advance guard of the future, but the trend of intellectual life is away from him. Medicine's multiplying capacities for therapeutic intervention *in utero* is changing how people think about the moral claims of fetal life. And there is a growing recoil from philosophies that misdescribe human beings as utterly autonomous individuals, unencumbered selves living in splendid self-sufficiency. There is heightened receptivity to philosophies that recognize that dependency on others is a universal and permanent fact of every life, throughout life. Dependency varies in kind and degree as people pass from birth to death but can never of itself be a reason for denying personhood.

Singer's defenders say that some of his most arresting statements have been stripped of nuance by being taken out of context. There is some truth to that. However, while utilitarianism has interesting permutations, nuance is never its strong suit. Which is why Singer probably will not be a powerful shaper of Princeton students or public discourse.

Powerful teachers are unfinished products, combining certainties with a capacity for uncertainty and revision. Singer enjoys the intricacy of applying his utilitarian calculus to thorny practical problems. But on matters more fundamental than applications of his calculus, his thinking is as fixed and lifeless as a fly in amber. Although he says startling things en route to shocking conclusions, his work lacks the real drama of the life of the mind. He seems to be a strangely unreflective—almost unphilosophic—philosopher. He does not really worry about the deep questions of meaning and value that are behind the questions of life and death. For utilitarians, there can be no truly deep questions, because human beings are no deeper than Bentham's depiction of them as under the sovereignty of pain and pleasure.

Given utilitarianism's unnaturally tidy conclusions about the human condition, utilitarian thinking serves a simple, even simpleminded, imperative:

adding pleasures and subtracting pains in this or that situation. The result often resembles mere logic chopping, without the risks of more wide-ranging reasoning about the deeper ambiguities surrounding life's possibilities. When moral reasoning is reduced to arithmetic—quantification involving categories as crude as pain and pleasure—moral reasoning is no more complex or interesting than the grinding of an adding machine.

A thoroughgoing utilitarian has the unlovely security and unenviable serenity of an inmate in what G. K. Chesterton called the clean, well-lit prison of one idea. Singer's utilitarianism is so dry and desiccated that it drains the drama from philosophy. Gone is the juice of life that human beings seek in poetry or religion or the poetry of religion. Students may, at first, experience a flush of fascination with Singer's rigor in applying his rules to recalcitrant reality.

Still, Singer, three of whose grandparents died in the Holocaust, brings to his vocation the earnestness of one who knows that ideas have consequences. He is engaging and accessible, and, unlike most contemporary philosophers, he is determined to bring philosophy to bear on urgent practical questions. He will do more to stimulate serious reflection—and more to stimulate opposition to his (literally) homicidal ideas—than he will to make his ideas acceptable.

Which is to say, Princeton can justify his appointment by utilitarian arithmetic. Such arithmetic has its uses, but not Singer's uses.

September 13, 1999

The Right to a Dead Baby

"**M**r. Vice President, do you favor passage of the Born-Alive Infants Protection Act, or do you believe, as your supporters at the National Abortion and Reproductive Rights Action League (NARAL) do, that a woman who seeks an abortion has an indefeasible right to a dead baby, no matter what?" Here is the story behind that question, which George W. Bush should ask Al Gore next week during the first debate.

The act, authored by Representative Charles Canady, Republican of Florida, would extend the law's protections—would protect the right to life—to infants who survive abortions. Such babies sometimes are born as a result of abortions sought because the babies have (or sometimes are mistakenly thought to have) defects such as Down syndrome or spina bifida. The House committee that passed Canady's bill 22–1 heard heartrending testimony about born-alive babies being discarded alive into soiled hospital linen or left on a baby scale, unattended, without warmth or nourishment, their hearts beating and limbs moving, until they died.

Canady's bill responds to the recent radical extension of the prochoice agenda. The federal court that overturned New Jersey's ban on partial-birth abortion cavalierly declared it "nonsensical" and "irrational" to believe that an infant's physical location relative to the mother has any relevance as to whether she may choose to have it killed. This pushes abortion rights beyond *Roe v. Wade's* framework. *Roe's* distinction—now a crumbling wall against infanticide—held that a child's legal status depended on whether the child was "unborn" or "born"—that is, the status depended on the child's location in relation to the body of the mother. Now the federal judiciary is close to saying that a child marked for abortion can be killed even if it is born alive. Canady notes that under this new radicalism, "a real child, with an objective existence, is treated as merely a conceptual construct, and in that way, swept aside as though he or she had no existence at all that anyone was obliged to recognize." The bill would acknowledge that, *at the very least,* when a baby is fully born it has an *intrinsic* dignity and a claim to the protection of law, irrespective of whether it is wanted.

The bill is a mild measure against the abortion-rights lobby's increasingly infanticidal agenda. Yet NARAL shrilly says the bill is an "anti-choice assault" that would interfere with "the medical decision making process." However, NARAL's opposition is understandable, given its mission. If a baby alive moments after an attempted abortion has a right to life, why exactly did it utterly lack such a right moments before? A week before that? A month?

But by its opposition NARAL is endorsing a central tenet of the right-to-life argument. The tenet is that it is arbitrary, and morally and philosophically problematic, to say that a baby has no intrinsic dignity and that its claim to respect for its life is contingent on its physical location or on whether it suits the convenience of anyone else. That tenet should, but does not, trouble the Supreme Court majority.

In June, when the Court declared unconstitutional Nebraska's ban on partial-birth abortion, Justice Stephen Breyer, writing for the majority, said that such abortions, although gruesome, might be safer for the woman than the common procedure of using instruments to dismember the child in the womb: "The use of instruments within the uterus creates a danger of accidental perforation and damage to neighboring organs. Sharp fetal bone fragments create similar dangers. And fetal tissue accidentally left behind can cause infection and various other complications."

But if avoidance of those dangers justifies killing an almost entirely delivered baby, why not be even safer and just deliver the baby and then kill it or let it die? After all, even partial-birth abortion requires insertion of some instruments into the woman.

Now that one of the nation's finest universities (Princeton) has given a prestigious position to an advocate of infanticide (Peter Singer suggests that for perhaps a month after birth parents should be entitled to dispose of unwanted children), it is not surprising that the Senate has what deserves to be called an Infanticide Caucus. The caucus has at least three members.

Two of them, Russ Feingold, Democrat of Wisconsin, and Frank Lautenberg, Democrat of New Jersey, identified themselves when, during the September 26, 1996, debate on partial-birth abortion, Rick Santorum, Republican of Pennsylvania, asked: Suppose during such an abortion [during which a baby is delivered feet first until all but a portion of the skull is outside the mother, then its skull is punctured, its contents vacuumed, then collapsed] the baby slips all the way out of the birth canal. Should killing the baby *even then* be a permissible choice? Neither senator would say "no."

During the October 20, 1999, debate Barbara Boxer, Democrat of California, joined the caucus:

SANTORUM: "You agree, once a child is born, separated from the mother, that that child is protected by the Constitution and cannot be killed. Do you agree with that?"

BOXER: "I think when you bring your baby home . . ."

She said more. What she would not say was "yes."

A Germantown, Maryland, teenager, who has been convicted of attempted first-degree murder, will soon be sentenced for trying to kill her newborn child. After giving birth in a bathtub, she abandoned the baby in an unheated trash room on a January morning. Considering that partial-birth abortion is a fundamental constitutional right and prochoice people such as NARAL oppose Canady's bill, the teenager will be forgiven for wondering what exactly she did that was so wrong.

Some prochoice people cast their opposition to Canady's bill almost as a matter of protecting consumer rights: A woman purchasing an abortion is entitled to a dead baby. Does Al Gore agree? If not, why not?

October 2, 2000

Infanticide: Ho-Hum

Ho-hum. It is becoming the sort of story that no longer rates much notice as news. *The New York Times* accorded it seven paragraphs at the bottom of an inside page, beneath this headline:

Girl, 15, Accused of Letting Her Daughter Drown at Birth

This is another case of a newborn baby consigned to the garbage, like the one whose brief life began and ended in a Delaware motel room last November, when the baby's parents, both college students, were away from their campuses. The *Times* story concerns another baby that was born and died in a bathroom, like the one in New Jersey whose birth and brief life recently interrupted, but only for a matter of minutes, the mother's prom.

This most recent (that we know of) instance of infanticide occurred in Queens. *The Times* reports that "Ms. Martinez told investigators she gave birth while sitting on the toilet. Ms. Martinez told them that she let the baby fall into the water, where her daughter cried for several seconds while her arms and legs flailed."

Judith Martinez has been arraigned on murder charges, as have the New Jersey prom mother and both parents in the Delaware case. These should make for interesting trials, given that: if, as soon as the baby's skull appeared, Martinez had opened a hole in the skull and extracted the brains, the most she could be charged with is practicing medicine (specifically, a partial-birth abortion) without a license.

New York, New Jersey, and Delaware must distinguish the salient differences between the kind of infanticide their state laws proscribe and the kind President Clinton protects with his vetoes of the ban on partial-birth abortions. Meanwhile, California's Supreme Court has given the nation fresh food for thought about legal and moral issues pertaining to very young life.

That court has held that Mikayla Snyder, who is three years old, can sue her mother, Naomi's, former employer for injuries (including permanent damage to Mikayla's brain and nervous system) that she, Mikayla, received four years ago. That is, she can sue for damages for injuries received in utero, when her mother, as a result of the employer's negligence, breathed carbon monoxide in amounts toxic to both mother and daughter.

Or toxic to mother and fetus. Or toxic to (in language preferred by some proabortion advocates) mother and "fetal material."

By its ruling, the court unanimously abandoned a prior doctrine that only the mother could seek compensation for workplace injuries because a fetus is "inseparable" from its mother. The court's new ruling turns on a physiological fact:

> *Biologically, fetal and maternal injury have no necessary relationship. The processes of fetal growth and development are radically different from the normal physiological processes of a mature human. Whether a toxin or other agent will cause congenital effects in the developing embryo or fetus depends heavily not on whether the mother is herself injured, but on the exact stage of the embryo or fetus's development at the time of exposure, as well as on the degree to which maternal exposure results in embryonic or fetal exposure.*

However, physiological facts can contribute to philosophical conclusions. Since 1872 California law has held that "a child conceived, but not yet born, is deemed an existing person, so far as necessary for the child's interests in the event of subsequent birth." Now California's court has said this: Although it is "tautologically true" that a fetus is "inseparable" from its mother, the fetus is legally distinguishable. It seems to have, in the logic of the law, attributes of a *person*.

Verily, it has the attributes of an American person, because it can have a lawyer, retroactively. The appellate attorney for Naomi and Mikayla Snyder, Paige Leslie Wickland, told the *Los Angeles Times* that the court's change of law might be explained by the fact that now three of the court's seven justices are women: "This may be an example of women having a different perspective on issues that concern children and the family."

If it is true that women are especially disposed to think about the fetus as a distinguishable and injurable person, that is full of potential for a rethinking of abortion policy. However, serious conclusions about the moral significance of physiological facts cannot be mere sentiments contingent upon gender. Rather, such conclusions must be grounded in philosophy informed by science. Today science and philosophy are tugging law away from the comforting premise of the abortion culture: that a fetus is nothing.

November 9, 1997

A Sacrament in the Church of "Choice"

It probably was inevitable that partial-birth abortion would become, as it did some while ago, a sacrament in the Church of "Choice." That sect's theology cannot risk conceding that what is killed in an abortion *ever* possesses more moral significance than a tumor. Hence it cannot concede that society's sensibilities should be lacerated by, or that its respect for life might be damaged by, *any* method of abortion.

But how did this surgical procedure become, as it did Wednesday, not just a constitutional right but a "fundamental" constitutional right—a right deemed integral to the enjoyment of liberty?

Nebraska's ban on partial-birth abortion, passed just one vote short of unanimity by the Legislature, and akin to bans enacted by twenty-nine other states, has not survived the Supreme Court's scrutiny. But scant scrutiny was required, given the logic the Court locked itself into twenty-seven years ago, when, in *Roe v. Wade,* the Court, with breathtaking disregard of elemental embryology, described a fetus as "potential life."

Nowadays proabortion forces, speaking with the mincing language of people who lack the courage of their squeamishness, speak of abortion producing "fetal demise." Remarkable, that—the demise of something only potentially alive. But not long ago proabortion forces denied that what they call "fetal material" and Nebraska calls "a living unborn child" can feel pain. In fact, partial birth abortion, which is generally used in the third trimester of gestation, is inflicted on beings that have reflexes and brain activity, and other attributes of newborn infants.

Not long ago proabortion forces argued that abortion involves no cruelty or gruesomeness from which society should flinch. Now they defend partial-birth abortion in order to defend all late-term abortions, all of which involve the violent dismemberment of "fetal material" that looks exactly like a baby.

Nebraska defined the prohibited practice as "delivering into the vagina a living unborn child" for the purpose of killing it. In this procedure (which the Court majority, in its delicacy, flinches from fully describing) the baby is turned, pulled by its kicking legs almost entirely from the mother. Then, with only the top of the skull still in the birth canal, the skull is punctured and its contents sucked out.

Divided 5–4, the Court held that Nebraska's law, as phrased, might criminalize another, more common procedure used primarily in second-trimester abortions. But Nebraska's attorney general has expressly vowed not to apply the law to this more common procedure.

The Court also faulted Nebraska's law for lacking an "exception for the preservation of the . . . health of the mother." But the American College of Obstetricians and Gynecologists, which opposes restrictions on abortion, says it can identify "no circumstances under which" partial-birth abortion "would be the only option to save the life or preserve the health of the woman." And the American Medical Association says "there does not appear to be any identified situation in which" partial-birth abortion "is the only appropriate procedure to induce abortion."

The primary reason the Court ruled against Nebraska is that it cannot find traction on the slippery slope onto which it so improvidently stepped twenty-seven years ago. America's subsequent slide into the culture of death was manifest September 26, 1996, during a Senate debate on partial-birth abortion.

Pennsylvania Republican Rick Santorum asked Democrats Russ Feingold of Wisconsin and Frank Lautenberg of New Jersey this: Suppose during an attempted partial-birth abortion the infant, instead of being just almost delivered, with only a few inches of skull remaining in the birth canal, slips entirely out of the canal. Is killing the born baby still a "choice"? Feingold and Lautenberg said it was still a matter between a mother and her abortionist. (C-SPAN captured this exchange. *The Congressional Record* was subsequently falsified.)

Feingold and Lautenberg anticipated the court. In *Roe v. Wade,* which arose in Texas, the court left standing a Texas law prohibiting "the killing of an unborn child during parturition," meaning the killing of an infant "in the state of being born and before actual birth." On Wednesday, such killing— what Justice Antonin Scalia, dissenting, accurately calls "live-birth abortion"— became a fundamental constitutional right.

Wednesday's decision will, as Justice Scalia said in dissent, rank with the cases of *Dred Scott* (1857, saying blacks could not be citizens and so could not seek judicial protection of their rights) and *Korematsu* (1944, upholding the internment of American citizens of Japanese ancestry) as acts of judicial infamy.

Al Gore, approving Wednesday's decision, and George W. Bush, deploring it, affirm strikingly different understandings of constitutional reasoning and elemental morality. With the Court and the culture in the balance, let no one say this is an unimportant election.

June 29, 2000

Fetuses and Carolinians

Suppose the number of months required for the full-term gestation of a human infant were a prime number—say, eleven. What would the nation's abortion policy be? For a quarter of a century now abortion policy has been made not by elected representatives but by the Supreme Court, so the question is: What would be the constitutional significance of that prime number? The question—How did we come to tickle constitutional law from the fact that nine is divisible by three?—reveals how peculiar and awkward the reasoning about abortion has become in the twenty-five years since *Roe v. Wade.*

Consider what the Supreme Court did—actually, declined to do—last week. It declined to review—that is, it let stand—a 3–2 decision by the Supreme Court of South Carolina declaring that under the state's law concerning child abuse and endangerment, the word "child" includes a viable fetus. Or as the state's attorney general, Charles Condon, says, "A viable fetus is a fellow South Carolinian."

Now, South Carolinians, a notoriously turbulent tribe, have a history— John C. Calhoun, nullification, and secession come to mind—of disturbing the nation's peace with strongly felt but dubiously reasoned constitutional doctrines. However, in this case they are doing the nation a service by forcing it to face the peculiar logic of the abortion policy that has been created by judicial fiats.

In *Roe v. Wade* the Court based constitutional law on biological nonsense, asserting that a fetus is "potential life." Every high school biology student knows that something living results when the DNA of the sperm fuses with that of the ovum to form a new and unique complex that controls the growth of the living thing through pregnancy and beyond, unless that life is ended by natural misfortune or deliberate attack. The argument about abortion concerns the moral significance and proper legal status of that living thing during pregnancy, not whether it is something alive.

When the Court waded waist deep into the abortion issue, it tried to impose tidiness by making much of the fact that the number nine is divisible by three. The Court announced in *Roe* that although the fetus is always only "potential" life, the status of the fetus would, as a matter of constitutional law, change with the trimesters of pregnancy. Although the trimesters are medically and morally meaningless, the court decreed that "meaningful" life begins in the third trimester, when the fetus attains "viability," meaning the ability to live outside the womb, and not just in South Carolina.

The Court held that even in the third trimester, fetuses are not "persons in the whole sense" and do not possess constitutional rights. However, dogs and cats are not persons and do not possess such rights; nevertheless, they can be protected by law from malicious injury or killing. Which is what Attorney General Condon has been trying to do by prosecuting pregnant cocaine addicts—twenty-three, so far—for child neglect and even manslaughter. Five other states' supreme courts have differed with Condon and South Carolina's court concerning whether a viable fetus can be cloaked with the protections government gives to a child.

South Carolina's practice should be considered in the context of today's prenatal medicine. Young couples, part of a solidly "prochoice" demographic cohort, often have framed pictures of sonograms revealing the fingers and heart chambers of their eighteen-week-old (second-trimester) fetuses. These couples have seen pictures of their fetuses responding to outside stimuli. An expanding arsenal of diagnostic and therapeutic techniques makes possible the intrauterine treatment of many forms of fetal distress and genetic problems. Drugs and blood transfusions can be administered, and excess fluids can be drained from fetal skulls and lungs. So this "potential life" can be a doctor's patient. Mothers have a constitutional right to end this life, but doctors are enjoined to do it no harm when it is a patient.

The political turmoil surrounding the abortion issue will not abate until the intellectual chaos is diminished. Therefore it is, perhaps, a pity that the U.S. Supreme Court decided not to review the South Carolina court's opinion. That would have been a way to revisit fundamental questions about abortion in the light cast by scientific changes and related changes in society's moral sensibility.

Jean Bethke Elshtain, professor of social and political ethics at the University of Chicago, rightly says that although the prochoice movement likes to present itself as an embattled insurgency, it actually is the establishment. Its position is given constitutional sanction and public subsidies. What Elshtain does not say, but what needs to be said, is that like many other establishments, the prochoice movement has grown intellectually lazy and arrogant.

South Carolina's policy regarding pregnant drug addicts is problematic, for several reasons. Some on the prolife side worry that it will encourage drug abusers to have abortions to avoid prosecution. Abortion-rights advocates reasonably wonder why South Carolina prosecutes only cocaine abusers, when alcohol creates far more infant casualties. Condon's answer—"I would be on a legal slippery slope if I tried to prosecute women who used legal substances"—is inadequate. Child abuse can be inflicted by any number of things the possession of which is legal.

Political life—the life of a community living by rules—is always lived on a slippery slope. Taxation could become confiscation; education could become indoctrination; police protection could become oppression. And for a quarter of a century abortion policy has been a particularly difficult struggle for traction on an alarmingly slippery slope, down which we have slid much too far. South Carolina has at least tried to slow the descent by asserting a public interest in protecting lives—not "potential" lives—from irreparable damage resulting from reckless and illegal behavior of persons who have been told by reckless legal reasoning that a fetus is never really owed the care due to other South Carolinians.

June 8, 1998

Protecting Viewers from Something "A Little Too Vivid"

The Republican establishment, which has the prominence and utility of a figurehead, had a bad day Tuesday when voters spurned its anointed candidate in a California congressional race. Perhaps—this is just a guess—it was unwise to anoint a man particularly distinguishable from his Republican rival by his tolerance of a form of infanticide. This contest became a skirmish in the abortion wars, wherein the celebration of tolerance is the first refuge of the intolerant.

When Representative Walter Capps of Santa Barbara, a Democrat, died, his widow entered the special election for his seat. So did two Republican state assemblymen, Tom Bordonaro, a conservative rancher of modest means, and Brooks Firestone, a liberal and wealthy winegrower. Predictably, but probably to the surprise of House Speaker Newt Gingrich and other prominent Republicans who endorsed Firestone, a crucial distinction between Bordonaro and Firestone was the former's support for, and the latter's opposition to, banning partial-birth abortion.

In Tuesday's election, Lois Capps finished first, as expected, but with less than 50 percent of the vote, so she will face a runoff with the second-place finisher, who is Bordonaro, even though Firestone outspent him at least 3-to-1. And even though the local affiliates of ABC, NBC, and CBS banned certain independent ads on Bordonaro's behalf.

The ads concerned partial-birth abortion. They featured no shocking pictures of dead fetuses, pictures that depict the reality behind the vacuity of the word "choice." They featured words—truthful descriptions of a medical procedure at the center of a national debate. The manager of the ABC affiliate called the ads' language "pretty strident" and "stronger than we were comfortable with." Well.

One ad pictured a newborn and said, "This baby was born just a few weeks early. Even at that age a partial-birth abortion can still be performed. This procedure starts with the entire body being delivered except for the head. An incision is then made into the skull and the brain removed."

The other ad pictured a group of conversing women, one of whom said, "First the baby's legs are pulled into the birth canal and the entire body is delivered except for the head. Then an incision is made in the skull and the brains are removed. After the head shrinks, the entire body is removed."

But *ABC World News Tonight* described the procedure this way: "A living fetus is partially withdrawn from the womb, then the skull is vacuumed out."

NBC Nightly News reported, "The fetus is pulled partially out of the birth canal, feet first. Then the skull is punctured and the brains suctioned out."

The manager of NBC's affiliate said the banned ad was "a little too vivid, a little too graphic" and "pretty tough. I can see it scaring little children to death." See? The censorship was to protect little children, not to protect partial-birth abortions of little children.

The affiliates ran censored ads that included the words "we won't describe this gruesome procedure." No independent ads by prochoice Republicans praising Firestone were banned or censored.

Many people who call themselves "prochoice" demand tolerance of the right to choose to kill almost-born babies but are intolerant of the right to choose one's public school, to smoke, to own a gun, to rent your basement apartment to whom you chose, to drive a sport utility vehicle—or to broadcast a truthful description of one way of killing almost-born babies. Republican opponents of Republican supporters of partial-birth abortion are called intolerant.

They are, in this sense: They do not think infanticide is a mere "matter of opinion" the way, say, tax reform or NATO expansion is. Hence their attempt to deny national party assistance to supporters of partial-birth abortion.

Critics say those who would ban party assistance should be more like the first Republican president, who detested slavery but made the goal of ending it subordinate to the goal of preserving the Union. However, the slavery controversy had two extremes: those who demanded immediate abolition and those who demanded the right to expand slavery into the territories. Abraham Lincoln—tolerant, up to a point—opposed abolitionists but countenanced civil war to stop expansionists.

Suppose the newly founded Republican Party had, in the name of tolerance, eschewed what today are disparaged as "litmus tests" and said that even slavery expansionists could expect party support. What would have been the point of founding such a party?

Given that the American Medical Association says there is "no identified situation" in which partial-birth abortion is necessary, it is reasonable to suspect that Republicans who support it do so partly because they consider the right-to-life movement generally déclassé. Reciprocated disdain is tolerable.

January 18, 1998

Solemnity at Texas High School Football Games

And you thought the Supreme Court could not further split repeatedly split hairs concerning what activities with a religious flavor, however optional or faint, in or around public schools violate the Constitution's ban on "establishment" of religion. Think again.

The Court conducts its business after a chant that concludes "God save the United States and this Honorable Court," and the Court sits across the street from Congress, both houses of which have taxpayer-paid chaplains who pray for divine guidance and blessings. But on Monday the Court ruled, 6–3, that the Constitution was violated by a suburban Houston school district's proposed policy of allowing students to elect a speaker to make remarks to "solemnize" football games, remarks that could, but need not, include a prayer.

Now, it is weird that anyone thinks Texas high school football needs a solemnity infusion. Nevertheless, the school district thought its policy would pass constitutional muster because it would involve private, not government-sponsored or -approved, student speech.

But not only was the policy not constitutionally bullet proof, it so swiftly drew legal challenges that it was never implemented. And on Monday the challengers won.

Justice John Paul Stevens, writing for the majority, which included Justices Sandra Day O'Connor, Anthony Kennedy, David Souter, Ruth Bader Ginsburg, and Stephen Breyer, said that such speech by students is not really private. The government "affirmatively sponsors" it. How can it be private speech, Stevens asked, when it is carried over a school's public address system? And it might make some people feel bad: "School sponsorship of a religious message is impermissible because it sends the ancillary message to members of the audience who are nonadherents that they are outsiders, not full members of the political community, and an accompanying message to adherents that they are insiders, favored members of the political community."

Hard feelings certainly can result when religious observances are not confined to gatherings of the like-minded. The first challenge to the school district's policy about football game prayers came in 1995, not from secularists but from a Catholic family and a Mormon family who were offended by what they considered abrasively sectarian and proselytizing prayers. It was then that the school district devised the policy to insulate itself from pregame student messages by having students vote first on whether to have a student speaker and then on who the speaker should be.

The majority opinion drew a robust dissent from Chief Justice William Rehnquist, who was joined by Justices Antonin Scalia and Clarence Thomas. Rehnquist charged the majority with "venturing into the realm of prophesy" because it was anticipating what the results of the school district's policy would be if it were implemented.

Conceivably, said Rehnquist, the procedure might have produced a majority of speakers who spoke, say, of sportsmanship, without religious references. Or it might have produced Christian prayer before 90 percent of football games. In that case the school might have reevaluated the policy. Certainly there would have been a record on which the Court could base a judgment about the policy's compatibility with the Establishment Clause of the Constitution. Instead, the majority rushed to judgment, saying that "regardless" of the student's use of their discretion under the policy, "the simple enactment of this policy" constituted an unconstitutional "school endorsement of student prayer."

This case lengthens the Court's meandering record of on-again, off-again, and occasionally partial, adherence to a three-pronged test to decide when public policy that touches religion, however tangentially, constitutes "establishment" of religion: the policy is constitutional if but only if it has a secular purpose, its primary effect neither advances nor inhibits religion, and it does not foster excessive government entanglement with religion.

The three-pronged test disregards the intention of the framers of the Establishment Clause, which was to ensure government neutrality between religious factions, not between religion and irreligion. And the test has produced some peculiar, even hilarious, rulings, such as the one in 1983, when the Court, allowing political prudence to trump the logic of its illogical precedents, said that Nebraska's Legislature could continue beginning each session with a prayer by a paid chaplain. Pity the poor chaplain, who suffered the indignity of a Court declaration that he did not have the primary effect of advancing religion.

Among the first acts of the First Congress, which wrote the First Amendment with its Establishment Clause, were the hiring of a chaplain and the urging of President Washington to proclaim a day of "public thanksgiving and prayer, to be observed by acknowledging with grateful hearts the many and signal favors of Almighty God." But then Washington at least did not proclaim it over a public address system.

June 21, 2000

Coping with the
—Well, Some of the—
Ten Commandments

The constitutional crisis began sixty-six years ago in North Carolina, but no one noticed. However, recently Richard Suhre (rhymes with surly) went ballistic and to court.

In 1932 Haywood County, North Carolina, built a courthouse that is now listed, in the National Register of Historic Places, among "the significant physical evidences of our national patrimony." Carved into the wall of one courtroom are two plaques listing ten commandments. Suhre, who advertises his atheism, lost a case in that courtroom and smolders with suspicion that the plaques disposed the jury against him.

But the list of admonitions on the plaques, which flank a bas-relief of Lady Justice, may not be "the" Ten Commandments. That is a question a judge must soon answer in deciding whether since 1932 Haywood County has been violating the First Amendment by fostering the establishment of religion.

This may seem to be just another skirmish along a familiar blurry border of First Amendment law. But Haywood County's defense did not consist just of splitting the usual constitutional hairs about the three-pronged test the Supreme Court concocted in 1971 for deciding what activities that bring government into contact with religion are constitutional.

By that test, permissible activity must have a secular purpose, must have a primary effect that neither advances nor inhibits religion, and must not foster excessive entanglement of government with religion. This formula looked clever until the justices were asked to declare unconstitutional the chaplain of Nebraska's Legislature.

They flinched, remembering that the first Congress, which drafted the First Amendment, hired a chaplain. So the Court fell back to asking if disputed activities "endorsed" religion.

Haywood County addressed this criterion by importing an expert witness to say that the courtroom commandments are not really religious. Haywood's commandments say, "Thou shalt have no other God before me. Thou shalt not make unto thee any graven image. Thou shalt not take the name of the Lord thy God in vain. Remember the Sabbath day to keep it holy. Honor thy father and thy mother. Thou shalt not kill. Thou shalt not commit adultery. Thou shalt not steal. Thou shalt not bear false witness. Thou shalt not covet."

Haywood's expert, Dr. Walter Harrelson, former dean of the divinity schools at the University of Chicago and Vanderbilt, said that the words on the courtroom plaques "are not the Ten Commandments of any known religion." This is because they "do not comport with the language of" the Torah, the King James or New Revised Standard Version of the Bible or the commandments as compiled by Augustine and others or as "kept by Lutheran, Roman Catholic, Orthodox Christian or Reformed Christian religions."

Rather, Harrelson testified, the courtroom plaques contain one of many "popular renditions" of the commandments. Such renditions are by now "inherently secular" and "Americanized" as "a familiar constituent of this nation's legal and moral heritage." Granted, they "might seem at first blush" to have "religious connotations." However, "their prevalence over time has caused them to evolve into a nonreligious, moral framework for a secular society."

Harrelson said the First Commandment, which "does not forbid atheism," actually means only "Do not have more than a single ultimate allegiance." The second nowadays means "Do not give ultimate loyalty to any earthly reality." The fourth just means "Do not treat with contempt the times set aside for rest."

The county noted that on the wall frieze in the U.S. Supreme Court, behind where the chief justice sits, there is a tablet bearing the Roman numerals I through X. The Office of the Curator of the Court insists that this merely "symbolizes early written laws," perhaps the Bill of Rights.

The county insisted that its commandments are like the phrases "In God We Trust" on coins (Mark Twain: "God was left out of the Constitution but was furnished a front seat on the coins of the country"), "one nation under God" in the Pledge of Allegiance, "so help me, God" in oaths, and "God save the United States and this Honorable Court." In all these expressions, the county argued, "religious connotations have become attenuated over time." That is, such religious expression by government is permissible because familiarity breeds innocuousness and hence indifference.

Defenders of religion have been reduced to such cringing arguments because the Supreme Court, which in 1952 said, "We are a religious people whose institutions presuppose a Supreme Being," has made a fetish out of scrubbing religion from the public square. Such arguments may be necessary to enable Haywood County to keep its commandments. But victories won with such arguments actually represent a surrender to secularism.

August 9, 1998

Censoring Zachary

Measured in terms of America's traditional causes of discord—antagonisms arising from class, race, ethnicity, and religion—there has never been more domestic tranquillity. Yet the sulfurous wrangling about religion in the fight for the Republican presidential nomination has made many Americans anxious about uncivil aggressiveness by some Christian factions bent on using government for sectarian purposes. But some Christians believe they are on the receiving end of aggression by government. Consider how growing up in America feels to Zachary Hood.

In 1996, when he was a first grader in a Medford, New Jersey, public school, his teacher rewarded students' reading proficiency by allowing them to bring from home, and read to the class, a story of their choice. The only requirement was that the selections be of age-appropriate brevity and complexity. Zachary chose the story "A Big Family" from *The Beginner's Bible*. This is the complete text:

> *Jacob traveled far away to his uncle's house. He worked for his uncle, taking care of sheep. While he was there, Jacob got married. He had twelve sons. Jacob's big family lived on his uncle's land for many years.*
> *But Jacob wanted to go back home. One day, Jacob packed up all his animals and his family and everything he had. They traveled all the way back to*

where Esau lived. Now Jacob was afraid that Esau might still be angry at him. So he sent presents to Esau. He sent servants who said, "Please don't be angry anymore." But Esau wasn't angry. He ran to Jacob. He hugged and kissed him. He was happy to see his brother again.

Although this mentions neither God nor God's manifestation in miracles, Zachary's teacher refused to allow him to read this "because of its religious content." The teacher said it amounted to reading the Bible and "might influence" other students. When Zachary's mother complained, the school principal backed up the teacher, saying the reading was "the equivalent of praying" and saying that Zachary and his mother "don't appear to be public-school material."

The choice of "A Big Family" was Zachary's second offense. When at Thanksgiving his kindergarten teacher assigned each student to make a poster of something for which he or she was thankful, Zachary drew a picture of Jesus. It was hung, with all his classmates' posters, in the hall outside the classroom. But school officials took it down because it had a religious theme. This was upsetting to Zachary, and his teacher got the poster put back up.

The incident about "A Big Family" sent Zachary's mother to court, where she is now represented by the Becket Fund, a Washington public-interest law firm specializing in defense of religious liberty. The trial court—the case is being appealed—supported the school. The court acknowledged that regulations of speech must be "viewpoint-neutral" and "reasonably related to a legitimate governmental purpose." But the court insisted that censoring Zachary's story was neutral.

Obviously if the story had been the same except that the names were Joe and Ed, it would not have been censored. But the court said, "It is irrelevant that the story had no overt religious theme; the speech was the book itself." The court said the censorship of Zachary's reading and poster had the reasonable pedagogical purpose of preventing the misperception by children that the school was endorsing religion.

But no school can function under the doctrine that it espouses whatever speech it permits. And two Supreme Court rulings and numerous decisions in other appeals courts have affirmed that, in the language of Zachary's mother's brief, "categorical discrimination against religious speech is *in and of itself* viewpoint discrimination." So when the court said the teacher had engaged only in permissible subject-matter discrimination, because she presumably would have censored all religious viewpoints, it got matters exactly backward. Not that a religious viewpoint can be tickled out of "A Big Family"; it was censored simply because it is known to come from a recognizable religious tradition, which makes the censorship viewpoint discrimination.

Had Zachary read a snippet from, say, the Koran, he probably would have been praised for his sensitivity to "diversity." As for the "impressionability" argument—that children might get the impression the school was endorsing religion—Zachary's mother says the argument backfires against the school: the only lesson the other children would learn from the censorship was that Zachary was being punished because he chose a Bible story.

Actually, it is the Medford school's clear hostility to anything biblical that violated the Establishment Clause, which the Supreme Court has said requires "the government to maintain a course of neutrality among religions, and between religion and nonreligion." Government action must not have the "primary effect" of advancing or *inhibiting* religion. The Court has said no law may "cast a pall of orthodoxy over the classroom" and orthodoxy can take the form of what the late Justice Arthur Goldberg called a "brooding and pervasive devotion to the secular and a passive, or even active, hostility to the religious." And Justice Sandra Day O'Connor has written that "the prohibition of all religious speech in our public schools implies . . . an unconstitutional *disapproval* of religion."

Today schools can require children to read "Heather Has Two Mommies" and other propaganda for "alternative lifestyles," and also can require that children not read something as innocuous as "A Big Family." Clearly there are more forms of extremism about religion than appear in the agendas of the most politically aggressive Christians. Given the Medford school's bullying of Zachary, he and his mother should take as a compliment the accusation that they may not be "public-school material."

March 20, 2000

Good News for Zachary

A Supreme Court ruling can be like a pebble tossed into a pond: ripples can radiate far. The Court's ruling last week in a case arising from a New York school's complaint may result in the Court implicitly reprimanding the New Jersey elementary school that considered Zachary Hood's reading preference unconstitutional. And last Monday's ruling may presage the rescue of many thousands of children in Cleveland and elsewhere from failing public schools. The ruling also may mean minimal constitutional impediments to President George W. Bush's "faith-based initiatives" for involving religious institutions in the delivery of some social services.

The Court has ruled, 6–3, that the Milford, New York, school district unconstitutionally barred the Good News Club from meeting in a school, after school hours, to instruct children in virtuous living from a Christian perspective. There are 4,622 such clubs in the United States, 527 of which meet in public-school buildings. The majority opinion by Justice Clarence Thomas asserted that opening school buildings to religious groups on the same basis as other groups would ensure government neutrality regarding religion, not threaten neutrality. His opinion was joined by conservatives William Rehnquist, Sandra Day O'Connor, Antonin Scalia, Anthony Kennedy, and Stephen Breyer, a liberal.

During oral argument about the case, Breyer asked a lawyer for the Good News Club: Suppose a city hall opened itself to after-hours use by community groups and a religious group wound up using it on Sundays for religious observance. Would not that be unconstitutional? By his question Breyer clearly implied that he thought so. But the club's lawyer replied that if the city hall was broadly opened for diverse uses, religious groups could not constitutionally be barred. Since the oral argument, Breyer may have learned the following from the Web site of Zachary's defender, the eponymously named Becket Fund, which defends religious liberty:

During President Thomas Jefferson's administration, when the ink was barely dry on the First Amendment's clauses barring "establishment" of religion but guaranteeing the free exercise of religion, Sunday services were held every week in buildings belonging to all three branches of government. Jefferson attended weekly services in the hall of the House of Representatives, bringing along the Marine Band for music. The speaker's chair served as a pulpit. Ministers included Anglicans, Presbyterians, Baptists, Quakers, Swedenborgians, a Roman Catholic bishop, a Unitarian, and a female evangelist. Presbyterians also used the War Office and Treasury Building.

Zachary Hood's case, discussed in this space in the March 20, 2000, *Newsweek,* began in 1996, when his first-grade teacher allowed proficient readers to read to the class a story of their choosing. He chose "A Big Family" from *The Beginner's Bible.*

The story mentions neither God nor miracles, and if it had been about, say, Bruce and Ralph, it would have aroused no objections. But Zachary's teacher said it amounted to devotional reading of the Bible and "might influence" other children. The school principal called it "the equivalent of praying" and said that Zachary and his mother "don't appear to be public-school material." Verily, they were recidivists. When assigned to make a Thanksgiving poster of something for which he was thankful, Zachary pictured Jesus. His poster was at first displayed in the hall with those of his classmates, then removed, and then put back up.

So far, Zachary has failed to persuade lower courts to heed Justice O'Connor's admonition that "the prohibition of all religious speech in our public schools implies . . . an unconstitutional disapproval of religion."

However, Zachary's lawyers hope that by the time you read this the Court will have ordered his case to be reconsidered in light of the *Good News Club* ruling.

The Court's commonsensical conclusion in that case—that true neutrality between religious and nonreligious organizations does not constitute "establishment" of religion—comes as Bush's faith-based initiatives proposal is encountering choppy water among legislators, some of whom say they consider it of dubious constitutionality. Furthermore, the Court's *Good News Club* ruling came as Cleveland's school-choice program is perhaps heading for the Court.

That program, which resembles programs in other cities, gives nearly four thousand low-income children in kindergarten through eighth grade scholarship vouchers redeemable at sectarian as well as secular schools. The Sixth Circuit Court of Appeals, contradicting Ohio's Supreme Court, has said the program violates the Establishment Clause. Proponents of school choice think the ruling about the Good News Club augurs well for the U.S. Supreme Court's taking the case and siding with Ohio's Supreme Court.

How many angels can dance on the head of a pin? Fewer than the number of distinctions the Court can draw between the constitutionality of this, and the unconstitutionality of that, contact between that religion and government. So last week's ruling is just a tantalizing suggestion of where the Court might go next. But in the unending—indeed, unendable—struggle over the proper scope for religion in the public square, last week may have brought, for the religious, radiating ripples of good news.

June 25, 2001

School Choice and the "Hecklers' Veto"

Roberta Kitchen of Cleveland, Tracy Richardson of Pensacola, Florida, and Tony Higgins of Milwaukee are black and have school-age children. And they are enemies of the American way. So say People for the American Way, teachers' unions, and others in the antichoice coalition waging a last-ditch resistance to people such as Kitchen, Richardson, and Higgins.

The three were in Washington, D.C., last week to talk about their lives because this Wednesday the Supreme Court will hold in its hands their happiness and that of millions of similarly situated parents and children. Their situation is perilous. The case the Court will consider on Wednesday has greater implications for equality of opportunity than any it has heard in the forty-eight years since *Brown v. Board of Education*.

The case comes from Cleveland, where Kitchen, who is raising five children abandoned by their alcoholic and drug-addicted mother, has participated in a program that provides $2,250 scholarships to low-income students to attend participating private or suburban public schools. The program empowers parents to choose alternatives to the Cleveland public schools, which Ohio declared to be in a state of "academic emergency" when the school district flunked twenty-seven of twenty-seven standards for student performance. At Euclid Park School, drug- and gang-infested, one of Kitchen's children reached sixth grade getting good grades—and essentially unable to read.

When Richardson's income was $11,000 a year, she rescued her daughter from a failing school through a Florida program similar to Cleveland's. Higgins's income was $14,000 when a similar Milwaukee program for his child that included after-school supervision enabled him to continue his education part-time. He gets his college degree this August.

Antichoice forces have lost six consecutive attempts to get the Supreme Court to declare unconstitutional—as violating the separation of church and state—all programs in which individuals were empowered to direct public funds to religious schools or programs. The Court says such empowerment is permissible on two conditions. The conditions are tailored to prevent the perception of government endorsement of religion and to guarantee that the primary effect of the program is not to advance religion.

One condition is that the choice of where to spend the money be a "true private choice"—what Supreme Court Justices Sandra Day O'Connor and Stephen Breyer have called a choice "*wholly* dependent on the student's private decision." Cleveland's program satisfies those justices' condition: scholarship checks are payable to the parents, who designate the recipient school.

The other condition is "neutrality." Educational assistance must be for a class—in Cleveland, poor children—defined without reference to religion; the program must contain no incentive to choose religious schools; and the range of choices must include more than religious schools.

The antichoice coalition attacks Cleveland's program by substituting a misleading statistic for the Court's carefully crafted principle. The coalition says the program must be unconstitutional because so many parents have chosen inner-city religious schools. But *of course* most have. They have severely restricted options because suburban public schools refuse to receive poor inner-city scholarship children. So the suburban schools have created the statistic that opponents of school choice say renders the program unconstitutional.

Were the Court to accept this perverse argument, it would be permitting a third-party veto over a program perfectly neutral regarding religion. Such a veto would be analogous to something the Court hitherto has disapproved.

Time was, communities would ban Party A from speaking publicly if there were a danger that Party B would be disorderly in disagreeing with Party A. The Court has declared this "hecklers' veto" unconstitutional.

Now, suburban schools, by shutting their doors to inner-city students, thereby create the fact that most schools that will accept those students are inner-city religious schools. Were the Court to say that this statistical outcome makes the scholarship program unconstitutional, the Court would be allowing the suburban schools' decision to control the constitutionality of a program designed for others.

The antichoice coalition's position is that because *some* schools—those in the suburbs—reject poor inner-city children, *no* school should be permitted to participate in the program. However, the Court has held that under the Individuals with Disabilities Education Act, when public schools fail to provide appropriate education, children can choose to receive it, at public expense, from private schools.

Children in Cleveland, and millions elsewhere, are *being* disabled—their opportunities as restricted as they would be by some physical or mental disabilities—by the antichoice coalition's campaign to turn the Constitution into a barricade to prevent poor children from escaping from the public school plantation.

This is "the American way"? Surely the Court will disagree.

February 17, 2002

The Supreme Court and the "Essence" of Golf

A doctrine prevalent in prestigious law schools is that language is "open-textured" and "indeterminate," and hence the users of words have vast latitude in infusing them with meanings. A moral theory in vogue is that one virtue trumps all competing considerations. That virtue, compassion, is a feeling that confers upon the person feeling it a duty to do whatever is necessary to ameliorate distress.

On Tuesday we saw what happens when judges are conditioned by that doctrine about language and convinced of that moral theory. The Supreme Court held, 7–2, that Casey Martin, a professional golfer handicapped by a degenerative disease that prevents him from walking a golf course, has a right to ride in a cart.

Martin, having successfully invoked the Americans with Disabilities Act, now can ride when competing against golfers who must walk five miles in PGA Tour tournaments. Because of this supposed enlargement of American rights, the PGA Tour and its millions of fans have lost their right to have tournaments conducted in accordance with their understanding of the proper nature of golf competition at the highest levels.

The ADA requires that "public accommodations" make "reasonable modifications" to help the handicapped, unless the modifications would "fundamentally" alter the nature of what the public accommodation does. Justice John Paul Stevens, joined by William Rehnquist, Sandra Day O'Connor, Anthony Kennedy, David Souter, Ruth Bader Ginsburg, and Stephen Breyer, said that the PGA Tour does not understand as well as he does what is fundamental to elite golf.

The PGA Tour says that such golf involves performing under the pressure of fatigue from walking. But the justices upheld a lower court, which also is composed of experts on playing professional golf. That court said that fatigue is not fundamental to such competition. Besides, that court said, it knew, simply *knew,* that Martin, even with his cart, was more fatigued than competitors who walked.

Stevens, not to be outdone by a lower court in the certitude sweepstakes, asserted his certainty that "pure chance may have a greater impact on the outcome of elite golf tournaments" than does the walking rule. He did not say how he knows that this is true or why it is relevant.

But the majority's ukase about what is "fundamental" in elite golf had to be preceded by two others. The point of the pertinent ADA provisions is to give enforceable rights to clients or customers of public accommodations (e.g., hotels, restaurants). So the Court had to decree this: A tournament featuring the world's best golfers—a *tournament,* mind you, not a golf course—is a public accommodation. That said, the Court also had to say this: A golfer who pays a tournament entry fee is a "customer" purchasing "competition."

Resisting this reduction of the English language to applesauce, Justice Antonin Scalia, joined in dissent by Clarence Thomas, said: Baseball players "participate" in games at Yankee Stadium and "use" it, "but no one in his right mind would think that they are *customers* of the American League or of Yankee Stadium. They are themselves the entertainment that the customers pay to watch."

As for Stevens's interesting claim to know golf's "essence," Scalia said, yes, sure, the Constitution's framers expected "the judges of this august Court would someday have to wrestle with that age-old jurisprudential question, for which their years of study in the law have so well prepared them: Is someone riding around a golf course from shot to shot *really* a golfer? The answer, we learn, is yes. . . . Either out of humility or out of self-respect (one or the other) the Court should decline to answer this incredibly difficult and incredibly silly question."

Many questions may now come to courts from athletes seeking court-ordered alterations—not, of course, "fundamental" ones touching the sport's "essence"—of this and that sport's rules in order to accommodate different disadvantages. Scalia envisions parents of a Little Leaguer with attention deficit disorder asking a judge to order that their child be allowed four strikes because his disability makes hitting that much harder.

And what of the mother who today is suing the San Francisco Ballet, charging that its weight and height standards illegally discriminate against her daughter? Suppose the daughter's physical attributes count under the ADA as "disabilities" in the context of her preferred profession. If that seems unthinkable, you have not noticed all that has been swept into the category "disability" under the ADA. What "reasonable modifications" of the Ballet's standards might Justice Stevens improvise? By what principle should the Ballet's standards survive while the PGA Tour's do not?

The work of compassionate courts never ends.

June 3, 2001

REASONABLE DOUBTS

Worrying Rationally

Americans probably watch the networks' evening newscasts with eyes as dull and lifeless as oysters on the half shell. The news Americans receive is that they are trapped in a tightening vise of risks.

Recently a network newscast (NBC's, but the three are alike, for reasons we shall come to) began with stories about Sonny Bono's accident and the risks of skiing. (Should helmets be mandatory?) There also was a story about the risks of "our everyday lives"—"even the simplest activities can be more dangerous than you may think." (Odds of "getting cancer from an average number of X-rays, one in 700. Your odds of dying in a home accident are one in 130; a car accident, one in 60.") There was good news on the risk front: a report that middle-aged men who eat certain kinds of fish once a week "can cut their heart attack risk in half." But the broadcast included bad news germane to that good news: the obligatory story of impending environmental calamity concerned "alarming new information about the state of the seas," which are "now very much at risk."

Just another day of journalism in this risky time.

Of course, there never has been a safer time (the biggest recent risk reduction was the dissolution of the Soviet Union); tomorrow almost certainly will be safer than today; many of today's risks can be minimized by routine urban wariness (stay out of the very few neighborhoods where the vast majority of violent crimes occur) and other forms of prudence (do not draw cash from an ATM at 2 A.M.); some risks result from demanded conveniences (e.g., ATMs); some risks are substantially optional (AIDS, coronary heart disease, and lung cancer, among other afflictions, are largely results of behavior well known to be risky); some risks are coveted consumption goods (skiing vacations in Aspen or Tahoe); some risks (driving small, "fuel-efficient" cars) are encouraged by "progressive" public policies; other risks are encouraged by pork-barrel politics (federally subsidized insurance encourages people to build homes where the insurance market tells them not to build, such as on floodplains, and artificial, meaning politically influenced, prices for many things, from grazing land to dairy products, encourage Americans to consume unhealthy amounts of fat in red meat, cheese, and other things); the elderly are increasingly at risk of suffering many afflictions because medicine has radically reduced the risk of dying earlier from other afflictions (such as pneumonia) . . .

Rational worrying is a learned skill. (White-knuckle fliers land in Los Angeles, sigh with relief, and relax in cabs that were last inspected at Studebaker dealerships and are driven in rush-hour traffic by strangers driven by strange demons.) Rational worrying requires weighing two primary variables: the probability of an event and the magnitude of that event. Living next to a nuclear plant involves a minuscule likelihood of a large disaster. Driving to the grocery store in this era of road rage—*that* is worrisome.

Irrationality about risks results in, among other wastes, public regulations and expenditures that do not fit reality. So just as young doctors should be told that all their patients are going to die, everyone needs reminding that there always will be a few especially important causes of death. Always.

One reason we live in an age of irrational anxieties is that television, a dispenser of perceptions, is an efficient instrument for erasing the distinction between measured risks and perceived risks. Furthermore, television news is produced largely by and for baby boomers, who in their narcissism constantly congratulate themselves on discovering new things (sex, cigars, injustice, martinis, risks). Now they are turning fifty and discovering a cosmic injustice: they are going to die. Is this *fair?* Can't Congress produce just one more entitlement?

If this generation of whiners had been born just fifty years earlier, many of its members would have died before learning how to whine. (Peter Brimelow reports in *Forbes* that U.S. infant mortality is less than one-tenth the rate in 1915. Soccer moms leading stressful lives in their station wagons are at least alive: today fewer than one in 10,000 women die in childbirth. In 1940, one in 300 did.)

Obsessing about physical risks comes naturally to a society that defines the good life in terms of material well-being and thinks the aim of politics is the ever finer fine-tuning of life's fairness. News you will not see reported on the evening newscasts: the parallel decline of the riskiness and the serenity of life in such a society.

January 11, 1998

Increasing Speed—and Safety: A Cautionary Tale

Statistics and probabilities can be puzzling, even paradoxical, as Willard Espy knew when he wrote:

> *Very, very, very few*
> *People die at ninety-two.*
> *I suppose that I shall be*
> *Safer still at ninety-three.*

Another example: In the movie *Fathers' Day,* Billy Crystal wants Robin Williams to facilitate a deception by pretending to cry. Crystal suggests that Williams imagine that he is a tragic hero like Lou Gehrig. Williams asks, "Who's that?"

Crystal, dumbfounded, says, "Everybody knows Lou Gehrig—the baseball player. He died of Lou Gehrig's disease."

Williams, flabbergasted that someone named Lou Gehrig died of something named Lou Gehrig's disease, exclaims, "Wow! What are the odds on that?"

Which is prologue to today's subject: What were the odds in 1987 that the increases in states' speed limits would result in decreasing statewide fatality rates? Herewith a story about the vagaries of statistical analyses and social policies, a story with a happy ending.

Two scholars who can explain the counterintuitive results of increased speed limits are Charles Lave and Patrick Elias of the department of economics at the University of California at Irvine. The story they tell begins with the 1973 Yom Kippur War, the oil embargo, and the federal law coercing states to enforce 55-mph limits. Federal highway funding would be reduced for states not meeting compliance requirements, which included speed-monitoring programs and reports of the proportion of drivers violating the new limit.

The primary reason for the 55-mph limit was fuel conservation, and when the energy crisis passed, Americans grew restless. In 1987 states were allowed to raise their limits on rural interstates, and forty adopted 65-mph limits. Opponents stressed not conservation but safety, predicting carnage. Their mantra was "Speed kills."

Concerning developments immediately after 1987, Lave and Elias note that construing the evidence is a more complex task than some analysts realize. Their conclusion is that, up to a point, higher speed limits save lives.

After 1987, the higher speed limits reduced statewide fatality rates by 3.4 percent to 5.1 percent, compared to the rates in states that did not raise limits. True, the actual number of fatalities continued to increase after 1987, but the volume of traffic increased even faster. The critical measurement is fatalities per vehicle mile traveled *in the entire state.* Some studies found that raising speed limits on particular highways increased, or did not decrease, fatalities on those particular highways. However, such studies failed to gauge the ways in which all of a state's highways make up a single interdependent system and to take into account the fact that highway systems and safety systems are also interdependent.

Lave and Elias say the 55-mph limit caused the misallocation of traffic and of police resources. The federal government had demanded strict compliance with the 55-mph limit, which forced state highway patrols to concentrate on speed enforcement on the interstate highways, which have the densest concentration of high-speed traffic. But these are also the safest highways.

And state police patrol resources were then decreasingly available for such safety programs as truck inspections and drunk driving checkpoints. Furthermore, many drivers who wanted to speed switched to less traveled, less patrolled, but less safe roads.

The 55-mph limit might have decreased fatalities on some roads by increasing patrolling and decreasing traffic volume from what it would have been without that limit. However, the effect on a state's total highways system was apt to be a net subtraction from safety.

Raising speed limits lured some drivers back to safer, more heavily patrolled roads and allowed highway patrols to shift resources back to the programs they thought most effective. And it decreased a real killer—speed variance among vehicles.

Many collisions occur when cars are overtaking and passing one another. Speed variance among drivers increases when speed limits are set so low that there is a high rate of noncompliance. Raising speed limits reduced turbulence in the traffic stream, leading Lave to say, "Variance kills, not speed."

When in November 1995 Congress empowered states to set such limits as they chose, fatalities did not increase by the 10 to 14 percent predicted by the Cassandras who foresaw 4,400–6,000 extra deaths per year. Neither did fatalities increase by even the 2 to 3 percent that would have been expected, extrapolating from recent trends. Instead, Lave concludes that fatalities have declined slightly (by 0.14 percent) even as total vehicle miles increased 2 percent.

This is a cautionary tale about the complexity of discerning reality in a welter of statistics. It also is an encouraging tale. Sometimes the unintended consequences of a policy—in this case, increased safety from speed limits that were increased for reasons other than safety—are good.

November 6, 1997

What Did We Know, and When Did We Know It, About Smoking?

"**S**ay, sport, have you got a coffin nail on you?" asks a character in an O. Henry short story *written in 1906. The New Dictionary of American Slang* dates the phrase "coffin nail" from the late nineteenth century. Which fact indicates that the government, in its suit against the tobacco companies, is committing the sin—fraud—that it supposedly is suing about.

Let us stipulate that the companies, without which the world would be better, have been deceitful about the addictiveness and harmfulness of cigarettes. But to prove fraud, government must show that its tobacco policy has been substantially affected by the companies' duplicities and that the companies prevented government and the public from knowing the truth. Good luck.

The government says, with a straight face, "Members of the public believed in the truth and completeness of the statements made by" the companies and "relied upon the statements . . . and demonstrated that reliance by purchasing and smoking cigarettes, and by refraining from trying to quit or reduce their consumption of cigarettes." But there are about as many ex-smokers as smokers in America, and history suggests why.

"In my early youth, I was addicted to tobacco," wrote former President John Quincy Adams in 1845, not in doubt about the addictiveness of tobacco, as many other people have not been in doubt, despite the tobacco companies' contrary assertions. After the Civil War, the abolitionist William Lloyd Garrison adopted some new causes, including abolition of tobacco. Is it plausible to say that the companies' behavior explains the fact that it was not until the 1970s that the military stopped providing free cigarettes to its personnel?

The government included cigarettes in combat rations in both world wars. But as early as 1892 *The New York Times* reported that because of health concerns the Senate "has received a constant stream of petitions against cigarettes." In a 1900 ruling the Supreme Court noted that "we should be shutting our eyes to what is constantly passing before them were we to affect an ignorance of the fact that a belief in [cigarettes'] deleterious effects, particularly on young people, has become very general, and that communications are constantly finding their way into the public press denouncing their uses as fraught with great danger."

The government, which now blames tobacco companies' duplicities for some substantial public health costs, has, since the 1964 Surgeon General's report, officially certified cigarettes as dangerous. For more than three decades the government has required increasingly stern health warnings to be printed on cigarette packs and advertising. Of course, this government still subsidizes the growing of tobacco and writes budgets with billions of tobacco tax revenues assumed.

Government pretends to be in a moral meltdown over fraud by the tobacco industry. The supposed fraud is a forty-five-year-long conspiracy (starting with a meeting of tobacco companies' executives in Manhattan's Plaza Hotel in 1953) to deny what most sentient people have surmised, with progressive certainty, for a lot longer than forty-five years—that cigarettes are dangerous enough to be called "coffin nails."

The government's suit seeks recompense from tobacco companies for expenditures the government, *because of the companies' fraud,* incurred treating smoking-related illnesses. Well. The government knows something about tobacco-related fraud.

Hundreds of jurisdictions have banned indoor smoking, partly because of a 1993 Environmental Protection Agency report that environmental tobacco smoke (ETS) kills three thousand Americans a year. In 1998 a federal judge accused the EPA of "cherry picking" the data for the report and said the EPA, "publicly committed to a conclusion before research had begun", violated procedural requirements in the pertinent law by excluding input from the tobacco industry; "adjusted established procedure and scientific norms to validate the Agency's public conclusion"; did not "disseminate significant epidemiologic information"; "deviated from its Risk Assessment Guidelines"; and "failed to disclose important findings and reasoning."

EPA's fraud was minor compared to the government's pretense that smoking costs it money. Various studies demonstrate that government reaps substantial savings because of the premature deaths of smokers, who (by the way, cigarettes are the most heavily taxed consumer good) collect few if any retirement, health care, and nursing home benefits.

When you hear a figure such as 427,743 "premature" deaths from smoking (according to the Centers for Disease Control, that was the annual average, 1990–94), bear in mind that nearly 60 percent of those deaths were of people seventy or older, nearly 45 percent were of people over seventy-five, and nearly 17 percent were of people over eighty-five. With what certainty in those cases can the government establish "smoking-attributable mortality"?

But then one certainty is that accuracy is not the hallmark of the government's tobacco policy.

October 3, 1999

Supersized Americans

Almost nobody knows who—or even what—the surgeon general is, so almost nobody noticed when David Satcher's term in that office recently expired. But notice what he did when stepping out the door. His warning about obesity, properly amplified, may demonstrate why the office of surgeon general sometimes is the government's most cost-effective institution.

In this mostly middle-class, broadly educated, information-acquiring country, often the most effective dollars government spends pay for the dissemination of public health information. In an affluent society, which has banished scarcity and presents a rich range of choice, many public health problems are optional—the consequences of choices known to be foolish.

Imagine how America's health profile would be improved by substantial reductions in coronary artery disease, lung cancer, AIDS, violence and vehicular accidents. All five are often results of behavior known to be risky. Now imagine Americans take to heart, so to speak, Satcher's warning that obesity may soon surpass smoking as the nation's principal cause of preventable death.

Although Americans spend more than $30 billion a year on weight-loss products or programs, obesity is, strictly speaking, epidemic. Scientists for the Centers for Disease Control and Prevention reported that in 1991 only four states had obesity rates of 15 percent or higher. Today 37 do and the obesity rate is increasing in every state and among all racial and ethnic groups. "Rarely," the report says, "do chronic conditions such as obesity spread with the speed and dispersion characteristic of a communicable disease."

A quarter of all Americans smoke (down from half in the two generations since the 1964 surgeon general's report connecting smoking with cancer). But most American adults—61 percent—are overweight or obese, primarily because they eat imprudently and exercise negligibly. Smoking-related illnesses kill 400,000 a year, but illnesses related to obesity—heart attacks, stroke, diabetes, some cancers—kill 300,000, are increasing faster than smoking-related illnesses and threaten to nullify recent gains made against those illnesses.

Unlike cigarettes, french fries—America's annual per capita consumption: 28 pounds—are neither addictive nor harmful when enjoyed in moderation. And public health information encourages moderation. But if you want to buy a weight-loss product, almost any bookstore has Eric Schlosser's best-selling *Fast Food Nation: The Dark Side of the All-American Meal*. It is a sure-fire appetite-suppressant.

Like a lot of people hell-bent on forcing root-and-branch reform of society, Schlosser's zealotry approaches monomania: He traces an amazing number of social ills to fast food. However, even allowing for the fact that fewer than one-third of Americans bestir themselves to get the medically recommended minimum amount of exercise, Schlosser plausibly argues this: There is more than coincidence in the correlation of the increase of obesity and the rise of the fast-food industry.

"What we eat," he writes, "has changed more in the last forty years than in the previous forty-thousand." He says half the money Americans spend on food—more than on higher education or new cars—is spent at restaurants, mostly at the fast-food sort. On any given day, a quarter of America's adults visit such restaurants. Every month 90 percent of children aged 3 to 9 visit a McDonald's. Commodity prices have fallen, so serving sizes have risen. McDonald's largest serving of french fries is three times larger than it was a generation ago. In the late 1950s the typical fast-food restaurant soft drink was eight ounces. Today McDonald's "large" Coke is 32 ounces—and 310 calories.

Now, food fascists are among the most annoying killjoys in our midst. They are immoderate in their animus against foods which are harmless pleasures if they are not a steady diet. But before tucking into your next double cheeseburger with bacon (70 percent of bacon sold in America is on fast food), calculate your BMI—Body Mass Index.

Divide your weight in pounds by the square of your height in inches, then multiply by 703. If the resulting number is below 25 you are not overweight. If it is 25 to 29 you, like 34 percent of Americans aged 20 to 74, are overweight. Since 1970 the percentage of children aged 6 to 11 who are overweight has almost doubled, from 7 to 13. The percentage for adolescents aged 12 to 19 has almost tripled, from 5 to 14, which may have something to do with the fact that for at least 2 hours a day 43 percent of persons in grades nine through 12 are immobile, watching television.

If your BMI number is 30 or higher you, like 27 percent of adults, have supersized yourself. You are obese. Bon appetit.

February 28, 2002

Boys Will Be Boys. So Drug Them.

A reaction is under way against drugging children because they are behaving like children, especially boy children. Colorado's elected school board recently voted to discourage what looks like drug abuse in the service of an ideological agenda. The board urged teachers and other school personnel to be more restrained about recommending drugs such as Ritalin for behavior modification of children and to rely more on discipline and instruction.

One reason for the vote is that some school violence has been committed by students taking psychotropic drugs. But even absent a causal connection between the drugs and violence, there are sound reasons to recoil from the promiscuous drugging of children.

Consider the supposed epidemic of attention deficit/hyperactivity disorder (ADHD), which by 1996 had American youngsters consuming 90 percent of the world's Ritalin. Boys, no parent of one will be surprised to learn, are much more likely than girls to be diagnosed with ADHD. In 1996, 10 to 12 percent of all American schoolboys were taking the addictive Ritalin. (After attending classes on the dangers of drugs?)

One theory holds that ADHD is epidemic because of the modern acceleration of life—the environmental blitzkrieg of MTV, video games, e-mail, cell phones, and so on. However, the magazine *Lingua Franca* reports that Ken Jacobson, a doctoral candidate in anthropology at the University of Massachusetts, conducted a cross-cultural study of ADHD that included observation of two groups of English schoolchildren, one diagnosed with ADHD, the other not. He observed them with reference to thirty-five behaviors (e.g., "giggling," "squirming," "blurting out") and found no significant differences between the groups.

Children, he says, tend to talk, fidget, and fool around—"all the classical ADHD-type behaviors. If you're predisposed to label *any* child as ADHD, the distracted troublemaker or the model student, you'll find a way to observe these behaviors." So what might explain such a predisposition?

Paul R. McHugh, professor of psychiatry at Johns Hopkins, writing in *Commentary,* argues that ADHD, "social phobia" (usual symptom: fear of public speaking), and other disorders certified by the American Psychiatric Association's *Diagnostic and Statistical Manual of Mental Disorders* are proliferating rapidly. This is because of a growing tendency to regard as mental problems many characteristics that are really aspects of individuality. So pharmacology is employed to relieve burdensome aspects of temperament.

"Psychiatric conditions," says McHugh, "are routinely differentiated by appearances alone," even when it is "difficult to distinguish symptoms of illness from normal variations in human life" or from the normal responses of sensitive people to life's challenges. But if a condition can be described, it can be named; once named, a distinct disorder can be linked to a particular treatment. McHugh says some experts who certify new disorders "receive extravagant annual retainers from pharmaceutical companies that profit from the promotion of disorders treatable by the companies' medications."

The idea that most individuals deficient in attentiveness or confidence are sick encourages what McHugh calls pharmacological "mental cosmetics." This "should be offensive to anyone who values the richness of human psychological diversity. Both medically and morally, encumbering this naturally occurring diversity with the terminology of disease is a first step toward efforts, however camouflaged, to control it."

Clearly, some children need Ritalin. However, Ken Livingston, of Vassar's Department of Psychology, writing in *The Public Interest,* says Ritalin is sometimes used as a diagnostic tool: if it improves a child's attention, ADHD is assumed. But Ritalin, like other stimulants such as caffeine and nicotine, improves almost everyone's attention. And Ritalin is a ready resource for teachers who blur the distinction between education and therapy.

One alternative to Ritalin might be school choice—parents finding schools suited to their children's temperaments. But, says Livingston, when it is difficult to change the institutional environment, "we don't think twice about changing the brain of the person who has to live in it."

This is an age that tries to medicalize every difficulty or defect. Gwen Broude, also of Vassar, believes that the rambunctiousness of boys is treated as a mental disorder by people eager to interpret sex differences as personal deficiencies. Danielle Crittenden of the Independent Women's Forum sees the "anti-boy lobby" behind the hand-wringing about the supposed dangers of reading the Harry Potter novels, which feature wizardry, witchcraft, and other really neat stuff.

The androgynous agenda of progressive thinkers has reduced children's literature to bland gruel because, Crittenden says, there is "zero tolerance for male adventurousness." The Potter books recall those traditional boys' books that satisfied boys' zeal for strife and adventure. Today, Crittenden says, that zeal causes therapists—they are everywhere—to reach for Ritalin.

Harry is brave, good, and constantly battling evil. He should point his broomstick toward Colorado, where perhaps boys can be boys.

December 2, 1999

The Mask of Masculinity

Professor Harvey Mansfield is Harvard's conservative. Well, all right, he is one of Harvard's handful of conservatives, a.k.a. The Saving Remnant. A few years ago he received a call when a distinguished colleague retired. The caller, a young woman journalist, wanted a comment on the retirement. Mansfield obliged, saying he particularly admired the colleague's manliness. An awkward silence ensued from the other end of the line. Then the reporter asked Mansfield, Could you think of another word?

What might be wrong with that word? That is a (literally) academic question, now that professors and somber quarterlies are creating a new discipline: masculinity studies. That subject is being, as it were, married to women's studies to round out gender studies, as at Hobart and William Smith Colleges, where there now is a Center for the Study of Women and Men.

Well. In olden days, before these things were understood with today's clarity, people thought that when they studied subjects such as philosophy, history, politics, sociology, anthropology, art, music, and literature, they were engaged in the study of women and men. But back to Mansfield's journalistic interlocutor. The problem she had with the word "masculinity" probably was twofold.

First, the word is stained with the supposition that manliness is a virtue. Advanced thinkers execrate the idea of a virtue that is not a gender-neutral,

equal-opportunity virtue. Both men and women can be brave, frank, aggressive, competitive, loyal, stoical. Is manliness anything more than a tossed salad
of those attributes? If so, can a woman be manly? (Was François Mitterrand
suggesting androgyny when he said Margaret Thatcher has the eyes of Ca-
ligula and the lips of Marilyn Monroe?)

Second, leave aside the question of whether manliness should be celebrated as a virtue rather than condemned as a social virus that causes wars,
sport utility vehicles, and other testosterone spills. But perhaps manliness is
(because everything is) a social construct. Here is the heart of gender studies:
If all human attributes are consequences of social arrangements, then clever
rearrangement of society can produce whatever results the rearrangers want.
If so, neither biology nor history nor nature is destiny. All is nurture and
ephemeral, nothing is instinctive, innate, permanent. Nothing is destined.
Everything is a matter of choice. Free at last, free at last . . .

One tool for striking the chains from women's wrists and ankles is a noun
that has become a verb: parent. It makes fathers and mothers interchangeable,
their differences fungible, their duties negotiable.

And why not, now that *The New York Times* reports this bulletin: "Masculinity is not monolithic"? Indeed. Mark McGwire cries. Male peacockery
flourished before and after Henry VIII donned silk stockings to show off his
legs. The *Times* cites a professor in Indiana who has written a book on masculinity as portrayed in the movies of Jimmy Stewart, Jack Nicholson, and
Clint Eastwood. The professor asks, What if masculinity is a construction,
something we unconsciously work very hard on making ourselves into that
we've all conned ourselves into believing is natural? The professor seems to
think he is entertaining a daring idea, but nowadays nothing seems more natural than disbelief in the natural.

Manliness is usually thought to involve, above all, courage, especially in
battle. In American literature, manliness is famously acquired by the young man
in *The Red Badge of Courage* who acquires that red badge—a wound. Manliness,
says Mansfield thoughtfully, celebrates action over thought, so one could even
say that thinking is in itself a challenge to the superiority of manliness.

If womanliness (which is not a synonym for femininity) is the opposite of
manliness, womanliness is more reflective, even philosophical, and less animal,
more human, hence higher. Males are not flattered by what Mansfield calls the
asymmetry of the sexes. Aristotle said men find it easier to be courageous and
women find it easier to be moderate. Mansfield suggests that this is because
women are more thoughtful. Would a really Nineties Man, caring and sensitive, want the largely animal attribute of manliness or regard it as virtuous? We
speak of speed being a virtue in a racehorse, but horses cannot be virtuous.

But wait. Perhaps the Nineties Man himself is inherently insidious. Perhaps he is sneaking patriarchy—the subordination of women—back into so-

ciety, from which it was so recently expelled. Gallantry, which everyone knows is condescension, may now come quietly, on little cat feet, disguised as sensitivity.

Perhaps what everyone knows is false. Maybe the gallantry of opening a door for a woman expresses disdain by asserting that the man is stronger. Then again, physical strength is a merely animal attribute. And opening a door may express sincere rather than guileful deference. Mansfield: The woman does go first.

Then again, male sensitivity was not born yesterday. Some of the stuffed animals that children cuddle are called teddy bears because on one famous occasion the man who was the rough-riding personification of self-conscious manliness was too sensitive to shoot a wee bear. Yes, Teddy Roosevelt. That (Eighteen-)Nineties Man thought that war was splendidly bracing for a nation and that if a war was not handy, war's moral equivalent, football, would have to suffice.

Mansfield says that feminists fault masculinity primarily for its antidemocratic exclusivity. They want society reconstructed so they can act as masculine as men have to, and they want men reconstructed so they will act a little less masculine, more sensitive. Feminists' real complaint, says Mansfield, is with femininity, the mystique (Betty Friedan) of mildness that men supposedly have foisted on women to keep them in their place, which is down, as the second sex (Simone de Beauvoir).

Why can't a woman be more like a man? ask some feminists. It is a fair, and complex, question famously asked in *My Fair Lady* by Professor Henry Higgins, no feminist.

July 19, 1999

Rethinking Puberty, and High School

Three great creations of American civilization in the nineteenth century were judicial review, the curveball, and high school. The first two are still robust. However, the time is ripe for rethinking the third.

For various reasons, some rooted in American history and others reflecting recent developments, education has become, for the moment, the most salient social concern and therefore the most potent political issue. The world is less menacing than at any time since the 1920s. Social learning about fiscal, monetary, and regulatory management has helped reduce the frequency and severity of business cycles. Demography (fewer young males), better policing, and more prison cells have helped reduce crime.

As a result, public attention is concentrated, even more than usual, on the Jeffersonian faith in education as the crucial ingredient in personal independence and upward mobility. The focus of today's anxiety is the highest institution from which a majority of Americans—more than 75 percent—graduate. It is the sea of denim and hormones called high school.

America's education debates usually run in deep ruts. Liberals want more money spent on schools, although there is scant evidence of a positive correlation between increased financial input into and increased cognitive output from schools as currently constituted. More constructively but still inadequately, conservatives call for mechanisms to expand parental choice among schools as currently constituted.

Now comes Leon Botstein with a radical argument for abolishing the high school as we know it. He argues that puberty is not what it once was, therefore high schools should not be what they have been since taking their current form about a hundred years ago.

Botstein, 51, has seen many products of America's high schools. He has the longest tenure among current presidents of major colleges. He has been president of Bard College since 1975. At age twenty-three he became the youngest college president in American history. He is musical director of the American Symphony Orchestra in New York and editor of *The Musical Quarterly*. In his spare time he has written a book-length manifesto, *Jefferson's Children: Education and the Promise of American Culture,* the third chapter of which argues that the American high school is "obsolete."

The problem, Botstein says, is that the high school was created for fifteen- to eighteen-year-olds who were still children, just approaching the brink of adulthood. Today people that age are, physiologically and psychologically, young adults who pose a teaching problem that the traditional high school cannot solve.

Medical and nutritional advances have changed the relationship between chronological age and physical development. Historians estimate that during the last half of the nineteenth century, menstruation began three to four months earlier each decade. The onset of puberty is substantially earlier today than a century ago, when the high school was invented. Then, says Botstein, the average age of the onset of menstruation was between fifteen and sixteen. Today it is thirteen.

As result, he says, educational practices no longer correspond to the freedoms and habits of young people's development. This is particularly so in today's adolescent culture, where money—meaning shopping—and ease of travel facilitate the young person's "self-declaration of independence."

Thus "today's first-year college students have lived the external appearances of an adult life for many more years than their counterparts fifty years ago did." Therefore, "what we have traditionally associated with the intellectual awakening during the college years must now occur in the high school."

Age eighteen is too old for the intellectual regimentation and social confinements of today's high school. As a result, teachers are demoralized by the demands of keeping order. And age eighteen is too old for starting serious education. It is too old to begin acquiring a love of reading, a level of comfort with mathematics and science, and good habits of concentration and memory.

Botstein believes that "linking learning to life in age-appropriate ways" requires "treating adolescents as young as thirteen and fourteen more the way we do college students and adults and less as children." Actually, he wants to abolish junior high, and he wants students in high school—which he would end at tenth grade—treated better than college students often are, with classes, including many seminars, that are smaller than those in grade school.

Botstein is a Roman candle of ideas about curriculum reform and other matters, but every one of them likely would strain the sclerotic educational system's capacity for adaptation. Still, the fact that the changes he proposes are probably impossible does not mean that his thinking is wrong or that lesser reforms will be satisfactory.

April 8, 1998

The Death of School Discipline

The contest between Al Gore and George W. Bush for the office of national school superintendent means Washington will expand its role in education. Until the Elementary and Secondary Education Act of 1965, the federal government had essentially nothing—certainly nothing essential—to do with elementary and secondary education. Today the federal government supplies only 7 percent of the money spent on such education, but 7 percent of $313.1 billion is a large lever for moving state and local education policies in directions that Washington favors. And money is not the full measure of the national government's impact on education. Consider school discipline.

Last month Al Gore endorsed a good idea, "alternative educational settings"—special "second chance schools"—for children expelled from schools for disciplinary reasons. However, one reason such schools are needed is that the federal government has complicated the task of maintaining school discipline. To understand how this happened, see "Who Killed School Discipline?" by Kay S. Hymowitz in *City Journal,* published by the Manhattan Institute.

Because schools reflect the families from which the pupils come, school discipline was bound to worsen as more broken families resulted in more troubled or badly reared children. And maintaining order was bound to become more difficult as popular culture became a sensory blitzkrieg of promptings to sexual and other self-assertion by adolescents. However, government has made matters worse.

In 1969 the Supreme Court held that a school violated five students' constitutional rights when it suspended them for wearing black armbands to protest the Vietnam War. The Court said students do not shed their free speech rights "at the schoolhouse gate" and schools cannot be "enclaves of totalitarianism." Thus did important matters of school discipline become federal cases. Thereafter, a principal who confronted, say, a student wearing a T-shirt emblazoned with "WHITE POWER" or with a swastika had to construe the Constitution. Could the principal prove that the behavior was "significantly disruptive"? Did he want to litigate the question?

In 1975, in a case concerning students suspended for fighting, the Court expanded students' due process rights, holding that students have a property right to their education. So lawyers and judges were pulled even deeper into school discipline procedures, presiding over—at a minimum—elaborate hearings with witnesses. Designed to make schools more "fair" and "responsive," such decisions, writes Hymowitz, made school administrators act defensively and look legalistic and obtuse:

> When a New York City high school student came to school with a metal-spiked ball whose sole purpose could only be to maim classmates, he wasn't suspended: Metal-spiked balls weren't on the superintendent's detailed list of proscribed weapons. Suspend him and he might sue you for being arbitrary and capricious.
>
> Worse, the influence of lawyers over school discipline means that educators speak to children in an unrecognizable language, far removed from the straight talk about right and wrong that most children crave. . . . Students correctly sense that what lies behind such desiccated language is not a moral worldview and a concern for their well-being and character but fear of lawsuits.

What also lies behind it is the therapeutic impulse.

In 1975 Congress passed the Individuals with Disabilities Education Act (IDEA), which requires schools to provide disabled children an "appropriate" education, within regular classrooms whenever that is possible. The act addressed real needs of many mentally and physically handicapped students. But since, and partly because of, the passage of the act there has been, as Hymowitz says, an explosive growth in the number of children classified under vague disability categories such as "learning disability" and "emotional disturbance."

Part of the legal definition of emotional disturbance is "an inability to build or maintain satisfactory interpersonal relationships with peers and teachers." So children who are unruly, for whatever reason, can claim—and litigate for—protected status within schools that, before 1975, would have had a freer hand to expel them.

IDEA arrived just as society was becoming suffused with the therapeutic impulse, which deemphasizes free will and moral responsibility and postulates social or physiological causes of behavior. This engenders a search for pharmacological treatments or such therapeutic "remedies" as role-playing games, breathing exercises, and learning to "identify feelings" and "manage anger." What Hymowitz calls "the skittish avoidance of moral language" by the therapeutically inclined indicates an enthusiasm for behavioral techniques and an aversion to "inducting children into moral consciousness."

If School Superintendent Gore or Bush wants school discipline that arises from a moral environment that socializes children, he should consider how schools stopped being moral communities and became cockpits for lawyers and playgrounds for therapists.

June 15, 2000

Disorder on Campus

The shaping of American minds is much on Americans' minds. A spate of recent news stories about higher education should direct attention to what it is higher than: secondary education. *The Chronicle of Higher Education* reports rising anxiety in the professoriate about declining decorum in classrooms. Students' incivilities include coming to classes late and leaving early, eating, conversing, reading newspapers, talking on cell phones, sleeping, watching portable televisions, and directing verbal abuse at teachers. The *Chronicle* reports that such problems have become common across the country.

Scruffy professors who dress slovenly and vent politics do not help. Coats and ties and other accouterments of dignity at the front of the classroom might be infectious. But the problem cannot be cured by Brooks Brothers. Neither can it be cured at the college level.

Academics being what they are, student incivility is producing a bumper crop of theories to explain the general coarsening of American life and various distortions of academic life. For example, one professor tells the *Chronicle* that when a student sits sixty rows back in a cavernous lecture hall, in a crowd of three hundred other students, such mass production of college credits is an incitement to disrespect for the setting. Furthermore, fewer and fewer students are receptive to the idea of the dignity of learning for its own sake. They respect only what they consider relevant to preparing them for the job market. Only 25 percent of undergraduates are liberal-arts majors. Twenty-five percent are business majors, and most of the rest are on vocational tracks such as health care and primary and secondary education. One professor says, "Consumerism is taking over college campuses. I'm hearing more students saying, 'After all, I pay your salary, and since I pay your salary, I should be able to tell you when I want to come to class and when my paper should be due.' Students live in a Wal-Mart society, where it's convenience that counts."

But the basic problem is that there are too many students who have neither the aptitudes nor the attitudes that should be prerequisites for going to college. More than 6 million students attend the country's 2,819 four-year institutions full-time, and 2.6 million more part-time. One in four freshmen does not return as a sophomore. Half who matriculate do not graduate even in five years. Still, colleges are churning out more graduates than the job market really requires. Anne Matthews, author of *Bright College Years: Inside the American Campus Today,* reports that a third of Domino's pizza-delivery drivers in the Washington, D.C., area have B.A.s, and an ad seeking a warehouse supervisor for the Gap reads, "Bachelor's degree required, and the ability to lift 50 pounds."

The vast majority of colleges and universities are, Matthews says, so hungry for students they are lowering admissions requirements, discounting tuitions, and advertising sushi and waffle bars in student unions and prime cable service in dorms. Rigorous institutions are more apt to have respectful students, but Matthews reports that the average student does twenty-nine hours of schoolwork a week, down from sixty hours in the early 1960s. And some of it is remedial work—learning that should have taken place in high school.

The *Los Angeles Times* reports that in the Cal State system, which has 344,000 students, almost half the freshmen need remedial work in math or English or both. At some high schools not a single student entering the Cal State system passed the basic skills tests—even though a criterion for admission is supposed to be ranking in the top third of high school graduates. There are many reasons that many high schools are not properly preparing students, but one glaring reason is this: because most institutions of higher learning have, essentially, open admissions, many high school students feel little incentive to exert themselves.

Necessity can be the mother of improvement, so if colleges got out of the remediation business, would high schools be jolted to become more demanding? That is not clear. What is clear is that as colleges become more thirsty for students, that thirst drives them to become less selective among applicants and less demanding of those admitted. So there is a trickling-down of sloth and mediocrity from higher education into secondary schools, which are not pulled toward excellence from above.

Last year Californians passed Proposition 209, barring the use of race and ethnicity as determinants of college admissions. Last week the University of California system announced a significant decline in the numbers of black and Hispanic applicants for next autumn's freshman classes. At Berkeley, blacks, Hispanics, and Native Americans, who made up 23.1 percent of 1997 admissions, made up 10.4 percent of 1998 admissions. At UCLA the decline was from 19.8 percent to 12.7 percent.

Because an expanding middle class is a source of social stability and because a college degree is a ticket to the middle class, it is desirable to increase minority enrollments. But it is imperative to do this without doing violence to the Constitution. And as Thurgood Marshall wrote in 1954 in the NAACP's brief in *Brown v. Board of Education,* "Distinctions by race are so evil, so arbitrary and invidious that a state bound to defend the equal protection of the laws must not invoke them in any public sphere." The post–Proposition 209 decline of minority admissions proves beyond peradventure that there has been systematic discrimination against whites and Asian Americans.

The decline also proves that the primary problems of American education are at the secondary school level, and in society beyond the schools. For whatever reasons, too many high schools serving minorities are failing to equip their most promising students for the most demanding institutions at the next level. Better high schools would enable colleges to be more selective and demanding, which in turn would require high schools to become yet better. By the time uncivil young adults destroy the decorum of a university, it is too late to do much about either them or it.

April 13, 1998

Education and the 9/91 Factor

With an energy that, were he a third-grader, would earn him a megadose of Ritalin, President George W. Bush this week will hopscotch from Washington, D.C., to Ohio to New Hampshire to Massachusetts for ceremonies celebrating the No Child Left Behind Act. The movable feast will wildly exaggerate the act's importance to primary and secondary education.

Its most important provisions are prerequisites for meaningful school choice, eventually. Information, generated by testing, is necessary for a market in which parents can, as comparison shoppers, hold schools accountable. Under the act, all children will be tested in math and reading every year from third through eighth grades. Students in schools that fail egregiously and protractedly will be empowered to choose other schools—but only other *public* schools *in the same school district*. Because failing schools are frequently in failing districts, the act's "choice" provisions are derisory.

Federal education legislation is rarely edifying. In 1994 the Senate, enacting the Goals 2000 education bill, issued, as is its wont, imperious commands to the future. Only two goals were quantifiable: By 2000, America's high school graduation rate would be "at least 90 percent" and students "will be first in the world in mathematics and science achievement." Senator Pat Moynihan, comparing these goals to Soviet grain production quotas, said, "That will not happen."

And of course it did not. In 2000 the graduation rate was about 75 percent, a figure inflated by "social promotions." The widely cited 86 percent figure included former high school students who pass "equivalency examinations," which are not equivalent to graduating from high school. American students ranked nineteenth among thirty-eight surveyed nations in mathematics (right below Latvia) and eighteenth in science (right below Bulgaria).

In 2000 the top five states in average SAT scores (with their ranking among the states and the District of Columbia in per-pupil spending) were:

1. North Dakota (41)
2. Iowa (25)
3. Wisconsin (10)
4. Minnesota (16)
5. South Dakota (48)

The bottom five were:

47. Texas (35)
48. North Carolina (38)
49. District of Columbia (4)
50. Georgia (31)
51. South Carolina (36)

Moynihan, being droll in order to be didactic, concluded that the best predictor of a school's performance must be its proximity to the Canadian border. He knew that ever since the baby-boom generation began moving through the school system like a pig through a python, policy makers have assumed that schools' cognitive outputs would vary directly with financial inputs to the schools. He also knew that by 1966 an ambitious government study had reached a conclusion so discomfiting the government considered not releasing it: "Schools are remarkably similar in the effect they have on the achievement of their pupils when the socioeconomic background of the students is taken into account."

Meaning: The crucial predictor of a school's performance is the quality of the children's families. Granted, many schools are heroic exceptions to this rule. Nevertheless, it is the rule.

A decade ago Paul Barton, then with the Educational Testing Service, estimated that about 90 percent of the difference among the average proficiency of the various states' schools could be explained by five factors: number of days absent from school, number of hours spent watching television, number of pages read for homework, quantity and quality of reading material in the home, and the presence of two parents in the home.

That fifth factor is supremely important, not least because it is apt to influence the other four decisively. When Barton wrote his study, "America's Smallest School: The Family," North Dakota ranked first in math scores and second in the percentage of children in two-parent families. The District of Columbia ranked next to last in math scores and last in the family composition scale.

Family decomposition should dampen this week's self-congratulatory focus on the latest education legislation. In 1958 the percentage of children born to unmarried women was 5; in 1969, 10; in 1980, 18; in 1999, 33. The especially chilling number: in 1999 almost half (48.4 percent) of all children born to women aged 20 to 24—women of all races and ethnicities—were born out of wedlock.

The importance of that for American education is in the 9/91 factor: Between birth and their nineteenth birthdays, American children spend 9 percent of their time in school, 91 percent elsewhere. The fate of American education is being shaped not by legislative acts but by the fact that, increasingly, "elsewhere" is not in an intact family.

January 6, 2002

Multiplying Knowledge at Monterey Bay

At the conclusion of his State of the Union Address in January, President Bill Clinton issued a remarkable bulletin: "The entire store of human knowledge now doubles every five years." It is not completely clear what exactly he meant.

What counts as knowledge? Every day that Congress meets results in a *Congressional Record* packed with things to know. Does the ever-expanding record of the thoughts of Al D'Amato count as an increase in the store of human knowledge? How about baseball box scores? And what of self-knowledge, as in "getting in touch with your feelings," as people do a lot of on daytime television? If such things count in the accumulation of knowledge, the reservoir of knowledge must be rising at least as rapidly as the president avers.

He spoke of the five-year doubling of knowledge about thirteen weeks ago, so the world's stock of knowledge has increased 4.89 percent since then. That augmentation of knowledge (remember, this is a 3.5 percent increase in what was already a pretty tall pile of knowledge) probably involves a quantity of the stuff greater than the sum of knowledge possessed by Leonardo da Vinci, or perhaps by all of Florence in his time. Gosh.

And consider the velocity of the multiplication of knowledge under way at California State University at Monterey Bay. It is a new institution trying to be true to the CSUMB mission of developing students who "understand the relativity of perception and hence the need to develop a sense of self-possession through a respect for self" and who "understand the creative, symbiotic interrelatedness" of humans with the earth and "the organic unity of all human cohabitation" with everything. CSUMB says:

> *Our system works a little bit like getting your driver's license. To get a driver's license, you need to demonstrate that you know how to drive and that you know the rules of the road. You can learn these things in a variety of ways. . . . When you get your license, you are not accountable for how you learned to drive, but rather for demonstrating that you are able to drive.*

There are thirteen "university learning requirements." You get the tang of the place by noting that one ULR is called "United States Histories." That plural noun signals diversity worship. CSUMB seems to consider sensitivity to "diversity" (the "English Communication" ULR stresses "empathic" listening and "sensitivity to the audience and occasion") a precondition for "learning in cross-cultural contexts" and for "cross-culturally competent citizenship in a pluralistic and global society." CSUMB says of students' "becoming their own historians":

> *They will demonstrate an understanding of their own positionality [sic], as well as a basic ability to research and evaluate a spectrum of evidence taken from any of the following areas: 1. Audio (e.g., music, radio); 2. Everyday Life (e.g., clothes, household goods and furniture, tools); 3. Oral (e.g., community storytelling, individual and family histories); 4. Performance and Ritual (e.g., ceremonies, re-enactments, theater); 5. Visual (e.g., advertisements, art, film,*

graffiti, photographs); 6. Written (e.g., government documents, magazines, newspapers, literature).

Another ULR, called "Vibrancy," serves "one of the seven academic goals of CSUMB which is: a holistic and creative sense of self." It requires students to "demonstrate an understanding of the factors that contribute to and enhance high level well-being, and an understanding of the interrelationship between intellectual, emotional, social, spiritual, environmental, and physical health as it relates to one's own life." In plain English, which does not seem to be a known dialect at CSUMB, this seems to mean eating and exercising sensibly.

There is a "Community Participation" ULR because CSUMB wants to "foster a sense of care and compassion in our students" so they can "participate in service in multicultural community settings." Under the "Creative and Artistic Expression" ULR, "each student must produce a work of art that communicates to a diverse audience." The first course listed under the "Ethics" ULR is "Environment, Culture and Ethics: Water and Humanity." The first course listed under the "Democratic Participation" ULR is "Politics of Everyday Life." Under the "Literature/Popular Culture" ULR, courses designed to help students understand "how race, ethnicity, class, gender, sexuality, disability, age and/or nationality inspire, inform, and influence writers, artists and audiences" include "Literary Analysis Through Global Narratives" and "Auto/biografias."

CSUMB is located on a recently closed army base. Some will see this as a reason to regret the end of the Cold War. Others, perhaps including the president, will see this as beating swords into the knowledge that is expanding so rapidly.

April 26, 1998

"Barkis Is Willin'"

An Address at Princeton's Sesquicentennial

Princeton is one of the few—the very few—American institutions in a position to contemplate its *next* 250 years. We are privileged to be asked to help Princeton look ahead. That said, this must be said by me: It is folly to ask journalists to say what the future will bring. After all, every four years the skies darken over Iowa and New Hampshire as journalists by the thousands fly in to give close scrutiny to the voters of those states, and every four years those journalists are surprised by what those voters do.

So do not ask journalists to prophesy. But feel free to ask them to lament, and to prescribe and proscribe. Journalists like nothing better than being normative, laying down the law about what the future *should* bring. I have been invited not to lay down the law but to make a few decorous suggestions and speculations. In the modern spirit of ruthless full disclosure, let me begin by confessing my meager qualifications for this task.

I am a faculty brat. Born into an academic family, I grew up on and around the University of Illinois campus, with two sojourns at Cornell University. In my well-spent early manhood I received nine years of higher education, a considerable expenditure of my time and other people's money. Of those nine years, the last and best three were spent here at the graduate school. Here I prepared to follow in my father's footsteps. He was a scholar, a professor of philosophy at the University of Illinois. You can perhaps gauge my seriousness as a scholar from this fact:

After receiving my B.A. degree from Trinity College in Hartford, I went abroad for a two-year degree program at Oxford. When the time came to leave Oxford, I was of two minds about my future. So I applied, successfully, to a fine law school and to a Ph.D. program at Princeton. It was a close call, but I chose Princeton because it, unlike the law school, is midway between two National League cities. If I had chosen otherwise, I would not have been in Philadelphia's Connie Mack Stadium for Sandy Koufax's last regular-season game. And I would be a lawyer. Gracious.

———

I DID indeed become a professor, for all of two and a half years, at which point I spent three years on the staff of the U.S. Senate. Then I went into—or, as my father was wont to say, I sank to—journalism.

But as a journalist, as a child of academia, and as lapsed scholar, I have had a continuing interest in the vicissitudes of America's institutions of higher education. My interest is not just that of a father with two children who have not yet been to college. And my interest is not just that of a citizen generally concerned about the vitality of the culture. I also have a vocational interest in higher education.

My vocation is public analysis of, and public argument about, public affairs, broadly understood. I understand public affairs broadly enough to encompass cultural as well as political conditions and events. And I am dismayed by the increasing thinness of the common cultural vocabulary that I can assume as I write for a mass readership. This is a particular problem for one who writes, as I do, primarily in 750-word bursts.

Brevity may be the soul of wit; it certainly is mandatory in periodic journalism. And compression is served by allusions and intimations that can move a narrative or argument with efficiency and elegance. So, as the public stock of shared cultural inheritance becomes thinner, effective writing—effective civic discourse—becomes more difficult.

Let me give some anecdotal evidence of the thinning of the common culture, bearing in mind that anecdotes are only anecdotes but that the plural of "anecdote" is "data."

In 1872 Theodore Roosevelt, Sr., took his family to Europe for an extended tour, during which his son Teddy did what fourteen-year-olds often do: he had a growth spurt. He had to buy a new suit because his wrists and ankles protruded comically from the suit he had brought from New York. Historian H. W. Brands, in his new biography *T.R.: The Last Romantic,* reports, without explaining or otherwise dwelling on the fact, that young Teddy said he and his family called this outgrown suit of clothes "my 'Smike suit' because it left my wrists and ankles as bare as those of poor Smike himself."

Well, now. When I was reading Brand's book, I was brought up short by this offhand, unelaborated reference to "Smike"—presumably a literary figure, with whom the Roosevelt family was obviously familiar and I was not. However, the name "Smike" did have a faintly familiar ring. It had, in fact, a Dickensian flavor, and in time I recalled its origin. Smike was one of the forty urchins so badly treated by the loathsome Wackford Squeers—talk about a Dickensian name—at Dotheboys Hall, the Yorkshire school that Dickens sketched so darkly in *Nicholas Nickleby.*

What struck me as a fascinating cultural datum was the fact that for fourteen-year-old Teddy and his family, this secondary character from a Dickens novel—a novel published thirty-four years before the Roosevelts' European tour—was so familiar to them. Smike was part of the shared vocabulary, the casual discourse of this family.

Obviously the Roosevelt family was not a typical American family. It was much better educated and more comfortably situated than most families of that day—or of ours, for that matter. And T.R. had a prodigious appetite for books. Brands notes that early in 1910, while T.R. was on safari in the African bush, hunting big game, he put his knife through the brain of a deadly puff adder and then said, "I slipped it into my saddle pocket, where its blood stained the pigskin cover of the little pocket 'Nibelungenlied' which that day I happened to carry." On the same trip Roosevelt wrote of reading Poe while on the upper Nile.

So let us stipulate that T.R. was an astonishing force of nature and therefore is of limited use as a retrospective cultural indicator. However, later on in Brand's book I was again brought up short by a similar literary reference that was casually used by a contemporary of Roosevelt.

Brand's narrative had reached 1910. Teddy Roosevelt was now a former president, had been for two years, and was not happy in that status. The polit-

ical mores of that day required would-be candidates to manifest a certain dif-
fidence, if not reluctance. But T.R. was hoping to be enticed—only pro forma
enticement would have been needed—to seek the 1912 Republican nomination, in a contest with his former friend and protégé, the incumbent president,
William Howard Taft.

During a trip to Boston, T.R. stayed at the home of a supporter. When
journalists asked the supporter if T.R. would be a candidate in 1912, the supporter answered simply, "Barkis is willin'." Barkis, my refreshed memory
eventually told me, was the wagon driver in *David Copperfield* who relentlessly
courted Clara Peggotty, Copperfield's childhood nurse. Dickens's readers remembered Barkis for his reiteration of the phrase "Barkis is willin'."

Surely this tells us something significant about America today that we do
not converse the way people did in T.R.'s yesterday. But what *is* the significance of the fact that, in the tenth decade of this century, you are unlikely to
encounter what Brands reports from the first decade—the easy, unaffected insertion of such a literary reference into the conversation between a political
person and journalists?

Before attempting to answer that question, let me give one more example
of interesting communication.

In June 1940 a British officer in the desperate circumstances of Dunkirk
beach flashed to London a three-word message: "But if not." What meaning,
if any, would we find in such a—to us—opaque message?

Far from seeming opaque in 1940, it was instantly recognized, as its sender
assumed it would be, as a biblical quotation. It is from the Book of Daniel,
from the passage in which Nebuchadnezzar commands Shadrach, Meshach,
and Abed-nego to either worship the golden image or be thrust into the fiery
furnace. The three threatened men respond defiantly, ". . . our God whom we
serve is able to deliver us from the burning fiery furnace, and he will deliver us
out of thine hand, O king. But if not, be it known unto thee, O king, that we
will not serve thy gods, nor worship the golden image."

This is, at least to me, an astonishing and deeply stirring episode. Here we
have an officer with his back to the English Channel and his face to the
Wehrmacht. In this extreme situation, he expresses his heroic defiance with
breathtaking elegance and economy. I especially stress, and envy, the economy.
He distilled his situation and moral stance into three words—three syllables,
actually. In the cacophony of war, in the deadly confusion of an evacuation
under attack, he deftly plucked from the then-common culture—mind you,
this was less than sixty years ago—an almost universally familiar fragment of a
passage from a book. With the fragment he connected himself, and his inter-
locutors, with a resonant story from the Western canon.

Now bear with me for one more example of discourse leavened by literature.

This is a quite contemporary example, from a column in *Newsweek*. The columnist is Meg Greenfield, the editor of *The Washington Post's* editorial page.

In one of her recent back-page columns in *Newsweek,* Meg marveled at the thinking, or want of thinking, that had brought President Bill Clinton to his current unhappy condition. Her subject is not just his interesting glandular life but his subsequent denials of it. Here is a bit of what Meg wrote about what he did after the scandal story broke in January:

> He is the president of the United States. He was in a very high-stakes conflict, and he knew it. He put his chips—his honor, and the prestige of his job—on a very big, cynical, overt lie, took a gargantuan gamble that he could bring it off and lost. His repeated assurances of his sincerity were so extreme, overimpassioned and finally, on those accounts, so unconvincing, that many people who at least suspected better believed him. Paradoxically, when it turned out that there was no fallback plan here, no thought for what could come next, the improvisation simply went forward until he ended up in the same unforgiving ditch as the other notorious deniers of truth in our 20th-century playbook. What, you can't help wondering, did they think was going to happen? Mr. Micawber himself would have found this an awfully laid-back program.

Well, hello, Wilkins Micawber, old friend. Micawber is, of course, David Copperfield's impecunious friend, the incurable optimist who, living always on the precipice of ruin, is forever reassuring himself and those around him not to worry because something will turn up.

Meg Greenfield's use of Micawber to illuminate presidential behavior is not just elegant and amusing. It is *economical.* We who discuss public affairs in public, for a large public, come to value economy of expression. The columnist's craft is a humble one, but it does have its rigors. A columnist is required to be brief and to change the subject frequently. But above all, be brief. To write newspaper columns is to learn to talk about important complexities, from nuclear weapons to the infield fly rule, in 750-word chunks. We who are given an entire page of *Newsweek* to fill can natter on at greater length—about 980 words.

In such writing, literary and historical allusions are not just pretty filigrees, they are practical necessities. They enable us to make a large point with a small reference. They help us to save time and words by triggering a response from the readership's reservoir of shared understandings. As that reservoir runs dry, writing—communicating—becomes more difficult, more tedious, more labored, less efficient.

You may have little interest in my parochial pleading on behalf of those who write in periodic journalism. But this should interest you: The various episodes I have cited, ranging from Teddy Roosevelt to Meg Greenfield, give rise to three questions. Has something—something directly pertinent to higher education—changed in a way that makes such dipping into a deep common culture less and less possible? If so, does that matter? If it matters, what is to be done?

My answers to those questions are: Something has changed; the change is profoundly disturbing; and if Princeton and places like it (not that there really are any places quite like Princeton) cannot do something about it, then we are all truly sunk.

Obviously something, or some set of things, has caused a thinning of the fabric of the common culture. The shared stock of literary and historical knowledge—the furniture of the public mind, or at any rate the mind of the portion of the public that is at least mildly interested in the national conversation about serious subjects—is not as plentiful and sturdy as it used to be.

The reason why can be reduced to a word: reading. Reading matters less to people than it once did. People, especially young people, do less of it than young people used to do. And people read less ardently, less passionately than they did, say, around 1840, when Dickens was publishing *The Old Curiosity Shop* serially in newspapers. Some of Dickens's devoted readers in New York City are said to have gone to the docks when transatlantic ships arrived with English newspapers, anxiously shouting up to the crew members on deck, "Did Little Nell die?"

Times and sensibilities change, and years later Oscar Wilde said that anyone who could read of the death of Little Nell without laughing must have a heart of stone. But without, perhaps, regretting the passing of the hunger for Dickensian melodrama, one can very much regret the passing of the passionate reading public.

On a more serious plane, it is simply impossible to imagine a book, any book on any subject, having the impact that Harriet Beecher Stowe's *Uncle Tom's Cabin* had when published in 1852. From Princeton's own Professor James McPherson, from his wonderful history *Battle Cry of Freedom,* we learn that Stowe's novel sold 300,000 copies in the United States alone in the first year of its publication. Relative to population, this is comparable to selling more than 3 million copies in a year today. And the literate population was much smaller then. Within a decade it sold more than 2 million copies in the United States. It is to this day the best-selling book of all time in proportion to population.

Lincoln may or may not have said to her, when she visited the White House, "So you're the little woman who started this big war." But because opinion drives events in a democracy, her book was a precipitant of the war.

Graham Greene used to distinguish between those of his works that were literature and those that were mere "entertainments." Let us say, for the sake of argument, that both *The Old Curiosity Shop* and *Uncle Tom's Cabin* were entertainments. Still, not all the ways that society entertains itself are of equal dignity and worth.

Contemporary America can still work itself into something of a swivel over the question of "Who shot J.R.?" (For the forgetful among you, J.R. was a nefarious character on the television drama *Dallas*. For the *really* forgetful who do not even remember *Dallas*, congratulations.) More recently, the American public became quite excited when anticipating the last episode of *Seinfeld*. In Saint Louis, this became a civic festival: a huge crowd gathered to see the episode shown on the side of a building. Now, just five months later, does anyone remember anything about the final *Seinfeld* episode?

A century and a half on, Micawber and Little Nell, Pickwick and Mr. Bumble, and a host of other Dickensian figures are still part, if a steadily diminishing part, of our common conversation. Who really thinks that even just ten years from now such *Seinfeld* characters as George Constanza or Kramer will remain fixtures in the public mind?

These somewhat dyspeptic ruminations of mine are perhaps partly a response to the current vulgarity of life in the town in which I live and work. The fact that vulgarians are thick on the ground in the nation's capital is not news; it is not a new phenomenon. But partly as respite from the sheer tawdriness of the company town in which I work, I have recently read Dumas Malone's six-volume biography of the most cultivated president the Republic has ever had, Thomas Jefferson.

In volume five, Malone discusses Jefferson's wonderful correspondence with his cultivated predecessor, John Adams, and also Jefferson's reading habits in retirement and his role in the creation of the Library of Congress. Malone writes, "Jefferson read ancient history with avidity and talked about the great Greek and Roman figures with more familiarity than most educated Americans of today speak of him and John Adams."

Remember Henry Adams's dark jest that the succession of presidents from Washington to Grant disproved the theory of evolution? What are we to make of the succession of presidents from, say, Teddy Roosevelt to the current one, of whom it was written, when he returned to Oxford as president, that he was returning to the place where he didn't inhale, didn't get drafted, and didn't get a degree? This is the president who during the 1996 campaign said, "The last time I checked, the Constitution said, 'Of the people, by the people and for the people.' That's what the Declaration of Independence says." The president was, of course, wrong—twice. He put language from 1863—from the Gettysburg Address—into documents from 1776 and 1787.

But why should we expect more cultural literacy of a president—even one who once taught constitutional law—than of a Harvard professor of English? One of those, testifying in the obscenity trial of the rap group 2 Live Crew, cited, as proof of the respectable poetic tradition of sexually explicit imagery, what he identifies as "Shakespeare's 'My love is like a red, red rose.'"

Perhaps a Princeton audience will take malicious pleasure from the fact that the Harvard professor confused Shakespeare with Robert Burns or that a future president seems to have passed through Yale's law school unscathed by close acquaintance with the Constitution. However, no one should take pleasure from living in what the writer Mark Steyn calls a "present-tense culture."

Ours is increasingly an electronic culture that lacks, as it were, a button to give the "save" command. Near many schools nowadays you see signs proclaiming a "Drug-Free School Zone." As Steyn says, we could more accurately have signs announcing "Latin-Free School Zones" or even "Dickens-Free School Zones."

Living remorselessly in the present tense, we treat school curricula as so much soft wax, taking the impress of the intellectual whims and fads of the moment. So assigned reading is forever being fine-tuned for "relevance," which is defined as service to fluid notions of multicultural "diversity." As Steyn says, such diversity reflects a society's narcissism, which produces, paradoxically, not true heterodoxy and cosmopolitanism but rather homogeneity and parochialism.

What is to be done? Schools, including universities, must insist upon the prestige of reading, and especially of reading old books. Americans are not reading the way they used to, and that is unfortunate. The printed word is doing well in America, principally because of newspapers and magazines. However, as purchasers of books, measured per capita, Americans fall far behind, for example, the British and Germans. American publishers produce about 50,000 new titles a year. So do the British, for a much smaller market. Germany, with a population less than one-third of that of the United States, publishes 60,000 titles.

Americans spend big sums on books—about $26 billion annually on books of all sorts, from cookbooks to Bibles to textbooks to novels. That $26 billion is equal to the amount Americans spend annually on cosmetics and hair care. The average expenditure on books by the approximately 100 million American households is $160. The average household buys eighteen books per year. But to prevent a premature outbreak of cheerfulness, let me put this in perspective.

A huge best-seller that "everyone is reading"—for example, *Angela's Ashes*—might sell 2 million copies. A John Grisham novel typically sells 2 million in hardback and another 3 million in paperback. This means that any World Wrestling Federation event on cable television draws an audience larger than the audience for the best-selling author in history. The video of the movie *Titanic* sold more copies in its first week on sale than the book *Midnight in the Garden of Good and Evil* sold in its first fifty-two weeks on *The New York Times'* bestseller list.

———

I DON'T want to sound like a curmudgeon . . .

Wait. Strike that. I do, of course, want to sound like a curmudgeon. I make much of my living sounding that way. It is called doing what comes naturally. A conservative's vocation—literally, his calling—is to affirm standards that are out of date. As a great wit (the playwright Alan Bennet) has said, standards are always out of date. That is why they are called standards.

Still, my aim is not to be just one more voice in the swelling chorus of complaint about the dumbing down of everything. So I shall not dwell on the fact that more high school students can name the Three Stooges than can name the three branches of government and many more can identify Leonardo DiCaprio than Al Gore.

Rather, my aim—and here I speak as a public commentator—is to warn that there is a seamlessness to cultural memory. A present-tense culture will forget more than who Smike, Barkis, and Micawber were. It also will forget who Clay, Calhoun, and Webster were and why they mattered and still do.

A common cultural vocabulary is more than just, in Burke's words, "the decent drapery of life." It is more than merely decorative. It is practical, because it facilitates adult conversation. As Steyn says, societies should be like icebergs: "beneath the surface, there's the unseen seven-eighths, the shared history on which the top eighth sits." Unfortunately, the bottom seven-eighths is melting because "a modern, electronic culture exists in a state of perpetual anticipation" of the new.

I am, I know, biting some of the hands that feed me when I say I agree with Steyn's warning that *all* institutions are in danger in a media age, an age of saturation journalism. It used to be that there was journalism from the early-morning chat shows until whenever Ted Koppel got sleepy. Now things are even worse. There is nonstop, wall-to-wall journalism. And much of it is, in its ravenous hunger for novelty and the new, increasingly indistinguishable from the entertainment wing of the media. A media-besotted age assumes the anachronistic nature of anything whose authority has anything to do with its longevity.

Cicero warned that "to know nothing of what happened before you were born is to remain ever a child." But as Steyn says, that warning loses its bite in a society that aspires to remain childlike—that is, aspires to live, as children do, in a perpetual present.

A society worthy of, and safe for, adults is one in which a wise person lives with a crick in his or her neck, a crick from looking backward. That may not seem a heroic stance, but it is prudent.

It also is a form of democratic politeness to the most numerous constituency—our ancestors. G. K. Chesterton understood this:

> . . . *tradition is only democracy extended through time. . . . Tradition may be defined as an extension of the franchise. . . . It is the democracy of the dead. Tradition refuses to submit to the small and arrogant oligarchy of those who merely happen to be walking about. All democrats object to men being disqualified by the accident of birth; tradition objects to their being disqualified by the accident of death.*

Which is why Woodrow Wilson worried that Americans were "in danger to lose our identity and become"—in Wilson's well-chosen word—"infantile in every generation. . . . We stand dismayed to find ourselves growing no older, always as young as the information of our most numerous voters. . . . The past is discredited among them because they played no part in choosing it."

A university can fulfill the role Wilson assigned it, as society's "seat of vital memory" and "organ of recollection," only if it sets out to reward reading by augmenting the prestige of readers.

I write for newspapers and magazines; I work on television. But this I know: Books remain the best, the primary carriers of ideas, and history is the history of mind. It is not only because ideas have consequences but because only ideas have large and lasting consequences. Ours is a proudly practical society that prefers people of "action" to people of mere contemplation. But the rise—the inundating rise—of graphic journalism and entertainment has at least served to remind us of a basic fact:

Reading is an *activity*. It involves the active engagement of the mind in ways that contrast sharply with the essential passivity that is possible with—passivity that is even required for—the ingestion of most electronic communication. So reading is demanding, often difficult—even, it is not too much to say, strenuous. Which is why most people, most of the time, would rather do something else.

Which is why it must be encouraged, not merely by being required but by being honored.

Which is as close as I am going to come to an agenda for action. If my lamentations are sound, Princeton will know better than I do what to do about them. In any case, I thank Princeton for the privilege of this opportunity to unburden myself of these thoughts, and I thank all of you for your patience in hearing me out.

I close by noting that there is still time, before dinner, to drop by a bookstore, which I intend to do.

October 23, 1998

Virtues Versus Values
Commencement Address at Lafayette College

Mr. President, members of the Board of Trustees, distinguished faculty, proud parents—proud and somewhat-lighter-in-the-wallet parents—and especially members of the Class of 2000—make that "fellow members of the Class of 2000."

What I say *may* come too late to do you a lick of good, you who today take your leave of this fine institution, but I will say it anyway: I think I have finally figured out the purpose of higher education. I have acquired this sunburst of understanding, if such it truly is, by thinking long and hard about an offensive—at least to me—aspect of American politics just now. I refer to the incessant and ubiquitous talk about "values."

Today our nation is enjoying peace and unprecedented prosperity. These happy circumstances allow, even seem to *demand,* a preoccupation with the teaching of what are nowadays called "values." The word "values" is a relatively new, and I believe regrettable, vocabulary for discussing a recurring American preoccupation: the possible decay of our national character.

When the Marquis de Lafayette returned to America for a hero's tour in 1824—which tour led to the naming of this college—his extended visit catalyzed the young republic's unease about what it sensed was a decline from the pinnacle achieved by the revolutionary generation, which by then had largely passed from the scene.

Then, as now, the nation was feeling its oats economically but was also feeling queasy about whether its character was as strong as its economy. Indeed, it worried that the *process* by which it was becoming rich—the banking, industrialization, speculation, and urbanization of early capitalism—was leading it away from the sturdy virtues of a yeoman's republic.

However, the anxiety of that day was not voiced in talk about values. Instead, Americans talked then as the Founders had talked: of *virtues.* You may well wonder: values, virtues, what's the difference? Consider. I think the difference is large.

Historian Gertrude Himmelfarb rightly says that political talk about values is now so ubiquitous we forget how new such talk is. It began, Himmelfarb says, just seventeen years ago, during Britain's 1983 general election campaign, when Prime Minister Margaret Thatcher jauntily embraced the accusation—and it was an accusation—that she favored "*Victorian values.*" Except, of course, that the Victorians themselves, those muscular moralists, never spoke of values but of virtues.

Once upon a time the word "values" was used most as a verb, meaning "to esteem," as in "I value your friendship." It was also a singular noun, such as in "inflation hurts the value of the currency." However in today's political discourse, "value" is becoming a *plural* noun denoting beliefs and attitudes of individuals and societies. And what this means is that Friedrich Nietzsche's nihilistic intent, the *de*-moralization of society, is advancing.

The de-moralization of society is advanced when the word "values" supplants the word "virtues" in political and ethical contexts. When we move beyond talk of good and evil, when the categories virtue and vice are transcended, we are left with the thin gruel of values-talk.

Oh, but how very democratic values-talk is. Unlike virtues, *everyone* has *lots* of values; *everyone* has as many as he or she chooses. Hitler had *scads* of values. George Washington had *virtues.* Who among those who knew him— surely not the Marquis de Lafayette—would have spoken of George Washington's values? No one.

Values-talk, alas, suits today's zeitgeist. It is the talk of a nonjudgmental age. Ours is an age judgmental *only* about the sin of being judgmental. Today it is a mark of broad-mindedness to say, "Oh, one person's values are as good as another's." But it is, of course, nonsense to say, "One person's virtues are as good as another's."

Values are an equal-opportunity business. They are mere *choices.* In contrast, virtues are habits, difficult to develop and therefore not accessible to all. Therefore, speaking of virtues rather than values is elitist, offensive to democracy's egalitarian, leveling ethos, which I say is precisely *why* talk of virtues *should* be revived and talk of values *should* be abandoned.

Another great Frenchman, Alexis de Tocqueville, who toured America not long after Lafayette did, noted that although much is gained by replacing aristocratic institutions and suppositions with democratic ones, something valuable is often lost. What is lost is the ability to recognize and the hunger to honor hierarchies of achievement and character. Therefore, democracy requires the cultivation of preventive virtues. Preventive virtues are those that counter certain unhealthy tendencies in democracies.

Let us hear about this from a man who is currently completing a new translation of de Tocqueville's magnificent *Democracy in America.* I refer to Harvey Mansfield. Harvey C. Mansfield, because of his opposition to grade inflation, is known at Harvard as "Harvey C-minus Mansfield." He is Harvard's conservative.

He notes that a theme of American literature, writ large, for example, in the works of Mark Twain, is the effect of democracy on the higher qualities of human beings. To counter democracy's leveling ethos, with its tinge of envy of those who possess scarce excellence, universities, Harvey Mansfield says, should teach students to *praise.*

Students, that is, should learn to look up, up to the heroic in thought and action, in politics and history and literature, in science and faith. After all, the few men and women who become heroes do so by looking up, by being *pulled up* by some vision of nobility, which makes a hero quite unlike, something quite different from, a role model. The concept of "role model" is also a very democratic notion. A role model is someone anyone can successfully choose to emulate.

Here, then, is higher education's special purpose in a democratic culture: to turn young people toward what is high.

A wit has said that in the nineteenth century England's ruling class developed its system of elite secondary schools for the purpose of making sure that Byron and Shelley could never happen again. The purpose of American higher education is *not* to serve as a values cafeteria where young people are encouraged to pick whichever strikes their fancy. Rather, the purpose of higher education for citizens of a democracy should be to help them identify excellence in its various realms and to understand what virtues make it so.

This message for a commencement season is also perennially germane to our political seasons. When you hear, as you frequently will this year, politicians speaking of their values and America's values, values here and values there, understand that you are in the presence of America's problem, not America's solution.

There, that is my message. I have said elsewhere that no matter *what* columnists say, they *must* say it briefly. Brevity is not among the columnist's *values*. Rather, brevity is a columnist's necessary *virtue*.

Again I thank this college for giving me the privilege of delivering the last lecture to the Class of 2000. I thank you all for the courtesy of your attentiveness. Now go forth and have fun, you've earned it. You have earned it by meeting the high standards of this college, a college worthy of its basketball team, a college whose founders named it for the Marquis de Lafayette, and who did that, they said, because of their respect for—listen to this language, I'm quoting the founders of your college—Lafayette's "talents, *virtues,* and signal services . . . [to] the great cause of freedom."

Virtues, not values. Thank you.

May 20, 2000

Rule by Microrules
Commencement Address at Washington University
in Saint Louis

I was *born* into university life as the son of a professor of philosophy at the University of Illinois. And at the beginning of my adult life, I was, briefly, a professor, at a time when campus turmoil was causing many Americans to consider America's professoriate a source of mischief and unwisdom.

I recall the night in 1976 when a former Harvard professor, my friend Pat Moynihan, won the Democratic nomination to run for the New York Senate seat held by Jim Buckley. That night Buckley said he looked forward to running against *Professor* Moynihan and that he was sure *Professor* Moynihan would conduct a high-level campaign suited to a Harvard *professor.* Over at Moynihan's headquarters, reporters told Pat that Jim Buckley was referring to him as "Professor Moynihan." Pat exclaimed, in mock dismay, "Ahh, the mudslinging has begun."

A commencement speaker is, awkwardly, the last obstacle standing between eager young people and the world which they think is their oyster. So I promise adherence to the rule that brevity is not only the soul of wit and the essence of lingerie; brevity is, on occasions such as this, mandatory.

You will be comforted to know that in practicing our craft, we columnists are required to be brief and change the subject frequently. However, speakers generally should have just *one* thumping point of great practicality—as, for example, the late Conrad Hilton had when he appeared on *The Tonight Show* with Johnny Carson. Carson said to Mr. Hilton, "You're a giant of American attainment, a legend in your own time, you've built hotels all over the world, turn to the camera right over there, look your fellow countrymen in the eye, and tell them the one thing based on your life's work that you would like your fellow countrymen to know." Like a great trooper, Hilton turned to the camera, looked America in the eye, and said, "Please, put the curtain inside the tub." If you owned a quarter of a million bathtubs, you would say the same thing.

Commencement speakers are supposed to send graduates forth full of pithy advice, so I recently reviewed some randomly selected commencement speeches given by others. One speaker said to the graduates: You are about to leave a beautiful campus devoted to the contemplation of beauty and the exploration of complexity. So, the speaker said, my advice is simply this: Don't go. Refuse to leave. Life is all downhill from here.

A make-believe commencement address, written by someone who claimed to have been overdosed on coffee and M&Ms, offered graduates two injunctions:

Use sunscreen and floss regularly. Good advice, but not as important as the advice that I herewith give you, drawing on my expertise in the field in which I most want to have expertise. To Washington University's Class of 1998, I say my cardinal rule of life is: With a runner on second and no outs, try to hit behind the runner.

These microrules—put the curtain inside the tub, use sunscreen, floss, hit behind the runner—may seem to you a tad too minor to merit attention, particularly on a day this momentous. However (and here we come to my macropoint), small rules illuminate a few huge truths about lives—about the lives of individuals, and the lives of nations.

One truth is this: follow the simple microrules and you might avoid a lot of macroproblems that will elicit ever more complex and coagulating rules, laws, and regulations.

Another truth is this: There are moments, and you are graduating into one, when people complain—well, journalists, who are not exactly people, complain—that there is scant news because the nation has a "miniaturized" political agenda. Well, Class of 1998, let me tell you: this miniaturized national agenda is a sign of national health. And this health has something to do with learning—rediscovering, really—simple rules.

Let me give you two examples. One concerns the physical health of individuals and health care policy. The other concerns our collective life—social policy, pertaining to poverty and education.

First, individual health. Does America want to improve its public health and significantly reduce the portion of GDP devoted to health care? If so then America needs to substantially reduce only *five* things: vehicular accidents, violence, coronary heart disease, lung cancer, and AIDS. And Americans *can* reduce these five by simply deciding to do so.

What do those five have in common? They are *all*, to a *significant* extent, results of *behavior*—behavior *known* to be risky. So a substantial improvement in public health could be achieved by people deciding to behave more prudently—by deciding not to smoke, and to eat and drink and engage in sex more sensibly.

You see? Simple rules, no more recondite or demanding than "put the curtain inside the tub" or "hit behind the runner." Now consider the role that can be played by simple rules in public policy. Consider what we have learned about the problem of intractable poverty.

It turns out there are three rules for avoiding long-term poverty—rules that make it unlikely that a person adhering to them will fall into such poverty. The three rules are: First, graduate from high school. Second, have no child out of wedlock. Third, have no child before you are twenty.

This is not a moral assertion, it is an empirical observation: the portion of the population that today is caught in long-term poverty consists *overwhelmingly* of people who have disregarded one or more of those rules.

Notice that, again, we are talking about a problem driven by behavior. Regarding poverty, we have in recent years done some impressive social learning. We have learned that a premise of social policy from the 1930s through the 1960s is no longer apposite.

The social policies put in place in those years were shaped by people who *themselves* were shaped by the searing experience of *material* deprivation in the 1930s—unemployment. And the premise of those policies was that long-term poverty existed in our wealthy nation *only* because we had not distributed our material abundance equitably and rationally. The premise was that poverty could be cured by government fiat, by the redistribution of goods and services that government knew *how* to distribute: money, housing, schools, transportation, jobs.

In 1966 Sargent Shriver, a good and intelligent man, was in charge of President Lyndon Johnson's "war on poverty." While testifying to Congress, Shriver was asked how long it would take to end poverty in America. Shriver said: Ten years. That was not a foolish answer—*if* the premise of social policy was correct—if poverty was *material* poverty, to be cured by *material* measures.

But at about that time, in the mid-1960s, two lines on a graph crossed, ominously. They crossed in a way that was counterintuitive. One was a *declining* line denoting the *decreasing* rate of unemployment. The other was a *rising* line denoting an *increase* in long-term welfare dependency. What did this mean?

It meant that in a portion of the nation, we were dealing with an impacted poverty that was—and is—immune to even powerful and protracted economic growth. Between 1940 and 1965 the portion of Americans living in poverty declined from about 30 percent to 17 percent. Since then it has declined only slightly, to 13 percent. This after more than *three* decades of formidable wealth creation by the economy and after *trillions* of dollars of government spending against poverty.

The problem, again, is behavior. The problem is not material poverty but rather a poverty of *intangible social capital*—a poverty of *inner* resources, of the habits, mores, values, customs, and dispositions necessary for an individual to thrive in a complex urban, industrial society. These missing attributes range from industriousness to sexual continence, from the ability to defer gratification to the determination to abstain from substance abuse.

This is a sobering diagnosis because government does *not* know *how* to replenish such intangible social capital once it has been dissipated. Any list of the government's most substantial successes in the century is apt to be long on *material* achievements: the TVA, the Manhattan and Apollo projects, the interstate highway system. Other successes include the civil rights acts, but with those, the government was *not* required to impart aptitudes *to* people; rather, government was removing *impediments to* the exercise of aptitudes by people.

Or consider two of the most successful social programs of the century: Social Security and the GI Bill. Social Security largely eliminated poverty in the elderly portion of the population. But this attack on poverty was *not complicated*. It involved nothing more complex than mailing checks to a stable population group. And the GI Bill, which did so much to make America a nation of upwardly mobile, college-educated homeowners, identified socially useful attributes, and rewarded those who *possessed* those attributes—attributes such as a drive for education, and the industriousness and thriftiness necessary to finance a mortgage.

We now know what is required to get those who are trapped in poverty onto the ladder of upward mobility. What is required is some mixture of incentives and other assistance for those people to live by some simple rules of prudence. Again, small rules of behavior.

Similarly, after forty years of trying to improve education from grades K through 12 by a mixture of money and educational fads, we now know that the best predictor of a school's performance is the caliber of the families from which the children come to school. Indeed, the four most crucial variables in determining a school's success are not variables at school. They are the number of parents in the home, the amount of homework done in the home, the quantity and quality of reading matter in the home, and the amount of television watched in the home. Government can do next to nothing to influence these variables.

So yet again: Small rules of behavior, not unlike putting the curtain inside the tub and hitting behind the runner.

We are nearing the end of a century that future historians may denote as "the century of the state." It has been a century during which governments have grown to hitherto *unimagined* proportions and in some places have committed *evils* hitherto unimagined. In our favored nation, government has made its share of mistakes but also has done much ameliorative good. However, in this century we became too enamored of government, too enthralled by the idea that clever experts in the upper reaches of government could concoct sophisticated solutions for all of our social ailments.

This faith in social salvation through "scientific" government—rule by experts—flared brightly at the dawn of this century. It was the Progressives' credo. Their program was to centralize power in Washington to enable the instructed few to direct the lives of the uninstructed many. *Unbounded* faith in a new science of society led to the election, in 1912, of a president who had been a professor—of political science, naturally—Woodrow Wilson.

We are wiser, now. Sadder, perhaps, but wiser, certainly. We now know that society flourishes when and only when its molecular unit, the family, flourishes. We know that lasting improvement comes only in the small increments produced by individuals adhering to the simple rules of life.

Professor Glenn Loury, an African-American sociologist at Boston University, recently gave one of his books a title that is a formula for improving society one person at a time. The title is: *One by One, from the Inside Out.* And always, that means living by the little rules with the big consequences.

A few years ago I wrote a book on baseball. One of my subjects now works here in Saint Louis: Tony La Russa, manager of the Cardinals. I may say that parenthetically that Tony is here in the quadrangle this morning. If any of you can pitch, please see him before tonight's game. From him I learned that there is only one way for a team to win consistently. It is all very well to have some prodigies of nature, such as Mark McGwire, who can hit the ball into another zip code. But Mark McGwires are rare, and even they, like all ballplayers, fail more often than not. Remember, the best hitter in baseball this year will fail about 65 percent of the time. So the only way to win consistently is by doing the little things—obeying the little rules of baseball—such as hitting behind the runner.

And with that reiteration of my point—my plea for the continuing relevance of life's little rules—I shall now close. I do not mind you looking at your watches, but you who are holding your watches up to your ears are telling me something.

However, as I speak here in Saint Louis, just a medium-length Mark McGwire fly ball from where the Cardinals play, I want to dispense one more dollop of advice.

It is: Take care of your children. In particular, do not let your children make momentous decisions at too young an age. I speak from bitter experience.

I grew up over in Champaign, Illinois, midway between Chicago and Saint Louis. And at an age too tender for life-shaping decisions, I made one. While all my friends were becoming Cardinals fans, I became a Cubs fan.

My friends, happily rooting for Stan Musial, Red Schoendienst, and other great Redbirds, grew up cheerfully convinced that the world is a benign place. So, of course, they became liberals. Rooting for the Cubs of the late 1940s and early 1950s, I became gloomy, pessimistic, morose, dyspeptic—in a word, conservative. It is well known, of course, that the Cubs last won the World Series in 1908, which is two years before Mark Twain and Tolstoy died. But that means, Class of 1998, that the Cubs are in the eighty-ninth year of their rebuilding effort, and remember, any team can have a bad century.

So, fellow members of the Class of 1998, my last piece of advice is "Mamas, don't let your babies grow up to be Cubs fans." But my advice is really more than that. It is another simple old rule that we are, as a nation, *belatedly* rediscovering. It is this: The most important business of one generation is the raising of the next generation. Nothing you do in life will be as deeply satisfying to you as what your parents are experiencing this morning—the joy of watching their children enter honorable adulthood with the momentum imparted by an education from a great university.

Again, I thank the university for allowing me to speak here. I thank all of you for your attentiveness. And I particularly thank my classmates for their patience with this, their last lecture at Washington University.

Now, classmates, go forth and have fun. You have earned it.

May 15, 1998

"Recognition" in San Francisco

SAN FRANCISCO—In this caricature by the bay there has been a ruckus over a requirement that high school students read works by "people of color." Nationally, there is an epidemic of "road rage"—aggressive drivers running red lights and venting high-speed hostility toward other drivers, toward the law, and perhaps toward the hand that life has dealt.

What might a battle over books and motorized strife have in common? Perhaps both pertain to the politics of recognition.

A member of San Francisco's school board says, "We are now the first district in the nation to require the reading of nonwhite authors. We also voted for a requirement that writers who are lesbian, gay, bisexual, and transgender be identified." The board, a nest of San Francisco moderates, rejected a proposal to require that 70 percent of the books be by nonwhite authors.

Supporters of the new requirement say it recognizes "marginalized" voices and rebukes the unjust, such as Mark Twain, who allegedly was disrespectful toward African-Americans, and Chaucer, who sank to portraying people based on their socioeconomic class. The board's action was justified with reference to "diversity," as though diversity would be lacking in a syllabus covering, say, Jane Austen, Mark Twain, and Thomas Mann. There also was much talk about the importance of readings that "reflect the culture" of the students, as though an Asian-American teenager born and raised here finds his or her culture reflected in a book written by an Asian in Asia.

When supporters of more color-conscious reading requirements explain their support, certain phrases recur. School reading lists should "validate who we are." "We are all here, so we might as well have a voice." The 87 percent of San Francisco students who are not white "deserve recognition."

This is the language of identity politics, which defines individuals by the groups into which they can be lumped. The premise of identity politics is that most groups have been "marginalized" by whites, who are no longer demographically dominant.

The language of this city's curriculum skirmish supports a thesis of a new book, *Speaking Respect, Respecting Speech.* In it professor Richard Abel of UCLA Law School argues "the centrality of the struggle for respect in contemporary political life."

But why has the competition for status become more intense and become focused more on cultural affirmations—recognition—than on government-distributed material rewards? Abel suggests that the political parties have become "indistinguishable on bread-and-butter issues." Certainly the liberal party has turned from material redistribution to status politics, promising a new hierarchy of respect through the redistribution of esteem.

One of Abel's surmises seems exactly wrong. He suggests that as economic growth slows, "frustrated ambitions are rechanneled into status claims." But status politics—the allocation by government of honor and social standing—is intensifying as (has Abel noticed?) the economy soars. It is more likely that status anxieties are actually sharpened by affluence, which blurs old status symbols.

Joseph Schumpeter said the invention of nylon reduced the social distance, as measured by consumption, between the duchess who wore silk and the shop clerk who wore cotton. Time was, the upper crust rode in carriages, the lower orders walked. No such dramatic difference distinguishes the driver of a Porsche from the driver of a Pontiac. So "conspicuous consumption" has lost much saliency as a signal of status. And public policies—from San Francisco's affirmative action reading requirements to apologies and other propitiations for various grievance groups—become the signalers.

This makes for rancid politics because status competition is fueled by envy, the only one of the seven deadly sins that does not give the sinner even momentary pleasure. And what becomes of those whose status anxiety is not assuaged by participation in group entitlements to government-affirmed esteem? Some vent their resentments in road rage.

As material abundance grows, society's relative scarcity of recognition and prestige (ranging from mere victimhood to today's platinum bliss, celebrity) becomes an intensifying ache. That imbecile in the BMW, who just endangered his life and yours by running a red light in order to get to the next one, has been deranged by a shattering realization: He is not eligible for the recognition sweepstakes that increasingly define politics. And as a conferrer of derivative status, a BMW is not what it—let alone what a carriage and six horses—used to be.

His driving is a cry for help, the poor thing. Of course, individuals craving esteem could stop waiting for someone or something to confer it. They could try earning it. Just an idea.

May 10, 1998

Sustainable San Francisco

SAN FRANCISCO—In this city of histrionic geography and ominous geology, the question about the Big One—the big earthquake—is not whether it will come but when. So people here have enough to worry about without being hectored about their perfume being a public health problem.

However, here you find the nation's highest metropolitan concentration of liberalism. Hence residents are being told that their well-being is menaced from every direction and they must modify their behavior in manifold ways or the city will no longer be "sustainable."

So says *The Sustainability Plan,* a report prepared for and endorsed by the city government. It is a wonderful window into the world of environmental worrying and illustrates the distillation of liberalism to an agenda of bodily health for individuals who are "educated" to appropriate social consciousness.

According to the report, a sustainable society meets its needs without sacrificing the ability of future generations "and non-human forms of life" to meet theirs. According to Beryl Magilavy, director of the city's Department of the Environment, who does her bit for a better world by owning neither a car nor a television, the report avoids the "sky-is-falling mode." But its cumulative effect is to sound this alarm: Time is running out because everything else is, too.

"Let me explain about that," she says, pausing over her vegetarian pasta dish and politely masking her weariness about being again asked to explain the report's recommendation that San Franciscans reduce their "personal impact on the shared indoor environment by limiting the use of scented personal-care products." Some people, she says, are bothered by such scents, so why not include in the report, which includes so much else, a recommendation of moderation—the report speaks only of *reducing* uses—about what the report calls "airborne emissions from fragrances"?

Here is why not. The recommendation is symptomatic of contemporary liberalism's aspiration to use the reduction of life's risks as the rationale for minutely monitoring, and improving, the behavior and consciousness of individuals.

The report begins at a Paul Revere–like gallop, warning that "our current course of environmental degradation and resource depletion" jeopardizes "our fragile ecosystems." How fragile? The problem is not just chemicals and other hazards (including that pervasive carcinogen, sunshine?), but also "everyday activities," such as firing up barbecues and fireplaces. "True sustainability, which implies eliminating"—yes, eliminating—"garbage collection and land-filling, will require dramatic changes to almost every economic transaction."

The report envisions lots of new jobs for the boys and girls of the "caring professions" who care for, by "educating," the masses who, without supervision by the caring, will carelessly foul San Francisco and the contiguous planet. The promise to educate recurs: "educate food stamp users to shop at farmers' markets . . . educate cooking students (future chefs) about organic, regionally produced foods . . ."

The report favors "culturally responsive" foods. Magilavy says such foods raise the consumer's consciousness of seasons and natural rhythms. The report encourages food grown locally, which will get people in touch with nature through "seasonal flavors" and minimize yucky trucking.

"Rooftops of new and existing buildings offer a vast amount of potential agriculture space." The report is a marvelous evocation of Soviet life, with its broth of slogans and quotas: "Initiate a 'fruit tree in every yard' campaign"; "Identify appropriate crops, such as apples, for citywide production quotas."

The report's animus against the internal combustion engine is, of course, strong, as is its endorsement of "secure bicycle and roller-skate storage at transit stations." For you out-of-towners, the report suggests "a procedure by which guests in San Francisco hotels can choose to have towels replaced less frequently than every day, to reduce water used in unnecessary laundry."

On page 63, just past the exhortation to "increase public education on the value of calcium in the diet" and just before the recommendation to "establish more sex education and self-esteem programs for youths," the report calls for a study of "the nature and causes of stress to San Franciscans." Well. One way to reduce that stress would be to burn—in an environmentally responsible incinerator, of course—every copy of this report, which says that virtually everything that everybody does is implicated in the impending unsustainability of everything.

Is it not somewhat disproportionate for people living by cheerful voice on the San Andreas fault to fret about the menace of disposable diapers? "That's true," says Magilavy brightly, "but we're already here." Not for long, if the report is right.

October 16, 1997

Making America Safe
—And Profitable—for Eminem

Got pissed off and ripped Pamela Lee's tits off . . .
My English teacher wanted to flunk me in junior high
Thanks a lot, next semester I'll be thirty-five
I smacked him in his face with an eraser, chased him with a stapler
and stapled his nuts to a stack of papers (Owwwwwwww!)

—EMINEM

Eminem, the rapper from whose hit "My Name Is" the above lyrics come, cannot serenely savor his triumph at the MTV Video Music Awards now that the Senate Commerce Committee is turning its disapproving glare upon the culture. Vice President Al Gore, too, is dismayed. He tells *The New York Times* ("his voice rising," says the *Times*) that "I am going to do something about this." So the culture is going to be fixed by the very connoisseurs who have vetted and confirmed all the federal judges who have done so much to ratify the premises of today's popular culture and to make resistance to it difficult—in fact, often unconstitutional.

The Commerce Committee (its witnesses including Senator Joseph Lieberman, who knows the importance of being earnest) called a hearing occasioned by a Federal Trade Commission report condemning the marketing of violent entertainment to children. But it would be better for the Judiciary Committee to consider its contribution, through liberal judges, to cultural decadence. And conservatives, too, should have uneasy consciences.

Light is shed on all this by two papers recently delivered here at the American Political Science Association by Christopher Wolfe of Marquette University and Harry Clor of Kenyon College.

Public morality, says Wolfe, concerns laws and public actions that, by reducing the incidence of certain acts and affirming certain values, shape the conduct, hence the habits, hence the character of citizens, hence society's moral ecology. By denying First Amendment protection to obscenity but defining obscenity in a way that makes it a category with virtually nothing in it and making pornography protected "expression" perhaps important to an autonomous individual's flowering ("one man's vulgarity is another's lyric," said the Supreme Court), the courts disarmed communities' attempts to define public morality. By inventing a privacy right as a scythe for mowing down virtually all restrictions on abortion and sexual activity, and especially in making abortion and contraception rights superior to parental rights, the courts further made radical personal autonomy—"choice"—trump the very notion of public standards of propriety. By cleansing the public square of religious expression (school prayer, crèches on public property, etc.), the courts undermined a traditional source of public morality.

Granted, judges may generally be, as Wolfe says, "less causes than conduits" of culture shaped by academic and media elites. However, court opinions have educative effects. And as Clor says, much besides jurisprudence is destroying what until relatively recently was a countervailing morality of self-restraint that moderated libertarian impulses.

The rationale for public morality, writes Clor, is that humans have powerful irrational or unsocial inclinations, the moderating of which is a precondition for self-control and civility—indeed, for civilization. And conservatives should face the fact that the customs and traditions that sustain good character are undermined by more than just legal protections of depersonalized sexuality and eroticized violence.

American conservatism's dominant strand shares modern liberalism's celebration of radical autonomy. Society, such conservatism says, is an aggregation of self-interested individuals choosing to associate not for the purpose of acquiring virtue, character, and culture but for liberty and property—security and prosperity. The mass-consumption society that is capitalism's crowning success has, Clor believes, a "privatizing" and "community-weakening dynamic." By encouraging people to act as radically autonomous bundles of appetites, it undermines self-control and moderation as much as does the dispensing of condoms to eighth-graders. Furthermore, "the celebrated 'nonjudgmentalism' of contemporary America is at least partly a phenomenon of bourgeois complacency rooted in a plenitude of bourgeois satisfactions."

Gore, with the myopia of a government lifer, would combat this cultural tsunami with—seriously—new rules about advertising directed at children. We will know he and his running mate (and their Republican rivals, for that matter) are truly serious when they acknowledge the consequences of some ideas.

The ideas of liberal jurisprudence, and the idea that "choice" is the essence of human dignity, and the idea that the very concept of public morality threatens the respect owed equally to all freely chosen "lifestyles," and the idea that Americans are united only by the belief that no public morality unites them, and the idea of conservative "nonjudgmentalism" that makes a fetish of consumer sovereignty—all these have helped make America safe and extremely profitable for the likes of Eminem.

September 13, 2000

Walker Percy,
Richard Petty, Whatever

Peace prevails on two formerly hot fronts in the culture wars: the National Endowment for the Arts and the National Endowment for the Humanities. But have they made a desert and called it peace?

Certainly they have made predictable accommodations with Congress. The result is a depressing embrace of cultural democracy, understood as emphasis on cultural forms that almost everyone can participate in or appreciate.

The congenial face of cultural democracy is that of a fifty-six-year-old Mississippian, William Ferris, the new chairman of the NEH. Nominated by President Bill Clinton and blessed by Mississippi's two Republican senators, he was confirmed without a discouraging word. Without words of any sort: there were no confirmation hearings.

That, in itself, is a cultural barometer. Three years ago, Republicans fresh from the 1994 elections were breathing fire and reciting the Tenth Amendment and saying that the NEA and NEH were frills the federal government should be shorn of. Now it is clear that the endowments will last longer than Mount Rushmore. Both the NEA and NEH have mastered adaptive evolution, defanging Republicans by becoming populist and perhaps philistine.

The NEA, operating on the circular reasoning that art is whatever an artist says it is and an artist is whoever produces art, has recently subsidized only as much obnoxiousness as is absolutely necessary to prove its willingness to shock the bourgeoisie. It has declared (in last October's report "American Canvas") that art should be *useful* by serving today's political fixation, multiculturalism—"pulling us as diverse groups and cultures together."

And it says "art includes the expressive behaviors of ordinary people," including "things that we make with our words (songs, stories, rhymes, proverbs), with our hands (quilts, knitting, rawhide braiding, piecrust designs, dinner-table arrangements, garden layouts), and with our actions (birthday and holiday celebrations, worship practice, playtime activities, work practices)."

Everything from singing in your morning shower to setting your dinner table is thus eligible for NEA support, which makes it easy to spread support, like honey on bread, across 435 congressional districts. The chairman of the NEA, William Ivey, is a folklorist.

Ferris, too, is a folklorist. As head of the University of Mississippi's Center for the Study of Southern Culture, he said, "The word 'culture' was chosen because it means 'lifestyle' and a lot more. It embraces everything about the region—politics, blues and country music, sports, art and religion. Everything."

Walker Percy, Richard Petty, it's all grist for the mills of "social history" and "cultural studies." Hence the center's "International Conferences on Elvis," with the lesbian impersonator Elvis Herselvis. The conferences were, according to an organizer, attempts "to shred the veil of academic elitism."

Ferris says that in the humanities "it's not so much the subject as how you do it." So the subject can be "Twain or Goo Goo Clusters." By studying food, such as that caramel, chocolate, marshmallow, and peanut candy, "you can understand a great deal" about regions. Ferris also believes that

> Today the lives of ordinary American people have assumed a place beside volumes of European classics in the humanities. . . . We must recognize those voices which seldom touch the printed page. A sharecropper in Alabama and a steelworker in Indiana have a voice in the humanities. Their view of truth and wisdom complements traditional learning in a new and exciting way.

That doctrine—"I hear America singing, and everyone sings equally well"—conforms to the categorical imperative of today's political utilitarianism: the greatest self-esteem for the greatest number. Besides, no one ever offended a congressional appropriator by being too solicitous of democratic sensibilities.

The NEH does much useful work, ranging from the preservation of brittle books, film, and photographs to supporting the publication of the papers of historic Americans. And Ferris's big idea—dividing the nation into, say, ten regions and funding regional humanities centers for the study of American particularities—could produce useful scholarship.

It could but probably will not, because the political class—Republicans at least as much as Democrats—wants the NEH's definition of the subsidizable humanities to be "inclusive," meaning so capacious that absolutely nothing is excluded. The NEA and NEH have become increasingly secure by becoming decreasingly defensible—by emphasizing low subjects as a matter of high principle.

It is, of course, not astounding that the majoritarian impulse has engulfed the culture agencies. They are funded by elected officials. By the logic of our politics, the two endowments will increasingly become cultural redundancies, "celebrating"—a word often heard in Washington culture talk—mundane things *because* they are ubiquitous.

April 5, 1998

Karen Finley's Major Tragedy

Karen Finley, a "performance artist," is one of those proudly independent souls whose pride and independence do not prevent them from cultivating a dependence on government subventions. She is one of those artists (broadly— *very* broadly—defined) who fancy themselves revolutionary. But she is not the type of militant who topples governments. Rather, she approaches the government not as a subversive but as a supplicant—less like Lenin than like any other lobbyist elbowing toward the public trough. She no doubt fancies herself as going through life giving the militants' salute—a clenched fist, raised. However, her other hand is forever extended for a government handout. She wants to *épater les bourgeois,* but she clearly considers herself entitled to have the bourgeoisie pony up money to pay for her attempts to scandalize it.

Finley's performance includes uttering "God is death" while smearing her nude self with chocolate, which is said to symbolize excrement. The meaning of all this is, evidently, that America is beastly to people like Finley (women, creative spirits, nonconformists, etc.). Another performer, who joined Finley in suing the government, urinates on stage and makes an altar out of a toilet bowl by putting a picture of Christ on the toilet lid. America has had a peculiar way of being beastly to such performers: it has enabled them to have careers performing, and has even paid them, through the National Endowment for the Arts.

However, the NEA is required to "take into consideration general standards of decency" in selecting recipients for its grants. Congress said so in 1990 as a sop to, and as a (successful) attempt to deflect, those who wanted to abolish the NEA. Those were the conservatives and other mossbacks who objected to forcing taxpayers to finance exhibits of photographs of a bullwhip in a rectum and a crucifix in a jar of urine.

The law directs the NEA to ensure that grants should be made "taking into consideration general standards of decency and respect for the diverse beliefs and values of the American public." Finley, a world-class whiner even by the standards of the "arts community," and three other performance artists were subsequently denied grants. They sued, claiming that the law was unconstitutionally vague and violated their freedom of expression by rejecting their applications because of the content of their expression. The Supreme Court rejected both claims, 8–1 (Justice David Souter dissenting).

Writing for the majority, Justice Sandra Day O'Connor noted that the NEA has limited resources and denies most applications, and she stressed the fact—or what she thinks is a fact—that the law only "admonishes" (her word) the NEA to give some "consideration" to decency. This, she suggested, means that there is no real disadvantaging of any particular kind of content or view-point of artistic expression. Because she made much of the fact that this "ad-visory" language did not prohibit subsidies of indecent art, her opinion suggests that if the law did more than admonish, with advisory language, in favor of the consideration of decency, it would indeed violate the First Amendment.

Justice Antonin Scalia would have none of this. Joined by Justice Clarence Thomas, he supported the judgment while eviscerating the reasoning by which the other six members of the majority reached it.

How, he wonders, is the law merely "advisory" when it says that the NEA "shall ensure" that decency is a consideration? That consideration need not be dispositive, but it must always be made. So NEA decision making, other things being equal, must always "favor applications that display decency and respect, and disfavor applications that do not."

Scalia tartly said that O'Connor devoted so much of her opinion "to ex-plaining why this statute means something other than what it says" that her opinion never got around to citing the pertinent constitutional text, the First Amendment proscription of laws "abridging the freedom of speech." He said that by requiring consideration of decency, "Congress did not *abridge* the speech of those who disdain the beliefs and values of the American public, nor did it *abridge* indecent speech." People so inclined are as unconstrained after the statute as they were before it to exercise their right to express themselves by urinating onstage and smearing themselves with chocolate. They just can-not expect the public to pay for such affronts to its sensibilities.

The implication of O'Connor's argument is that government cannot flatly oppose funding some projects rather than others because of their con-tent. But, Scalia notes, when Congress established the National Endowment for Democracy, it was not constitutionally required to fund rival forms of gov-ernment. There is no constitutional infirmity in the fact that the NEA is *re-quired* to discriminate in favor of artistic (as opposed to, say, scientific or theological) expression.

Neither is there a constitutional problem with Congress's *determination* (it is more than a mere exhortation) that the NEA "shall" discriminate in favor of decency over indecency: "Because such favoritism does not 'abridge' anyone's freedom of speech." The majority's mincing opinion tiptoes around the plain fact that it was constitutional for Congress to do what it obviously did when it established content- and viewpoint-based criteria upon which grant appli-cations are to be evaluated. So, Scalia says, the majority sustains the law only "by gutting it."

In spite of that, Newt Gingrich, the revolutionary, hailed the ruling, which he misconstrued as a vindication of "the right of the American people to not pay for art that offends their sensibilities." Finley, whose most memorable performance is as a solipsist, announced that it was a "major tragedy" that "I spent years on this case, and I lose." *The New York Times* reported that in her despondency she was thinking of abandoning performances, "although she felt she might have to confront repression even as an author and visual artist."

On the day of the ruling, midway through the fourth year of the Republican revolution, the House Appropriations Committee voted to continue funding the NEA.

July 6, 1998

CONTINGENCIES
LARGE AND SMALL

History and Contingency

S uppose.

Suppose the car had hit the pedestrian slightly harder. What car? The one on Fifth Avenue in New York on the evening of December 13, 1931, when an English politician on a lecture tour momentarily forgot the American rules of the road and looked the wrong way when stepping into the street. Winston Churchill could have died. Then, perhaps in 1940 or 1941, a prime minister less resolute and inspiriting than Churchill might have chosen to come to terms with Germany before Hitler attacked the Soviet Union. Imagine the hegemony of a National Socialist Germany stretching across the Eurasian landmass from the Atlantic to the Pacific.

Suppose Robert E. Lee had occupied Cemetery Hill on the first night at Gettysburg, which he might have done if Stonewall Jackson had not accidentally been killed two months earlier by Confederate soldiers. The dynamic of the next few days would have been entirely different. Lee probably would have prevailed there, and this might now be two nations. (Actually, there probably would be lots of nations in the territory that was the Confederacy, because those fractious people would have improvidently established a weak central government and the right of secession.)

Suppose the northeast wind blowing across New York harbor had not suddenly turned into a southwest wind on the night of August 29, 1776. Or that a thick fog had not rolled in the next day. There might never have been an independent United States for Lee to try to dismember if those climatic changes had not facilitated the evacuation whereby George Washington and 10,000 soldiers—about half the entire Continental Army—escaped capture by the British after the Battle of Long Island.

These are among the "might have beens" that some distinguished students of military history consider in the new issue of *MHQ,* a quarterly of military history. That their speculations about history-altering contingencies are deeply satisfying says something about intellectual currents of modern history.

Two converging intellectual tendencies have had demoralizing—and demoralizing—effects on the way we are encouraged to understand history. This matters because the way we think about the past conditions how we act—or do not act—to shape the future.

The first tendency has been to blur the picture of human beings as responsible, consequential actors in history. Marx argued that the unfolding of history is governed by vast impersonal forces obeying iron laws of social development impervious to, and largely controlling, the volitions of individuals. Darwin, presenting the human species as continuous with the slime from which the species has only recently crept, seemed to embed mankind in the necessities of nature. Freud said the individual has uncharted depths with turbulences that the individual, whose "self" is a kind of fractious committee, cannot master.

The second tendency is a consequence of the first, of postulating that individuals are inconsequential. It is a degenerate democratic impulse in the historians' craft—"history from the bottom up" or "history with the politics left out." All "elitist" history that stresses great individuals and events—political, military, diplomatic, intellectual—supposedly insults common people. The corrective—call it "affirmative-action history"—allots at least as much attention to the ordinary activities of the many as to the extraordinary activities of the few.

The trouble is, this involves painting mankind's story without the bright primary colors of personal greatness, which has two bad consequences. Pastel history teaches that mastery of events is a chimera, so why bother with politics? And it makes the idea of "leadership" suspect, so who cares about the character and caliber of leaders? The salutary effect of *MHQ*'s "what if" exercises is a keener appreciation of the huge difference that choices and fortuities make in the destinies of nations.

Perhaps the pleasure of that appreciation helps explain the astonishing popularity of the movie *Titanic*. The story is dramatic and this is a three-hanky movie, but among people who have been plied with philosophies denigrating the role of choice and chance in the human story, the story of the *Titanic* has more than merely tragic resonance.

The sinking of the "unsinkable" ship on its maiden voyage, a ship with a social order replicating society's classes, quickly became a metaphor for the fragility of civilization and a rebuke to technological and other hubris: So, mankind, you really thought you could iron the future flat, removing risk and the need to pay attention to what might be in the fog dead ahead?

Which is the moral of history's many crucial "might have beens": Pay attention.

February 22, 1998

. . . The Iceberg Too

Paul Volcker, former chairman of the Federal Reserve Board, puts the scale and velocity of America's current wealth creation into this perspective: In just the first half of 1999, the *increase* in the net worth of American households was approximately equal to the *total* annual income of the 2.5 billion people of China, India, Russia, and Brazil.

The political consequences of such an economic fact are difficult to anticipate, but this seems likely: the surge in wealth is both a current cause of political tranquillity and a potential cause of volatility. People, said someone not overly fond of them, have feelings in all their possessions. America, which has more than four times as many stock owners as union members, has a lot of exposed nerve endings in the stock market.

After years of economic growth, many giddy people may assume that the market is governed by an upward-clicking ratchet. A rapidly rising stock market is a pleasure, and in contemporary America pleasures quickly come to be considered entitlements. The market and the American pain threshold move inversely, so imagine the political furies that will be let loose when a market plunge pulses fear through the ganglions of a society of stockholders.

A successful society needs a Cassandra or two to keep it properly wary, but all America has at the moment are the likes of Ross Perot and Pat Buchanan hearing the "great sucking sound" of American prosperity being swallowed by a Mexican economy that is 10 percent the size of the American economy.

Imagining the future and its hazards is increasingly difficult. A businessman recently said the future might look like 1950, when milk trucks crept through neighborhoods delivering their products: people may buy groceries the way they increasingly buy books, through e-commerce. But such a change would be minor and predictable compared to past surprises and those with which the future is surely pregnant. Consider the thoughts of several contributors to the current issue of *Forbes ASAP.*

Why do we have mass mobility—and immobility (congestion)? Because, says science writer James Burke, a nineteenth-century German engineer used a perfume sprayer and gasoline to invent the carburetor. A nineteenth-century English chemist, prompted by the empire's problems with malaria, tried to invent artificial quinine from coal tar. He failed, but when he dipped a strand of silk into it, he had the first aniline dye. Fifty years later, a German medical researcher accidentally spilled some of the new color into a sample of bacteria and noticed that the dye preferentially stained and killed certain bacilli: chemotherapy was born.

Remington firearms company, using machine tools developed for the Civil War and a mechanism developed for pianos, produced the typewriter. It facilitated an explosion of commerce and, says Burke, "freed women from the drudgery of the kitchen to become involved in the drudgery of office work." Social and political emancipation followed.

Increasingly, America has an entertainment economy. Michael J. Wolf, a media and entertainment specialist at Booz, Allen & Hamilton, says the entertainment share of GDP is well over $1 trillion if, in addition to traditional entertainment products (movies, TV, music, sports, etc.), you add much of the consumer electronics sector and things like "fun" vehicles, such as SUVs and Harley-Davidsons.

Some entertainment products are, Wolf says, "largely inexhaustible." Disney's movie *Snow White* cost $1.5 million and made $8.5 million in its initial release cycle (1937–1943). Rereleased and incorporated into games, toys, and apparel, it has made $1 billion. Through various tie-ins and spin-offs, *The Lion King* has already made $9 billion—less than the $10 billion in commerce Michael Jordan is estimated to have generated, but *The Lion King* can do it over and over with each generation of children.

America's economic performance is generating understandable pride, and we know what pride goeth before. The editors of *Forbes ASAP* allow Mark Helprin, the novelist and essayist, an elegant dissent from the triumphalism of those who, intoxicated by modern marvels, abandon themselves to what he calls "faith in emerging perfection, reason, justice, the linear concept of history." As an antidote to all that, Helprin offers some lines from Thomas Hardy's poem "The Convergence of the Twain: Lines on the Loss of the *Titanic*":

> *And as the smart ship grew*
> *In stature, grace, and hue,*
> *In shadowy silent distance grew the Iceberg too.*
>
> *Alien they seemed to be:*
> *No mortal eye could see*
> *The intimate welding of their later history.*

Are there icebergs in America's path? None just now. None, that is, that any mortal eye can see.

September 26, 1999

Neurologically Wired to Wall Street

Treasury Secretary Lawrence Summers recalls that only ten years ago he called his wife just to tell her he was talking on a car phone. Seven years later, in a canoe off the Ivory Coast, he was handed a mobile phone to talk to then Treasury Secretary Robert Rubin.

At a time when 1 billion of the world's 6 billion people have never made a telephone call, technology drives America's economic giddiness. Millions of amateur investors (the Consumer Federation of America reports that only 38 percent of investors know that interest rates and bond prices vary inversely) believe that investing profitably is effortless.

In these fat years, Americans eat and drink constantly, so airport corridors—in 1975, 80 percent of Americans had never traveled by air—are lined with eateries. At one in Phoenix there is a ticker giving stock prices in streaming red lights. There is a ticker at Shea Stadium so New York Mets fans can monitor their investments between innings. America is neurologically wired to Wall Street.

Only 29 percent of persons filing tax returns itemize deductions; 74 percent of households pay more in payroll taxes than in federal income taxes; 15 percent of households do not have bank accounts. However, since 1995 the number of households with a net worth of $1 million has doubled, to 7.1 million (about one in fourteen) and the investor class now is a majority. In a country in which retirement was a rarity when Social Security was established 65 years ago, about half of households have stock holdings, and enough Americans are sufficiently attentive to the stock market that market tickers are becoming ubiquitous.

So are morally dubious incitements to do-it-yourself investing. In a recent *Business Week* cover story, Marcia Vickers and Gary Weiss report that advertising by brokerage firms rose 95 percent in 1999, to $1.2 billion, and that CNBC has become to investors what ESPN is to sports fans. The long bull market and cable television have turned many financial analysts into celebrities, making them less researchers than pitchmen, some of whom, say Vickers and Weiss, "own the stocks they pitch on the air." They say, "Studies show that buy recommendations outnumber sells by a staggering 72 to 1. The ratio 10 years ago was 10 to 1." Of Mary G. Meeker, chief Internet and e-commerce analyst for Morgan Stanley Dean Witter, they say, "Even though she stated in December that 90 percent of Internet stocks are overvalued, she has never placed an actual sell on a Net stock."

Investors are urged to take "control" of their financial destiny by buying on margin and restlessly churning their portfolios (in 1990, the average NASDAQ stock was held for two years; today, five months) with the manic energy of Stuart, that redheaded twentysomething lunatic in the Ameritrade commercials. But is the bull market apt to stampede on indefinitely?

Andy Serwer, *Fortune* editor-at-large, challenges skeptics to ask themselves: How many of these are you likely to buy in the next twelve months: a PC, a laptop computer, a printer, a scanner, a cell phone, a pager, a Palm-like device, a DVD player, a digital camera, a handheld GPS (global positioning system) device, a PlayStation? "How many of those items," he asks, "did you buy in 1990?"

Granted, this is the first economic expansion since the 1920s driven almost entirely by the private sector, especially by higher productivity because of information technologies. Granted, the profusion of new consumer goods astounds—although that profusion is a difference only of degree, not of kind, for America's economy, which usually is driven primarily by consumers.

Shawn Tully, senior writer at *Fortune,* speaks for skeptics when he counters that a tech stock is not a collectible, it is a financial instrument. Like any other stock, its real value is "the sum of its future cash flows, adjusted by an interest rate that reflects the stock's riskiness and the yields available on other investments." The anticipation of huge cash flows presupposed by the current price-earnings ratios of many tech stocks presupposes huge profits.

But they can come only from "the ability to sell a product far above cost for a very long time." Are there really enough such products to fulfill the current market's implicit prophecies? Want another 1920s parallel? Robert Kuttner, *Business Week* columnist, notes, "The price-earnings ratio of the market as a whole is now far in excess of 1929 levels."

The great political event of this election year may yet be a Great Correction that gives some fliers a taste of real turbulence—think downdraft—before they board their flights from Phoenix.

April 13, 2000

What Began with Jim Clark's Boat

God, a wit warns, is going to come down and pull civilization over for speeding. The stock market has done that to America's economy.

Time was, the economy drove the stock market. Now causation can work the other way, at least when the market controls confidence. However, although surveys show plunging consumer confidence, consumer behavior is producing a negative savings rate—spending outstripping after-tax income. Consumer spending makes up two-thirds of GDP, and in this year's first quarter such spending probably was 3 percent higher than in last year's first quarter.

Today's economic events constitute a $4 trillion puzzle, that being the amount of wealth (exceeding the combined GDPs of Britain, France, and Italy) that has quickly come and gone among NASDAQ stocks—so quickly that all of the $4 trillion was here only on March 10, 2000, NASDAQ's apogee. Which may explain why Americans do not miss it more than they do: They hardly had time to become attached to it.

The Wall Street Journal's Holman Jenkins recalls John Maynard Keynes's warning that low trading costs (Keynes never imagined online trading) in a context of abundant liquid capital make it too easy for investors to buy or sell on whim, rumor, or perceived portents (Keynes never imagined CNBC). Yet investors remain remarkably free from the volatility that was predicted because of the new demographics of stock ownership. A majority of households own stocks, and mutual funds have surpassed banks as the major repository of savings. Investors' money is still flowing into equities.

Furthermore, the budget surplus may help divert more money from cautious investors to stocks. Such investors often have favored thirty-year Treasury bonds, a species endangered by the government's reduced borrowing.

Investor stoicism, as Gretchen Morgenson of *The New York Times* calls it, has been remarkable, considering that if the shares of Yahoo!, Cisco, Oracle, Sun Microsystems, Intel, AT&T, and Microsoft were now to begin rising in price by 15 percent a year, it would take them twenty, ten, nine, nine, seven, seven, and six years respectively to regain their recent peaks.

Could it be that the birth, and the bursting, of the tech stock bubble came about because Jim Clark, Netscape's founder, craved a new boat? Journalist Michael Lewis, in his book *The New New Thing,* says the decision to take Netscape public in August 1995 came when the company was eighteen months old and had not earned a cent. But Clark, eager to finance a grandiose yacht, launched one of history's most successful share offerings.

Thus died the axiom that tech companies went public only after at least four consecutive profitable quarters. Soon we were in the brief, giddy life of capitalism without profits, during which some investors decided that only premodern investors thought that the value of shares should be a function of the firm's future cash flows. Such investors became fixated on what are known in New Economy jargon as "nonfinancial metrics." Those are supposedly ways of measuring value in a company when monetary measurements do not show value.

One such measurement is Web site traffic. Another is "engaged shoppers," measured by (no kidding) page views per viewer per month. Then there is a company's ability to claim shares of consumers' minds. Morgan Stanley research has reported that one company (Homestore.com) had a "leading mind share among consumers." This, translates the *Times*'s Morgenson, means that "approximately 72 percent of the total time spent by Internet users on real estate–related Web sites in September was spent on Homestore's properties." However, what often is missing from these recondite measurements is how, if at all, they translate into revenues, not to mention (and often this is not mentioned) profits.

The Wall Street Journal first used the phrase "Internet bubble" in 1995. In 1996 Alan Greenspan put the phrase "irrational exuberance" into our economic lexicon. But what exuberance is rational nowadays?

Earlier this month there was a remarkable one-day rally when NASDAQ surged 8.9 percent, the Dow 4.2 percent. This happened for two reasons. Dell

Computer announced that it would hit its quarterly revenue target—but that target had been lowered in anticipation of the first quarter-by-quarter decline in the company's sales in seven years. And an uptick in the number of persons applying for unemployment benefits suggested that the economy was slowing and thus the Federal Reserve might again cut interest rates, which it did on Wednesday.

The market's eager response to such meager good news does not indicate a recession mentality. Can there be a recession without one? Probably not.

April 22, 2001

Capitalism is a Government Project

Washington—narcissistic and even solipsistic, as usual—thinks Enron's collapse is primarily a Washington, meaning a political, story. Actually, the debacle is, so far, primarily a tale of two other cities. Houston is Enron's hometown. New York is the center of the financial system that Arthur Andersen is supposed to serve. Andersen is the document-destroying accounting firm that failed—assuming, generously, that it tried—to report Enron's activities accurately.

However, Washington will star in subsequent acts of this drama, which may live on, in litigation, longer than anyone reading this column. Events since September 11 have confirmed Randolph Bourne's 1918 axiom that "war is the health of the state." Enron's collapse is a reminder that economic scandal, too, causes the state to wax.

It will remind everyone—some conservatives, painfully—that a mature capitalist economy is a government project. A properly functioning free market system does not spring spontaneously from society's soil as dandelions spring from suburban lawns. Rather, it is a complex creation of laws and mores that guarantee, among much else, transparency, meaning a sufficient stream—torrent, really—of reliable information about the condition and conduct of corporations.

Always necessary to economic health, transparency has increasingly become crucial to civic health because of the changed demographics of stock ownership. A nation in which a majority of households own equities is neurologically wired to the stock market. Hence corporate corruption quickly begets political demoralization and cynicism.

Off and on over the years, a few capitalists have done more to delegitimize capitalism than America's impotent socialist critics ever did or today's moribund Left could hope to. It is the Republicans' special responsibility to punish such capitalists.

Democrats are properly put on the defensive by corruption in organized labor and the ditziness of the cultural Left. Similarly, Republicans, beginning with their post–Civil War coziness with corporate America (tariffs and all that), have had a special responsibility to police business outlaws.

Fortunately, those in the Bush administration who were approached on Enron's behalf evidently did exactly what government should do for fools and clever knaves who are ruining a corporation: nothing. But now there are things to be done.

Indignation is a precondition for whatever new laws and regulations are required to prevent behavior such as Enron's. It has been said that the absence of honest emotion is the shared characteristic of American politics and professional wrestling. One would like to hear from President George W. Bush regarding Enron's executives, the sort of anger he expressed over the possibility that the crybaby Secret Service agent whose behavior caused an American Airlines pilot to bar him from a flight might have been a victim of illegitimate profiling.

Instead, we have heard Bush's slippery—Clintonian, actually—assertion that Enron's CEO, Ken Lay, "was a supporter of Ann Richards in my run in 1994" for governor. Well, yes, but no. Lay contributed to Richards. And he contributed much more to Bush.

When the president finds his proper voice, he should say: Arthur Andersen was both accountant and consultant for Enron. The resulting coziness reeked of conflict of interest and surely helped produce Enron account books that should be filed under "fiction." Enron never reported even a bad *quarter* before collapsing. Consulting by accounting firms should be proscribed. And what is the point of "peer reviews" by the big accounting firms of one another's work if they do not discern an approaching train wreck such as Enron's?

A few senior Enron executives sold their Enron stock when they realized they were steering their ship onto the rocks. In some crucial final days, employees, locked in steerage like the lower orders on the *Titanic,* were blocked from selling the Enron stock that made up, on average, 62 percent of employees' 401(k) holdings. (At 120 large corporations, employees' 401(k) plans have at least one-third of their value in their employers' stocks.) If insider trading and other laws do not proscribe such things, they should.

Amid the debris of Enron, the functions and liabilities of boards of directors need fresh scrutiny. Many boards have proved themselves unwilling (there are myriad forms of coziness between corporations and their directors) or unable to stop the most scandalous practices regarding senior executives' compensation, practices not easily distinguishable from the looting of shareholders' wealth. Let us have, at a minimum, congressional hearings that embarrass the looters, if they are capable of embarrassment.

Now Washington takes center stage. By casting a cool eye on Enron's debris and those who made it, government can strengthen an economic system that depends on it.

January 15, 2002

America's Long-Term Leveling

O nly a mind as closed as an oyster could miss the dominating fact of contemporary politics. It is that American society is creating wealth at an astonishing rate, yet the government is so strapped it can barely fund basic domestic programs.

Only a mind as acute as Chris DeMuth's can fully construe this fact. DeMuth, president of American Enterprise Institute, argues that as America rapidly becomes rich beyond the dreams of even our parents, it is also becoming freer and more egalitarian. And this wealth, freedom, and equality are causing the welfare state to unravel.

That we are rapidly becoming richer is clear. People who deny that equality is increasing are fixated on the recent small increase in income inequality. That increase, the subject of an unceasing journalistic drumbeat, is, DeMuth argues, a small incongruity in the long-term "leveling of material circumstances" that has been under way for three centuries and is accelerating.

Since 1700, the average life span in Western societies has doubled. Today material necessities—food, shelter—are so universally available that the problem of poverty, understood as material scarcity, has been solved. Poverty, DeMuth notes, is now a problem of individual behavior, social organization, and policy, not of society's material scarcities.

Two centuries ago, land was the essential source of wealth. One century ago, physical capital was. Today, human capital—knowledge, cognitive skill—is, and such capital is widely distributed by nature and augmented by universal education. Furthermore, sexual equality has advanced so far that young men and women of comparable education and training now earn essentially equal incomes.

As societies become more wealthy, DeMuth argues, money income becomes a less informative measure of individual welfare, as is demonstrated by this fact: Western democracies have become so wealthy that, for the first time in history, "voluntary reduction in time spent at paid employment has become a major social and economic phenomenon." This reduction appears in expanded education of the young and, even more, in longer retirement of the elderly.

When Social Security was enacted in 1935, the idea of retirement was, for most Americans, exotic. DeMuth says most men worked until they dropped, and they dropped early. Today, the explosive growth of the sports, entertainment, and travel industries indicates a social revolution quantified by Robert Fogel, one of the University of Chicago's stable of Nobel Prize–winning economists.

He estimates that since 1880, the time devoted each week by the average American male head of household to nonwork activities has risen from 10.5 hours to 40 hours, while time at work has been cut nearly in half, from 61.6 to 33.6. So income inequality has widened as social equality has increased. It has widened, in part, because of the ability of people to choose to substitute leisure for income-producing work.

Today, DeMuth notes, government's principal activity consists of transferring income from workers to nonworkers for the subsidization of two things that were virtually unknown just a few generations ago: nonwork (retirement, extended schooling) and ambitious medical care (replaceable body parts, exotic diagnostic and pharmacological technologies—a far cry from 1900 medicine, which consisted largely of making patients comfortable until nature killed or cured them). But the welfare state's core functions are being made obsolete by technological and economic developments linked to the growth of social wealth and equality.

For example, access to financial expertise has been democratized: anyone who mails $100 to a mutual fund thereby hires top-grade investment management. Which is one reason why, while privatization of Social Security is languidly debated in Washington, private savings (including mutual funds, pension plans, and other investments such as housing) have already surpassed Social Security as a source of retirement income.

The modern age's expansion of individual autonomy has not only diminished the importance of many social insurance and regulatory functions of the government bequeathed by the Progressive and New Deal eras. This expansion has, DeMuth argues, recast the great question of social life, from What should government do? to How should we behave?

Expanded autonomy frees individuals for admirable and improving pursuits—and for unworthy and self-destructive behavior. With the growth of wealth, freedom, and equality has come an equally astounding explosion of social pathologies, from family disintegration and illegitimacy to drug abuse and vulgar popular entertainment.

The banality of current politics and the miniaturization of the political class result, as DeMuth says, from the marginalization of government. Citizens are turning their attention, as individuals and as members of civic and religious groups, to the question: What is freedom for? The question is itself among the luxuries of a wealthy, free, and equal society.

August 21, 1997

The "Strip Mall Socialism" of Government

Extraordinary affluence is obviously changing the nation's political agenda. Less obviously, and ominously, it is changing the nation's political sensibility, reducing to the vanishing point the once sturdy concern for limited government.

The nation's freedom and prosperity have been secured. The problems that dominate day-to-day legislative business—e.g., reducing pollution and congestion, improving medical care, providing more police—are not resource problems: The sacrifices involved in paying for such things are not prohibitive. Christopher DeMuth, head of the American Enterprise Institute, argues that although Americans are unprecedentedly prosperous, self-sufficient, and at peace with one another, government continues to grow prodigiously because of little-understood dynamics.

Government outlays (federal, state, local) and regulatory costs—largely imposed on the private sector—have grown more than 50 percent faster than the economy for fifty years and now claim more than one-third of GDP. The federal government owns one-third of all land, pays for 40 percent of medical care, manages nearly 50 percent of individuals' retirement funds, and regulates many industries. Most Americans live and work in a web of government rules.

Forces working to inhibit government include globalization—the ability of capital and services to move to hospitable jurisdictions—and the pace of technological change. For a quarter century, says DeMuth, the government has been trying and largely failing to regulate the computer industry: "Although it may lasso an individual firm such as Microsoft, it has no hope of corralling the entire industry as it did trucking and railroads in an earlier age."

However, more private wealth means more resources for the traditional lobbying of government and more incentives for government to try something new. It is what DeMuth calls "the New Executive State" expanding through extortion.

Consider the extraordinarily complex Clean Air Act, which has, in effect, been written mostly by the Environmental Protection Agency, courts, and environmental groups, negotiating rules that put flesh on what was at first a thin skeleton of congressional sentiments. The EPA's new ozone standards, now being appealed, would cost $100 billion *per year* if fully implemented and would yield negligible, if any, public health benefits, says DeMuth. The New Executive State's technique is not to fully implement such rules but to force firms and localities to negotiate waivers—with many strings attached.

The executive branch has used Title IX of the Education Act as an excuse for writing rules that are compelling many colleges to abolish some men's sports to achieve equal expenditures and participation in men's and women's sports. But Congress mentioned no such requirement in Title IX. The executive branch now engages in taxing and spending: the Federal Communications Commission established by regulation a tax—now producing more than $5 billion annually—on long-distance service. The FCC sets the rate and adjusts it to suit its plans for spending on computers for schools and other projects. DeMuth says dryly, "When the telephone companies announced plans to itemize the tax on their long-distance bills, the FCC chairman told them it would be better if they didn't."

DeMuth says the latest wrinkle in "executive taxation" is "recoupment litigation," such as the tobacco and gun suits. Government selects targets—in the tobacco and gun instances, legal industries manufacturing legal products. Government hires private lawyers, working for a percentage of the take, to force the targets, under the threat or actuality of litigation, to pay some of government's expenses—and to change some of their business practices.

We are not just now losing limited government as the Founders conceived it and as Americans debated it from the founding until the second half of the twentieth century. That conception and that debate are history. Several presidencies, particularly those of FDR and LBJ, and compliant Supreme Courts long ago interred the ideas that the federal government is limited by the Constitution's enumeration of its powers; that significant spheres of life are fenced off from the federal government; that there are some human wants and grievances that are not properly public business.

The new worry is that the government is not only unlimited in scope, it also is not limited by the politics of legislatures: public deliberations, accommodations to rival constituencies, pressures to moderation and compromise inherent in logrolling, and the competition for finite appropriations. And increasingly, government is not limited by the rule of law, understood, perhaps quaintly, as power controlled by laws enacted by Congress.

Congress is complicit in all this because Congress could stop it. Until it does, we will have more of what DeMuth calls "strip mall socialism," sprawling government, ubiquitous and undistinguished, with "no theme or theory, just momentum."

February 24, 2000

Hillary Clinton's
Insouciant Insincerity

The increasingly gothic tale that is Bill Clinton's current crisis was missing a savory ingredient until his wife, breathing fresh life into the paranoid style in American politics, blamed his problems on a "vast right-wing conspiracy," a phrase with an interesting pedigree. Joseph McCarthy, echoing J. Edgar Hoover's 1919 warning about a Communist conspiracy "so vast, so daring," warned in 1951 about "a conspiracy on a scale so immense" that it was everywhere.

Anticipating the Oliver Stone movie version of all this, Hillary Clinton supplied the "man on the grassy knoll" culprit. And, lo, the man is . . . Jerry Falwell!

Well. Paranoiacs can have real enemies, as does Bill Clinton. But neither he nor his wife is a paranoiac. Her insouciant insincerity in playing the conspiracy card is understandable, given that it is a Clinton habit and given the alternative, which is to discuss the facts—those known and those still concealed by her husband.

In the taped conversations with Gennifer Flowers, first heard in 1992, Bill Clinton suggested to her that if he became the subject of sexual accusations, "it would be extremely valuable" if she would "have an on-file affidavit explaining that, you know, you were approached by a Republican." (Should you consider those tapes accurate? Clinton did. He called Mario Cuomo to apologize for his taped statement that Cuomo "acts like a mafioso.")

Today's controversy has come with uncommon speed to the traditional "vast conspiracy" accusation. Fifty years ago it took Alger Hiss much longer to postulate that the FBI had fabricated a perfect duplicate of his Woodstock typewriter to link him to stolen State Department documents.

It is a lawyer's axiom: if you have the law on your side, argue the law; if you have the facts on your side, argue the facts; if you have neither, pound the table. Hillary Clinton's table pounding about the vast conspiracy continued Wednesday morning when she said on ABC, "I'm interested in what the facts are, and we know very few facts right now."

"We"? The man across from her at the breakfast table surely has lots of pertinent facts right now. So Hillary Clinton might begin to slake her thirst for facts by saying, "Pass the marmalade, and by the way, is *The New York Times* right that Monica Lewinsky met alone with you late last month, two weeks after being subpoenaed by Paula Jones's lawyers and a week before Lewinsky filed her affidavit saying she had not had sexual relations with you? Help yourself to the bacon, dear, and what *did* you and 'that woman' talk about, other than saving Social Security?"

"That woman" is the president's dismissive designation of her to whom he reportedly gave that private December meeting, and an inscribed book of poetry, and he alone knows what else. (Hillary Clinton is not surprised by all this giving, because "he is an extremely generous person"—"I mean, I've seen him take his tie off and hand it to somebody.")

Lewinsky seems to have had a remarkable interest in the intricacies of the law. She reportedly says on one of the tapes made by Linda Tripp that "perjury is rarely prosecuted in civil cases."

Perhaps she got that insight from "Vernon." That apparently is her way of speaking of Vernon Jordan, who Hillary Clinton says is so "outgoing and friendly" that there is just no telling what he will do for little people.

On Monday the president took care to seem quite cross about what is being said about him. What else is he angry about?

As chief executive he is charged with seeing that the laws are faithfully executed. So presumably he is furious that *someone* wrote the memo that Lewinsky had, suggesting how Tripp should amend her memory and testify concerning another woman, who supposedly had an unsolicited and unwanted sexual encounter with the chief executive. Is he consumed by curiosity about who wrote it and who gave it to Lewinsky? What steps is he taking to find out? More breakfast table talk for his wife.

Twenty-four years after President Nixon said in a State of the Union address that "one year of Watergate is enough," Hillary Clinton, the point of the White House spear, is saying that one week of Monica Lewinsky suffices and it is time to get on with the agenda the president outlined Tuesday evening. But first he may have to drive a stake through the heart of a right-wing conspiracy on a scale so immense that perhaps it even had Lewinsky as an agent in place. Gosh.

January 29, 1998

Friendship

I regret that what began as a friendship came to include this conduct.

—PRESIDENT CLINTON, AUGUST 17, 1998

Such is Bill Clinton's fecundity as a liar, there still are darkly illuminating lies that are just now being scrutinized for the first time, even by people who have been attentive to this scandal. Consider the lie printed above.

Like Poe's purloined letter, Clinton's lie has been in plain view. For five months. And it was neither a slip of the tongue nor a flustered response to an unexpected question. It was a carefully written part of a crafty script, coldly calculated and finely calibrated. It was in the written statement he read to the grand jury when he was asked the first question about his relationship with Monica Lewinsky.

But this relationship that supposedly "began" as a friendship actually became something else *very* quickly. The "conduct" that included oral sex (and e-mail describing the effect of chewing Altoids before performing oral sex) began the very *day* in 1995 that Clinton first met Lewinsky. As Representative James Rogan said to the Senate, within *hours* after Clinton met and spoke with Lewinsky for the first time, "he invited her back to the Oval Office to perform sex acts on him." Lewinsky has testified that even a month later, a month into both the "friendship" and "this conduct," she was still doubtful that Clinton even knew her name.

In the days before Clinton's August 17 grand jury appearance, various Republicans and Democrats pleaded with him not to lie. By then the spectacle of national leaders begging the chief executive not to intentionally commit additional crimes was no longer spectacular. Five months ago—seven months into this debacle—the scandal implicit in such begging had become banal. Such is the moral chaos Clinton has sown.

The lie quoted above, which Clinton read to the grand jury, should be kept in mind as Clinton's lawyers argue to the Senate that even his cumulative lies do not constitute an impeachable offense. The Senate will weigh Clinton's comportment against the Harkin Standard, which Iowa's Democratic Senator Tom Harkin clarified—perhaps improvidently, from his and Clinton's point of view. Consider the path the Senate took to that standard:

Two things are infinite: God's mercy, of course, but also the Senate's vanity. The House did its duty, as it saw it, by impeaching the president, thereby forcing the Senate promptly to do a minimal duty: to agree on rules for a trial. So the Senate produced a "bipartisan" agreement, in which each side got *exactly* what it wanted. This was not amazing, considering that both sides wanted precisely the same thing: praise. Even if the praise were to be, as it mostly was, self-bestowed.

The senators decided to decide some other day about whether to have—imagine this—a trial with witnesses. Still, such is Washington's hunger for reasons to (as is said nowadays) "feel good about itself," this exercise in kicking the can down the road was heralded by the kickers as an act of statesmanship akin to Lend-Lease.

Then, after hearing two days of the House managers' presentations about the facts and the law, Harkin successfully asked Chief Justice William Rehnquist to affirm the obvious: in impeachment trials, senators are more than mere jurors and hence are not bound to consider only the facts and the law. Harkin's eagerness to emphasize this point may be taken as a measure of the queasiness the president's supporters feel about relying on the facts and the law.

Harkin, who calls the House's articles of impeachment a "pile of dung," is agreeably free of the Senate's undignified preening about its dignity. And, eschewing the mock solemnity of his Democratic colleagues, Harkin does not pretend that he is interested in anything—say, facts, or the law—other than Clinton's survival. ("I am undecided until I hear all the facts," says Vermont's Democratic Senator Patrick Leahy gravely, moments after having disdained the "partisan impeachment" by the House, based on work by "an out-of-control special prosecutor.") Furthermore, Harkin is right: the Senate must consider the public good.

Which means Harkin, and others like him, must explain why the public good is served by leaving in the highest elective office the man who craftily wrote and coldly read the statement "I regret that what began as a friendship came to include this conduct." That senatorial task is actually much more difficult than Clinton's lawyers' mundane task of filling the air with dust about the facts and the law.

January 21, 1999

The Silence of the Law and "the Silent Artillery of Time"

The times may seem out of joint, but suddenly at least some names fit. Republicans are acting like Republicans, Democrats like Democrats.

Republicans have chosen a steep path strewn with hazards. However, by their choice they have pledged allegiance to the republican principle. They are trying to spike "the silent artillery of time."

For Democrats, "responsive" is the highest encomium for government. They favor maximum feasible directness in the translation of public opinion into government policy. They want opinion to be only minimally mediated. They believe that in polities larger than city-states, representatives are necessary but a representative's duty is deference—faithful, immediate, emphatic replication of opinion into action.

The Founders and subsequent republicans believe public opinion is the starting point of popular government, but opinion should be refined by deliberative processes. The "republican principle . . . does not require an unqualified complaisance to every sudden breeze of passion, or to every transient impulse." When "the interests of the people are at variance with their inclinations" it is the representatives' duty "to give them time and opportunity for more cool and sedate reflection" (Alexander Hamilton, *The Federalist,* no. 71).

By leaning against the wind of opinion regarding impeachment, the reflective Republicans are exercising leadership. That is perilous in a democratic age because leadership suggests if not a defect, at least an insufficiency on the part of the people. Although people clamor for leadership, when it occurs they are apt to regard it as an act of lèse-majesté because it implies that deliberative processes of representative institutions are required to "refine and enlarge" their opinions (James Madison, *The Federalist,* no. 10). The Founders and subsequent republicans, not being sentimentalists, have worried more than democrats have about the importance of, possible scarcity of, and provision for, virtue, absent which popular government will fail.

In his most famous utterance, the first Republican president and most profound president wondered whether a nation like America "can long endure." A quarter century earlier, in his extraordinary speech to the Young Men's Lyceum of Springfield, he had worried about the damage done to nations by "the silent artillery of time." In this Abraham Lincoln echoed Edward Gibbon's last volume of *Decline and Fall of the Roman Empire,* where the first answer Gibbon gave to the question of why Rome had fallen was "the injuries of time."

Gibbon's last volume was published in 1788, as the ratification of the U.S. Constitution was being debated. Benjamin Franklin, asked as he left the Constitutional Convention what it had wrought, replied, "A republic, if you can keep it." America's Founders were haunted by history's record of the failure of republics. In his Farewell Address, President George Washington pondered what could "prevent our nation from running the course which has hitherto marked the destiny of nations."

The Founders knew the ancients' assumption that virtue tends to be a wasting asset, that morals tend to deteriorate, and therefore that fatalism is wisdom: nations rise and fall by natural cycles. The boldness—audacity, even—of America's Founders was in their belief that history could be beaten by reflection that results in institutions: our constitutional order.

Republicans flying in the face of today's political ethic—its categorical imperative: to thy polls be true—should take comfort from the fact that their resistance to Clinton's lawlessness has a pedigree that runs back to the Founders' thoughts about the perils that make republics perishable. Clinton's calculated, sustained lying has involved an extraordinarily corrupting assault on language, which is the uniquely human capacity that makes persuasion, and hence popular government, possible. Hence the obtuseness of those who say Clinton's behavior is compatible with constitutional principles, presidential duties, and republican ethics.

It is axiomatic: Worse than a society with no law is one with only law. As law metastasizes in America, codes of personal behavior wither. Increasingly, our leaders—disproportionately lawyers—behave as though the silence of the law confers permission: What is not proscribed is permitted.

One manifestation of the degeneration of private judgment is the president's evident incapacity even to imagine that honor might require his resignation. For eleven months the nation has lived with a paradox: If he had the moral sense to resign, he would not be in the position to need to.

The Founders provided impeachment to cope with the likes of Clinton, a president who, by recidivist lying without remorse, has fallen below the threshold of minimal truthfulness and has traduced political discourse. He cannot speak credibly on grave matters, such as war. He should go, for the public good. Public opinion is neither sufficient nor necessary to justify that.

December 20, 1998

Closing the Lewinsky Parenthesis

As the Lewinsky Parenthesis in America's political conversation comes to a close, consider two changes it has accelerated. One is a revision of the job description of president. The other is the conservatives' collapse of confidence.

The first is partly the result of a conservative impulse and partly a product of conservatives' excesses. The second requires conservatives to practice the cardinal virtue of their creed: prudence, which involves facing facts and distinguishing between those that can be changed and those that must be accommodated. To begin understanding both changes, consider the three reasons why the public has steadily (showing none of the volatility the Founders feared) held to its judgment that Bill Clinton is both a bad man and a good president.

First, conservatives, in their sensible desire to dampen Americans' enthusiasm for government, have indiscriminately portrayed the political class as contemptible. The public has been convinced of that by conservatives, to a degree now inconvenient to conservatives, and so has not been scandalized by Clinton's scandals.

Second, between 1952 and 1988 Republicans controlled both houses of Congress only two years (1953–54) but won seven of ten and five of the last six presidential elections during that span. Republicans held the presidency for all but twelve of the forty years prior to 1992. As a result, conservatives became fixated on the presidency and opportunistically adopted the vocabulary of watery Caesarism, arguing that social progress is a measure of, because it is a consequence of, presidential aptitude. The quite unconservative premise—its pedigree traces to turn-of-the-century Progressives—is that government, particularly the executive branch of the central government, is the most important creative agency in society. So today's high approval by a content, prospering country of its president's job performance rests on an assumption that conservatives embraced.

Third, why are many conservatives shocked that the first modern nation, the United States, is embracing a distinction made by the founder of modern political thought, Niccolò Machiavelli? He (see *The Prince*, Chapter 8) argued that one could be a "most excellent captain" without being "among the most excellent men." Time was, conservatives relished Conservative Prime Minister Harold Macmillan's answer when he was asked if he would give people moral direction. For that, he said, they should consult their bishops, not their politicians.

Machiavelli earned a bad reputation by severing the assessment of a politician's job performance from the assessment of his moral qualities. Less radical thinkers—temperate Machiavellians—know that a morally exemplary leader is an occasional bonus in political life and occasionally is imperative, but is not necessary for the functioning of a well-founded regime. As James Madison wrote, with dry understatement, in *The Federalist*, no. 10, "Enlightened statesmen will not always be at the helm."

Clinton is surviving because the public wants him to, and it wants this *for essentially conservative reasons.* Conservatives, not recognizing the conservative roots of the public's reasoning, are disconcerted by this and by the fact that the political market is ratifying conservatism's successes of recent years.

Many conservatives crankily charge Clinton with intellectual larceny in his macroissues (balanced budget, welfare reform) and microissues (V chips, school uniforms). Now he has moved rightward regarding what is arguably the most important issue of the 1990s—missile defense—and some conservatives' gloom has deepened.

As recently as September, forty-one Democratic senators filibustered to prevent a vote on a Senate resolution declaring it U.S. policy to deploy effective antimissile defenses of the territory of the United States as soon as that is technologically possible. Five months later that resolution expresses administration policy.

And some conservatives, in their almost clinical obsession with Clinton, have responded by talking of themselves as *victims* of an *unfair* expropriation of their policy property. Cannot such conservatives hear their own larceny? They are stealing the whiny language of contemporary liberalism.

Some conservatives who celebrate the working of markets in petroleum and potato chips seem to dislike market forces affecting political ideas. They complain when demand for a political program they advocate causes Clinton to move toward supplying what is demanded. But that is how things are supposed to work when conservatives succeed in moving the center of political gravity to the right.

Even before the Lewinsky Parenthesis began, many conservatives were quite cross with the public because that center had not moved enough to permit implementation of conservatives' plans for pruning government. Now Clinton is wielding his popularity to advocate a huge and potentially popular new entitlement: Medicare coverage of prescription drugs. This will reveal whether conservatives' capacity for persuasion has been crippled by self-pity.

January 28, 1999

Sorry About That

SOUTH POLE, January 19, 2001—President Clinton today apologized to Antarctica.

Speaking to an audience composed of the traveling press, Clinton said he repented for America's "sin" of neglecting this continent except when America paid a kind of improper attention to it. He regretted that during the Cold War, U.S. policy "subordinated the true interests of Antarctica to geopolitical calculations arising from the conflict with the former Soviet Union."

Last year, Mr. Clinton apologized to Russia for U.S. policies that he said had caused the collapse of communism. He said this diminished the world's political "diversity."

In words barely audible here over polar winds, Mr. Clinton expressed regret for the "insensitivity of American stereotyping." He said that "for too long American ethnocentrism and cultural chauvinism have caused us to think of Antarctica only as a cold and icy place."

Mr. Clinton praised the recent decision of San Francisco authorities to require high school students to read at least one novel from "the canon of Antarctic classics." America, he said, is "a gorgeous mosaic of multiculturalism" and should be ashamed of educational practices that "through centuries of cultural oppression, have privileged European contributions to art and literature over the contributions of others."

"We must not fear differences," Mr. Clinton said. "We have extended curriculum recognition far, but you can never extend it too far. Now it is time for inclusion of snow and ice."

Mr. Clinton, who has been traveling outside the United States every day since the middle of March 1998, came to this frozen setting to complete what he calls "this tour of tears." Aides say that Mr. Clinton, who has spoken often of his "legacy," believes that history will remember him not for pioneering new dimensions in executive privilege but for his "foreign policy of creative contrition."

The policy was born in Uganda on March 24, 1998, when Mr. Clinton, for the first time, apologized to an entire continent in one fell swoop. In Uganda, which in the 1970s was governed by General Idi Amin, Mr. Clinton encouraged Africans to dwell on the foreign sources of their sufferings.

He announced that slavery was "wrong," and he essentially apologized to all Africans for all the white people who bought African slaves captured by African sellers of slaves. He also apologized because during the Cold War, America had been more apt to be friendly to African nations that were friendly to America.

By telling Ugandans that "the United States has not always done the right thing by Africa," Mr. Clinton began a foreign policy built around apologies to all other peoples, nations, and continents toward which American behavior has not always been perfect. In Uganda he noted that Americans were precocious sinners, having had slavery to be ashamed of "before we were even a nation." But slavery was not the worst: "Perhaps the worst sin America ever committed about Africa was the sin of neglect and ignorance."

Mr. Clinton's first post-Ugandan stop in his penitential travels was Outer Mongolia. Presidential polling revealed deep American ignorance of, and unrepentant neglect of, Outer Mongolia. Mr. Clinton told a cluster of Outer Mongolians and their horses that the United States is a nation in North America and that it would try to do better by them.

The State Department, responding to Mr. Clinton's determination to be compassionate to all victims of American neglect and ignorance and sin, has organized a Bureau of Abasement. It is headed by an Assistant Secretary of State for Regrets.

However, Mr. Clinton has insisted that "being ashamed does not have to be all sackcloth and ashes." Last year he ordered the Air Force to give *Air Force One* a new name for the remainder of his presidency. The plane's new name has been painted on the nose of the fuselage: *"Sorry About That!"*

In his nearly thirty-four months of incessant traveling, Mr. Clinton has offered a generic apology for America being big, rich, powerful, and happy. However, he has also regretted specific American "sins," such as forcing other nations to drink Coca-Cola, watch *Dallas* reruns, accept foreign aid, and put up with the presence of the American troops that liberated them or kept them free.

Mr. Clinton insists that being volubly embarrassed by one's country's actions is a form of patriotism. "Love of country," he says, "means always having to say you're sorry."

On the last full day of his presidency, Mr. Clinton flew home from

Antarctica on *Sorry About That!* to what one adviser noted was the only country Mr. Clinton has not apologized to.

March 29, 1998

Clinton's Legacy: An Adjective

B ecause of his political monomania and because he is a perpetual preener
who can strut even while sitting, Bill Clinton relished being president. The
pomp, the cameras, the microphones make that office a narcissist's delight. But
other than by soiling the office, he was a remarkably inconsequential president, like a person who walks across a field of snow and leaves no footprints.

It is axiomatic: Some people want public office in order to do something;
others in order to be something. Clinton was the latter sort. Which is why he
never seriously considered dealing with America's most serious policy problem and why he was an unserious president.

Some problems come as bolts from the blue, unanticipated, not because of
negligence but because of the general opacity of the future: the Depression,
the AIDS epidemic. Other problems are seen coming, but the time at which
they will reach critical mass is unclear: the environmental toll of industrialism,
African-Americans' struggle for access to opportunity.

But both the size and arrival time of America's great impending problem
were known when Clinton became president and chose not to address the
problem pre-emptively. That problem is the coming collision between the
baby boomers' graying and the welfare state's promise to palliate the consequences of illness and old age.

Serious historians probably will rate Clinton as perhaps more consequential than Chester Arthur—although Clinton had no achievement as substantial
as Arthur's civil service reform—but much less consequential than, say, Lyndon Johnson or Richard Nixon. Clinton's great accomplishment was negative.
He inherited a rising economy—although he campaigned in 1992 as though
the country were in a recession, it ended a year and a half before he entered
the White House. Partly because there was a Republican Congress during
three-quarters of his presidency, his policies did not interfere with the private
sector's wealth creation, which made possible his proudest, but not notably
Democratic, boasts: a balanced budget, then a surplus.

The two most important policy developments of the Clinton years were
the enhancement of free trade (NAFTA, GATT, normalized trade with

China) and welfare reform. The former happened because Clinton favored it and most Republicans, unlike most Democrats, supported it. The latter happened because he did not dare to veto a third time what Republicans persisted in sending to him. Regarding two things he would never compromise about, racial preferences and abortion on demand, he was on the cutting edge of twenty-five years ago, when he and those policies were young.

Clinton's greatest effect has been on his party. He repositioned it as the servant of the comfortable middle class eager for more comforts. He reaped his reward where the comfortable live, in the suburbs, where Republicans won between 55 percent and 61 percent of the vote in 1980, 1984, and 1988. Political analyst Charles Cook says Clinton carried the suburbs by two points in 1992 and five points in 1996. In 2000, 43 percent of the votes were in the suburbs, where George W. Bush beat Al Gore by just two points.

Fortunately, America has enjoyed something of a holiday from history since the Gulf War. For eight years America's armed forces have been diminished while their tempo of operations has increased. To the question "Are you better off than you were eight years ago?" Saddam Hussein and Yasser Arafat can answer a resounding "Yes."

Some presidents' names become adjectives: Lincolnian gravity, Rooseveltian reassurance, Kennedyesque charisma, Nixonian deviousness, Reaganesque leadership. To understand the meaning of "Clintonian," parse this from a 1997 news conference: "I don't believe you can find any evidence of the fact that I have changed government policy solely because of a contribution."

It is reasonable to believe he was a rapist fifteen years before becoming president, and that as president he launched cruise missiles against Afghanistan (a nearly empty terrorist camp), Sudan (a pharmaceutical factory), and Iraq to distract attention from problems arising from the glandular dimension of his general indiscipline. As president he was fined $90,000 for contempt of court, and there is no reasonable doubt that he committed and suborned perjury, tampered with witnesses, and otherwise obstructed justice. In the words of Richard A. Posner, chief judge of the Seventh Circuit Court, Clinton's illegalities "were felonious, numerous and nontechnical" and "constituted a kind of guerrilla warfare against the third branch of the federal government, the federal court system."

Clinton is not the worst president the republic has had, but he is the worst person ever to have been president.

January 11, 2001

A College Education

Political hypochondriacs again are urging Americans to fear and be offended by the system of choosing presidents by electoral votes. Criticism of this system recurs whenever a close contest poses the possibility that a candidate might win an electoral vote victory while receiving fewer popular votes than his opponent. It is said, with more passion than precision, that this happened three times: 1824, 1876, 1888.

Even if that is true, it means that in fifty of fifty-three elections since 1789—in 94 percent of elections, and in twenty-seven consecutive elections—the system has not produced the outcome that troubles the sleep of its critics. Besides, the assertions about those elections can be true without being pertinent.

In 1824, before the emergence of the two-party system, all four candidates appeared on the ballots in only six of the twenty-four states. Six states, including New York, had no elections: their state legislatures picked the electors. Nationally, only about 350,000 of the 4 million eligible white males voted. In 1828 Andrew Jackson received 38,149 more votes than John Quincy Adams, but neither received a majority of electoral votes. So the House of Representatives decided, picking Adams. In 1888 fraud on both sides may have involved more votes than the victory margin (90,596).

There *never* has been an Electoral College victory by a candidate who lost the popular vote by a substantial margin. And only simpleminded majoritarianism holds that "the nation's will" would be "frustrated" and democracy "subverted" (this is the language of Electoral College abolitionists) were an electoral vote majority to go to a candidate who comes in a close second in the popular-vote count. In such a case, the Framers' objective—a president chosen through state-by-state decisions—would be achieved.

The Electoral College has evolved, shaping and being shaped by the two-party system, which probably would not survive abandonment of winner-take-all allocation of electoral votes. Direct popular election of presidents, or proportional allocation of states' electoral votes, would incite minor parties to fractionate the electorate. This might necessitate runoff elections to guarantee that the eventual president got at least 40 percent of the vote—and runoffs might become auctions in which minor parties sold their support.

The electoral vote system shapes the *character* of winning majorities. By avoiding proportional allocation of electoral votes, America's system—under which Ross Perot in 1992 got 19 percent of the popular votes and zero electoral votes—buttresses the dominance of two parties and pulls them to the center, producing a temperate politics of coalition rather than a proliferation of ideological factions with charismatic leaders.

Furthermore, choosing presidents by electoral votes is an incentive for candidates to wage truly national campaigns, building majorities that are geographically as well as ideologically broad. Consider: Were it not for electoral votes allocated winner-take-all, would candidates campaign in, say, West Virginia? In 1996 Bill Clinton decisively defeated Bob Dole there 52 percent to 37 percent. But that involved a margin of just 93,866 votes (327,812 to 233,946), a trivial amount compared to what can be harvested in large cities. However, for a 5–0 electoral-vote sweep, West Virginia is worth a trip or two.

Some Electoral College abolitionists argue that a candidate could get elected with just 27 percent of the popular vote—by winning the eleven largest states by just one vote in each and not getting a single popular vote anywhere else. But it is equally pointless to worry that a candidate could carry Wyoming 220,000 to 0, could lose the other forty-nine states and the District of Columbia by an average of 4,400 votes, and be the popular-vote winner while losing the electoral vote 535 to 3. Serious people take seriously probabilities, not mere possibilities. And abolitionists are not apt to produce what Madison was too sober to attempt, a system under which no unwanted outcome is even theoretically possible.

Critics of the Electoral College say it makes some people's votes more powerful than others'. This is true. In 1996, 211,571 Wyoming voters cast presidential ballots, awarding three electoral votes, one for every 70,523 voters, whereas 10,019,484 California voters awarded fifty-four electoral votes, one for every 185,546 voters.

So what? Do critics want to abolish the Senate as well? Delaware, the least populous state in 1789, was understandably the first to ratify the Constitution with its equal representation of states in the Senate: Virginia, the most populous, had eleven times more voters. Today Wyoming's senators' votes can cancel those of California's senators, who represent sixty-nine times more people. If that offends you, so does America's constitutional federalism.

The electoral-vote system, like the Constitution it serves, was not devised by, and should not be revised by, simpleminded majoritarians.

November 2, 2000

435 May Be 565 Too Few

A s George W. Bush prepares to exchange the pleasures of rusticity at his ranch for the capital's political climate that he vows to improve, here is a proposal for doing so: Increase the size of the House of Representatives to 1,000 seats.

Today's number, 435, is neither written into the Constitution nor graven on the heart of humanity by the finger of God. It was set by a 1911 statute, which can be changed in a trice.

In 1910, when America's population was 92,228,496, the ratio of representatives to citizens was one for every 212,999. The House has had 435 members since 1912 (except briefly after Alaska and Hawaii became states in 1959, when there were 437 representatives until after the 1960 census).

The first Congress had 65 representatives for about 3.9 million Americans, one for every 60,000. Not until 1860 did the ratio top one for every 100,000. Today the ratio is one for every 646,947. In 1790 only Virginia had that many residents (692,000). Today, four states (Alaska, North Dakota, Vermont, Wyoming) do not have that many. So now representatives, whom the Founders intended to represent smaller numbers than senators, represent more people than most senators did in the Founders' era.

If there were 1,000 representatives today, the ratio would be one for every 281,000, about what it was in 1930. Candidates could campaign as candidates did in the prebroadcasting era, with more retail than wholesale politicking, door to door, meeting by meeting. Hence there would be less need for money, most of which now buys television time. So enlarging the House can be justified in terms of the goal that nowadays trumps all others among "progressive" thinkers: campaign finance reform.

Much of the political class and the media, with the special irresponsibility each brings to campaign finance reform, saluted and swooned in admiration when John McCain recently vowed to force prompt action on his reform bill. The swooning saluters were undeterred by the fact that the contents of McCain's bill had not yet been—and still have not been—divulged.

However, one of Bush's published reform proposals, although potentially hugely important, goes largely unremarked. It would ban lobbyists from making campaign contributions to any senator or representative while Congress is in session. This, even more than the seating problems in a 1,000-member House, would be a *powerful* incentive for Congress to have shorter sessions.

Critics will say, correctly, that the House chamber cannot seat a thousand members, that it would be crowded and uncomfortable, that office space would be so severely rationed that staffs would have to be trimmed, so the House, and therefore Congress, could not do very much. Sensible people

would be dry-eyed about such conditions, which would encourage representatives not to tarry here.

Besides, congestion would be constructive. The greatest democratic
statesman of the last century understood this.

On May 10, 1941, an air raid badly damaged the House of Commons,
which moved its sitting to the House of Lords. On October 28, 1943, Winston Churchill delivered a short, brilliant speech concerning reconstruction.
"We shape our buildings," he said, "and afterwards our buildings shape us."
Hence he said that the House "should not be big enough to contain all its
Members at once without overcrowding, and that there should be no question
of every Member having a separate seat reserved for him."

In a House that could accommodate everyone, most debates would be
conducted in the depressing atmosphere of an almost empty chamber. (As any
viewer of C-SPAN knows, this is the case in the House of Representatives today.) But, said Churchill, good parliamentary dialogue—quick, informal, con-
versational—"requires a fairly small space, and there should be on great
occasions a sense of crowd and urgency." Besides, the House's vitality and its
hold on the nation's imagination "depend to no small extent upon its episodes
and great moments, even upon its scenes and rows, which, as everyone will
agree, are better conducted at close quarters."

Of course, the House of Representatives will not more than double its
size, thereby diluting the majesty of membership and the power of each member. In truth, there are reasons for not doing so, including considerations of
sheer cumbersomeness.

Nevertheless, it is well to acknowledge arguments for enlargement. They
point to possible connections between institutional attributes and the tone and
quality of representative government, which, as the president-elect has repeatedly said, has room for improvement.

January 14, 2001

What the Remorseless
Improvers Have Wrought

The nation held its breath. Or was it stifling a yawn? In any case, presidential
politics became *serious* last week because a bunch of candidates broadcast
television ads. Consider how far American politics has come to be this sort of
spectator sport.

Once upon a time, Americans' zest for politics astonished the world. In Jules Verne's *Around the World in Eighty Days* (1873), Phileas Fogg, passing through San Francisco, gets swept up in a tremendous election hullabaloo. Fogg asks if the awesome commotion is for "the election of a general-in-chief, no doubt?" He is told, "No, sir; of a justice of the peace."

Nineteenth-century political speeches, writes Michael Schudson, were "long enough to help kill two presidents—William Henry Harrison, who died from complications of exposure at his own inauguration, and Zachary Taylor, who died following the dedication ceremonies for the Washington Monument." In 1858, the first of seven Lincoln–Douglas debates, in Ottawa, Illinois, a city of about 7,000, was witnessed—you cannot say heard—by about 20,000, none of whom, in those days before direct election of senators, could vote for either candidate.

American politics, at that time the best entertainment money did not have to buy, was entering its era of maximum popular participation. But soon "progressive" high-mindedness would help put a stop to that.

Schudson, of the University of California, San Diego, argues in his book *The Good Citizen: A History of American Civic Life* that politics from the colonial period through the Revolution was a "politics of assent." Elections were acts of deference, ratifying rule by the gentry, which regarded political office as an obligation connected with social standing.

But urbanization produced heterogeneous populations, newspapers (by 1794 they made up 70 percent of the weight in the postal system) fueled argumentation, and immigration produced fierce rivalries among ethnic communities. Soon mass-based parties replaced the politics of deference with the "politics of affiliation."

Between Lincoln and Teddy Roosevelt, writes Schudson, no president captured the public's imagination, yet "these were the years of the highest voter turnout in our entire history. Americans of that era *enjoyed* politics." It was not elevated politics. It was a sport of rival social groups organized into teams (parties) around "ethnocultural" issues—immigration, church schools, temperance—at least as bitterly divisive as today's social issues.

But in the late nineteenth century in the North, 70 percent or more of those eligible usually voted in presidential elections. This was partly a tribute to political machines: Pennsylvania's Republican organization had 20,000 wage-earning workers—more employees than most of the state's railroads. And Schudson says that during the Gilded Age as many as 20 percent of New York City voters may have been paid in some form or other as Election Day workers. Then righteous reformers and caring government took much of the fun, and a lot of the voters, out of politics.

Reformers wanted fewer parades and more pamphlets—voting should be not an act of group solidarity but an individual act of informed competence.

Parties, said well-bred reformers, should not just rally committed followers, who often were, well, not the sort of folks who knew which fork to use with the fish course. Rather, parties should persuade the uncommitted. The progressive aspiration, says Schudson, was a "citizenship of intelligence rather than passionate intensity."

The coming of solicitous government gave people rights to things they had once received for services rendered to the party. In the nineteenth century, Schudson says, people could "smell and taste the material benefits in politics." Under the twentieth century's sanitized, omnipresent, and omniprovident government, services became less connected with elected officials than with bureaucracies, so "self-interest in political life became more of an imaginative leap."

By 1924 *The New Republic* was wondering about "the vanishing voter." But by then World War I propaganda had proved that opinion could be manufactured. And Freudians, crowd psychologists, and sociologists (sociology, virtually untaught in 1890, was taught at more than three hundred universities by 1910) were suggesting that individual autonomy is a chimera. This theory emancipated intellectuals from the obligation to respect democracy and became an (unspoken) axiom of modern liberalism and judicial activism.

Today government does more and more for citizens who vote less and less. Celebrating expertise and stigmatizing partisanship, the remorseless improvers of our politics have the reformers' perennial aspiration of replacing politics with administration. Witness John McCain's John Brown–like passion to purge politics of "special interests": only unspecial interests should be heard from.

The improvers have always aimed at reducing the passionate and increasing the cognitive ingredient in voting. Think of that as you watch the candidates' ads.

November 21, 1999

A Free-Love Nominating System

L ast week the Supreme Court heard arguments in a case that, if correctly decided, will strengthen First Amendment freedoms of speech and association and demonstrate that much of John McCain's strength in the primaries was made possible by state election laws inimical to those freedoms. The question at issue is whether California's "blanket" primary abridges the freedom of individuals to associate in political parties that serve as their right to express their chosen philosophies.

In closed primaries, only registered members of a party can vote. In open primaries, any registered voter can get any party's ballot. In blanket primaries, no party has its own ballot or primary.

On a "blanket" ballot, voters can choose among all parties' candidates for each office. All candidates of all parties for a particular office are listed together under that office. The Republican who gets the most votes among Republican candidates gets the party's line on the general election ballot, and so with candidates of all other parties. (California treats only presidential primaries differently: ballots are coded, and only votes of registered party members count in the allocation of national convention delegates.)

Californians want the blanket primary: they established it by initiative with 60 percent of their votes. However, constitutionalism limits the wants that are permissible. As the Supreme Court has said, the purpose of the Bill of Rights is to put some things "beyond the reach of majorities"—things like First Amendment freedoms.

Four California parties—Republican, Democratic, Libertarian, and Peace and Freedom—last week told the Court that the blanket primary annihilates their freedom to associate for the expressive purpose of advocating their political philosophies. It does so by stripping party members of control of the selection of their candidates and hence of their message. In a blanket primary, a party's nomination can be won by a candidate other than the one who gets a majority of the party members' votes.

The Court has said states can require parties to select candidates by primaries but do not have carte blanche to dictate the nature of the primaries. In 1986 the Court overturned Connecticut's law requiring closed primaries, siding with Connecticut's Republican Party, which wanted an open primary as a means of broadening its base.

Proponents of blanket primaries say that by enabling lightly committed, barely partisan voters to opt for any candidate, they produce more "moderate," less ideological nominees. Opponents say that even if it were (which it is not) obviously good to blur the philosophical clarity and dampen the ideological warmth of parties, government has no right to break parties to the saddle of such a state-imposed orthodoxy—to mandate a primary the purpose of which is to change the nature of the parties' speech.

Proponents say that by multiplying choices, blanket primaries increase voter participation. Indeed, California's assistant attorney general defended the blanket primary by asserting, "The more people you have voting, the more representative the candidates are going to be."

Opponents ask, In what kindergarten is *that* theory of representation taught? There is much more to representation than elementary arithmetic. Parties are indispensable instruments of representation because they aggregate interests and articulate distinctive doctrines of justice. But parties cannot do this if they can be hijacked by drive-by voters with no durable interest in the parties, acting on transitory whims or even to make mischief by burdening a party with a weak candidate.

The Court might flinch from ruling against blanket primaries because such a decision would have serious implications for the twenty-three states that have open primaries. It should not flinch.

If a blanket primary is (as the lawyer for California's Democratic Party says) "a free-love nominating system where [voters] go from party to party and no one has to declare any fidelity," an open primary is comparable. For many voters, such as many Democrats and independents who gave McCain victories in New Hampshire's and Michigan's open Republican primaries, open primaries are one-night stands.

The Court has said that freedom of association "plainly presupposes a freedom not to associate." But blanket and open primaries force party members to associate with persons indifferent or hostile to the aims that party members join together in order to advocate. And such primaries can allow people completely unassociated with the party to foist upon it nominees—messengers—who express messages contrary to those the party members wish to express. Whatever can be said in support of California's desire to pump up the turnout in primaries, that desire cannot trump First Amendment freedoms.

April 30, 2000

FDR Pays His Taxes

A seasonal foreboding again settles on the Republic. H & R Block, which prepares the income tax forms of about one in seven taxpayers, is broadcasting television commercials featuring the ingeniously cryptic slogan "We know. Do you?"

Those four words capture the ominous mood of March in this country. In America, home of the free and land of due process, most taxpayers find it impossible to know if they are complying with tax law.

As a taxpayer wrote to the commissioner of Inland Revenue (as it then was) in March 1938, "I am enclosing my income tax return for the calendar year 1937, together with my check for $15,000. I am wholly unable to figure out the amount of the tax." And figuring tax obligations was relatively simple when President Franklin Roosevelt wrote that.

In the 1960s the *H & R Block Income Tax Guide* was 196 pages long. In 1988 it was 317 pages. By 1998 it was 574. In 1997, forty-five daring tax professionals participated in *Money* magazine's annual experiment, each one preparing the magazine's sample tax return. Result? Forty-five different bottom lines. Fewer than one in four came within $1,000 of the correct answer.

Also in 1997, a Congress controlled by Republicans, who profess to favor tax simplification, passed legislation with the Orwellian title "Taxpayer Relief Act." It added to the tax code 800 amendments, 290 new sections, and 36 retroactive provisions. No wonder when you drive downtown or to a mall you are four times more apt to see an H & R Block office than a Gap store.

These depressing facts are supplied by Amity Shlaes of *The Wall Street Journal*. Her scalding new book, *The Greedy Hand: How Taxes Drive Americans Crazy and What to Do About It,* makes clear that no matter how indignant you are about the tax code, you are not keeping up with the multiplying reasons for indignation. Consider the experience of John and Barbara Zwynenburg.

When in December 1988 their son was killed in the terrorist bombing of Pan Am Flight 103 over Lockerbie, Scotland, they expected some sort of settlement from Pan Am. But before receiving anything from Pan Am they heard from the IRS, which demanded $6 million—its estimate of its share of the coming settlement. (Which eventually was for thousands, not millions.)

Such anecdotes usefully get the public's dander up, but they concern episodes less injurious to the public than are the broad consequences of tax policies.

Shlaes shows how estate taxes kill family businesses, 70 percent of which do not make it from the founding generation to the next. The family that owns, say, a Burger King franchise, which is valuable but does not generate a large cash flow, may have to sell it to pay the tax on the value of it.

Job creation is hurt by the payroll tax. Just the *visible* half paid by the teenager behind the McDonald's counter (the half the employer pays does not show up on a worker's pay stub) is at a higher rate (7.65 percent) than the rate Congress imposed on millionaires (7 percent) when it inaugurated the income tax in 1913.

High property taxes intended to fund good schools drive away affluent homeowners, depress property values, and hurt schools. The reduction (this is effectively a tax) of Social Security benefits to seniors who earn "too much" idles vigorous, productive workers in a time of labor scarcity. And so it goes.

Shlaes twice cites former Treasury Secretary William Simon's acerbic remark that America should have a tax system that looks as though someone designed it on purpose. But Shlaes and Simon are political sophisticates who know that the metastasizing tax code (it is twice the length of *War and Peace,* and the code regulations are more than four times longer than the code) actually embodies the purposes of the political class.

For that class, amending the tax code amounts to appropriating by other means. Every wrinkle in the code was put there to please some constituency, which becomes attentive to the defense—if not the enlargement—of the favor.

Which is why radical tax simplification would not be merely a step toward a more rational use of economic resources, it would also be a *political* reform, restraining the political class and crippling the coterie of lawyers and lobbyists who are parasites on the ever more baroque tax code.

Which is why simplification is one of two reforms (the other is term limits) the political class opposes in spite of their popularity. The limits of that class's desire to please the public are reached when what pleases the public limits that class.

March 14, 1999

A Democrat Learns to Love Trickle-Down Economics

O nce when Paul Hindemith, composer of very modern music, was rehearsing one of his especially dissonant compositions, he interrupted the orchestra, saying, "No, no, gentlemen. Even though it sounds wrong, it's still not right."

Contemporary politics, a kind of atonal music, produces moments like that. Consider the proposed legislation by Representative Patrick Kennedy, Democrat of Rhode Island, to succor the yacht industry and assuage the pains of its most put-upon customers.

The Omnibus Budget Reconciliation Act of 1990 was the budget agreement by which President Bush broke his "read-my-lips" vow not to agree to new taxes. The act was, as omnibus bills tend to be, an eye-of-newt-and-hair-of-toad brew of this and that and some other things, and it included—in the name of fairness, of course—a stern tax on "luxury items."

Those items included automobiles, aircraft, jewelry, and furs over certain prices. And yachts costing more than $100,000.

In 1990 there were no luxury excise taxes, all of them having been repealed in 1965. But perhaps every quarter century or so government—it cannot help itself—must go on a "fairness" bender, the memory of the hangover from similar misadventures having faded.

In 1990 the Joint Committee on Taxation projected that the 1991 revenue yield from the luxury taxes would be $31 million. The actual yield was $16.6 million. Why? Because—surprise!—the taxation changed behavior: fewer people bought the taxed products. Demand went down when prices went up. Washington was amazed. People bought yachts overseas. Who would have thought it?

According to a study done for the Joint Economic Committee, the tax destroyed 330 jobs in jewelry manufacturing, 1,470 in the aircraft industry, and 7,600 in the boating industry. The job losses cost the government a total of $24.2 million in unemployment benefits and lost income tax revenues. So the net effect of the taxes was a loss of $7.6 million in fiscal 1991, which means the government projection was off by $38.6 million.

This illustrates the shortcomings of "static analysis." Concerning which, consider an imaginary case.

It has been calculated that if the federal government imposed—in the name of fairness, of course—a 100 percent tax on all the earnings, from the first penny, of all millionaires, which is to say if the government confiscated all their earnings, the sum would suffice to run the government for just six weeks. The problem with that calculation is that it reflects "static analysis." That is, it does not allow for the behavioral changes the tax would provoke: No one would earn the one-millionth dollar, thereby triggering the confiscation, so the revenue yield from the 100 percent rate on millionaires would be zero.

But back to reality. "Practical politics," Henry Adams famously said, "consists in ignoring facts." But facts are famously stubborn things, particularly when they involve unpleasantness for one's constituents. In 1993 Congress repealed the excise taxes on boats, aircraft, jewelry, and furs. It also indexed, phased down, and scheduled the expiration of the tax on cars.

Now comes Kennedy with the Boat Building Investment Act, which he calls "exactly the opposite of a luxury tax." Indeed it is.

Its centerpiece is a 20 percent tax credit for purchasers of American-made luxury yachts over 50 feet long. So the purchaser of a $1 million yacht would get a $200,000 credit against his federal income taxes.

However, this would not be an unlimited benefit for the upper crust. The credit would be capped at $2 million, so the government would help only with the first $10 million that a purchaser spends on a yacht.

You probably have not heard of Kennedy's legislation. Do you think you might have heard a media uproar about it if its author were a Republican? Just a thought.

Kennedy says America lags behind other nations in "supporting" boat manufacturers, so this bill also would spend $25 million annually on "export assistance"—for example, marketing American-made yachts at overseas expositions—and training employees of America's yacht builders. This is necessary, Kennedy says, to "continue the revitalization" of the industry after the "near-fatal experience when the luxury tax was implemented."

This legislation is a matter of fairness, says Kennedy, who acknowledges that hitherto he has supported "targeted tax cuts" targeted at people of modest means. But his proposal, as he explains it, is really sort of like that. The benefit of up to $2 million for each purchaser of a luxury yacht would benefit the nearly six thousand Rhode Islanders working in the state's more than $1 billion a year boatbuilding industry, and workers elsewhere.

You see, the subsidy to the wealthy would, to coin a phrase, *trickle down.*

October 28, 1999

Conservatism: Freedom Plus

Conservatives in this summer of their discontent are suffering from political hypochondria. They have a real problem, of which their hypochondria is symptomatic. They are not thinking clearly.

And their somewhat surly bewilderment reveals conservative variants of two sins of this era: self-pity, expressed in a sense of victimhood, and the entitlement mentality. Some conservatives feel victimized by various villains (the media, conservatives in office, etc.) and entitled to an unresisted sweep for their ideas.

This week twenty-eight contributors to *The Weekly Standard* discuss whether there is a conservative crack-up, a supposed sign of which is that conservative ideas are ascendant while conservative politicians are being "battered." Actually, some conservative ideas are ascendant because, lacking the ballast of convincing content, they are lighter than air. And the idea that America's conservative politicians are downtrodden reveals an unconservative fixation with the presidency.

Since the Clinton era began, Republicans have gained fifty-one members in the House, thirteen senators, fifteen governors (about three quarters of the electorate today chooses to live under Republican governors), and more than five hundred state legislators. The two largest cities have Republican mayors. Politically, Clinton is the man who walked across a field of snow and left no footprints.

Granted, Democrats, after losing seven of ten and five of six presidential elections, have now won two. But the Clinton presidency's most important initiative—the health care plan—never even came to a vote. And the only events of the Clinton years that historians twenty-five years hence are apt to dwell upon—welfare reform (repeal of an entitlement, forced by Republicans) and trade liberalization (opposed by a majority of Democrats)—limit government.

Michael Barone, author of *The Almanac of American Politics,* notes in *The Weekly Standard* that in the 1950s welfare statism advanced while Dwight Eisenhower, Winston Churchill, Harold Macmillan, Konrad Adenauer, and Charles de Gaulle—not a liberal on the list—were heads of government. Today, liberals lead governments rightward. They do so because memories of the material hardships of the 1930s have faded and now "the recalled bad times are the 1970s." Then government was hubristic and incompetent, tolerated or sanctioned much pathological behavior (crime, illegitimacy, welfare dependency), and unleashed inflation that penalized virtue (thrift, industriousness).

However, the welfare state does express, in part, an ethic of common provision—the idea that some of life's risks should be socialized—and conservatives cannot prosper by preaching that this ethic is categorically unethical. Furthermore, Walter Berns of the American Enterprise Institute reminds *The Weekly Standard*'s readers that conservatives cannot distill conservatism's aspirations into the word "freedom." They cannot because their principal anguish, which they struggle to transmute into a governmental agenda, concerns an insufficiency of virtue revealed by the uses Americans make of their vastly expanded freedom from the restraints of government or social stigmas.

Conservatives often become conservatives because they are alarmed by the encroachment of the state on the sphere of individual sovereignty. But that sphere must have boundaries. And conservatives sometimes need to be reminded that conservatism is a *political* philosophy: it concerns *collective* aspirations and actions.

Regarding which, *The Weekly Standard*'s most pregnant piece, by Eliot Cohen of the Nitze School of Advanced International Studies, notes that the Founders neither envisioned nor desired "feeble government." Cohen warns against "mindless opposition to the state" and wonders, for example, whether conservatives who decry liberal history textbooks are willing to spend adequate sums to acquire and protect Civil War battlefields.

Much of conservatism's oppositional agenda has been fulfilled (opposition to communism, to irrational regulation of entire industries—airlines, trucking, etc.). Important work remains, such as opposition to racial preferences. But now: What is conservatism for?

Let the conservative rethinking revolve around two questions and a challenge. The questions are: What do we love when we love our country? What do we wish for when we wish for national greatness? The challenge is for conservatism to find a place in its pantheon for three great nationalists: Alexander Hamilton, Henry Clay, and Theodore Roosevelt.

Hamilton understood the role of an energetic national government in facilitating individual striving. Clay fired the nation's imagination (including young Abraham Lincoln's) with a program—the "American system"—for using national exertions (tariffs, "internal improvements") to nurture the social solidarity that is a prerequisite for patriotism. And from trustbusting to canal building, T.R. used invigorating strenuousness by government to foster the national thinking necessary for a citizen's sense of identity in a continental nation.

Here, then, is a third question. Twenty years ago many of today's conservatives rallied 'round keeping control of the Panama Canal. But would such conservatives have built it in the first place?

August 17, 1997

Relearning the Lessons of "the Most Important Law"

I t is sometimes called the most important law ever passed by Congress—quite a claim, considering the radiating consequences of the 1850 Fugitive Slave Law, the 1935 Social Security Act, the 1965 Voting Rights Act, and others. However, when in 1944 Congress passed the GI Bill, it could not have anticipated how profoundly this would shape modern America. The bill's story, told in the PBS program *The GI Bill: The Law that Changed America,* is pertinent to current controversies about the utility of government and the remoralization of social policy.

The bill was partly intended as a prophylactic measure against prospective discontents: the rise of European fascism had been fueled by the grievances of demobilized servicemen from the First World War. It is not correct to say, as the program does, that hitherto American veterans had been neglected. In 1865 one-fifth of Mississippi's state budget went for artificial limbs to replace limbs left in places such as Shiloh and Cold Harbor. And in the 1890s more than 40 percent of the budget went to one entitlement: pensions for Civil War veterans. Still, veterans of the First World War had not been well cared for.

However, for liberals the GI Bill's primary purpose was to jump-start the social project that the war had interrupted, the completion of the New Deal program of social amelioration. That purpose was different, and better, in decisive ways than the purposes of some social policies in the 1960s. The bill, which subsidized education and home buying for veterans, employed liberal means and had profoundly conservative consequences. A middle-class form of striving replaced the working-class path to upward mobility.

In 1940 only one in nine Americans was a high school graduate, there were fewer than 1.5 million college students, and only one in twenty Americans had a college degree. By the spring of 1947 the 1.6 million veterans enrolled in college made up 49 percent of all registered students. Sixty percent of the veterans enrolled in science and engineering programs, including many of the four hundred whose dormitory was the ice rink at the University of Illinois. That university had been expecting at most 11,000 students, but 15,000 showed up.

By the time the program ended in 1956, 2.2 million veterans had gone to college and 3.5 million to technical school, and 700,000 had received off-campus agricultural instruction. By 1990 there were 14 million Americans in college and one in five Americans had a degree. The GI Bill contributed mightily to making college a middle-class expectation. And in modern America, expectations mutate into entitlements: under President Clinton's policies of promiscuous social promotion beyond high school, at least two years of college is becoming a quasi entitlement.

In 1940 two-thirds of Americans were renters. By 1949, 60 percent of Americans were homeowners, partly because of subsidized loans for veterans. A veteran of the Navy Seabees, Bill Levitt, bought a lot of Long Island farmland and marketed a basic house for $7,990, a bargain at a time when the average family income was about $2,500. A veteran interviewed for the PBS program remembers, "No money down. I can afford that. And I get four rooms, and there's a washing machine. In those days people didn't have washing machines in their houses. They went to the corner to a launderette. But Levitt houses came with a washing machine! Oh, it was unbelievable!" Levitt himself saw a political dimension to Levittown: "No man who owns a house and lot can be a Communist. He has too much to do." (Well, think about it: Would the Winter Palace have been stormed if more Leningraders had had lawns to mow?)

In 1957, the year after the GI Bill programs ended, *Sputnik* reinforced America's attention to education, particularly in science, and to the world of white-collar work. Simultaneously, the 1957–58 recession underscored the value of education as insurance against life's vicissitudes.

The total cost of the GI Bill was $14.5 billion, which was serious money back then. However, the bill was not akin to today's entitlements. Its benefits were contingent on the recipients' having rendered service of the most serious sort. And the bill was congruent with the broad social strategy described by Michael Barone in *Our Country,* his history of American politics from FDR to Reagan. It was a strategy of honoring "those who worked their way up in society" and of placing "society's stamp of approval on their affluence and success." It was a strategy "which aimed not at servicing a lower class but at building a middle class." With the GI Bill, social policy sent strong cues to young Americans, telling them to stay in school, grind out good grades, defer marriage past the teenage years, defer children until the family income began to rise.

At the end of the war American confidence was at an apogee, in part because American society then was characterized by cultural homogeneity, buttressed by a bourgeois judgmentalism. Social policy reflected a broad consensus about the proper behavior for facilitating socially useful aspirations. But twenty years later liberalism became bifurcated between economic and lifestyle liberals. The latter, despising as "repressive" all social policies that promoted behavior deemed worthy, sought to de-moralize policy. By the late 1960s liberalism's tone and content were deeply influenced by liberalism's political base in the so-called "caring professions." They served "clients" in the urban population disorganized by behavior, particularly involving drugs and sex (illegitimacy), that was an insuperable impediment to the aspiration of economic liberals—greater equality of incomes.

The most important development in social policy since the 1960s has been the recent recasting of welfare policy to reform recipients' behavior. This stems from renewed appreciation of the behavioral basis of much poverty. Perhaps the judgmentalism of the GI Bill is having useful echoes in the 1990s, as a dose of the 1940s becomes an antidote to the disease of the 1960s.

October 27, 1997

A GI Bill for Mothers

Although his cultured despisers are loath to admit it and he was probably ambivalent about it, Richard Nixon skimmed more cream off the American professoriate than most presidents have done, packing his administration with, among others, Henry Kissinger and Pat Moynihan (Harvard), James Schlesinger (University of Virginia), George Shultz (University of Chicago), and Arthur Burns (Columbia). Yet Moynihan, Nixon's urban affairs adviser, insistently, and for a long time unsuccessfully, urged Nixon to consult with another professor, then at Harvard. Finally Moynihan prevailed by exclaiming, "Mr. President, James Q. Wilson is the smartest man in the United States. The president of the United States should pay attention to what he has to say."

Since then, many officials, from mayors through presidents, have done so, and recently the large Washington, D.C., audience at the American Enterprise Institute's annual Francis Boyer Lecture did so. Wilson, who has recently retired from UCLA, gave Washington, a proudly practical city, a demonstration of the unity of theory and practice. He offered a theory about why America is materially better off but spiritually worse off than it was not long ago. And he suggested programmatic responses, one of which has the potential to make "family values" a matter for practical rather than merely rhetorical treatment by the political class.

Wilson's worry, and much of the nation's, is that America is being poisoned by a subculture that is both cause and consequence of many children being born to unwed girls, raised in neighborhoods where there are more male sexual predators than committed fathers and matriculating, as it were, into gang life for protection and self-advancement. It is a subculture "armed to the teeth, excited by drugs, preoccupied with respect, and indifferent to the future. Its children crowd our schools and fill our streets, armed and dangerous." It is dominated by "young, marginally employed, sexually adventuresome, socially aggressive young men who reject the idea of hard work and social conformity that made their elders successful." As "bastardy has become more common, children more criminal, and marriages less secure," policy makers have tried this and that. "Much has happened but little has changed."

However, Wilson does note one change: more than half the public, and 70 percent of Americans under the age of thirty-five, think no shame should attach to having children out of wedlock. That fact is surely related to this one: social pathologies have multiplied during a burst of wealth creation without precedent in world history. America's poverty problem is not one of material scarcities but of abundant bad behavior. Wilson, seconding William Galston, says there are three simple behavioral rules for avoiding poverty: finish high school, produce no child before marrying, and produce no child before age twenty. Only 8 percent of families who conform to all three rules are poor; 79 percent of those who do not conform are poor.

In recent decades there has been some pertinent social learning. We have learned that the trajectory of a child's life is largely determined in the earliest years. "The human personality emerges early; if it is to be shaped," Wilson says, "it must be shaped early." The best predictor of a child's flourishing is the fervent devotion of two parents. Wilson warns that if the work requirements of the 1996 welfare reform are implemented, young mothers will be told to spend much of each week away from their children who, "already fatherless, will now not even be raised by their mothers."

Wilson's ameliorative ideas for American families include making adoption easier in order to minimize foster care. ("The average foster child lives with three different families, and ten or more placements are not rare.") Another idea is to require unmarried teenage mothers to live with their babies in a home supervised by experienced mothers. A third idea is this: given that religiosity and decency are correlated, and given that it is a reasonable surmise that the former causes the latter, and given the remarkable success of a religious-based program such as Alcoholics Anonymous, and given the evidence that religious programs in prisons reduce recidivism—given all this, large cities should have "the religious equivalent of the United Fund" to deliver services for the underclass through churches.

However, the most intriguing idea suggested by Wilson, which he credits to Richard and Grandon Gill, pertains to parents outside as well as inside the underclass. It would offer the equivalent of the GI Bill for a parent—usually a mother—who will postpone a career until her children reach school age.

No parent, Wilson says, can "have it all," and in the clash between family and work, the former must be favored. "If we care about how children are raised in their early years, and if, as is now the case, how they are raised is left to overwhelmed women or institutional arrangements, the only way we can restore the balance is by committing money to the task of inducing actions that were once the products of spontaneous arrangements." Hence a GI Bill–style educational entitlement that would enable a parent who stays home with a young child to finish school, attend college or graduate school, or take technical training courses after the child's most formative years.

The original GI Bill's benefits were entitlements of a sterner sort than we have become used to. They were linked to services rendered—services of the most serious sort, involving war. A new version of that entitlement would compensate a parent who forgoes earnings in order to render the vital social function of putting children on the path to social competence.

Politics has come to seem demoralizingly disconnected from practicality because leaders have been unable to connect their rhetoric with programs. They have failed to find ways for government to get a grip on the nation's principal problem—the coarsening of the culture that is produced by the brew of toxic behaviors associated with family decomposition. With reference to "family values," Wilson and the social scientists he cites are pointing to a way for the political class to reacquire relevance.

December 22, 1997

In Need of Another Moses

NEW YORK—Someone droll in Senator Pat Moynihan's office has provided a one-page "unfinished history" of Governors Island, which sits, like an unloved orphan, in New York harbor, hard by the Statue of Liberty. The history says: "1708: Lord Cornbury, New York's first transvestite governor, builds a mansion on Governors Island, possibly misusing defense funds, including proceeds of New York's unusual wig tax."

Perhaps in Year One A.M. (after Monica) we have to bring up the fact that his lordship, who was not the soul of discretion (he was arrested by his creditors), did have the, shall we say, eccentricity of going about in public dressed like his cousin, Queen Anne. But we are straying from the subject, which is: Why is a perfectly good 173-acre island, with a stunning view and some Revolutionary War constructions, going to waste? The answer says something about modern governance and tells us that we shall not see another Moses—Robert Moses, that is.

The island, which had a hotel and racetrack in the fun-filled 1780s, became a military headquarters in the nineteenth century. In 1901, dirt and rock from construction of the city's first subway line were used to double the island's size. On September 29, 1909, Wilbur Wright took off there on the first flight over American waters.

George Patton played polo there, and Mayor La Guardia, affronted by such amusements of the upper crust, tried to wrest the island from the federal government. The army successfully resisted. In 1966 the army left, replaced by the Coast Guard, which in 1995 announced that it was departing. At that point the government entertained a good idea: sell the island.

During an October 1995 helicopter flight over it, President Clinton, in the persuasive presence of Moynihan, offered to sell it to the city for $1, which is less than the cost of a toxic hot dog from a street vendor. The city recoiled from this offer as from an adder, fearing annual maintenance costs of maybe $25 million. Moynihan summarizes the city's less-than-spacious thinking as "Who is going to mow the lawn?"

So it came to pass that, in the masterpiece of creative writing called the 1997 Budget Agreement, the government stipulated that the island will be sold for $500 million in 2002. This stipulation is part of Washington's way of creating surpluses—never mind that no one thinks anyone will pay anything like that. (Although Moynihan rightly says, "There are plenty of people in Congress who would sell it to Saudi Arabia if that meant half a billion dollars.")

A telephone call to someone you might think would pay a lot reveals why buyers are scarce. "Ferries don't work," says developer Donald Trump, citing the long struggle toward profitability of Fisher Island in Miami but ignoring the many contented people on Puget Sound. Trump says modern Americans are too antsy to wait on even very good ferry service. He says even Staten Island did not prosper until ferry service was supplemented by the Verrazzano Narrows Bridge.

The usual rule of thumb among developers concerning projects with high risks but potential high yields is that "the second guy in will make money"—after the first guy goes broke. Concerning Governors Island, Trump says, "The third guy in will make money."

A big problem, he says, is that government is chock full of blocking mechanisms. Environmentalists are particularly nimble at litigating development to a money-eating standstill.

Once upon a time, Robert Moses, the master builder of modern New York, could drive the construction of bridges, highways, and other large-scale public works. Arguably, some might have been better left unbuilt or done differently. But on balance the city is better off because, for a while, it was able to act with dispatch. Such dispatch is a distant memory today, when time and money are consumed by filing environmental impact statements, negotiating racial set-asides, and generally being nice to snail darters and other grievance groups.

It is passing strange that a congested city with a shortage of housing, green space, and Revolutionary War landmarks cannot find a moneymaking use for an island that is going to waste within hailing distance of the capital of money-making, Wall Street. Strangeness compounded: One bad idea for making the island profitable has been refuted by a bad argument.

Mayor Rudolph Giuliani has suggested building a casino and luxury hotel on the island, making a Monaco off the tip of Manhattan. One argument against this was: Gambling would attract people who would spoil the ambiance of New York City.

Think about that.

May 14, 1998

On April 1, 2002, President George W. Bush, citing New York's post-September 11 needs, agreed to sell it Governors Island for a "nominal" fee.

Congress's "Nuremberg Defense"

When in 1996 Congress ended wool and mohair subsidies, liberals said this proved they were serious about "reinventing" government, conservatives said it proved they were serious about shrinking government, and realists said the subsidies would be back. Some are back.

Wool subsidies grew out of World War II, when uniforms were woolen. Worried that domestic producers would not be able to supply enough for future wars, in 1954 Congress voted for subsidies. Mohair was included because . . . well, just because.

In spite of the subsidies, wool production declined, a lot. Never mind. Wars hot and cold came and went without a wool crisis. Still the subsidies endured, until ended with great fanfare. Last week, mohair subsidies reappeared (this time as zero-interest loans rather than direct payments) in the omnibus appropriation bill.

Together with the $250,000 for an Illinois company to research caffeinated gum, the $750,000 for grasshopper research in Alaska, the $1.1 million for manure handling and disposal in Starkville, Mississippi, the $100,000 for Vidalia onion research in Georgia, the . . .

The 4,000-page bill's garbage-pail nature can be gauged from these two consecutive sentences in the conference committee's report: "The conferees believe that the responsibilities of Nurse Corps officers necessitate that they should be required to have baccalaureate degrees.

"This provision extends the 1998–1999 duck hunting season in the State of Mississippi."

Maybe there should be a law that no bill passed by Congress can have more pages than *Moby-Dick*. Why *Moby-Dick?* For no reason. Why should reason enter into the legislative process at any point? But, then, what is the point of pretending to have lawful lawmaking?

The "Nuremberg defense," used by war criminals, is "I was only obeying orders." Usually it means "I was only obeying orders I gave myself." Congress's "Nuremberg defense" is "We were only disobeying orders we gave ourselves."

Congress recently imposed upon itself certain spending caps. Now Congress has made them porous by saying that whatever it designates as "emergency" spending does not count against the caps. An emergency is supposed to be a onetime, unforeseen disaster. Only a small fraction of the omnibus bill's approximately $20 billion in "emergency" spending qualifies.

In light of that, imagine the anticonstitutional behavior Congress will engage in if it ever "restrains" itself with a constitutional amendment "requiring" balanced budgets.

Voting against the omnibus bill on Wednesday, Senator John McCain noted that the only copy of the bill available to Republicans on Tuesday was "scattered in pieces around the Republican cloakroom." He asked not that Republican views prevail on everything but that Republicans have recognizable views and: "We ask only that we adhere to a little truth in advertising. . . . When we call something an emergency, we should be able to say it with a straight face."

Another of the twenty-nine senators voting against the unamendable bill, Pat Moynihan, said there might be much good in it, but "How would anyone know?" He recalled that last year, when he was floor manager of an 820-page tax bill, there was only one copy to be had for the Senate floor. The Senate, he says, has become "ominously careless with our procedures" and is "beginning to resemble a kind of bastard parliamentary system," in which loud floor debate proceeds while "the real decisions are made in a closed room by three or four people."

Meetings of conference committees are, he says, rarely convened. The rule, dating from 1884, that prohibits legislating in appropriations bills is now so shredded that last Sunday the House Appropriations Committee's Web site listed "significant legislative provisions in appropriations bills."

Such is Congress's creeping lawlessness, Moynihan says, "The Senate has, by unanimous consent, 'deemed' bills passed before they are received from the

House of Representatives. In 1997, a provision giving a $50 billion tax credit to the tobacco industry was slipped into a conference report *after* the conference committee had completed its work. (That provision was repealed soon after its existence was discovered.)"

Represenative Chris Cox, Republican of California, remembers the first bill he voted on when he came to Congress in 1989. The 776 pages of the savings-and-loan bailout bill were pasted together by staff between a Friday and a Sunday vote, at which point not a single voting member had read it. The 1990 budget bill came to the floor in a large corrugated box containing more than 1,000 unpaginated, uncollated pages "tied together," Cox said, "in twine, like newspapers headed for recycling."

Under Republicans, as under Democrats, the degradation of Congress, and of the idea of deliberative democracy, continues. This is the "bipartisanship" so much praised by advanced thinkers.

October 25, 1998

The Appendix of the Body Politic

Conservatives rightly say that the Corporation for Public Broadcasting is akin to the body politic's appendix: vestigial, purposeless, and occasionally troublesome. But the CPB is currently useful in revealing the emptiness of Republican praise of limited government.

Louisiana Congressman Billy Tauzin was one of the two Democrats who supported the Republicans' 1994 Contract with America, and in 1995 he changed parties. He is a conservative who favors the theory of limited government and the practice of protecting, with tariffs, Louisiana crawfish from the competition of Chinese crawfish. His enthusiasm for the CPB indicates that he is having a hard time getting the hang of being a Republican. But then, so are many other House Republicans.

The Commerce Committee subcommittee Tauzin chairs was poised to increase funding for the CPB, which subsidizes public television and radio, when the fuss erupted about public television stations swapping mailing lists with political organizations, mostly Democratic. The resulting uproar, a distraction from the larger point, may actually have benefited public broadcasters: By promising to desist from such political stupidity, the broadcasters have quelled any remaining resistance to their role as expensive examples of cultural redundancy.

Created in 1967 as a filigree on Lyndon Johnson's Great Society, the CPB was supposedly necessary because over-the-air broadcasting allowed few competitors, who were driven to seek broad audiences by catering to the lowest common cultural denominator. The rationale for public broadcasting was marvelously sealed against refutation: government must subsidize alternative programming precisely because few people want it.

Thirty-two years later, in a five-hundred-channel environment, this rationale is as absurd as public television's recent slogan "If PBS doesn't do it, who will?" Who? The History Channel, Discovery, Arts & Entertainment, Bravo, the Outdoor Channel, the Travel Channel, Nickelodeon, CNN, and scores more. And all of them do something public television does not: they pay, as opposed to consume, taxes.

The public television lobby still argues that no matter how many choices the market offers, government must offer other programming. The lobby also argues, with antic illogic, that such programs as *Sesame Street* serve sizable audiences but no private, taxpaying broadcast entity would be interested in broadcasting them. Still, "concern" for "children" is the card that presumably trumps all others nowadays, and the CPB plays that card vigorously in defense of its subsidies.

At the June 30 hearing of Tauzin's subcommittee, Robert Coonrod, CPB's president, said that loss of government support would be "devastating." But government provides just 15 percent of public broadcasting's funds, while various private interests parasitic off public broadcasting make huge sums selling paraphernalia based on the characters from *Sesame Street, Barney & Friends, Teletubbies, Arthur,* and other programs.

Newspapers, which should recoil from government participation in media (what would newspaper editors think of a Corporation for Public Newspapers?), continue to editorialize about the necessity of public television. And at the June 30 hearing some public broadcasting officials even asserted that the economy gets a $12 billion boost from workers made more productive by basic adult education on public television.

At that hearing Kevin Klose, president of National Public Radio—about 700 federally subsidized stations; the government thinks America's almost 9,500 commercial stations are insufficient—gave a virtuoso rendition of the self-congratulatory gush characteristic of subsidized broadcasters. NPR, he said, "is beyond public service—it's a national treasure" providing "enlightened reporting" and "cultural programs that celebrate the human experience."

But the prize for preposterousness was taken by LeVar Burton, actor (he played Kunta Kinte in the miniseries *Roots*) and host of the PBS children's television series *Reading Rainbow.* He let loose the requisite gush (PBS is a "shining light"; "It is about the kids"; PBS helps "to grow young minds into thoughtful individuals and caring human beings . . . seeing in every one of them a seed of greatness" and doing everything "to nurture that seed"). Then he displayed a cell phone that flips open and said the reason we have such phones is that "some kid grew up watching *Star Trek* and saw Captain Kirk reach behind to that place on his hip and pull that thing out and call Scotty on the ship. That kid then grew up, became an engineer, and designed a device that is as common to us today as the bread toaster."

Well. Burton gave no evidence, there being none, for his fanciful history of the cell phone. But even if his history were not nonsense, *Star Trek* was on commercial television, so how did his fairy tale about technology justify subsidies for public television? There is no justification for it, nor for a Republican-controlled Congress that continues it.

August 1, 1999

The Politics of Pathos

In the first minute of his fifty-five-minute interview with C-SPAN's Brian Lamb, Texas Governor George W. Bush was asked to explain his goal of "prosperity with a moral and spiritual center." Bush answered by citing the need to "rally what I call the armies of compassion all across the state of Texas to interface with our young, to help and to mentor," and so on. But he finally said, "It's really all based around a story."

The story is that Bush visited a juvenile justice facility, where a boy asked him, "What do you think of me?" Bush says, "It was a question that was just so profound and so right." It meant, Bush says, "Is there a role for me in society?"

Maybe that is what the boy meant. Certainly Bush's answer means he is attuned to the times. He is fluent in the emotive language of today's therapeutic ethos. This fluency of a Republican raised in Midland, Texas, testifies to the ubiquity of the culture of emotional vulnerability.

Early in his presidency, Bill Clinton took his Cabinet to Camp David for a sensitivity session, complete with "facilitators" to facilitate the sharing of feelings by participants who were in recovery from reticence. A participant told *The Washington Post,* "Don't try to make this sound weird." Heaven forfend.

One of Newt Gingrich's first acts when elected speaker was to hire a "corporate psychotherapist" to help Republicans communicate their feelings to the public. Such recourse to the "caring professions" is now normal. The sensitivity industry is booming, there being more therapists than firefighters or librarians or mail carriers, and twice as many as there are dentists or pharmacists.

Government cannot be hermetically sealed against the culture. Bush's rhetoric, like Clinton's, which it mimics, is evidence of more than just conservative panic about the public's receptivity to Clinton's belief that pathos is the primary business of politics. Rather, Bush's manner of speaking is evidence that Clinton's political style is not idiosyncratic but symptomatic. The conflation of culture and government is far advanced.

James L. Nolan, Jr., professor of sociology at Williams College, understands the implications of the dialectical relation between compassionate government and the therapeutic culture. In his book *The Therapeutic State: Justifying Government at Century's End,* he argues that government tends to expand; that expansion tends to produce a crisis of legitimacy; that the therapeutic mission both fuels and legitimizes government's expansions into new spheres of society's and individuals' lives.

The therapeutic ethos increasingly infuses civil case law that elevates the status of emotions by awarding damages for distress unrelated to physical injury. It treats crimes as pathologies, in drug cases especially but also sometimes regarding burglary, prostitution, domestic violence, writing bad checks, and other offenses. Defendants are "clients." The aim is "healing" or "recovery." Recidivism is not proof of failure in "treatment" because relapse is part of recovery from the "sickness" of crime. Proof of recovery is the "client" pleasing his government therapist by assenting to the pathological interpretation of his behavior and thus to the ideology of victimization: crime is caused by an abusive or otherwise pathological childhood.

The therapeutic orientation of education postulates that a prerequisite for learning is a government-approved and -encouraged frame of mind: "self-esteem." Government occasionally makes mandatory a pharmacological "remedy," Ritalin, for the suddenly epidemic problem of attention deficit disorder. Nolan says therapeutic welfare policy also involves government concern not only with behavior but with the internal workings of individuals: intentions, motives, family relationships, and so on.

Clintonesque, meaning self-referential, rhetoric is part of the substance of therapeutic politics. Count the times Clinton says "I feel good about" this or "I feel comfortable about" that. Count the ways government insinuates itself into intimacy with citizens.

Governor Bush, avatar of "compassionate conservatism," began his answer to Brian Lamb by endorsing "limited government." However, compassion means the prevention or amelioration of pain, including the emotional pain of disappointment or hurt feelings. A compassionate government's work is never done. That work, and the government that undertakes it, is thus unlimited.

The truthful answer to the question the boy put to Bush—"What do you think of me?"—would be "Young man, I don't know you, and it is not the business of government to get to know everyone personally. Society would be suffocated, and individual liberty jeopardized, by a government that tried to."

But Bush, like all thoroughly modern masters of the politics of pathos, understands that the therapeutic ethic sternly forbids such sternness.

February 7, 1999

Listening to Politics with a Third Ear

The period for a new election of a citizen to administer the executive government of the United States being not far distant . . .

—THE OPENING WORDS OF PRESIDENT GEORGE WASHINGTON'S
FAREWELL ADDRESS, 1796

Time was, that is how presidents were understood—modestly, as administrators who executed the will of others. Nowadays, presidents permeate the federal leviathan with their wills, and they, like it, are everywhere. So a presidential election is a great national temperature taking, measuring how Americans feel about *everything.*

Some elections, such as that of John Kennedy in 1960, are continental shrugs, in which the country says, "What's the difference?" Historian Arthur Schlesinger, Jr., a Kennedy supporter, felt impelled to publish a book, *Kennedy or Nixon: Does It Make Any Difference?* and the popular vote difference was only 118,574 votes—about one per precinct. Some elections, such as that of Ronald Reagan in 1980 (the Iran hostage crisis, the "misery index"—the sum of the inflation and interest rates—at 20), are akin to the country slapping its palm on the kitchen table and exclaiming, "We'd better try something different."

Of course, no matter how a Republican wins the presidency, Democrats, including most of the media, deny that a mandate resulted. When Dwight Eisenhower carried eighty of ninety-eight states in two elections, his victory was dismissed as "purely personal" because, it was said, his smile was his political philosophy. When Reagan won decisively in 1980, the result was minimized as a negative judgment on President Jimmy Carter, who was devoid of positive content.

Two days after the 1984 election, *The Washington Post* carried this unintentionally hilarious eight-column headline: "Democrats Challenge President's Landslide as a Mandate." Asked who could have beaten Reagan, an aide to Walter Mondale said: "Robert Redford. Maybe Walter Cronkite." Thus was Reagan's forty-nine-state nonmandate (he won forty times more electoral votes than Mondale's total from Minnesota and the District of Columbia) dismissed as purely personal—more proof of the Smile Theory of history.

This year's campaign was uncommonly substantive—its subjects ranged from ballistic-missile defense to prescription drug entitlements to partial privatization of Social Security—and remarkably civil. It also reflected, and advanced, the ongoing revision of political categories and stereotypes.

Al Gore, candidate of the liberal party, ran vowing to conserve the status quo—to defend Social Security against partial privatization, to defend public education against competition from school-choice programs, to defend unrestricted abortion and myriad racial preferences against adverse judgments from a reconfigured Supreme Court. George W. Bush, candidate of the conservative party, effectively ended the sixty-year-old conservatism that was born in reaction against the New Deal. He accepts that the primary domestic responsibility of the next president is to strengthen the emblematic achievement of the New Deal, Social Security—and to enlarge the entitlement menu of the emblematic achievement of the Great Society, Medicare.

It is well said that to understand politics you need a third ear, to hear what is *not* said. Think of the things that were not issues this year. Gore did not call for restoring the 70 percent marginal income tax rates that existed until the most important congressional action of the 1980s, the Reagan tax cuts. Gore did not call for repeal of the most important congressional action of the 1990s, the welfare reform act of 1996. On the other hand, Bush did not talk, as Republicans did just six years ago, of abolishing four Cabinet-level departments, including, and especially, the Department of Education.

Leadership has been defined as the ability to inflict pain and get away with it, or to persuade people to accept pain—short-term pain for long-term gain. Neither candidate sought a mandate for that sort of leadership. Bush asked the country to be brave and endure a tax cut; Gore said the country was entitled to even more entitlements than it has or than Bush envisions. Neither candidate has an adversarial stance toward the political or moral culture of the day; neither feels Flannery O'Connor's prompting "to push as hard as the age that pushes against you." But then, pushing change through Washington—liberal or conservative change—is going to be slow going.

In the 1938 off-year elections the country, partly recoiling against President Franklin D. Roosevelt's overreaching in his plan to pack the Supreme Court by expanding its membership, produced a Congress in which Republicans and conservative—mostly Southern—Democrats could largely control the parameters of government activism. Congress did not again have a liberal legislating majority until the anti-Goldwater landslide of 1964 gave President Lyndon Johnson a two-year window of opportunity with the do-everything 89th Congress. The 1966 elections brought a Republican resurgence in Congress—and the election of a new governor of California, Ronald Reagan. So in the last sixty-two years, there has been a liberal legislating majority in Congress for only two years. It will be a long time before there is another.

As for conservative change, this year's candidates, in their attempted seductions of the electorate, touched all the erogenous zones on the body politic. The siren song of modulated conservatism was: accept leviathan, but leaven its operations with a modest expansion of the range of choices (of schools, of retirement investments, of health care providers).

A country in which personal computers are selling at the pace of one every two seconds and Internet usage is doubling every hundred days (and accounts for 13 percent of electricity consumption) is a country comfortable with, and insistent upon, more choices. The country has a rapidly broadening sense of competence and empowerment. Americans, who of late have been subject to moral hypochondria, do not equate material improvement with moral improvement. But they may be correct in concluding that some of today's material changes, such as broad mastery of new information technologies, come coupled with promising moral change.

Theologian Richard John Neuhaus, reflecting on the idea of moral progress, notes that until about 1900, most people lived half their lives with toothaches, but few people born after 1960 know what a toothache is. In some ways, moral progress has been as striking: Try explaining segregated buses to someone born after 1970. One reason politics has lost some of the sizzle of olden days is that some stark injustices have not merely been corrected, they have been relegated to the realm of unintelligible things.

As always, the election-year surfeit of blather called to mind the complaint about the person who lost the talent for communicating with the loss of the faculty of speech. But judging by what was said and unsaid, it has been a good year.

November 13, 2000

"Let Us . . ." No, Let's Not.

Come Saturday, on the Capitol's west front, the forty-third president, immediately after becoming such, will look out, figuratively speaking (and as F. Scott Fitzgerald wrote at the conclusion of *The Great Gatsby*), toward "the dark fields of the republic" rolling on and will unburden himself of his inaugural thoughts. Whatever they are, and whatever his manner of expressing

them, the event will supply evidence of the evolution of the nation's preoccupations and sensibilities.

His inaugural address, the nation's fifty-fourth, presumably will make no
reference, as James Monroe's did, to coastal fortifications, and no reference to
polygamy, which James Garfield's said "offends the moral sense of manhood"
and Grover Cleveland's said is "destructive of the family relation and offensive
to the moral sense of the civilized world." We have come a long way, in every
way, from the day when the first inaugural address was delivered in the Senate
chamber of Federal Hall on Wall Street on the inhabited southern tip of Manhattan, an island that then was mostly fields and forests. Here is the second sentence of George Washington's address:

> On the one hand, I was summoned by my country, whose voice I can never
> hear but with veneration and love, from a retreat which I had chosen with the
> fondest predilection, and, in my flattering hopes, with an immutable decision,
> as the asylum of my declining years—a retreat which was rendered every day
> more necessary as well as more dear to me by the addition of habit to inclina-
> tion, and of frequent interruptions in my health to the gradual waste commit-
> ted on it by time.

We will get to the "on the other hand" anon. But first, ask yourself this:
What would happen if a president today addressed such an eighty-seven-word
sentence to an American audience? The audience would become bewildered,
then restive, then headachy. What does that say about the direction we have
traveled, rhetorically and therefore intellectually, since 1789?

Granted, when Washington spoke as he did, the country was not wired,
so it was not listening. Still, there was an audience in the room, and presumably it had no difficulty following his words. His listeners, their ears trained by
the oral culture of Protestant sermons, could cope with a serpentine thought
expressed in a sentence of sinewy syntax. Besides, Washington's listeners were
raised on the King James version of the Bible, Thomas Cranmer's *Book of
Common Prayer,* and John Bunyan's *Pilgrim's Progress.* Their mental muscles had
not gone flaccid from a steady diet of advertising, situation comedy repartee,
and "See Spot run" journalese.

The late Herbert Stein, who for sixty years was an economist and connois-
seur of America's political culture, discovered that in inaugural addresses from
Washington through James Buchanan, the average number of words per sentence was 44; from Abraham Lincoln through Woodrow Wilson, 34; since Wilson, 25. However, only one inaugural address merits a place in the nation's
literature. No one who has a pulse, or deserves to have one, can read Lincoln's
second inaugural ("Fondly do we hope, fervently do we pray, that this mighty

scourge of war may speedily pass away. . . . With malice toward none, with char-ity for all . . .") without a *frisson* of patriotic awe. And in its context, the most eloquent sentence in Lincoln's address is four words long: "And the war came."

The general shortening of sentences reflects, in part, a change in the na-ture of inaugural addresses. Stein noted that beginning with Woodrow Wil-son, they often took on hortatory cadences as presidents came to think it their job, and the government's, to incite Americans to change their behavior ("The only thing we have to fear . . ." "Ask not . . ."). Wilson, who missed his calling (he should have been a fierce Presbyterian divine), in his first Inaugural waxed prophetic: "At last a vision has been vouchsafed us of our life as a whole."

The presidency, which Teddy Roosevelt called a "bully pulpit," really has become awfully like a pulpit, with presidents toiling to establish the oral and visual relationship of pastors exhorting their congregation: "Let us . . ." Kennedy used that phrase—its approximate meaning is: "For Pete's sake, pull up your socks and shape up"—sixteen times in his inaugural address, and Richard Nixon used it twenty-two times in his second. Good grief.

But *let us* get back to Washington's first inaugural. He expressed remark-able modesty, all things considered. And he was hardly a Uriah Heep. The president's pride, dignity, reserve, and aura of command were not only uni-versally admired; they were the towering political facts of—indeed, the ce-ment of—the infant republic whose birth he had brought about by waging war against the world's mightiest power. Furthermore, he had just become the first (212 years later, he is still the only) president to win all the electoral votes. Yet in his third sentence—at a mere sixty-nine words, it was of almost Hem-ingwayesque terseness—Washington said:

> On the other hand, the magnitude and difficulty of the trust to which the voice of my country called me, being sufficient to awaken in the wisest and most ex-perienced of her citizens a distrustful scrutiny into his qualifications, could not but overwhelm with despondence one who (inheriting inferior endowments from nature and unpracticed in the duties of civil administration) ought to be peculiarly conscious of his own deficiencies.

Yes, there really was a time when American leaders wrote and spoke like that and Americans understood. Washington's protestations of inadequacy may seem a tad overdone, but they were tactical. At that time the country, hav-ing just emancipated itself from a monarchy, had a lively suspicion of execu-tive power and of anyone whose grandeur might tempt him to take the unformed presidential office in that direction. George W. Bush need not as-suage that anxiety, which on a list of today's anxieties ranks somewhere below worries about coastal defenses and polygamy.

January 22, 2001

Missing Coolidge

The Georgia state legislator thought, Yuk! Dorothy Pelote, a fastidious representative from Savannah, noticed supermarket bag boys licking their fingers to help them separate bags. So, feeling the modern itch to have government scrub away all of life's imperfections, she introduced a bill to require "at each bagging station a device designed to wet the fingers of any employee separating the bags." Is the era of big government really over?

Maybe. The Pelote bill died. Perhaps the spirit of the thirtieth president lives.

This summer marks the seventy-fifth anniversary of the coming to the presidency, upon the death of Warren Harding, of a man born in Vermont in 1872—on the Fourth of July, wouldn't you know. Walter Lippmann had this to say about him:

> *Mr. Coolidge's genius for inactivity is developed to a very high point. It is far from being an indolent activity. It is a grim, determined, alert inactivity which keeps Mr. Coolidge occupied constantly. Nobody has ever worked harder at inactivity, with such force of character, with such unremitting attention to detail, with such conscientious devotion to the task. Inactivity is a political philosophy and a party program with Mr. Coolidge, and nobody should mistake his unflinching adherence to it for a soft and easy desire to let things slide. Mr. Coolidge's inactivity is not merely the absence of activity. It is, on the contrary, a steady application to the task of neutralizing and thwarting political activity wherever there are signs of life.*

Lippmann was being arch but was onto something: some political inactivity is the opposite of lethargy. Often the real sloth is activity resulting from nonresistance to the constant urge to "do something." Consider, for example, the current Congress, which has done one big thing and is threatening to do two more.

The thing already done is perhaps the biggest public works bill in the history of the planet. Maybe the bill that paid for the Pyramids was bigger, relative to the relevant GDP, than this year's $203 billion highway extravaganza. However, calculating inflation-adjusted Pyramid construction costs is dicey, and pharaohs skimped on costs by using nonunion labor. Anyway, Scott Hodge, a budget analyst in Washington, calculates that at $30 per square foot of heavy gold electroplate, the highway bill could gold-plate one lane of highway four and a half times around the Earth's circumference.

Next may come the 753-page tobacco bill. Ostensibly, its primary purpose is to do something about the 3 percent of cigarettes sold to underage smokers. For that, a one-page piece of legislation would suffice, denying driver's licenses to underage smokers. But the bill's real purpose is to siphon money from smokers for myriad spending programs. Hence the careful calibration of the tax so that it is high enough to generate a cataract of revenues while *not* seriously curtailing purchases of cigarettes. The tax would be phased in to *avoid* jolting smokers into changing their behavior too much.

The depressing trifecta of this legislative year will be completed if Congress enacts rationing of political speech. That goal of campaign-finance reform received a timely rebuke last week when a federal appeals court declared unconstitutional some low Arkansas limits on political contributions ($300 to statewide executive officials, $100 to all other candidates). One argument offered for the necessity of such limits was that a legislator had received contributions from tobacco sources and had introduced a bill favored by those sources. The court scoffed, "If it were reasonable to presume corruption from the fact that a public official voted in a way that pleased his contributors, legislatures could constitutionally ban all contributions except from the public official's opponents, a patent absurdity."

Unfortunately, the appeals court spoke of the Arkansas limits' being "too low to allow *meaningful* participation in protected speech and association" and "too low to allow for *appropriately robust* participation" (emphasis added). Governmental callousness about violating the First Amendment has advanced to the point where courts presume to protect not free speech but only the speech that they deem "meaningful" and "appropriately robust." The court's drawing (and Congress's desire to draw) such constitutionally impermissible distinctions is akin to Congress's incontinent spending in the highway bill and its unseemly grasping through the tobacco bill. Today there are too few politicians with Coolidge's "steady application to the task of neutralizing and thwarting" the activities of the political class.

Coolidge is thought of today, if at all, as humorless (Alice Longworth thought he looked like someone weaned on a pickle) and inconsequential. (When told he had died, Dorothy Parker wondered how anyone could tell.) But while he was president, ice cream production rose 30 percent. And his reticence (When a woman told him she had bet she could get more than two words out of him, he replied, "You lose.") lent itself to aphorism ("Inflation is repudiation"). And subtlety: when reporters asked him about some new biographies that criticized George Washington, he pulled aside the curtain, looked at the Washington Monument, and said, "I see it's still there." As for wit:

When he and Mrs. Coolidge (a stunner; see the White House portrait of her in a red sheath dress) were being given separate tours around a farm, she asked her guide if the rooster copulated more than once a day. "Dozens of times," she was told. "Tell that to the president," she replied. When the president was told, he asked, "Same hen every time?" He was told, "Oh, no, a different one each time." "Tell that to Mrs. Coolidge," he said. (The technical term for the rearousal of a male animal by a new female became "the Coolidge effect.")

When asked why he chose not to seek re-election in 1928, he said, "Because there's no chance for advancement." Who believes the current crop of politicians represents advancement beyond Coolidge?

June 22, 1998

Al Sharpton's Parricide

The Democratic Party's nightmare is abstemiously breakfasting on oatmeal and skim milk. Al Sharpton, 47, is in fighting trim. He has lost the weight of a ten-year-old boy—eighty-plus pounds—and is spoiling for a fight.

The Brooklyn-born and New York–based preacher-agitator thinks he has dethroned Jesse Jackson as the reigning heavyweight among African-American leaders. He will take his rhetorical flair—a street preacher at age four, at ten he toured with Mahalia Jackson and preached to 10,000 at the 1964 World's Fair—into the 2004 Democratic presidential primaries. He will "raise a progressive agenda," "energize minority voters," and "develop enough leverage to leverage the party."

"We"—his plural pronoun intermittently signals identification with Jackson—"went from 1988, being number two to Dukakis, to '96 in Chicago begging to get a prime-time speech—which he didn't get. We can't tolerate that."

When reminded that every four years someone says Democrats can win by turning left, he serenely replies, "Well, I'm the someone this time." He says, "I'm better known than Daschle and Gephardt" in inner cities and "I'm better known now than Jackson was in 1982." ("You have to look at Jesse two years before his first run.") He says black radio is "much stronger" than when Jackson was running, there is Black Entertainment Television, and students and activists are on the Internet. Furthermore, the Democrats' moving many primaries to early in 2004 will help him. It will reward name recognition and "in the base I'm trying to bring out, I'm well known."

Now picture the other candidates in 2004, mostly senators with their pretty red ties and not a hair out of place, decorously debating Sharpton, who talks like this: "In the language of the 'hood, Clinton pimp-slapped Jesse on Sister Souljah." Sharpton is talking about Clinton's 1992 criticism of a black rap singer to distance himself from, among others, Jackson.

Sharpton says Jackson, 60, has been his mentor, friend, and "surrogate father" but now is an exhausted volcano, viewed by young blacks as "an establishment figure." Besides, he says, since Jackson acknowledged fathering a child with an aide, he has lost the unlimited access he had to black churches. Sharpton compares Jackson to Muhammad Ali: great once; can't fight anymore. He says Jackson learned from Martin Luther King during a few years of association, but he, Sharpton, has benefited from observing thirty years of Jackson's mistakes. Parricide isn't pretty.

Sharpton is free of reverence and reticence. Referring to the ex-president's office: "It is appropriate that Bill Clinton is in Harlem so he can welcome" those tossed off welfare by the legislation he signed in 1996. Sharpton says all thirty-eight members of the Congressional Black Caucus are, or can be, threatened by insurgents. The thirty-eight "must side with me or I'll support the insurgents."

The "progressive agenda" is mostly the Left's leftovers—no death penalty, less incarceration, more generous welfare—with one addition. On September 10 Jackson, Sharpton, and others were close to forcing Democrats to face the issue of reparations for slavery. Blown away, the issue is coming back. Sharpton will see to that.

His critics will see to the revival of interest in what has been called "Sharpton's Chappaquiddick," his riotous support of Tawana Brawley, the black fifteen-year-old who in 1987 fabricated a story of rape and abuse by some white men. She was thoroughly discredited. Sharpton stops well short of remorse: "I did what I believed."

Today he says he shares some of the cultural conservatism—"I never knew I was underprivileged until I went to a sociology class at Brooklyn College"— of churchgoing African Americans. He denounces "decadence and low expectations in our community," saying "this hip-hop thing has a lot to do with it—glorifying decadence."

A long-distance runner—hyperkinetic, he travels incessantly, "mostly to B and C cities" such as Flint and Tallahassee "because I'm known in A cities"— he has put away the jogging suits he wore to hide his previous bulk. In his chalk-striped gray flannel he is more conservatively dressed than many in the Four Seasons hotel dining room. "I am conservative on everything but race," he declares with a straight face, a declaration somewhat vitiated by the fact that, for him, everything is race.

Sly, clever, witty, incapable of embarrassment, and uninterested in the ceremonial politeness of national politics, Sharpton is going to have fun in 2004. Democrats, can't we all just get along? Give him at least a prime-time convention speech. On reparations.

January 10, 2002

REGULATING CAMPAIGNING: THE MANY MISADVENTURES OF REFORM

The "Latin Americanization" of Campaign Finance Law

Almost nothing that preoccupies Washington, D.C., is as important as Washington thinks almost all its preoccupations are. But soon Congress will consider some version of the McCain-Feingold bill, which raises "regime-level" questions. It would continue the change for the worse of American governance. And Washington's political class hopes the bill's real importance will be underestimated.

With a moralism disproportionate to the merits of their cause, members of that class—including the exhorting, collaborative media—are mounting an unprecedentedly sweeping attack on freedom of expression. Nothing in American history—not the Left's recent campus "speech codes," not the right's depredations during the 1950s McCarthyism or the 1920s "red scare," not the Alien and Sedition Acts of the 1790s—matches the menace to the First Amendment posed by campaign "reforms" advancing under the protective coloration of political hygiene.

Such earlier fevers were evanescent, leaving no institutional embodiments when particular passions abated. And they targeted speech of particular political content. What today's campaign reformers desire is a steadily thickening clot of laws and an enforcing bureaucracy to control both the quantity and the content of all discourse pertinent to politics. By the logic of their aims, reformers cannot stop short of that. This is so, regardless of the supposed modesty of the measure Congress will debate next month.

Reformers first empowered government to regulate "hard" money—that given to particular candidates. But there remains the "problem" of "soft" money—that given to parties for general political organizing and advocacy. Reformers call this a "loophole." Reformers use that word to stigmatize any silence of the law that allows unregulated political expression. So now reformers want to ban "soft" money. But the political class will not stop there.

Its patience is sorely tried by the insufferable public, which persists in exercising its First Amendment right of association to organize in groups as different as the Sierra Club and the National Rifle Association. One reason people so organize is to collectively exercise their First Amendment right of free speech pertinent to politics. Therefore reformers want to arm the speech police with additional powers to ration the permissible amount of "express advocacy," meaning speech by independent groups that advocates the election or defeat of an identifiable candidate.

But the political class will not stop there. Consider mere issue advocacy—

say, a television commercial endorsing abortion rights, mentioning no candidate and not mentioning voting but broadcast in the context of a campaign in which two candidates differ about abortion rights. Such communications can influence the thinking of voters. Can't have that, other than on a short leash held by the government's speech police. So restriction of hard money begets restriction of soft, which begets restriction of express advocacy, which begets regulation of issue advocacy—effectively, of all civic discourse.

The political class is not sliding reluctantly down a slippery slope, it is eagerly skiing down it, extending its regulation of political speech in order to make its life less stressful and more secure. Thus is the First Amendment nibbled away, like an artichoke devoured leaf by leaf.

This is an example of what has been called "the Latin Americanization" of American law—the proliferation of increasingly rococo laws in attempts to enforce fundamentally flawed laws. Reformers produce such laws from the bleak, paternalistic premise that unfettered participation in politics by means of financial support of political speech is a "problem" that must be "solved."

One reason the media are complacent about such restrictions on (others') political speech is that restrictions enhance the power of the media as the filters of political speech and as unregulated participants in a shrunken national conversation. Has the newspaper in which this column is appearing ever editorialized to the effect that restrictions on political money—restrictions on the ability to buy broadcast time and print space and other things the Supreme Court calls "the indispensable conditions for meaningful communication"— do not restrict speech? If this newspaper ever does, ask the editors if they would accept revising the First Amendment to read, "Congress shall make no law abridging the freedom of the press, but Congress can restrict the amount a newspaper may spend on editorial writers, reporters and newsprint."

When Senator Mitch McConnell, the Kentucky Republican, and others filibuster to block enlargement of the federal speech-rationing machinery, theirs will be arguably the most important filibuster in American history. Its importance will be attested by the obloquies they receive from the herd of independent minds eager to empower the political class to extend controls over speech about itself.

September 28, 1997

One-Third of the Senate Versus the First Amendment

L ast week Washington was a sight to behold. Two sights, actually, both in-volving hardy perennials. The city was a riot of cherry blossoms. And senators were again attacking the First Amendment.

Thirty-three senators—thirty Democrats and three Republicans—voted to amend the First Amendment to vitiate its core function, which is to prevent government regulation of political communication. The media generally ignored this: evidently assaults on the First Amendment are now too routine to be newsworthy. Besides, most of the media favor what last week's attack was intended to facilitate, the empowerment of government to regulate political advocacy by every individual and group *except the media*.

The attempt to improve Mr. Madison's Bill of Rights came from Fritz Hollings, the South Carolina Democrat, who proposed amending the First Amendment to say Congress or any state "shall have power to set reasonable limits on the amount of contributions that may be accepted, and the amount of expenditures that may be made by, in support of, or in opposition to, a candidate for nomination for election to, or for election to, federal office."

So this license for politicians to set limits on communication about politicians requires that the limits be, in the judgment of the politicians, "reasonable." Are you reassured? Hollings, whose candor is as refreshing as his amendment is ominous, says, correctly, that unless the First Amendment is hollowed out as he proposes, the McCain-Feingold speech-regulation bill is unconstitutional.

Russ Feingold, the Wisconsin Democrat who is John McCain's coperpetrator, voted against Hollings in order to avoid affirming that McCain-Feingold is unconstitutional. McCain voted with Hollings.

The standard rationale for regulating the giving and spending that are indispensable to political communication is to avoid "corruption" or the appearance thereof. Hollings, who has been a senator for thirty-three years, offered a novel notion of corruption. He said the Senate under Montana's Mike Mansfield (who was majority leader in 1961 to 1976) used to work five days a week. But now, says Hollings, because of the imperatives of fund-raising, "Mondays and Fridays are gone" and "we start on the half day on Tuesdays," and there are more and longer recesses. All of which, says Hollings, constitutes corruption.

Well. The 94th Congress (1975–76), Mansfield's last as leader, was in session 320 days and passed 1,038 bills. The 105th Congress (1997–98) was in session 296 days and passed 586 bills. The fact that twenty-two years after Mansfield's departure there was a 7.5 percent reduction in the length of the session but a 43.5 percent reduction in legislative output is interesting. But it is peculiar to think that passing 586 bills in two years—almost two bills every day in session—is insufficient. Is the decline in output deplorable, let alone a form of corruption, and hence a reason for erecting a speech-rationing regime?

The Framers of the First Amendment were not concerned with preventing government from abridging their freedom to speak about crops and cockfighting, or with protecting the expressive activity of topless dancers, which of late has found some shelter under the First Amendment. Rather, the Framers cherished unabridged freedom of political communication. Last week's thirty-three votes in favor of letting government slip Mr. Madison's leash and regulate political talk were thirty-four fewer than the required two-thirds and five fewer than Hollings's amendment got in 1997. Still, every time at least one-third of the Senate stands up against Mr. Madison, it is, you might think, newsworthy.

Last week's campaign reform follies included a proposal so bizarre it could have come only from a normal person in jest, or from Al Gore in earnest. He proposes to finance all congressional and Senate races from an "endowment" funded with $7.1 billion (the .1 is an exquisite Gore flourish) in tax-deductible contributions from individuals and corporations.

An unintended consequence of Gore's brainstorm would be to produce, in congressional races across the country, spectacles like that in the Reform Party today—federal money up for grabs and the likes of Pat Buchanan rushing to grab it. But would money flow into the endowment?

With the scary serenity of a liberal orbiting reality, Gore says, "The views of the donor will have absolutely no influence on the views of the recipient." Indeed, but the views of particular recipients also would be unknown to particular donors because all money would pour into and out of one pool. So what would be the motive to contribute?

Still, Gore has dreamt up a new entitlement (for politicians) to be administered by a new bureaucracy—a good day's work for Gore.

April 2, 2000

The McCarthyism of
the "Progressives"

McCainism, the McCarthyism of today's "progressives," involves, as McCarthyism did, the reckless hurling of imprecise accusations. Then the accusation was "communism!" Today it is "corruption!" Pandemic corruption of "everybody" by "the system" supposedly justifies campaign finance reforms. Those reforms would subject the rights of political speech and association to yet further government limits and supervision, by restricting the political contributions and expenditures that are indispensable for communication in modern society.

The media, exempt from regulations they advocate for rival sources of influence, are mostly John McCain's megaphones. But consider how empirically unproved and theoretically dubious are his charges of corruption.

What McCain and kindred spirits call corruption, or the "appearance" thereof, does not involve personal enrichment. Rather, it means responding to, or seeming to respond to, contributors, who also often are constituents. However, those crying "corruption!" must show that legislative outcomes were changed by contributions—that because of contributions, legislators voted differently than they otherwise would have done.

Abundant scholarship proves that this is difficult to demonstrate and that almost all legislative behavior is explainable by the legislators' ideologies, party affiliations, or constituents' desires. So reformers hurling charges of corruption often retreat to the charge that the "real" corruption is invisible—a speech not given, a priority not adopted. That charge is impossible to refute by disproving a negative. Consider some corruption innuendos examined by Bradley Smith, a member of the Federal Election Commission, in his new book, *Unfree Speech: The Folly of Campaign Finance Reform*.

In April 1999 Common Cause, McCain's strongest collaborator, made much of the fact that from 1989 through 1998 the National Rifle Association had contributed $8.4 million to congressional campaigns. However, that was *just two-tenths of 1 percent* of total spending ($4 billion) by congressional candidates during that period. How plausible is it that NRA contributions—as distinct from the votes of 3 million NRA members—influenced legislators?

Common Cause made much of the fact that in the ten years ending in November 1996, broadcasting interests gave $9 million in hard dollars to federal and state candidates and in soft dollars to parties. Gosh. Five election cycles. Changing issues and candidates. Rival interests within the industry (e.g., Time Warner versus Turner). And broadcasters' contributions were only *one-tenth of*

1 percent of the $9 billion spent by parties and candidates during that period. Yet as Smith says, Common Cause implies that this minuscule portion of political money caused legislative majorities to vote for bills they otherwise would have opposed or to oppose bills they otherwise would have supported, each time opposing the wishes of the constituents that the legislators must face again.

As Smith says, to prove corruption one must prove that legislators are acting against their principles, against their best judgment, or against their constituents' wishes. Furthermore, claims of corruption seem to presuppose that legislators should act on some notion of the "public good" unrelated to the views of any particular group of voters. With the reformer's characteristic hyperbole, Wisconsin Senator Russell Feingold, McCain's partner, attempts to reconnect reform with "corruption." He says, "Members of Congress and the leaders of both political parties routinely request and receive contributions for the parties of $100,000, $500,000, $1 million."

Well. There are 535 members of Congress. In the last two-year (1999–2000) election cycle, there were 1,564 contributions of $60,000 or more from individuals and organizations. So all those legislators supposedly "routinely" receiving such contributions for their parties receive, on average, fewer than two a year. The total value of all 1,564 was $365.2 million, a sum equal to one-fourteenth the amount Procter & Gamble spent on advertising during the same period.

The New York Times accurately and approvingly expresses McCainism: "Congress is unable to deal objectively with any issue, from a patients' bill of rights to taxes to energy policy, if its members are receiving vast open-ended donations from the industries and people affected." Oh. If only people affected by government would stop trying to affect the government—if they would just shut up and let McCain act "objectively."

Although reformers say there is "too much money in politics," if they really want to dilute the possible influence of particular interests (the NRA, broadcasters, whatever), they should favor *increasing* the size of the total pool of political money, so that any interest's portion of the pool will be small. And if reformers really want to see the appearance of corruption, they should examine what their reforms have done, have tried to do, and have not tried to do.

Smith notes that incumbent re-election rates began to rise soon after incumbents legislated the 1974 limits on contributions, which hurt challengers more than well-known incumbents with established financing networks. After 1974, incumbents' fund-raising advantages over challengers rose from approximately 1.5 to 1 to more than 4 to 1.

Early 1997 versions of the McCain-Feingold and Shays-Meehan reform bills would have set spending ceilings—surprise!—just where challengers become menacing to incumbents. Shays-Meehan set $600,000 for House races. Forty percent of challengers who had spent more than that in the previous cycle, won; only 3 percent who spent less, won. In 1994, 1996, and 1998, *all* Senate challengers lost who spent less than the limits proposed in the 1995 and 1997 versions of McCain-Feingold.

There are interesting limits to McCain's enthusiasm for limits. His bill does *not* include something President Bush proposes: a ban on lobbyists making contributions to legislators while the legislature is in session. Such a limit would abridge the freedom of incumbents. Campaign finance reform is about abridging the freedom of everyone but incumbents—and their media megaphones.

March 21 and 29, 2001

A 100 Percent Tax on Political Speech?

At a stroke, Bill Bradley recently refuted the bromide that he is boring, and in doing so he usefully illuminated the upcoming Senate debate on campaign finance reform. He did all this with a remarkable proposal—one flagrantly unconstitutional and amazingly inimical to democratic values, but definitely not boring.

On a call-in program on New Hampshire public radio, Bradley was at first boring: he advocated public financing, saying we spend $900 million a year promoting democracy abroad and for about the same sum we could supplant all private money with public money in campaigns. This would "totally take special interests out of our election process." His unremarkable, because familiar, thought raises questions:

By what criteria would he sort the "special," and impliedly disreputable, interests from the nonspecial, reputable ones that deserve to be in our election process? When the sorting is done, what will that process be about? Is Bradley a modern mugwump, trying to scrub the stain of politics from politics? Bradley is a practicing liberal who (therefore) is comfortable with the regulatory state, which, with all its regulating and subsidizing, is waist-deep in the business of allocating wealth and opportunity. Does he understand that the way to reduce the role of money in politics is to reduce the role of politics in the acquisition of money?

But let us move on to Bradley's remarkable idea.

The host of the radio program, noting that Bradley is ardent for campaign reforms, asked about "issue ads," noting that "nonprofit advocacy groups" of many persuasions are alarmed about the regulation of such ads envisioned by the Shays-Meehan bill, the House-passed version of campaign finance reform. Bradley replied that the way to deal with issue ads is to "simply say if somebody is going to buy an issue ad, that there's got to be an equal time on the other side." That, he said, is "the regulatory way. The market way to do it is simply say, when an issue ad is put on, there's a 100 percent tax, and the 100 percent tax is then given to the other side so that you get both points of view presented and you simply don't have the point of view that has the most money behind it dominating the airwaves."

A caller declared it "appalling" and "scary" to say "if I'm going to express my opinion I have to support somebody else who wants to express his opinion." And the caller added that Bradley, by talking about giving money to "the" other side so that people would hear "both" points of view on an issue, assumes, unrealistically, a tidy bipolarity of public debate, rather than a variety of opinions on particular issues. Bradley called that "a very good point" and "food for thought."

Here is more such food: the campaign finance reformers' assault, in the name of political hygiene, on the First Amendment is now so sweeping, and so untroubled by even twinges of conscience, that a mainstream politician like Bradley can casually propose such a tax on political communication. Note well: the tax is intended not to raise revenue but to change behavior—to extinguish an entire category of political advocacy.

Bradley suggests this in the name of a chimera. It can be called "equality of political efficacy." The reformers' preferred metaphor is "leveling the playing field." They should listen to the logic of their language: fields are leveled by bulldozers. Speaking of scary, imagine the government as a bulldozer used to produce equality of political advocacy for each point of view and "the" other side.

Fortunately, the Supreme Court has said government cannot require people "to pay a tax for the exercise of that which the First Amendment has made a high constitutional privilege." And "the power to tax the exercise of a privilege is the power to control or suppress its enjoyment" and is "as potent as the power of censorship." And "the concept that government may restrict the speech of some elements of our society in order to enhance the relative voice of others is wholly foreign to the First Amendment."

Bradley has usefully compared money in politics to ants in the kitchen: "Without closing all the holes, there is always a way in." This is a useful metaphor because it explains why the law regulating political speech *must* metastasize.

Controls on "hard" money, which is given directly to particular candidates, do not allow the political class to ration political speech as effectively as that class desires. So it wants to supplement those controls with controls on "soft" money, which is given to parties to fund advocacy and other activities not specifically supportive of particular candidates. But even controls on "hard" and "soft" money will be largely vitiated unless "express advocacy"—

urging the election or defeat of specific candidates—by private groups is controlled. But even those three kinds of restrictions on political communication will not give the political class the control it desires over communication about itself unless restrictions are imposed on issue advocacy by private groups. Hence Bradley's 100 percent tax.

His proposal is not of practical importance: in the unlikely event Congress enacted it, the Supreme Court would hurl the law back across First Street, N.E., with "Are you out of your collective minds?" scrawled across it. But Bradley's proposal is profoundly important as a symptom of the indifference—no, hostility—of campaign reformers to First Amendment values.

Now that it has become "progressive" to "reform" politics by restricting political speech, reformers are constantly dreaming up refinements to the restrictions. As a result, the nation is acquiring a speech code that, like the tax code, is constantly in play, subject to endless tweakings by groups seeking additional advantages. Speech-rationing laws, once present, proliferate, like ants in the kitchen.

October 11, 1999

Congress and the "Misuse" of Political Speech

The Senate this week revisits campaign finance reform, making another attempt to broaden regulation, by the political class, of public communication about that class. So consider remarks Representative Lois Capps, Democrat of California, made during the debate on the House version of speech regulation, the Shays-Meehan bill.

Her husband, a congressman, died in October 1997. In January 1998 she finished first in an all-party primary, and in March she won a runoff to complete the remainder of her husband's term. Then came the June primary for the November election. In November 1998 she won a full term.

Her arduous year—four elections in eleven months—included the involvement of issue-advocacy groups that ran ads, some beneficial to her, some beneficial to her opponent. When praising Shays-Meehan, she said, "Last year . . . I endured four grueling elections and watched as wave after wave of attack ads flooded my district under the guise of informing voters. These ads distorted both my record and the record of my opponent. The Shays-Meehan bill effectively ends the misuse of issue advertising. It does so by requiring all ads which clearly urge the support or defeat of a candidate in a federal election to be treated like what they are, political ads."

She is right—and wrong. Many ads were distortions. But that does not justify expanding government policing of the "misuse" of political speech.

The political class understandably resents having lost control of the country's political conversation. In every election candidates have issues they want to stress or avoid. Increasingly, interest groups use issue ads to force new subjects onto the political agenda. However, elections are not the political class's private property, and that class cannot construct a quasi property right by regulating, as Shays-Meehan would, what can be said by interest groups about candidates in the months immediately before elections.

Those regulations have been dropped from the Senate's version of reform, the McCain-Feingold bill, in an attempt to get the eight votes that were lacking last year when the bill's supporters failed to get cloture to bring the bill to a vote. However, by dropping those regulations, McCain-Feingold lost the support of one group of ardent speech rationers, the League of Women Voters.

The Senate will debate campaign reform amid fresh reports about what reformers consider the intensifying "problem" of "too much money" in politics. The problem, reformers say in effect (when they are not lamenting the "apathy" of an electorate "disconnected" from politics), is too many people participating in politics by contributing too much to parties and candidates.

If fund-raising continues at the current pace, candidates for the House, Senate, and presidency will spend $3 billion in the 1999–2000 cycle, an $800 million increase over the 1995–96 presidential election cycle. But to put that $800 million—in eight quarters—into perspective: $655 million was spent on advertising on the Internet *in just the last quarter of 1998.*

That $3 billion would come to $14.60 per eligible voter for political communication about the determination of public policy—about the presidential contest, 435 House contests, and 34 Senate contests. Too much? By what standard?

If today's fund-raising pace is maintained, the two-year total for congressional races could be $1 billion. But before fainting, consider:

In a *single year,* 1998, the nation's largest advertiser, General Motors, spent almost $3 billion communicating about its products. The fourteenth-largest advertiser, McDonald's, spent more than $1 billion in 1998 communicating about food.

The Senate debate takes place after the Bush campaign's announcement that it has raised $56 million in seven months. However, Holman W. Jenkins, Jr., of *The Wall Street Journal* reports that in 1967–68 Eugene McCarthy, whose insurgent campaign against President Lyndon Johnson for the Democratic presidential nomination lasted about seven months, raised $11 million. In current dollars, that is almost $53 million. And most of it came from five people. Under the political-speech regulations put in place since then, it is impossible—it is illegal—to mount a McCarthy-style insurgency against the political status quo. The political class, which *is* the status quo, wants it that way.

It is indeed wrong that the political class must spend so much time raising money. It also is that class's fault: it has not repealed the $1,000 limit on contributions imposed, unindexed to inflation, twenty-five years ago. That limit has created an artificial scarcity of something—money—that is stupendously plentiful in booming America.

The political class could do what it most likes to do—do itself a favor—by deregulating political speech, including repeal of limits on political giving. Then Representative Capps could more easily raise enough money to answer what she considers "misuses" of political speech.

October 10, 1999

A (Speech) Policeman's Lot Is Not Easy

The coming debate on campaign finance "reforms" that would vastly expand government regulation of political communication will measure just how much jeopardy the First Amendment, and hence political freedom, faces. The recent evidence is ominous.

In 1997 thirty-eight senators voted to amend the First Amendment to empower government to impose "reasonable" restrictions on political speech. Dick Gephardt has said, "What we have is two important values in direct conflict: freedom of speech and our desire for healthy campaigns in a healthy democracy." Bill Bradley has proposed suppressing issue advocacy ads of independent groups by imposing a *100 percent tax* on such ads. John McCain has said he wishes he could constitutionally ban negative ads—ads critical of politicians.

The basis of political-speech regulation is the 1971 Federal Election Campaign Act. Bradley Smith, a member of the Federal Election Commission and author of *Unfree Speech: The Folly of Campaign Finance Reform,* calls the FECA "one of the most radical laws ever passed in the United States." Because of it, for the first time Americans were required to register with the government before spending money to disseminate criticism of its officeholders.

Liberals eager for more regulation of political speech should note the pedigree of their project. The first FECA enforcement action came in 1972, when some citizens organized as the National Committee for Impeachment paid $17,850 to run a *New York Times* ad criticizing President Richard Nixon.

His Justice Department got a court to enjoin the committee from further spending to disseminate its beliefs. Justice said the committee had not properly registered with the government and the committee's activities might "affect" the 1972 election, so it was barred from spending more than $1,000 to communicate its opinions. After the expense of reaching a federal appellate court, the committee defeated the FEC, but only because the committee had not engaged in "express advocacy" by explicitly urging people to vote for or against a specific candidate.

In 1976 some citizens formed the Central Long Island Tax Reform Immediately Committee, which spent $135 to distribute the voting record of a congressman who displeased them. Two years later this dissemination of truthful information brought a suit from the FEC's speech police, who said the committee's speech was illegal because the committee had not fulfilled all the registering and reporting the FECA requires of those who engage in independent expenditure supporting or opposing a candidate. The committee won in a federal appellate court, but only because it had not engaged in "express advocacy."

In 1998, with impeachment approaching, Leo Smith, a Connecticut voter, designed a Web site urging support for Bill Clinton and defeat of Representative Nancy Johnson, Republican of Connecticut. When Johnson's opponent's campaign contacted Smith, worried that his site put him and its campaign in violation of the FECA, he sought an FEC advisory opinion.

Although Smith had neither received nor expended money to create this particular Web site, the FEC said the law's definition of a political expenditure includes a gift of "something of value," and the FEC noted that his site was "administered and maintained" by his personal computer, which cost money. And that the "domain name Web site" was registered in 1996 for $100 for two years and for $35 a year thereafter. And "costs associated with the creation and maintaining" of the site are considered an expenditure because the site uses words that bring on the speech police: it "expressly advocates" the election of one candidate and the defeat of another.

The FEC advised Smith that if his site really was independent, he would be "required to file reports with the Commission if the total value of your expenditures exceeds $250 during 1998." If his activity was not truly independent, his "expenditures" would have to be reported as an in-kind contribution to Johnson's opponent. Smith ignored the FEC, which, perhaps too busy policing speech elsewhere, let him get away with free speech.

Today Internet pornography is protected from regulation, but not Internet political speech. And campaign finance "reformers" aspire to much, much more regulation because, they say, there is "too much money in politics."

Actually, too much money that could fund political discourse is spent on complying with FECA speech regulations. To cover compliance costs, the Bush and Gore campaigns combined raised $15,135,382.54. And Bradley Smith notes that because of the law's ambiguities and the FEC's vast discretion, litigation has become a campaign weapon: candidates file charges to embarrass opponents and force them to expend resources fending off the speech police. Consider this legacy of "reforms" during this month's debate about adding to them.

March 11, 2001

The Speech Police Find "Offending Passages"

Even more scandalous than the political class's continuing assault on the First Amendment is the journalistic class's complicity in this assault. The threat, advanced under the antiseptic rubric of "campaign finance reform," is a speech-rationing system to solve the "problem" of "excessive" political giving and spending.

Such a system already exists, but reformers always want new laws to make the system more elaborate. And even without new laws, the Federal Election Commission is trying to punish some "offending" journalism. Consider the FEC's attempt to fine Steve Forbes $94,900 for the content of his magazine column.

Like his father and grandfather before him, Forbes writes a biweekly column for *Forbes* magazine, of which he is editor in chief. The column is primarily about public policy, although it also contains short book reviews, restaurant recommendations, and other whimsy.

The FEC's speech police have decided to permit the whimsy. However, there are limits to their liberality. They have scoured the columns Forbes wrote while campaigning for the Republican presidential nomination in 1996 and have culled what they call "offending passages."

What passages offend the government? Passages on, say, Brazil pass muster, but those on Bosnia were, the speech police say, illegal. Why? Because Bosnia was, and Brazil was not, an issue in the 1996 campaign. Forbes's thoughts on Canada are fine because no one cares about Canada. However, thoughts on partial-birth abortion get Forbes fined.

Sifting permissible from impermissible content, FEC bureaucrats—your tax dollars at work—have calculated a fine of $95,000. The FEC believes *Forbes* magazine made an impermissible corporate contribution of that size to Forbes's campaign. The FEC arrived at that sum by calculating what an advertiser would pay for the same space occupied by these passages in the magazine and in a small New Jersey newspaper that Forbes owns and that carries his column.

Forbes could pay the fine out of petty cash but instead is going to court. The Supreme Court and numerous lower courts have told the FEC, as Forbes says, that "the threshold question for determining if *any* activity or disbursement is subject to regulation by the FEC is whether that activity expressly advocates the election or defeat of a federal candidate."

The FEC admits there was no "express advocacy" in *Forbes* magazine on behalf of Forbes. However, for twenty years the FEC has unsuccessfully tried to turn American politics into a game of "Mother, may I?" in which candidates must constantly traipse to the FEC to seek permission for contemplated campaign activities.

Once upon a time, defenders of the First Amendment applauded when Justice William Douglas explained the indissoluble link between freedom of speech and freedom to give and spend money for the dissemination of speech: "It usually costs money to communicate an idea to a large audience. But no one would seriously contend that the expenditure of money to print a newspaper deprives the publisher of freedom of the press."

Nowadays *The New York Times, The Washington Post,* and other members of the media favor circumscribing everyone else's freedom of speech by circumscribing the freedom to give and spend on behalf of political expression. Why? Perhaps partly because such circumscription enlarges the importance of the media's unregulated political expression, relative to the expression permitted to people covered by speech-rationing laws.

But will the media remain immune to regulation? The FEC's ham-handedness regarding Forbes demonstrates how any speech-rationing system will tend to become steadily more rococo.

Controls on "hard" money (given directly to particular candidates) are ineffective unless supplemented by controls on "soft money" (given to parties for "party-building" activities), and even those controls are vitiated unless express advocacy by private groups is controlled, but those controls are nullities unless control encompasses issue advocacy by private groups. And in time we come, as the Forbes case shows, to government attempts to excise "offending passages" from a magazine.

Where is the media outrage? This year is seeing the crack-up of several causes and the ruin of reputations. By their uncharacteristic and unprincipled quietude concerning the president's comportment, many feminists have devalued their past protestations and forfeited their place in the nation's political conversation. Similarly, much of the media are shredding their credentials as defenders of free speech.

With scant help from them, Senator Mitch McConnell, Republican of Kentucky, and other congressional friends of the First Amendment last week defeated this year's speech-rationing legislation, thereby sparing the Supreme

Court the chore of nullifying it. But the First Amendment is weaker because of the silence of the media lambs who once were lions in its defense.

September 13, 1998

Minnesota Takes Exception to the First Amendment

Curiouser and curiouser, said Alice, who was in Wonderland, although she could have been in Minnesota. The misguided Supreme Court of that state will soon answer to the U.S. Supreme Court, trying to defend the indefensible: provisions in the state's Code of Judicial Conduct, promulgated by the state court, that push campaign regulation, meaning the official supervision of political speech, to new levels of offensiveness.

Like a sizable majority of states, Minnesota elects judges, which is a bad idea but historically understandable. The state constitution mandating this was adopted on the eve of the Civil War, when abolitionist feelings were running high and so was resentment of the judicial high-handedness that produced the 1857 *Dred Scott* decision. Be that as it may, Minnesota says there shall be judicial elections but that candidates for judicial office are forbidden to say anything pertinent—and, by the way, so are candidates' family members. Really.

The code contains various provisions that are constitutionally dubious. The "announce" clause prohibits judicial candidates from announcing "their views on disputed legal or political issues." The "endorsement" clause forbids candidates "to seek, accept or use" an endorsement from any political party organization. The "attend or speak" clauses prohibit candidates from "attending political gatherings" or speaking at political party gatherings. However, they can attend and speak at meetings of other interests: the NAACP, the NRA, the Minnesota Trial Lawyers Association, etc. Go figure.

What, you may wonder, is the point of conducting elections if candidates are forbidden to say anything that might enable voters to make informed choices? Minnesota's Republican Party wonders, and so do such ancillary groups as—isn't this an interesting country?—the Indian Asian American Republicans of Minnesota and the Muslim Republicans of Minnesota. They have enlisted the James Madison Center for Free Speech, and the U.S. Supreme Court will hear their argument on behalf of Gregory Wersal.

Minnesota's judicial elections are conducted with "nonpartisan" ballots:

candidates do not run with party designations, which is a bad idea compounded. If you are going to have elections, why forbid politicking? In any case, when in 1996 Wersal sought election to Minnesota's Supreme Court, he attended Republican gatherings and—scandal compounded—said informative things, such as that he favors strict judicial construction and is critical of certain Minnesota Supreme Court rulings.

This violated the "announce" clause. Threatened with an ethics complaint, which threatened his livelihood as a lawyer, he dropped his candidacy. But in January 1997 he announced for the 1998 campaign. In December 1997 Minnesota's Supreme Court made matters worse by adding the "endorsement" and "attend or speak" clauses and requiring judicial candidates to encourage family members to adhere to the standards of conduct for candidates, who are forbidden to knowingly permit any person "to do for the candidate what the candidate is prohibited from doing."

Wersal lost in the primary but ran again in 2000, when, although he did not seek it, he received the Republican Party endorsement. When his opponent attacked him for this, Wersal sought permission from the board that enforces the code to respond to this attack, which would require him to mention the endorsement. Permission denied. Such is life under speech police empowered to enforce someone's idea of political hygiene.

Minnesota defenders of these restrictions on political speech and association say they "guarantee the independence" of the judiciary "from political, economic and social pressure"—whatever "social pressure" might include. So Minnesota is to have elections designed to guarantee the winners' "independence" from the electorate. This is pure McCainism—John McCain's vision of campaign "reforms" that will produce a *faux* politics without the "appearance" of the "corruption" of actual politics.

But note this: the justices of the state Supreme Court have created a speech code that controls the conduct of candidates for that court. Does that not trouble Minnesota's fine-tuners of "appearances"?

When the dust from the terrorism crisis settles, attention should be paid to the perversely selective concern some people have shown about civil liberties these past few months. The same sort of people who insist that unlawful noncitizen belligerents be accorded the full panoply of legal protections accorded to Americans accused of burglary are simultaneously eager to abridge Americans' core First Amendment right, that of unrestricted political speech. Curiouser and curiouser.

Meanwhile, another year has passed and McCain-Feingold has not. The House version of that bill, which would further empower the federal government to ration political speech, is bottled up in committee, so "reformers" are in the slough of despond, not to mention high dudgeon. Rejoice.

January 3, 2002

The Scandal the Media Are Missing

The media are missing a scandal because the media *are* the scandal. They are complicit with the portion of the political class currently attempting to impose on the public, in the name of campaign finance reform, speech restrictions of the sort to which the media are immune. But the rationale for this immunity, as explained by the Supreme Court in the First Amendment case most cherished by the media, refutes the argument for the campaign reforms most of the media favor.

The Senate is currently debating the McCain-Feingold bill to ban "soft money" contributions to political parties. Such money can be used only for certain purposes, such as issue ads, voter registration, and turnout drives, and cannot be spent in support of particular candidacies for federal offices.

One possible effect of outlawing soft money might be what the reformers desire: reducing corruption or the appearance of it. One certain effect would be a diminution of political communication, exhortation, argument—in a word, speech.

In the 1976 *Buckley v. Valeo* ruling, the Supreme Court struck down limits on what candidates could spend, arguing on First Amendment grounds that money is indispensable to political communication, so limiting spending limits speech. That ruling was a direct descendant of a 1964 ruling, *New York Times v. Sullivan,* which began when the *Times* published a political advertisement that supported civil rights groups in the South.

The ad communicated information, expressed opinions, cited grievances, and alleged abuses. An elected city commissioner in Montgomery, Alabama, filed a libel action against the *Times'* publisher and some clergymen whose names appeared in the ad. An Alabama court awarded the commissioner $500,000, and the case went to the U.S. Supreme Court, where Justice William Brennan, writing for a unanimous Court, reversed the Alabama judgment.

He said the judgment had violated the "profound national commitment to the principle that debate on public issues should be uninhibited, robust, and wide-open, and that it may well include vehement, caustic, and sometimes unpleasantly sharp attacks on government and public officials." Indeed, "neither factual error nor defamatory content" nor a combination of those elements "suffices to remove the constitutional shield" from political speech such as the ad.

Today many in the media, comfortable behind that undentable shield, urge Congress to impose speech-regulating measures that *must* mean less "uninhibited, robust and wide-open" debate. The media's influence is increasing as the political speech of everyone else is brought under an increasingly complex regime of regulation. Also, the media's enthusiasm for speech-regulating reforms is applied liberalism, the impulse to have the state put a leash on everything in the name of equality.

However, defenders of unfettered speech should not support raising the $1,000 limit that was legislated in 1974 and mistakenly allowed to stand by the Court in 1976. Because the real value of $1,000 has declined as the costs of campaigning have risen, the limit inflicts on candidates the misery of spending disproportionate amounts of their time raising money in dribs and drabs.

But to acquiesce in raising the $1,000 limit would be to endorse the insupportable—the principle that limits on giving, unlike those on spending, are compatible with the Constitution. Here, worse is better: the more such limits on contributions make life difficult for the political class, the more likely that class is to throw up its hands and, as a desperate last resort, do the right thing—deregulate political speech.

The time is not ripe for the audacious concept that Congress shall make no law abridging freedom of speech. Meanwhile, the prize for perverse audacity goes to Arizona's campaign reformers, who persuaded voters to approve, by a slender majority, a baroque campaign-financing system, the awfulness of which only begins with partial public funding and a 20 percent reduction in existing state limits on private contributions. To discourage independent groups from participating in politics, extra public funds are given to candidates when independent groups campaign against them.

The pot of money for Arizona candidates is filled in part by a $100 annual fee on certain lobbyists—those who represent for-profit entities or trade associations. This is constitutionally dubious because it conditions the exercise of the First Amendment right to petition for redress of grievances.

In addition, there is a 10 percent surcharge on all civil and criminal judgments. So when on June 9 Steve May got a $27 parking ticket in Tempe, he sent the city a check for $24.30, subtracting the coerced political contribution. May thereby practiced what Jefferson preached: "To compel a man to furnish contributions of money for the propagation of opinions which he disbelieves, is sinful and tyrannical."

October 17, 1999

Surprise!

What is liberalism's appeal? Surely less its plausibility than the surprises it provides. Liberals constantly experience the excitement of the unexpected, the thrill of being startled by the unanticipated—if only by them—consequences of their actions.

After Senate passage of the McCain-Feingold campaign finance bill became a foregone conclusion, *The Washington Post,* which adores the bill, carried this front-page headline: "Campaign Bill Could Shift Power Away from Parties." *Could?* McCain-Feingold would ban soft money contributions to political parties, so *of course* money diverted from that channel will flow into unblocked channels. The *Post* considers this news?

Do reformers consider this progress? Since when? Not long ago, political action committees were the root of all evil—refusing PAC contributions was, indeed still is, a form of moral grandstanding by some candidates.

Disregard the rhetoric by McCain-Feingold enthusiasts about their bill curing the "problem" of "too much money in politics." Here are two safe bets: there will be more money spent in the 2001–2002 off-year election cycle than was spent in 1997–1998, and more spent in 2003–2004 than in 1999–2000.

The realistic way to reduce the amount of money in politics is to reduce the amount of politics in money—the importance of government in allocating wealth and opportunity. Does the *Post* advocate less government as a path to less political money? No.

The day after the *Post's* story, *The New York Times,* a McCain-Feingold zealot, trumpeted this "news": "Campaign Finance Overhaul May Enhance Influence of Big Political Action Committees." *May?* This is not a close call.

Alighting upon the obvious with a self-congratulatory sense of original discovery, the *Times* reported that "suddenly, the large labor groups, corporations, trade associations and ideological organizations that funnel their political largess through PACs may find that they are the largest players on the field because their soft-money competitors can no longer participate." Then the *Times,* constantly liberal and thus incessantly surprised, used the U-word, "unexpected": "The prospect that PACs will become only more influential marks an unexpected turn because for years those committees were portrayed as the villains."

If McCain-Feingold becomes law, by next year liberals, and McCain, will be describing PACs the way they describe all sources of political communication not yet rationed by regulations—as "loopholes" to be closed. They will propose closing the loophole by banning (their favorite word) PACs, or narrowing the loophole by, say, limiting the proportion of a candidate's contributions that PACs can provide.

Three days after that *Times* story, the lead story in *Roll Call,* the newspaper that covers Congress, was headlined "Soft-Money PACs Banned." Do tell.

More than forty House and Senate members operate so-called leadership PACs funded by soft money. But some members seem to have been too busy praising McCain-Feingold to read that bill. While voting for its ban on soft-money fund-raising by the national party committees, they neglected to read what *Roll Call* calls "a little-noticed provision" prohibiting federal legislators or candidates for federal office from raising unregulated money for their PACs.

Roll Call—written, mind you, for professional legislators and their staffs—says dryly, "That came as news to some Senate leaders who have opened leadership political action committees that operate outside of federal regulations." On March 19, the day debate on the bill began, Joseph Lieberman, a McCain-Feingold supporter, filed papers with the Federal Election Commission for his new leadership PAC. House Minority Leader Richard Gephardt, who says "the Senate passed a good bill," recently launched a soft-money PAC. Senators and representatives might have assumed, understandably, that they would be exempt from a soft-money ban because Congress has often exempted itself from regulations it imposes on others.

The governors' associations of both parties have been funded substantially by soft money. Both parties' conventions are funded in part by ad hoc entities that raise large amounts of soft money that may or may not be impacted by McCain-Feingold. Now what?

Common Cause, the League of Women Voters, and many of the other liberal lobbies backing McCain-Feingold candidly say that it is inadequate, other than as a step toward public funding of all campaigns. That is, a system in which the only permissible political communication by parties and candidates would be what the government pays for.

If McCain-Feingold becomes law, liberals (and McCain, a conservative infected by liberalism's faith that good intentions, cleverly codified, can scrub the naughtiness from this fallen world) will soon demand more reforms to correct the unanticipated (by them) consequences of their reforms. That, too, is part of liberalism's appeal: It provides steady work.

April 12, 2001

Virtue at Last!
(In Ten Months)

Presidential Press Secretary Ari Fleischer, pioneering new frontiers of fatuity, says some parts of the Shays-Meehan campaign finance bill please his boss and others do not. "But ultimately the process is moving forward, and the president is pleased." Ultimately, in Washington, the celebration of "process" signals the abandonment of principle.

President George W. Bush's abandonment of his has earned him at least $61 million (see below) and the approval of *The New York Times*. It praises his "positive role" and gives him "considerable credit" for the passage of the bill, which has received so much supportive editorializing from the *Times,* in news stories and editorials, that it should be called Shays-Meehan-*Times.*

What pleased the *Times* is that Bush did next to nothing to discourage—in fact, Fleischer issued a statement that encouraged—passage of a bill chock-full of provisions that Bush, who swore an oath to defend the Constitution, has said violate the First Amendment. Two years ago he affirmed this principle expressed by Supreme Court Justice Clarence Thomas: "There is no constitutionally significant distinction between campaign contributions and expenditures. Both forms of speech are central to the First Amendment." When asked about the principle that it is hostile to First Amendment values to limit individuals' participation in politics by limiting their right to contribute, he said, "I agree." Asked if he thinks a president has a duty to judge the constitutionality of bills and veto those he considers unconstitutional, he replied, "I do."

Now he seems ready to sign Shays-Meehan-*Times.* Why? Could it have something to do with the fact that the bill raises from $1,000 to $2,000 the limit on individuals' contributions to House, Senate, and presidential candidates? Candidate Bush got $1,000 contributions from 61,000 people. If he can get just that many to give $2,000—for a sitting president, that should be a piece of cake—the bill that he says "makes the system better" will be worth an extra $61 million to him in 2004.

The ardent-for-reform *Washington Post*—the bill should have been called Shays-Meehan-*Times-Post*—baldly asserts (talk about the triumph of hope over experience) that the bill "will slow the spiral of big-money fundraising." Actually, the 2003–4 election cycle probably will see the normal increase in political spending. The difference will be that in the next cycle much more of the political giving will be more difficult to trace. The soft money that Shays-Meehan-*Times-Post* bans—contributions to parties—must be reported. Henceforth much of that money will go to independent groups that will not have to report the source of the money that finances their issue advertising.

One of the bill's incumbent-protection measures says that a candidate whose opponent is very wealthy can receive contributions larger than $2,000. But the Supreme Court has held that the only constitutional justification for limiting political contributions is to prevent corruption or the appearance thereof. So this bill claims, in effect, that the appearance of corruption from a large contribution varies with the size of one's opponent's wallet.

Another incumbent-convenience provision makes it much more difficult for independent groups—labor unions, corporations, nonprofit entities (individuals are another matter; see next paragraph)—to run ads that so much as *mention* a House, Senate, or presidential candidate within thirty days of a primary or *sixty* days of a general election—in effect, after Labor Day.

In the name of protecting regular people from rich people, the bill has this effect: a millionaire can write a check for $1 million and run a political ad that the National Rifle Association or the Sierra Club could not run using $1 contributions from 1 million individuals.

Most representatives who voted for the bill probably do not know half of what is in it. They cannot know. No one will know until there have been years of litigation about Federal Election Commission regulations issued to "clarify" things. What, for example, is meant by "coordination"? Consider.

There are dollar limits on contributions to candidates, but not on spending for political advocacy by independent individuals or groups—unless they are coordinated with the candidate. In that case they are counted as contributions to the candidate and thus limited. The bill says coordination includes "any general or particular understanding" between such an individual or group and a candidate. If proper law gives due notice of what is and is not permitted, this is not the rule of law.

Opinion polls invariably show negligible public interest in campaign-finance reform, but almost every congressional district has at least one newspaper hot for reform. Media cheerleading for the bill has been relentless. For example, NBC's Katie Couric, advocating passage of what should be called the Shays-Meehan-*Times-Post*-Couric bill, wondered whether Enron's collapse would make "people say, 'Enough is enough! This has got to happen!'" The media know that their power increases as more and more restrictions are imposed on everyone else's ability to participate in political advocacy.

The bill repeals the politicians' entitlement to buy advertising at the lowest rate stations charge any buyer. This will mean hundreds of millions of dollars of extra revenue for broadcasters. Is this a reward for the media's support? Is there an *appearance of corruption* here? Never mind. But note this. Repeal of the entitlement is another gift from incumbents to themselves: challengers usually have less money, so they will be most hurt by higher ad rates.

The bill's authors say soft money is (a) scandalous and (b) not to be tampered with until after they have re-elected themselves. That is, they refused to ban soft money until they have spent all that their parties have raised and will frenetically raise until November. It is going to be that kind of year.

February 25, 2002

The Next Mess Reformers Will Make of the Last Mess They Have Made

Campaign finance reformers have had their way in Washington, which should keep them content—or at least muted—for maybe two years. But what will they attempt when next they announce, as they did this time, that the system they have created is scandalous and again needs their purifying touch? Events in Arizona suggest an answer.

The Clean Elections Act, enacted by a 1998 initiative, establishes public funding for all campaigns for state offices. To qualify for public subsidies, candidates need only collect a prescribed number of $5 contributions—different numbers for different offices. Recipients of subsidies are not allowed to spend any other money. Subsidies range from $10,790 in primaries and $16,180 in general elections for state legislative candidates, up to $409,950 in primaries and $614,930 in general elections for governor.

Reformers say the system is voluntary. Not exactly. Consider the incentives designed to compel participation.

Candidates who choose not to participate are severely penalized. To cripple their ability to participate in politics outside the "voluntary" system, statutory contribution limits for nonparticipating candidates are reduced by 20 percent and reporting requirements are made more onerous. If nonparticipants manage, in spite of the imposed handicaps, to spend above the limits stipulated for participants, matching funds are provided to participants.

In this 2001–2 election cycle, Arizona's subsidies will amount to an estimated $16 million. The money is supposed to come from four sources.

Two are voluntary. Taxpayers can dedicate $5 of their state income taxes to the fund. And, remarkably, for additional contributions they choose to designate for the state pool, they get a dollar-for-dollar tax *credit*—a reduction of their tax bill—of up to $530 or 20 percent of their liability, *whichever is greater.* So funding the public financing of campaigns is cost-free for taxpayers. Yet taxpayers have chosen to provide only 29 percent of required revenues. (Only 12.5 percent of federal taxpayers use the checkoff for funding presidential campaigns.)

Two sources are coercive. The most important is a 10 percent surcharge imposed on all civil and criminal fines—even parking tickets. And a $110 fee is imposed on all lobbyists for *for-profit causes*—for example, the Chamber of Commerce but not teachers' unions or Planned Parenthood.

The Institute for Justice Arizona Chapter is challenging both coercive measures as unconstitutional "compelled speech." The reformers' mantra that "money is not speech" is answered by the California Supreme Court, which has neatly said that "speech results, from money's enabling." The U.S. Supreme Court has repeatedly held that government cannot force individuals to finance political speech against their will. By this the court has implicitly accepted the premise that "speech results, from money's enabling."

To see the future, look back eight years. In 1994, a year of liberal over-reaching, Hillary Clinton's crusade for government domination of health care collapsed. Subsequently, liberals have taken a more incremental approach toward that goal. Much the same has happened regarding campaign finance reform.

In 1994 the reformers' bill included taxpayer-funded campaigns, state-by-state spending limits varying with population, and a ban on soft money (for parties, not candidates, for uses such as voter registration and turnout). That bill failed. But this year reformers achieved a soft-money ban that soon will have consequences that the reformers will say justify more reforms.

The more candid, or less circumspect, reformers acknowledge that their goal is complete public financing of campaigns, a system in which government will control the amounts of money used (and the times, places, and manners of using it) to debate the composition of the government. Reformers will demand this when, in a few years, they declare it scandalous that their ban on soft-money contributions to the parties has—by the predictable hydraulics of political money flows—diverted money to independent groups, some of them created for the purpose of receiving it.

The reformers' 1974 success, limiting contributions to candidates, gave rise to soft money and political action committees—and to the reformers' demand for what has just been passed, a ban on soft money and restrictions on speech by independent groups. After the Supreme Court makes short shrift of those restrictions, independent groups will become even more important conduits of political money. Political parties, deprived of soft money, will have been pushed by reformers toward the margins of politics. Reformers will be shocked.

Then reformers will advocate measures foreshadowed by Arizona's, including government as a monopolist of money for political advocacy and co-erced contributions to the pool of money the government disburses. They will advocate this in, perhaps, 2004, declaring it urgent to correct the scandalous consequences of what they did in 2002.

February 21, 2002

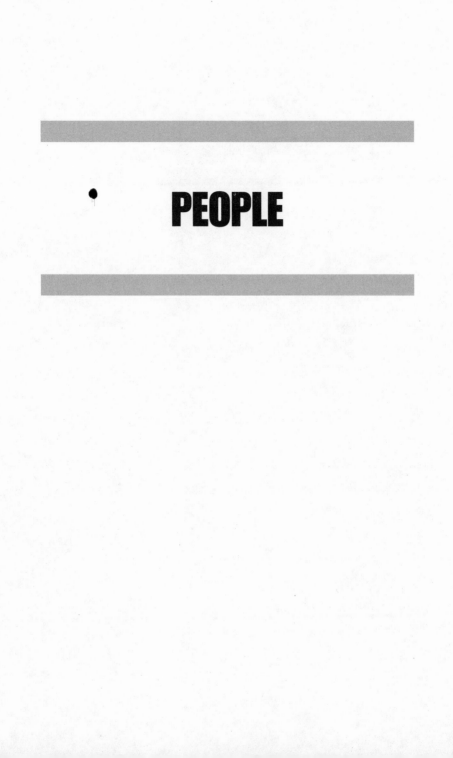

PEOPLE

The Forfeiture of Princess Noor

LONDON—Turn a corner in this city where Thomas Becket lived and Christopher Wren built, and you may come upon a church. It may only be what Father Ronald Knox called "a rather anyhow little church." Saint Paul's of Knightsbridge might seem such, at first glance. Look closer.

Look not just at its glittering roster of past worshipers, which includes the Duke of Wellington. When the widow Lady Randolph Churchill remarried in 1900 (to a man twenty-one years her junior; there was talk), witnesses who signed the register included her twenty-five-year-old son, Winston.

Look mostly at two modest plaques on the church's outside north wall. One, "In memory of old boys of St. Paul's School who gave their lives for freedom, honor and right 1914–1918," contains thirty-seven names. Three Hawkins boys. Three pairs of boys with the same last names. Incalculable heartache.

The other plaque commemorates fifty-two women who lost their lives in the Second World War, for which the Great War—in 1914–1918 it was unimaginable to call that the First World War—was prologue. The women were members of the Women's Transport Service, a.k.a. FANY—First Aid Nursing Yeomanry, which during the war was headquartered in the vicarage. Thirteen of the fifty-two died in German prison camps, including the woman listed on the plaque as "N. Inyat-Khan G.C."

The G.C. stands for George Cross. Awarded for gallantry, it is the civilian equivalent of the highest military honor, the Victoria Cross. Princess Noor Inyat-Khan earned it en route to death, in September 1944, by a bullet fired by an SS man into the back of her skull as she knelt on the sandy, blood-spattered soil of Dachau concentration camp.

The great-great-granddaughter of a Muslim ruler who died resisting Britain's conquest of India, she also was related, on her mother's side, to Mary Baker Eddy, founder of Christian Science. Her parents moved to London shortly before the outbreak of war in 1914, then to Paris. She received a degree from the Sorbonne and became an author of children's stories.

Fleeing to England when France fell in 1940, she received training as an operator of wireless radios, which brought her to the attention of the SOE (Special Operations Executive). Having been duly warned about the risk of capture, torture, and execution, she and two other women stepped from a plane on a French meadow before dawn on June 17, 1943. By that evening she was in Paris. Within a week the Gestapo had arrested so many British agents that her radio was one of the few still operating—intermittently, as she was dodging German direction-finding trucks.

Refusing repeated offers of evacuation to England, she lived for a while in

an apartment house largely occupied by German officers. She was perhaps un-
suited to such work. One of her tutors in the clandestine arts called her "a
splendid, vague, dreamy creature, far too conspicuous—twice seen, never forgotten." Various habits, such as putting the milk in her cup before the tea, revealed her English origins, and she was careless with her cipher book.

When an informer betrayed her to the Gestapo, Noor was living near the
Gestapo's Avenue Foch headquarters. The Germans continued for months to
impersonate her, using her set to send misleading messages to England.

The Gestapo did not treat her harshly until she made two escape attempts.
Soon she was in a German prison, in solitary confinement, her hands and feet
chained and a chain connecting her hands and feet. After the war, the prison war-
den told a British interrogator that he thought "the tranquility did her good."

In *Bodyguard of Lies,* his history of "the clandestine war of deception" between the Allies and the Axis, Anthony Cave Brown writes, "These men and
women had volunteered for operations in the lonely, gray outer marches of
the war. . . . It was in the very nature of their work that their lives must be
considered forfeit the moment they left the shores of England." Noor's was
just one life sacrificed in the last century so that we could live in this one,
oblivious of such sacrifices.

The guns of August 1914 devoured the generation to which "the old boys
of St. Paul's School" belonged. Twenty-five Augusts later Europe was in the final days of its slide into the war that swept Noor into its vortex. All is quiet
this August. The wall of St. Paul's Church, in Knightsbridge, records a small
portion of the pain that purchased this quiet.

August 26, 2001

Princess Diana and the Law of Inverse Ratio Rhetoric

Within hours of the death of Princess Diana, two unfailing fountains of
banalities and bromides had been heard from. President Bill Clinton,
whose gift for self-absorption has a kind of grandeur, interrupted his vacation
to deliver a bulletin on his inner life, making a statement in which he talked
about his feelings and his wife's feelings and, oh yes, the princess. Several Sunday-
afternoon football announcers took advantage of a pause in the play to note
that Diana had been "a hero." These leading indicators of cultural froth clearly
indicated the beginning of a bull market in bathos.

The media were already revved up in Marathon Grief mode. Television networks were trying, as it were, to bite their lower lips, emulating the president's preferred manner of advertising his very solemnest sincerity. Early in this century a wit defined a newspaper as a device incapable of distinguishing between a bicycle accident and the collapse of civilization. At the century's end we have mass media with wondrous capacities for subtracting from understanding by adding to the public's inclination for self-deception and autointoxication.

By turning everyone everywhere into bystanders at events, and by eliciting and amplifying their "feelings," the media turn the world into an echo chamber and establish for the promptable masses the appropriate "reaction" to events. Mass hysteria is a riveting spectacle, whether it occurs at a Nuremberg rally or a rock concert. It is nonetheless hysteria when muted in the form of mass lugubriousness, but at least a funeral-as-rally is, unlike a Nuremberg rally, revolting without being a prelude to anything evil—or anything at all. Because the media are part of this story, they are missing the news.

Evidently many scores of millions of people lead lives of such anesthetizing boredom, emotional aridity, and felt insignificance that they relish any opportunity for vicarious involvement in large events. And Princess Diana's death has been a large event precisely and only because the public, in a spontaneous act of mass parasitism, has fastened onto the event for the catharsis of emotional exhibitionism.

Even by the standards of today's confessional culture, people certainly have been remarkably "sharing" with their "feelings" about Diana. They have been sharing them with strangers, and their feelings have been about the death of a stranger who, they say, although she never made laws or poetry or shoes or butter, nevertheless "made a difference" and mattered to them more than they knew until she died. The media have been more than merely dutiful in reporting on the "grief" from which millions have been "suffering." Listening to language used this way is like watching an infant play with a Steuben vase.

During the 1979 malfunction at Three Mile Island nuclear plant, a hyperventilating journalist on TV referred to the event—no deaths; no public-health impact—as a "catastrophe." Viewers were left to wonder what words remained to describe, say, war. The premature death of any young mother is, of course, sad. But when it is the celebrity of the deceased that triggers behavior that is identified as "grief" and "suffering," what words remain to describe what occurs in, say, a pediatric oncology ward?

It is unclear how individuals, let alone clumps of millions, can grieve and suffer for a celebrity stranger whose death illustrates the Law of Inverse Ratio Rhetoric. The law is: hyperbole about a deceased person expands to fill the vacuum of the person's substantive significance. Diana evidently was what she appeared to be, eager to use for social betterment the celebrity that came from her marriage. But that virtue does not begin to explain why people stood in line all night for the opportunity to jot their thoughts about Diana in a book at St. James's Palace, or why people left flowers at the British Embassy on Washington's Massachusetts Avenue.

Such people were clutching at the flying coattails of history. And so for the world, or at least the wired world of the North Atlantic community, last week was deeply pleasurable, even exhilarating.

All the world's a stage—well, a television studio—and those who join a mass grieving become bit players, briefly able to exclaim, "History has happened to me, personally!" The North Atlantic community consists of societies in which scarcities of food, shelter, and clothing have been banished. But material abundance may make certain other scarcities more chafing, particularly the scarcities of power and, if not celebrity, at least recognition. This may partially explain another current form of mass irrationality, the epidemic of aggressive driving. One theory, unprovable but plausible, is that this epidemic is a welling-up of brutish assertiveness on the part of people who lead lives of quiet exasperation in the anonymity of bureaucracies.

The fact that supposedly mature societies can be so fixated on royalty suggests just how lightly childishness sleeps, when it sleeps, in such societies. It is perhaps unjust, but poetic justice, that the ramshackle House of Windsor is being faulted for exhibiting insufficient passion in the current grieving sweepstakes. Critics wonder if the Royal Family is emotionally crippled and out of touch. Do you suppose?

Members of that family are isolated from birth on, cosseted in unearned luxury, bereft of even a family memory of productive labor, and forbidden to utter in public virtually any serious thought. And people wonder why, when the wind rises, the Windsors want to go to earth in Scotland.

If there is any comfort for sensible people to take from the amazing amount of sheer fakery last week, it is that the British public seems to have cast a semiconscious vote against the Royal Family's seedy style of fantasy and for another—"the people's princess," which fortunately is an oxymoron that must ultimately be subversive of the infantile idea of royalty. As for the American public, its healthiest reaction now would be chagrin akin to a hangover. That would be condign punishment for becoming inebriated with a spectacle both empty and degrading.

September 15, 1997

Princess Diana, Conjuror

One cause of Princess Diana's death was the modern form of fame, "the frenzy of renown." The frenzied, meaning people who are intoxicated by synthetic significance, are complicit in her death.

Death came when she and her companion of recent weeks were in high-speed flight from photographers hell-bent on supplying the highly remunerative market for snapshots of her life. Hers was a life somehow always rich in opportunities for photographs of the sort she deplored. Greta Garbo she was not. She had a great fondness for café society, which is not the milieu of the reclusive.

She died in, and to some extent because of, the vortex of publicity that surrounds—no, that *is*—the modern British monarchy, into which she fell by marriage at age twenty. Once upon a time, the justification for the monarchy was clear: It was God's will. No one now believes that, and few really believe the subsequent justification, which, unlike the first, was more or less true for a while: that the monarchy is a constitutional necessity.

The monarchy is a residue of the infancy of the British people. They still like it, and it is their right to retain it, rationality being broadly optional. But there is no evading the fact that an occupational hazard of royalty is infantilism, now that royalty is shorn of serious duties and exists primarily to do public relations for itself.

One manifestation of infantilism is a sense of entitlement to incompatible things. Princess Diana felt entitled to be forever the social fiction that she became by marriage: royalty. In negotiations about her divorce she fought for, and bitterly resented the forced surrender of, the title "Her Royal Highness."

However, she also wanted the sort of privacy often claimed by the privileged, meaning publicity on her terms. She wanted to be listened to concerning various social causes (the latest being a ban on antipersonnel land mines). But she had a claim—make that a hold—on public attention only because she was a celebrity, as Daniel Boorstin has defined that term. That is, she was known for her well-knownness.

Thirty-six years ago, in his book *The Image,* Boorstin argued that the graphic revolution in journalism and other forms of communication had severed fame from greatness, which generally required a gestation period in which great deeds were performed. This severance hastened the decay of fame into mere notoriety, which is very plastic and very perishable.

This severance was apparent by 1905, when the narrator of Edith Wharton's *House of Mirth* spoke of living in "a world where conspicuousness passed for distinction, and the society column had become the roll of fame." The noun "flack" pertaining to modern communications was prefigured by a proper noun, George Flack, the journalist in Henry James's *The Reverberator* (1888), who thought of himself as a servant of democratic values:

> *You ain't going to be able any longer to monopolize any fact of general inter-est . . . it ain't going to be possible to keep out anywhere the light of the Press. Now what I'm going to do is set up the biggest lamp yet made and make it shine all over the place. We'll see who's private then . . . and who'll frustrate the People,* the people that wants to know. *That's a sign of the American people that they do want to know.*

All democracies want that. They want royalty of their own making—and unmaking. Democracy's leveling impulse is served by democracy's powerful, if fickle, machinery of elevation through publicity.

Princess Diana died, in a sense, at the intersection of a premodern insti-tution, royalty, and the modern sensibility, which holds that privacy is a denial of a democratic entitlement, the public's entitlement to any fact that enter-tains. She seems to have understood that her life was a constant conjuring trick. There was an incurable precariousness to her position as she tried to live off derivative dignity from an anachronistic institution while cultivating the royalism of a democratic age: celebrity.

In one of her last interviews she, who kept the company of the flamboy-antly rich, struck a populist note: "I am much closer to people at the bottom than those at the top, and the latter won't forgive me for that." What proved to be fatally unforgiving was the insatiable craving of society, from top to bot-tom, for details of Diana's life as princess for a democratic age. It was a drama on which the curtain came down with a crash.

September 3, 1997

Magic in Broad Daylight

Fifty years ago Wednesday, a twenty-five-year-old woman was awakened in a hunting lodge—a posh treehouse, actually—in Kenya and told that her fa-ther had died. Therefore she was immediately Elizabeth II, sovereign.

Tony Blair, the tenth prime minister of Elizabeth II's reign, was not yet born when she ascended to the throne. Winston Churchill was then the first among her ministers. How much has changed since her June 1953 coronation? The decision to televise it was deeply controversial. Most television sets were in pubs, where, it was feared, decorum among the lower orders might lapse during the ceremony.

Since then, the House of Windsor, including some of its much-too-merry wives, has often resembled a soap opera. But then, sovereignty has never been a shield from life's vicissitudes: the longest-surviving child of Queen Anne's (ruled 1702–14) eighteen pregnancies died at age eleven.

Elizabeth II's coronation coincided with Edmund Hillary's conquest of Mount Everest (and, almost as inspiriting, with the end of tea rationing, a relic of the war), which stirred hopes of a "New Elizabethan Age." Instead, there was the continuing loss of empire, a diminishing world role, watery socialism, and worsening economic anemia. By the mid-1970s Britain was reduced to the status of the sick man of Europe. Then came revival, but the woman who authored it was named not Elizabeth but Margaret—Thatcher.

Once upon a time, in mankind's political immaturity, monarchy was the best available answer to the problems of sovereignty and succession as nation-states evolved. And being a monarch was risky. Richard III (ruled 1483–85) was the last English king to die in battle, and George II (ruled 1727–60) was the last to fight alongside British troops.

Sovereignty has been leaking away from British sovereigns since regular meetings of Parliament became normal during the reign of Edward I (ruled 1272–1307). The power of the Cabinet grew because George I (ruled 1714–27), a German from Hanover, knew so little English he rarely met with his ministers. (When he asked how much it would cost to close St. James's Park to the public and plant it with turnips, an aide replied, with studied ambiguity, "Only three crowns, sire.") Under Britain's unwritten constitution, what is constitutional is whatever you can get away with. For the monarch, that is not much.

In 1936 Edward VIII committed a constitutional impropriety when, shocked by Welsh unemployment, he exclaimed, "Something must be done!" In 1938 it was similarly improper when Prime Minister Neville Chamberlain returned from Munich and George VI (ruled 1936–52) appeared with him on a Buckingham Palace balcony, thereby signaling a royal opinion (approval) about a subject of debate in Parliament. Elizabeth II knows what Shakespeare's Henry V meant: "And what have kings, that privates have not too, save ceremony, save general ceremony?"

The British monarchy is Europe's oldest political institution, but some of its trappings are surprisingly young—presidents had been living in the White House for thirty-seven years before the first sovereign (Victoria, in 1837) lived in Buckingham Palace. And the monarchy has an almost adolescent awkwardness in coping with one facet of the modern age, the publicity industry. The queen has not made a memorable mistake in fifty extremely public years, but her extended and very dysfunctional family is a new phenomenon: *lumpenroy-*

alty. Well, not so new. William IV (ruled 1830–37), who died in 1837, perhaps of exhaustion, had ten illegitimate children by one of his mistresses.

In the nineteenth century Walter Bagehot, the most profound of all journalists, noted that the modern monarch is part of the "dignified" as distinct from the "efficient" aspect of the state and warned, "Above all things our royalty is to be reverenced, and if you begin to poke about it you cannot reverence it. . . . We must not let in daylight upon magic."

The question now is: Even if magic can coexist with television and tabloids, does a mature nation need magic, particularly magic emanating from monarchy in a nation too susceptible to snobbery? Actually, any nation does need *something* in the way of regularly recurring national communions that reaffirm the nation's unity and identity.

At her coronation, Elizabeth was divested of the robes she wore to Westminster Abbey. Then, standing in a white shift, she was invested with symbols of her authority (sword, orb, etc.) and of authority over her (a Bible). Properly understood, it was an antimagical moment; it was the very public manufacturing of a monarch.

Britain's monarchy adds to the public stock of pretty-much-harmless pleasure. *Of course* it is irrational, but so are many things we love, including love.

February 3, 2002

Hitler and Epistemological Optimism

Don't judge a book by its cover. But begin judging Ron Rosenbaum's book by its brilliant dust jacket, which features an old, grainy black-and-white photograph of a cherubic infant, less than a year old, dressed in a white gown with a ruffled collar, staring at the camera with wide, dark eyes, his delicate lips slightly parted, a look of mild curiosity on his round face. How did this small bundle of potentialities become Adolf Hitler?

In *Explaining Hitler: The Search for the Origins of His Evil,* Rosenbaum, a novelist and literary journalist, takes readers on a mind-bending tour of "the garden of forking paths" in "the trackless realm of Hitler's inwardness." Rosenbaum tells an astonishing story of the lengths to which people have gone to explain Hitler without coming to terms with the stark fact that evil is a capacity of human nature.

Rosenbaum asks: Was Hitler "some ultimate, perhaps never-before-seen extension of that capacity"? Was he on the extreme end of the spectrum of human types that includes Gandhi, or was he "off the grid, beyond the continuum, in a category of his own"?

Why did Hitler kill the Jews? Because he wanted to. But was he capable of choosing what he wanted? Or was he merely a cultural product, soft wax on which the hard edges of "society" left a lasting impress? We are all, to some extent, such wax. Hence the current preoccupation of our politics with the condition of the culture. But clearly Hitler was unusual, and surely he was not just unusually susceptible to this or that prompting by "society."

It is not enough simply to say Hitler was a spectacular anomaly and leave it at that. However, what fascinates and at times horrifies Rosenbaum is the tendency of explanation to evolve into extenuation and exculpation. Furthermore, many explanations of Hitler raise the tormenting possibility that Hitler's career could have been prevented by some timely therapeutic intervention.

Rosenbaum's exploration of the Hitler explanation industry is a product of exhaustive historical research and meticulous contemporary reporting. But more than an intellectual tour de force, it is a practical primer on thinking about the largest political problems and perennially pertinent historical judgments. Those are judgments about free will and historical determinism, about whether supposed great men are igniters of events or themselves mere social products and symptoms, and about the putative history-making role of impersonal ideological or anthropological forces.

Some instinct for proportionality causes people to seek large causes for large events. People rightly recoil from the idea that the Holocaust was produced by a figure of burlesque—a Chaplinesque corporal. Yet intellectual fashion disparages as unsophisticated the idea that an individual can be large enough to shake history violently.

Hence the multiplication of explanations of what Rosenbaum calls the "transformation from baby picture to baby killer." Too often the explanations amount to what courts call a "diminished capacity" defense. Such explanations arise from the simpleminded scientism of the semieducated, the belief that somehow everything explains everything.

The explanations seek to reduce Hitler to, for example, a mere catalyst of preexisting "eliminationist anti-Semitism" in a Germany "pregnant with murder." (Never mind that anti-Semitic literature in Russia, Poland, Romania, and France was at times more virulent than that in Germany.) Or to present Hitler as unhinged by this or that formative experience, such as his mother's horrific suffering from primitive, turn-of-the-century cancer treatment administered by a Jewish doctor.

Or perhaps he was deranged because of his—if this is true—absent left testicle. Or by the unassuageable dread that his father was born from the illegitimate union of his grandmother and a Jew. Or because he caught syphilis from a Jewish prostitute. And so on and on.

There is an unending process of discovering reasons why Hitler could not help himself. Perhaps people cannot bear the thought that Hitler was being himself.

Scholarship about the Nazi era has revealed the special horror of banal atrocities, those committed by "ordinary men"—by, that is, people without even the excuse of ideological intoxication. But more horrible—Rosenbaum's research suggests that it is, for most people, unendurable—is the possibility that Hitler was simply extraordinarily evil and that evil cannot be explained.

That this is so unsettling speaks volumes, Rosenbaum believes, about our age. It is an age of "epistemological *optimism,* a faith in an explicable world." By showing how Hitler refutes that facile faith, Rosenbaum's book should teach caution to a chastened age.

October 29, 1998

The "Ah!" of Avery Dulles

BRONX, N.Y.—Fordham University, a Jesuit institution, looks appropriately gothic in a December gloaming, and especially so as a backdrop for its most eminent teacher, all of whose six-foot, two-inch frame beneath his black beret is clothed in black against the night chill. Avery Dulles, 81, distinguished son of a famous father, remembers the letter he sent to his parents fifty-nine years ago, announcing his first steps on the Catholic path of service to the faith whose founder's birth is celebrated this season.

"Something of a shock" was, he says, the initial reaction of his father, John Foster Dulles, a flinty Presbyterian, who as a Princeton undergraduate had studied under an especially austere Presbyterian: professor Woodrow Wilson. However, in the 1950s Secretary of State Dulles found that having a Jesuit son gave him special stature with American Catholics, gave him a shared experience with Germany's Chancellor Konrad Adenauer, whose son was a priest, and helped him with Catholic politicians in France and Italy.

Avery Dulles, a son of the establishment (his father, the grandson of a secretary of state, was a Sullivan and Cromwell lawyer and a colleague of Bernard Baruch during World War I), was at Choate and Harvard with John F. Kennedy. The great Catholic medievalist Étienne Gilson had recently been at Harvard and his teachings lingered. And it was from Harvard in autumn 1940 that

Dulles wrote home to say he was converting to Catholicism. After one year at Harvard Law School and four years in the Navy, he decided on the priesthood.

From the vantage of his ninth decade, Dulles is not greatly impressed by this year's big news in Christianity, the joint declaration of Lutherans and Catholics in Augsburg, Germany, in October. It stated that "a consensus on basic truths of the doctrine of justification exists between Lutherans and Catholics."

Some press reports suggested that the purported consensus proves that the Reformation, which made the sixteenth century the incubator of modernity, was, it turns out, about an arcane misunderstanding. Other reports suggested that the Catholic Church has surrendered on the subject at the heart of Luther's theology: "justification by faith alone."

Salvation, that is, by faith rather than good works. In the sixteenth and seventeenth centuries much ink, and not a little blood, was shed over whether faith is the unmerited gift of God's grace or whether free will, manifested in deeds, participates in earning salvation.

Over a plateful of veal in a restaurant in Little Italy near the campus, Dulles delicately suggests that real differences still divide Lutherans and Catholics concerning the acquisition of faith, the interior renewal wrought by faith, and manifestations of this renewal. The fact that Luther and the Council of Trent are dinnertime topics in the Bronx pleases people who believe that history is dignified by its serious quarrels. And that fact satisfies those Christians who regard the continuing vitality of Christianity's divisions as evidence of spiritual vigor: you cannot split rotten wood.

But there is a common Christian sensibility, elegantly expressed by a priest who lived just slightly more than half as long as Dulles has lived, Gerard Manley Hopkins (1844–89): "Time has three dimensions and one positive pitch or direction. It is therefore not so much like any river or any sea as like the Sea of Galilee, which has the Jordan running through it and giving a current to the whole."

That may strike the secular-minded as optimistic, but for Dulles, optimism about the long run is not optional. It is a vocational imperative. "The long run," he says dryly, "includes the eschaton."

That is, "the fullness of time," meaning the Second Coming and the Kingdom of God. Meanwhile, Dulles's time is full of writing. The manuscript of his twenty-first book has just gone to the printer, and the list of his publications during the last fifteen months includes two new books, the reissue of a third, and thirty-nine shorter pieces in books and periodicals.

Among sociologists and other advanced thinkers it has long been, so to speak, an article of faith that modernity is inimical to religious faith. Which makes them regard America with scandalized disbelief—America, the most modern of nations, and one planted thick with people who feel, as Hopkins put it in a poem, a religious "ah!" about the presence of the divine:

. . . the Holy Ghost over the bent
World broods with warm breast and with ah! bright wings.

That is how the Bronx, and everything contiguous thereto—the world—seems to Dulles, a place constantly burdened by sin but unceasingly solicited by grace. Quite a drama. It keeps him spry.

December 23, 1999

Francis Cardinal George, Unenthralled

CHICAGO—Given ancient traditions and contemporary resentments of America's global ascendancy, it is fanciful to think that the priest who lives here, hard by Lake Michigan, might one day be summoned to the west bank of the Tiber River to hold the world's oldest office. However, Francis Cardinal George, sixty-four, the first Chicagoan to be Chicago's archbishop, is temperamentally and intellectually suited to continue the work of Pope John Paul II.

But, then, George is invaluable here as a critic—loving but unenthralled—of American culture at a moment when complacency obscures reasons for anxiousness. A holder of doctorates in theology and political philosophy, George, who laughs easily and often, wears his learning lightly but wields it seriously. He casts a cool eye on today's triumphalism, which is the sin of pride tarted up for the post–Cold War victory parade.

The evaporation of Marxism, with its beguiling (to intellectuals) brew of pseudoscience and messianic promise, and the collapse of other collectivist creeds have left no rival to the American model of market-oriented social arrangements. But George argues that America once was and needs to be again more Lockean and less Hobbesian.

John Locke, so important to America's Founders, tempered his philosophic individualism by stressing shareable norms that come to us from nature and common experience and require us to take into account something other than our own desires. But Locke's intellectual precursor, Thomas Hobbes, portrayed human beings not as possessing personhood, not as rational or responsible, least of all as free. Rather, Hobbes said, they are subject to irresistible stimuli and are, George says, "as determined as any physical object." Human rights as Hobbes understood them are banal, arising from, and being defined by, irresistible urges.

People comfortable with such a characterization will, George warns, lose their ability to stand "outside" their actions and witness their self-creation though moral choices. And a society morally anesthetized by the reduction of persons to bundles of impulses and by the definition of rights in terms of power (powerful desires) should not be surprised by 1.3 million abortions a year and one in three children born out of wedlock.

Hobbes famously said that life in the state of nature is completely presocial ("solitary, poor, nasty, brutish and short"). But a society that postulates, as Hobbes did, a world void of natural norms will be a barely social society. Such a void, says George, will be filled exclusively by every individual's interests and drives. This limits our horizons to our own experiences. The classic American antidote to such truncation of moral vision is education. But there can be, George tartly notes, "well-instructed moral cretins."

Man, said the philosopher and novelist Iris Murdoch, is a creature who makes pictures of himself—and comes to resemble the pictures. George warns that Hobbes's picture of mankind, or any radically individualist depiction, can be self-fulfilling. Against such depictions, the Church bears witness to a particular and universal notion of the good.

This puts—or should put—believers in perennial, and healthy, tension with any society, but particularly with pluralistic societies and especially with those permeated with modernity's mentality, which eschews the idea of a transcendent source of norms. George celebrates evangelical Christians' "model of discipleship." He says "they understand faith as a surrender" that prevents surrender to the culture and "the collapse of religion back into culture."

The three great carriers of American culture—universities, entertainment, and the law—currently teach, George says, the supreme value of something value-free—a mere process, "choice." So politics is becoming a mere "ensemble of procedures" for "regulating the pursuit of our personal satisfactions." The resultant culture is comfortable with merely comfortable religion—religion that is, George says, a "personal motivator" but not "an organizer of life."

In an increasingly secular society, in what Max Weber called the "disenchanted world," faith decreasingly infuses life. It organizes neither space (towers of commerce, not a cathedral, are at the center of the city) nor time (even Catholic schools take spring breaks, not Easter breaks). This result is what George calls "religious indifferentism."

In an era of watery convictions and thin theological gruel, George's forthrightness must be bracing even to the unchurched: "Although the Catholic Church does not embrace religious pluralism as an ideal, she understands it in the context of her eschatological confidence." John Paul II's calendar for 2003 is filling up. Long may he remain full of humor and remarkably robust for one well stricken in years. But a worthy successor could be found just off Lake Shore Drive.

May 13, 2001

C. S. Lewis's Cult of the Ordinary

Clive Staples Lewis was known as Jack to his friends and is known as C. S. Lewis to his still-growing legion of readers. Many more than 50 million copies of his books—no one knows how many—are in print thirty-five years after his death. When he died on November 22, 1963, the world paid scant attention, having another death on its mind. So let us now praise this famous man—as famous now as when his picture filled *Time* magazine's cover in 1947—on the centenary of his birth in Belfast on November 29, 1898.

What twentieth-century writer has had the largest influence? In terms of effect on history, David Remnick, editor of *The New Yorker,* nominates Aleksandr Solzhenitsyn, whose *The Gulag Archipelago* made impossible what had seemed incorrigible—many intellectuals' belief in the Soviet Union as a moral advance for civilization. Timothy Garton Ash, author and journalist, nominates George Orwell, who coined such locutions as "Big Brother," "newspeak" and "doublethink" to describe modes of mendacity now called "Orwellian."

However, C. S. Lewis ranks among the century's most influential writers. His influence was—is—closely connected not to the century's great struggles against totalitarianism but to the religious sensibility's struggle against the century.

His outwardly uneventful life—he taught English literature at Oxford and Cambridge—turned on his adult conversion to Christianity. After which he became an oddity, a learned celebrity in tweeds, finding, on radio and in print, remarkable resonance for his apologetics, the most famous of which is *Mere Christianity.* However, his best-known work is *The Chronicles of Narnia,* a seven-volume children's fable in which faith is advanced obliquely, by insinuation.

Lewis was led to Christianity not by logic of the sort he wielded in his apologetics but by a sense that the everydayness of life is permeated by glory. The "man on the Clapham omnibus" is a British locution akin to Americans' "man on the street," and Lewis had a mystical sense of divine presence while on a bus.

Another episode on his road to religion was (literally) pedestrian: a walk around Addison's Walk at Magdalen College, Oxford, during which he believed he felt the immediacy of the divine. The kind of path Lewis took to belief was understood by an earlier, much more theologically sophisticated Oxford man. In *Apologia pro vita sua,* perhaps the greatest record written in English of an individual's religious transformation, John Henry (later Cardinal) Newman wrote, "It was not logic that carried me on. As well might one say that the quicksilver in the barometer changes the weather. It is the concrete being that reasons; pass a number of years and I find my mind in a new place: how? the whole man moves; paper logic is but the record of it."

What one biographer calls Lewis's cult of the ordinary, plus his nostalgia for childhood, were facets of a coherent sensibility. Lewis lived, as a specialist in medieval literature might be expected to do, a romantic's reaction against the segmentation, routinization, and bureaucratization of modern life. First the horrors of war, then the banal materialism of welfare statism, built a receptive audience for him.

In "The Abolition of Man," his essay most pertinent to today's discontents, Lewis refuted the crux of modern radicalism, the idea that human nature has no constancy, being merely an unstable imprint of the fluctuating social atmosphere. That fallacy emboldens politicians as social engineers. So Lewis warns, "If man chooses to treat himself as raw material, raw material he will be."

One of Lewis's contemporaries, another Oxonian, novelist Evelyn Waugh, created the character Scott-King, a teacher at a boys' school whose headmaster admonishes him that parents are interested only in preparing their boys for the modern world: "You can hardly blame them, can you?"

"Oh yes," Scott-King replies, "I can and do," adding, "I think it would be a very wicked thing indeed to do anything to fit a boy for the modern world."

When Lewis came to see the world—the sky, a grain of sand, friendship— through the spectacles of faith, he felt completely at home in the world. And alienated from his time.

In Lewis's light masterpiece *The Screwtape Letters,* a seasoned devil warns a novice devil that their work is frustrated by great moralists. Such moralists, the devil says, do not inform men, they remind them. Lewis's deceptively modest mission was to remind readers that they—their natures; their susceptibility to the numinous—are among life's constants. Evidence of which, his millions of readers might say, is the continuing hunger for his adversarial stance toward life in our time.

November 26, 1998

P. D. James, In Earnest

LONDON—Baroness James of Holland Park is the somewhat forbidding title of the energetic eighty-one-year-old grandmother known to millions of readers worldwide as P. D. James, author of elegantly crafted and morally complex detective novels, the latest being *Death in Holy Orders.* However, Holland Park is just a nice swath of urban green space across a busy street from her modest home here, and she functions as a baroness only when in the House of

Lords as that seven-hundred-year-old body does what it can to cause whatever government controls the House of Commons to have second, or perhaps first, thoughts about what it cannot really be stopped from doing.

It is instructive to solicit the judgment of the elderly about contemporary conditions, because, as James has written, episodes long past "catch on the threads of memory as burrs stick to a coat" and provide benchmarks for marking progress, or what passes for it. Her formative years were dominated by reverberations of the catastrophe of 1914–18, which cast "a shadow of uncomprehended vicarious sadness." Her generation "was born under a pall of inarticulate grieving." Measured against *that* benchmark, contemporary Britain is blessed.

Yet the "devolution" of power from Westminster to Welsh and Scottish assemblies is but one, and not the most profound, sign of a country less unified than it once was by certain common beliefs. Those, she says, centered on the empire, the monarchy, and the Church of England and its liturgy. The attenuation—to put it mildly—of those beliefs and the replacement of religion by sport, particularly tribal loyalties to soccer teams, has resulted, James says with mingled regret and complacency, in a "less moral country, but a more equal and fair one." Time was, "ordinary people certainly were more honest— but, then, many lived under the fear of hell and the law." Progress. Perhaps.

She is mildly disdainful of what she calls "the climate of compensation," which Americans call the entitlement mentality of a therapeutic culture. "People," she says bemusedly, "expect to be *counseled* if they suffer trauma." Recalling the soldiers returning from two wars, she says tartly, "I don't remember them all coming home expecting to be *counseled* about what they went through." Remembering what fell upon London six decades ago, she dryly wonders, "Would there be enough *counselors* to go around after a bad bombing?"

Her judgments have the edge of a survivor from a sterner age. Five years ago, heeding Samuel Johnson's dictum that "At 77 it is time to be in earnest," she published "a fragment of autobiography" titled *Time to Be in Earnest*. In it she approvingly recalled a similar astringency in a letter Jane Austen wrote when she learned that a neighbor had given birth to her eighteenth child: "I would recommend to her and Mr. Dee the simple regimen of separate rooms."

James believes that her vocation, writing novels, has a mildly moral as well as entertaining purpose. She recalls that Victorian novelists rather defensively claimed a moral mission because then there "hung about novel-reading the sulphurous whiff of indolent and almost decadent self-indulgence." She knows that novels are unlikely instruments for the reform of institutions or individuals, but she thinks most novelists have an "urge to nudge society's inclinations in a direction more agreeable to our own beliefs and prejudices."

Women, she says, have an eye for details and hence for clues, are more interested in motive than violence, and are gifted with psychological subtlety and the exploration of moral choice. Besides, "bringing order out of disorder is a female function." This thought has two virtues: in addition to scandalizing a certain stripe of feminist, it is explanatory.

It explains why women (Dorothy Sayers, Josephine Tey, Ruth Rendell, Elizabeth George, and James herself, among others) are such masters of the detective genre: they have a natural aptitude for it. Especially for detection about murder, because death underscores "the fragility of life." Hence, again, the female function: women as agents of order. Furthermore, as a Christian, James believes detective fiction "provides for the reader the comforting reassurance that, despite our apparent powerlessness, we yet inhabit an intelligible universe."

Although she is fond of Henry James's statement that "We trust to novels to maintain us in the practice of great indignations and great generosities," she doubts that it is still accurate. Less demanding entertainments—television, principally—have largely displaced novels. But not entirely. Today's readers, too, have their James.

September 9, 2001

Rough Rider in Green Bay

America had seen something like Vince Lombardi's Chiclets-teeth grin before. His face often radiated competitive fury, but when it crinkled with happiness, you saw the visage—and spirit—of Teddy Roosevelt, apostle of the strenuous life, who could have said, as Lombardi did, that fatigue makes cowards of us all. T.R. thought an occasional war could invigorate the nation, tuning its spirit and teaching it teamwork, and thought football could serve as a substitute. However, he found college football—the NFL was two decades away—alarmingly rough. Being the first busybody president, he convened a White House conference on rules changes to cut down the number of undergraduates being killed and maimed.

In 1959, half a century after T.R.'s last full year in office, Lombardi drove his mauve-and-white Chevy from his native New York, where he was the Giants' offensive coach (Tom Landry coached the defense), to Green Bay. In the turbulent next decade, stalking the sideline in his camel's-hair coat and fedora, he would become emblematic of the counter-counterculture. Today, twenty-nine years after his death from cancer, he remains a remarkably durable embodiment of values that the nation, when waxing nostalgic, thinks got lost along the way.

David Maraniss says in his new biography, *When Pride Still Mattered*, that

Lombardi is the "patron saint of American competition and success." If so, the 1990s may be a Lombardi moment in America. The nation currently has the swagger and success of Lombardi's Packers, who from 1960 to 1968 won five NFL championships, including three in a row, and the first two Super Bowls.

Maraniss, a *Washington Post* associate editor, was drawn to Lombardi as a subject by "cultural geography." Maraniss was an undergraduate at the University of Wisconsin when it was a roiled sea of radicalism and Lombardi, 130 miles north, was vivifying martial values. He imbibed those values as assistant to coach "Red" Blaik at West Point in the early 1950s. In those days Lombardi took game films down to Manhattan, to the Waldorf Towers, to delight a former superintendent of the academy, Douglas MacArthur, who said what Lombardi believed: "There is no substitute for victory."

Such aphorisms appealed to Lombardi, whose father, a butcher, said, "No one's ever hurt. Hurt is in your mind." Lombardi's grandparents came in the wave of immigrants drawn to America by ads seeking workers to build the Brooklyn Bridge. Lombardi grew up in Brooklyn, became muscular carrying slabs of meat, then traveled to the northern Bronx to play football at Fordham. There the coach was Jim Crowley, one of the "Four Horsemen" of Notre Dame's 1924 backfield. Crowley's high school coach in Green Bay, Curly Lambeau, founded the Packers.

Color-blind and extremely nearsighted, Lombardi, a five-foot-eight, 175-pound lineman, played, Maraniss says, with the abandon of someone nearly blind. Fordham's Jesuits taught Lombardi to understand virtue in terms of freely chosen subordination to a collective enterprise. Football entices many writers to commit dubious sociology—football's conquest of territory is Manifest Destiny redux, and all that. But Maraniss sensibly writes, "The contradictory ideals of unity and independence, conformity and rebellion, run deep in the American psyche, and along that divide football is the sport most closely aligned with unity and conformity, for better and worse."

Although aging flower children paint the 1960s in pastels, the NFL prospered then in part because it fit that decade's celebration of the military—remember the Kennedys' fascination with the Green Berets—and the modern, meaning the intricate, the technically proficient, the specialist. Hence the apotheosis of the coach as "scientific" tactician.

In football's early days, coaching during the game was forbidden as unsportsmanlike. When Illinois's Bob Zuppke invented the offensive huddle in 1921, referees joined the huddles when substitutes entered the game, to prevent surreptitious coaching. But the man most responsible for the early growth of football, Yale's coach Walter Camp, preached that football coaches trained the managerial elite who would command the big battalions of American industry in the wars of commerce.

In 1878, when football was just becoming a staple of life on American campuses, some credit for Princeton's unbeaten season went to an unathletic but cerebral undergraduate who helped coach the team: Tommy Wilson. He went on, did Thomas Woodrow Wilson, to become the bane of Teddy Roosevelt's existence. *"Everything,"* wrote young Tommy, foreshadowing Woodrow, "depends upon the character of the captain and president [of the team]."

In chaotic 1968, both Hubert Humphrey and Richard Nixon, Maraniss says, considered Lombardi as a running mate. (Lombardi was a Kennedy Democrat, having met Jack during the 1960 Wisconsin primary.) Instead, Lombardi, like Alabama's Bear Bryant and Ohio State's version of George Patton, Woody Hayes, stayed on the sidelines but remained a center of attention at a time when Howard Cosell and Muhammad Ali were setting a different tone in sports.

Maraniss's balanced biography is not a "pathography," obsessive about its subject's defects. But it is a cautionary tale about the cost of athletic success, the collateral damage done by an obsession with winning. What has been said of the study of the law—that it sharpens the mind by narrowing it—can be true of coaching. Lombardi was an inattentive parent and a negligent husband, whose wife took solace from alcohol.

Football, writes Maraniss, blends elegance and violence into contact ballet, but at bottom football is hitting, and hitting causes pain to most players on most plays. Hence football fit what Maraniss calls Lombardi's premodern heritage from southern Italy's "history of pain": earthquakes, volcanic eruptions, revolts, famines, invasions, "a communal memory of the works of man collapsing."

Lombardi's Packers were such a work. Having won Super Bowls I and II, the Packers next won Super Bowl XXXI.

November 8, 1999

Joe Dimaggio's Seamless Life

There is a peculiar pathos to the lives of most great athletes because their careers compress life's trajectory of aspiration, accomplishment, and decline. Then what? For most, the rest of life, which is most of life, is anticlimax, like that of

> *Runners whom renown outran,*
> *And the name died before the man.*

But there was a seamlessness to Joe DiMaggio's life in and after the game. The patina of age did not dull the luster of his name. Baseball, sport of the long season and much history, has an unusually rich statistical geology—a sediment of numbers. Some numbers are so talismanic that simply citing them suffices to identify the achievement and achiever.

Examples are 116 (victories in a season, 1906 Cubs); 511 (career victories, Cy Young); 1.12 (season earned run average, Bob Gibson, 1968); 130 (stolen bases in a season, Rickey Henderson, 1982); 755 (career home runs, Hank Aaron); 60, then 61, and now 70 (home runs by Babe Ruth in 1927, Roger Maris in 1961, and Mark McGwire in 1998); .406 (most recent .400 season, Ted Williams, 1941). And baseball's most instantly recognized number, 56: Joe DiMaggio's consecutive game hitting streak in 1941.

The Streak, as it is still known, was stunning, even if a sympathetic official scorer at Yankee Stadium may have turned an error or two into hits. It took two sensational plays by Indians third baseman Ken Keltner to stop The Streak, and the next day DiMaggio started a sixteen-game streak. His 56 has not been seriously challenged in fifty-seven seasons. His 1933 minor-league streak of 61 has not been matched since then.

Because of baseball's grinding everydayness, professionals place a premium on consistency. DiMaggio brought his best, which was baseball's best, to the ballpark every day. What he epitomized to a mesmerized nation in 1941—steely will, understated style, heroism for the long haul—the nation would need after December 7.

However, the unrivaled elegance of his career is defined by two numbers even more impressive than his 56. They are 8 and 0.

Eight is the astonishingly small difference between his thirteen-year career totals for home runs (361) and strikeouts (369). (In the 1986 and 1987 seasons, Jose Canseco hit 64 home runs and struck out 332 times.) Zero is the number of times DiMaggio was thrown out going from first to third.

On the field, the man made few mistakes. Off the field, he made a big one in his marriage to Marilyn Monroe. But even that enlarged his mythic status. As when they were in Japan and she visited U.S. troops in Korea. Upon her return to Tokyo, she said to him, ingenuously: You've never heard cheering like that—there must have been fifty or sixty thousand. He said, dryly: Oh, yes I have.

They had gone to Japan at the recommendation of a friend (Lefty O'Doul, manager of the San Francisco Seals), who said that in a foreign country they could wander around without drawing crowds. The friend did not know that Japan was then obsessed with things American, especially baseball stars and movie stars. When the most famous of each category landed, it took their car six hours to creep to their hotel through more than a million people.

As a Californian, he represented baseball's future—he and San Diego's Ted Williams, a twenty-one-year-old rookie in 1939, when DiMaggio was twenty-four. DiMaggio, a son of a San Francisco fisherman, was proud, reserved, and as private as possible for the bearer—in the second generation—of America's premium athletic tradition, the Yankee greatness established by Babe Ruth and Lou Gehrig. DiMaggio felt violated by the sight of Marilyn filming the famous scene in *The Seven Year Itch* when a gust of wind from a Manhattan subway grate blows her skirt up above her waist.

Pride, supposedly one of the seven deadly sins, is often a virtue and the source of others. DiMaggio was pride incarnate, and he and Hank Greenberg did much to stir ethnic pride among Italian-Americans and Jews, respectively. When as a player DiMaggio had nothing left to prove, he was asked why he still played so hard, every day. Because, he said, every day there is apt to be some child in the stands who has never before seen me play.

An entire ethic, the code of craftsmanship, can be tickled from that admirable thought. Not that DiMaggio practiced the full range of his craft. When one of his managers was asked if DiMaggio could bunt, he said he did not know and "I'll never find out, either."

DiMaggio, one of Jefferson's "natural aristocrats," proved that a healthy democracy knows and honors nobility when it sees it.

March 9, 1999

Gentlemen in Spikes

Joe DiMaggio was the first Michael Jordan, the first athlete who transcended his sport, and sport generally, to become his generation's archetype of a gentleman. But thirty years before DiMaggio there was Christy Mathewson, who did more than anyone to prepare the nation to make DiMaggio a grace note of the twentieth century. Mathewson did this by placing baseball firmly in a new and unrivaled position in the nation's imagination.

Mathewson is buried next to the campus of Bucknell University in Lewisburg, Pennsylvania. Although he did not get a degree there, he attended that school before becoming a big leaguer, at a time when college men were thin on the ground in the professional game. Not until 1988 did California surpass Pennsylvania as the state that has supplied the most major leaguers. For a long time players were hard men fleeing hard lives in coal mines and steel mills and on hardscrabble farms.

Mathewson was born in 1880 in a tiny town with the no-nonsense name of Factoryville, Pennsylvania. There, according to his biographer, Ray Robinson, many young men went to work in the mines as soon as they came of age. At the time, says Robinson of professional baseball players, "too many of them spit on the carpet or threw up in public to allow any in their profession to be canonized." In 1900, he says, ballplayers ranked below circus clowns and itinerant actors in the order of social acceptance.

However, the country hungered for athletic heroes, a hunger only somewhat satisfied by the fictional Frank Merriwell. That paragon from Yale excelled in many sports, his heroics recounted between 1896 and 1914 in *Tip Top Weekly*. By 1914 Mathewson had become Merriwell.

On the field he was brilliant. Four times he won thirty or more games in a season. In some years he had more wins than walks. In the 1905 World Series he won three games—all shutouts. In three games, only one Philadelphia Athletic reached third. In 1909 his ERA was 1.14. Off the field, he was that elusive ideal, a gentleman a democracy could be comfortable with. With wavy brown hair and blue eyes, wearing neatly pressed tweeds and a necktie, Mathewson, says Robinson, "defined baseball in a new, acceptable way for millions."

Back then, baseball had the nation's undivided attention. Nowadays, there are about six weeks between the last NBA championship game and the first NFL preseason game. But before the late 1950s, Major League Baseball was essentially unchallenged by other professional team sports. Soon after Mathewson made it easier to admire players, baseball produced a very different kind of hero, whose name—Babe—suited his off-field comportment. The bear hug with which the nation embraced him proved that the public was ready to make allowances for a sports star, who could get away with being a manchild. Then Babe left the stage, and on strode DiMaggio, no child.

By the time DiMaggio left the stage, after just thirteen seasons—he lost three to the Second World War—he had a place in the nation's pantheon that was remarkable for an athlete and probably possible only for an athlete who played baseball. Ballplayers can partake of a mystique that attaches to one of America's oldest and least changed institutions. (The only substantial rules change since 1903, the designated hitter, is not an argument for change.) And DiMaggio's understated style suited the game of grinding everydayness, which has an ethic suited to a republic—an ethic against flamboyance, against showing up the other guy.

DiMaggio burst upon the nation just nine years after Charles Lindbergh almost inadvertently invented celebrity of a degree—of a kind, really—never before experienced. DiMaggio played a team game but somehow knew, in the intuitive way an artist has of knowing things, that our rough-and-tumble democracy, leveling though it is, responds to an individual with an aura of remoteness. How many times did the obituaries mention DiMaggio's "class"?

Now, no one who spent as much time as DiMaggio did in Toots Shor's Manhattan saloon was an enemy of conviviality, and anyone allergic to celebrity would not have married Marilyn Monroe. However, DiMaggio seemed somehow private when in public, at work in front of the throngs.

Baseball players have a low-key way of praising other players, a way that expresses the ethic of their craft. They say they like the way a player "goes about his business." They often mean how methodically he makes sure he is ready to play hard through the long season, and particularly how he works at the skill of catching the ball. DiMaggio patrolled Yankee Stadium's center field, one of baseball's biggest and a good place to demonstrate Koppett's Law. Baseball writer Leonard Koppett says: Poor fielding will lose many more games than good hitting will win. You can score only one run and still win, but you must get twenty-seven outs.

DiMaggio was a link in baseball's chain of understated excellence that stretches from Mathewson to Cal Ripken to twenty-three-year-old Alex Rodriguez. Mathewson would be named, in 1939, as one of the five original inductees (with Ruth, Ty Cobb, Honus Wagner, and Walter Johnson) into the Hall of Fame. But he died in 1925 at forty-five of tuberculosis, to which he may have become susceptible as a result of exposure to mustard gas during World War I.

"Show me a hero and I will write you a tragedy," wrote an emblematic figure of the 1920s, F. Scott Fitzgerald. Not necessarily. DiMaggio died full of years and honors. It has been well said (Charles Evans Hughes said it of Lindbergh) that we judge a great person the way we judge a great ship, by displacement. The Yankee Clipper still takes up a lot of space in the nation's memory.

March 22, 1999

Don Zimmer: The Face of Baseball

T AMPA—Want to see the face of baseball? Turn the page. What? You expected the sunburst smile of Ken Griffey beneath a backward-turned Reds cap? Or Pedro Martinez's assassin stare from the Fenway Park mound? No, such superstars come and go, but Don Zimmer is a baseball lifer.

Currently he is the Yankees' bench coach, whose job during games consists of sitting next to manager Joe Torre and dispensing advice based on intuition—intuition that distills more than half a century of experience. Understand Zimmer, and you will understand baseball—and one reason why today's Yankees are so successful. No other sports franchise has the Yankees' glamour—the pinstripes, Yankee Stadium, twenty-five World Series won, Ruth, Gehrig, Mantle, Jeter. But beneath baseball's glitter there always is the grit of men like Zimmer.

He is the last former Brooklyn Dodger still wearing a major-league uniform. His number this year is 52, the number of years he has been a profes-

sional ballplayer. His number will be 53 next year, unless the grinding pain in his knee finally drives him out of the game. Sitting next to Zimmer in the dugout this morning at Legends Field, the Yankees spring training camp, stirs to life is number 8, another lifer with an artificial right knee. But Yogi Berra earned his knee problems in a Hall of Fame career of catching. Zimmer acquired his aches and pains in a more mundane career that began in places such as Hornell and Elmira, New York. Beginning in 1954, it included twelve seasons in the big leagues. He was a utility infielder with a great team, the 1955 World Series champion Dodgers, and with the 1962 Mets, who lost a record 120 games. His career batting average was .235. He was a journeyman whose journey, which included winter ball in Latin America, ended in one of baseball's dead ends, with the expansion Washington Senators. Yet within baseball's little family he is, in his way, a legend.

He was born where professional baseball was, in Cincinnati. At fifteen he was playing sandlot ball with Pete Rose's father. (In a 1962 stint with Cincinnati he became the last Reds player to wear 14 before Pete Rose.) At home plate before an Elmira night game in 1951, Zimmer married Soot (Jean), the girl he had started dating in tenth grade. In 1953 Soot was nearly widowed at home plate in Columbus when Zimmer—this was before batting helmets—was beaned on the left temple. He was not fully conscious for thirteen days, during which holes were drilled in his skull to relieve the pressure of swelling. His vision was blurred, he could neither walk nor talk, and his weight plunged from 170 to 124. He was told he was finished at twenty-two.

Not exactly. The next spring he was at the Dodgers' spring training camp. The climb to the big leagues was steeper back then. The Dodgers had fifteen farm teams, compared with six today. Zimmer's climb got steeper when, in an exhibition game, he fouled a ball off his forehead. But he made the climb. In 1956 a Cincinnati Reds fastball broke his cheekbone. Go ahead, tell him baseball is not a contact sport.

He managed in the minors (Knoxville, Buffalo, Indianapolis, Key West, Salt Lake City) before coaching with the Expos, Giants, and Rockies and managing the Padres, Red Sox, Rangers, and Cubs. With the Red Sox he managed in one of the most famous games in history. In 1978 the Sox blew a fourteen-game lead, ending the season in a tie with the Yankees, who won the play-off game with a home run by light-hitting Bucky (Expletive Deleted) Dent, as he is known in New England. A few years later in Zimmer's baseball wanderings, he rented Dent's apartment, in which the walls were covered with pictures of Dent hitting the home run. Zimmer's biggest thrill in baseball? Going to Fenway for the 1978 playoff game. His biggest disappointment? The outcome of that game.

Coaching with the Rockies in 1995, Zimmer told management what he was going to do, and did it: he retired in the fifth inning of a game. He didn't want any fuss. He was out of baseball just long enough to get from Social Security the only check he ever received outside baseball. Then Torre called, and Zimmer called Social Security to say, "Don't send no more."

Now we are in the era of big bang baseball, right? Last year there were 5,526 home runs, a 9 percent increase over 1998's record of 5,064. In 1989 the American League home run champion, Fred McGriff, hit thirty-six home runs. Last year, twenty big leaguers hit at least thirty-six. In the five seasons 1990–94 only one player hit fifty home runs (Detroit's Cecil Fielder, fifty-one in 1990). In the five seasons 1995–99, six different players did it a total of ten times. So why are the Yankees, who last year had no one hit even thirty, champions?

Perhaps for the same reason that not since 1985 (when Steve Balboni hit thirty-six homers) has the World Series been won by a team with a player who hit thirty-five home runs for it during the season. *Sports Illustrated*'s Stephen Cannella notes that it has been twenty years since the major-league home run champion played on a World Series winner (Mike Schmidt, 1980 Phillies), and only twice in the 1990s did a league home run leader's team even reach the play-offs. Teams become champions not primarily by big blasts, but by doing the little things right. The Yankees do them, often with an assist from their bench coach.

Bob Klapisch of the Bergen (New Jersey) *Record* gives an example of Zimmer and Torre working in tandem. It was in 1998 in Oakland, in a 5–5 game going into the ninth. On a 3–2 pitch Tino Martinez walked. (In the 1996–99 span, the patient, selective Yankees pushed pitchers deeper into counts—more pitches per batter—than any other team. The Oakland As have noticed. Last year the overachieving As received more walks than any team since the

1949 Boston Red Sox.) Martinez is not fleet of foot, so as he reached first, Torre asked Zimmer if he would pinch-run for Martinez. Martinez was the Yankees' best late-inning hitter, but the next hitter was Chad Curtis, who often drives extra-base hits into the outfield gaps, so a runner faster than Martinez would have a much better chance of scoring the go-ahead run on a double. "Not now, not in a tie game," said Zimmer, thinking about the need for Martinez's bat in extra innings.

But then Curtis worked the count to 2–2, a good count for a fast runner to steal on. So Torre asked Zimmer, "How about now?" The Yankees had speedy Homer Bush on the bench. Zimmer said, "Not yet. Not at 2–2. But I might at 3–2." Having a full count with a fast runner on first would make Curtis a better hitter because the pitcher would throw a strike to avoid walking him and moving Martinez to second, where even he could score on a double or long single. The next pitch was ball three, and Torre told Zimmer, "All right, get Homer in there."

The threat that Bush might steal caused the pitcher to throw over to first twice to hold Bush close to the bag. Then, the pitcher's concentration perhaps frayed, he tried to avoid a walk by throwing Curtis a ball over the plate. But it was over the middle of the plate. Curtis hammered it for a two-run home run. The As scored two in the bottom of the ninth, so the Yankees had to win it in the tenth, but they were able to do that only because of the Torre-Zimmer nuances in the top of the ninth.

When Torre hired him, Zimmer told him to feel free to ignore his advice: "You're not going to hurt my feelings. I'm too old to have feelings." Torre spends a lot of time with Zimmer off the field, too. Other coaches carry stopwatches, timing batters from home to first, runners from first to second, pitchers getting the ball from the stretch position to the plate, catchers getting the ball to second. "Zimmer," says Torre, "has a clock in his head." Zimmer's secret? Says Torre, laconically, "It's just things that he senses." Zimmer has an old man's disapproval of many modern things. Guaranteed contracts, for one: insecurity is a splendid spur. And five-man pitching rotations: "If I was paying someone $9 million, I'd want him out there every four days." And he thinks the designated hitter takes the challenge out of managing: "If you want to relax, without having to think much about what's going on, you want to be in the American League."

But he knows baseball is in many ways better than ever. "When I was playing," he says, "after the last game of the season you put your glove and spikes on the shelf and the next time you touched them was when you went to spring training." Now baseball is an around-the-calendar job. He thinks there are four future Hall of Fame shortstops playing in the American League: the Mariners' Alex Rodriguez, the Red Sox's Nomar Garciaparra, the Indians' Omar Vizquel, and the Yankees' Derek Jeter (whose pregame ritual includes rubbing Zimmer's stomach and head and patting his hips).

Zimmer played with the man who opened the door for African-Americans—Jackie Robinson—and came to the big leagues five years before the Red Sox became the last team to field a black player. Today, when three of the five most common surnames in baseball are Martinez, Rodriguez, and Garcia, more than one-fifth of major leaguers are from foreign countries. A team of players from the Dominican Republic might beat an All-Star team formed from all the rest. It would if the Dominicans pitched Pedro Martinez, who last year had one of the finest years in major-league history.

Last year he started the All-Star game, facing six batters, fanning five. In the 23–4 season that he wrapped around that gem, his 2.07 earned run average was less than half the average for American League starters (5.03). With runners in scoring position, batters hit .204 against him. With runners in scoring position in late innings of close games, they batted .134. He had 313 strikeouts, while no other American Leaguer had more than 200. His 13.2 strikeouts per nine innings is the best by a starter *ever*. No pitcher ever matched his eight consecutive games with eleven or more strikeouts, and in seventeen postseason innings last year he allowed no runs and struck out twenty-three. Has Zimmer ever seen anything like that? As a matter of fact he has, in that fateful year 1978, when the Yankees' Ron Guidry was 25–3 with a 1.74 ERA. Guidry started the Bucky (Expletive Deleted) Dent game. Where is Guidry today? Right here, imparting wisdom to rookie pitchers. You see why they call it Legends Field?

Zimmer, who has seen it all, hasn't seen enough, because as the seasons roll by, greatness follows greatness and records fall. Certainly this year he is going to see a crackerjack (so to speak) season. If on opening day—make that Opening Day; capital letters for this civic festival, even if it occurs in Japan this year—Rey Ordoñez of the Mets plays his usual flawless game, he will extend to 101 his major-league record streak of consecutive errorless games. (Last year he broke Cal Ripken's record of 95 consecutive games.) Hall of Famer Rod Carew holds the record of fifteen All-Star game starts. Ripken, who is nine hits from 3,000, could start his sixteenth in Atlanta in July. If the Rangers' catcher Pudge Rodriguez starts the All-Star game, he will tie Johnny Bench's record of nine straight starts—and Pudge is just twenty-eight years old. If the Padres' Tony Gwynn hits .300 for the eighteenth time in eighteen seasons, he will trail only Ty Cobb's record twenty-three consecutive .300 seasons. Mariano Rivera, the reliever who gets outs numbers 25, 26, and 27 in Yankees wins, has not been scored on since last July—33⅔ regular season innings, plus another 12⅓ in postseason play.

The pain in Zimmer's knee permitting, he will see this season through, and don't bet against seeing number 53 at Legends Field next spring. He will be leaning not on a cane, which he thinks has no place on a baseball field, but on a fungo bat. Perfect.

April 3, 2000

John Adams, Popular at Last

From an early age John Adams longed to "shine" on the public stage, but "popularity was never my mistress, nor was I ever, or shall I ever be a popular man." Adams did not reckon on David McCullough.

McCullough does not write "pathographies." That neologism, coined by novelist Joyce Carol Oates, denotes a kind of biography that, of late, has been too much with us. Such biographies portray their subjects not just warts and all, but as mostly warts—the sum of their pathologies. It speaks well of McCullough that he abandoned writing a biography of Picasso because he could not stand to be so long in the company of such an unpleasant man.

McCullough's biographies are of Americans he thoroughly admires—sometimes, perhaps, a tad too thoroughly, as in his (deservedly) Pulitzer Prize–winning 1992 treatment of Harry Truman. It is said that the ideal biographer is a conscientious enemy of his subject, eager to depict defects and otherwise demystify the once mighty but scrupulous. However, McCullough is drawn to people he thinks insufficiently honored. His latest, on John Adams, today tops *The New York Times'* best-seller list.

The Founding Fathers are having a banner year in bookstores. Joseph Ellis's Pulitzer Prize–winning *Founding Brothers* is in its twenty-sixth week on *The New York Times'* list. Ellis's slender *The Passionate Sage* (1993) began the revival of Adams's reputation. But McCullough's 651 pages of *John Adams* really redress the neglect of the man who "made the Declaration happen when it did."

As a British spy said, Adams thought about "large subjects largely." (Entries in Adams's diary: "At home with my family. Thinking." "At home. Thinking.") He read broadly and deeply in political philosophy, and, like Machiavelli, he took man as he is, "a dangerous creature."

Adams proved that the category "constitutional revolutionary" is not an oxymoron: he was for independence early, even though it meant "to brave the storm in a skiff made of paper." Then he worked at taming the political furies with paper—the Constitution.

McCullough wonderfully tells the life of this brave, sometimes vain and ill-tempered man as, first and always, a love story, his marriage to Abigail being one of America's greatest collaborations. McCullough's gift for detail—the stormy seas, fleas, and bedbugs of eighteenth-century travel; the social graces of the period—makes his narrative sprightly. At a Paris dinner a lady said to Adams, "I never could understand how the first couple found out the art of lying together." McCullough writes:

Assisted by an interpreter, Adams replied that his family resembled the first couple both in name and in their frailties and that no doubt 'instinct' was the answer to her question. "For there was a physical quality in us resembling the power of electricity or of the magnet, by which when a pair approached within striking distance they flew together . . . like two objects in an electrical experiment."

The lady replied that, in any case, "it is a very happy shock."

McCullough's enthusiasms are infectious, and his book has added fuel to the latest outbreak here of monumentitis, an attempt to place near the Tidal Basin a monument to Adams "and his family." Well before McCullough wrote, this monument was a project of Representative Tim Roemer, an Indiana Democrat and history buff whose heart is in the right place but whose Adams monument would not be.

Although Adams' Braintree, Massachusetts, home is splendidly preserved, there is, inexcusably, no Boston monument to the author, in 1779, of the Massachusetts Constitution, the oldest operative written constitution in the English-speaking world. That is the proper place for a monument to him, not in Washington. Adams lived in Washington only briefly as the first occupant of the White House, during his single term as Washington's successor. The term began when the capital was in Philadelphia and proved to be, as Abigail had warned, "thorns without roses."

But if a monument in Washington is to honor Adams and "his family," it should include not just Abigail and son John Quincy but also the gifted great-grandson, Henry Adams. He was one of America's greatest historians; *The Education of Henry Adams* is America's greatest autobiography and among the greatest in world literature; his *Mont-Saint-Michel and Chartres* expressed his stained-glass mind's recoil from modernity as manifested in the Gilded Age.

Yes, let us have, staring balefully toward Capitol Hill, a statue of Henry Adams, author of the novel *Democracy,* creator of Senator Silas Ratcliffe: "The beauty of his work consisted in the skill with which he evaded questions of principle." No one ever said that about Henry Adams's great-grandfather.

June 24, 2001

James Madison, the Subtlest Founder

There is no monument to James Madison in Washington. There is a tall, austere monument to the tall (six-foot-two), austere man for whom the city is named, a man of Roman virtues and eloquent reticence. There is a Greek Revival memorial to Madison's boon companion, the tall (six-foot-two), elegant, eloquent Thomas Jefferson, who is to subsequent generations the most charismatic of the Founders. But there is no monument to the smallest (five-foot-four) but subtlest of the Founders, without whose mind Jefferson's Declaration and Washington's generalship could not have resulted in this republic.

So this Friday, as an insufficiently grateful nation gives scant notice to the 250th anniversary of Madison's birth, pause to consider what he wrought, such as the Constitution and the first ten amendments, called the Bill of Rights. Pretty good work, that, but not more impressive than Madison's thinking, which was the Constitution's necessary precursor. He became the Father of the Constitution only because he was the founder of modern democratic thought.

Before Madison produced his revolution in democratic theory, there had been a pessimistic consensus among political philosophers: if democracy were to be possible, it would be only in small societies akin to Pericles' Athens or Rousseau's Geneva—"face-to-face" societies sufficiently small and homogeneous to avoid the supposed threats to freedom—"factions." In turning this notion upside down—that is what a revolution does—Madison taught the world a new catechism of popular government:

What is the worst result of politics? Tyranny. To what form of tyranny is democracy prey? Tyranny of the majority. How can that be avoided? By preventing the existence of majorities that are homogenous, and therefore stable, durable, and potentially tyrannical. How can that be prevented? By *cultivating* factions, so that majorities will be unstable and short-lived coalitions of minorities. Cultivation of factions is a function of an "extensive" republic.

Which brings us to what can be called Madison's sociology of freedom, explained in his contributions to the most penetrating and influential newspaper columns ever penned: *The Federalist,* to which Alexander Hamilton and John Jay also contributed.

In *The Federalist,* no. 10 Madison wrote that "the extent" of the nation would help provide "a republican remedy for the diseases most incident to republican government." He said, "Extend the sphere, and you take in a greater variety of parties and interests; you make it less probable that a majority of the whole will have a common motive to invade the rights of other citizens." Because "the most common and durable source of factions" is "the various and unequal distribution of property," the "first object of government" is "protection of different and unequal faculties of acquiring property."

The maelstrom of interestedness that is characteristic of Madisonian democracy is often not a pretty spectacle. However, Madison knew better than to judge politics by esthetic standards. He saw reality steadily and saw it whole, and in *The Federalist* no. 51 he said that people could trace "through the whole system of human affairs" the "policy of supplying by opposite and rival interests, the defect of better motives."

Madison's 250th birthday comes at a melancholy moment. A banal and muddleheaded populism—call it McCainism—is fueling an assault this month on Madison's First Amendment freedoms of speech and association. In the name of political hygiene, advocates of "campaign finance reform" are waging war against the Madisonian pluralism of American politics.

Madisonian doctrine considers factions to be inevitable and potentially healthy and useful. McCainism stigmatizes factions as "special interests" whose rights to associate and speak politically for their interests should be strictly limited and closely regulated by government. Madison's First Amendment says, "Congress shall make no law . . . abridging the freedom of speech . . . or the right of the people . . . to petition the government for a redress of grievances." McCainism advocates speech rationing by the multiplication of government-imposed limits on the right of individuals and groups to spend money for the dissemination of political speech.

McCainism says money "taints" politics. Madisonian theory asks: What would politics consist of if it were "untainted" by the vigorous, unfettered participation of factions on whose interests government impinges? McCainism aims to crimp the activities of political parties by banning contributions of "soft money" (used for party building, not for particular candidates' campaigns or for expressly advocating the election or defeat of specific candidates).

The Founders did not anticipate the necessity of political parties. However, Madison quickly came to think that parties could moderate factions by channeling and disciplining them. Campaign-finance reformers are always unpleasantly surprised by the unintended consequences of their reforms. Were they to succeed in banning soft money, they would be startled by an utterly predictable result of the hydraulics of political money: money banned from the parties would flow instead to other—often wilder—factions.

Then the reformers, who cannot see a freedom without calling it a "loophole" that needs closing, would try to extend government regulation of political speech to the speech of those factions. Madison, wise about the untidiness of freedom, would respond by reminding the reformers of his reform: the First Amendment.

Madison undertook the thankless task of explaining the implications for democracy of the unflattering fact that men are not angels, and posterity has not thanked him with the sort of adulation bestowed upon Jefferson. However, in 1981 the Library of Congress, which began with Jefferson's donation of his library, needed a new building and named it after the most supple intellect among the Founders: the James Madison Memorial Building. Perhaps that should suffice as a monument to Madison. Or maybe his monument is our constitutional government, which proves the possibility of liberty under law in an extensive—a continental—republic.

March 19, 2001

Barry Goldwater, Cheerful Malcontent

Barry Goldwater not only represented Arizona politically, he reflected it physically. The geometry of his face—the planes of his strong jaw and high forehead—replicated the buttes and mesas of the Southwest, and the crow's-feet that crinkled the corners of his eyes seemed made by squinting into sunsets.

He was called "the cheerful malcontent." It takes a rare and fine temperament to wed that adjective with that noun. His emotional equipoise was undisturbed by the loss of forty-four states as a presidential nominee. Perhaps he sensed that he had won the future. We—27,178,188 of us—who voted for him in 1964 believe he won, it just took sixteen years to count the votes.

It is commonly said that the sixties began as a decade of dissent in 1964 with the Free Speech Movement in Sproul Plaza on the Berkeley campus. Wrong. It began in Chicago in 1960, when Arizona's junior senator strode to the podium of the Republican convention and growled, "Let's grow up, conservatives. If we want to take this party back, and I think some day we can. Let's get to work."

The residue of dissent on the left has long since gone to earth on campuses, there to nurse frustrations and fantasies. Dissent on the right rose to power.

Goldwater's candidacy captured his party for conservatives, sealing for them victory in an internecine struggle that had simmered and sometimes raged since 1912, when a former Republican president, Theodore Roosevelt, challenged an incumbent Republican president, William Howard Taft. T.R. represented what today are called "moderates," Taft the conservatives. Since 1964, no one opposed by the party's conservatives has been nominated for president.

Goldwater lacked reflectiveness but also lacked malice and pomposity. The man who said, "I haven't really got a first-class brain" enjoyed telling of the time he tested a speech on his wife, Peggy, and a few of her friends. They were unenthusiastic. "So I said, 'What the hell is the matter?' and Peggy said, 'Look, this is a sophisticated audience. They're not a lot of lamebrains like you, they don't spend their time looking at TV Westerns. You can't give them that corn.'"

He gave people his 100-proof opinions, which did not originate in focus groups and were not mediated by consultants. He casually told a columnist, "You know, I think we ought to sell TVA," and then shrugged off the howls of dismay: "You either take Goldwater or you leave him."

In 1964 an extraordinary grassroots movement, energized by *National Review* magazine, took him to heart and to the Republican nomination in San Francisco, where he scandalized polite society by saying that extremism in defense of liberty is no vice and moderation in pursuit of justice is no virtue. Hearing this, a journalist exclaimed in disbelief, "He's going to run as Goldwater!" What a concept.

He was one of the creative losers—William Jennings Bryan was another—of American politics. Which means that neither he nor Bryan was really a loser, having left larger marks on the nation than many a winner has done.

Thrice Bryan sought and lost the presidency as the Democrats' nominee but in the process gave voice—and what a voice it was—to a rising anxiety about private-sector power concentrated in entities of industrial capitalism: corporations, banks, trusts, and especially railroads, which held the prairies, from which Bryan sprang, in their thrall. He midwived the birth of the modern Democratic Party, creator of the regulatory state as a countervailing power.

Goldwater gave somewhat raspy voice to a growing anxiety about the incontinent growth of government and its pretensions. This westerner's platform could have been sung in four words: "Don't fence me in." Goldwater's message was as new as the booming cities of the Sunbelt and as old as the philosophy of the Founder who lived at Monticello. In 1980 Goldwater's message was given wings by Reagan's mellifluous voice, which had first been heard by a broad political audience in October 1964 in a nationally telecast speech for Goldwater.

In retirement Goldwater lived in Phoenix in a house built on a hill to which he, as a boy, had ridden on horseback to sleep under the stars. He never really left home.

In 1949, when he decided to give politics a fling, he wrote to his brother, "It ain't for life and it may be fun." It was to occupy a good portion of his life, but at no point did it absorb all of his life, and it was a lot of fun, for him and for we few, we happy few, who joined his parade.

May 31, 1998

Robert Kennedy, Conservative?

The abrupt extinguishing of any life before it reaches a natural apogee is an irresistible occasion for speculation about what might have been. When the life was that of a formidable politician with a large and passionate following, such speculation becomes an important civic act, clarifying the nation's trajectory and the possibilities that may have been closed by the person's death. For American liberals, the past thirty-five years seem haunted by sad hypotheses that linger in the air, like echoes of three silenced voices.

Thirty years ago the assassination of Robert F. Kennedy, then forty-two, occurred less than five years after the assassination of his forty-six-year-old brother, the president, and less than two months after the assassination of the thirty-nine-year-old Martin Luther King, Jr. By a total of just six bullets fired in Dallas, Memphis, and Los Angeles, all Americans should have been somewhat immunized against historicisms that disparage the importance of contingencies in deflecting the direction of the human story.

Now comes Michael Knox Beran to further trouble the equanimity of liberals and tantalize the imaginations of everyone else. In *The Last Patrician: Bobby Kennedy and the End of American Aristocracy*, Beran, a New York lawyer, argues that what Sirhan Sirhan ended the night Kennedy won the California primary was not a reinvigoration and restoration of Rooseveltian liberalism. Rather, he believes, the loss was larger than that because Kennedy was by then a more original force than liberals understood or can yet comfortably acknowledge. If Beran is correct, what was stopped in the kitchen of the Ambassador Hotel was Kennedy's unenthralled reassessment, tantamount to rejection, of what liberalism then was. Kennedy's criticism, as Beran tickles it from his words and deeds, looks like a close cousin of conservatism.

But is Beran correct? That is difficult to determine, because his argument is occasionally chaotic—which makes his book more stimulating than convincing. However, he is such a lively writer, and such a risk-taking thinker, that the sparks he promiscuously strikes from his literary flint are, cumulatively, illuminating. And what he says is clear enough that it will provoke liberals to accuse him of an intellectual train robbery. They have suffered enough, not least at the hands of the current president, and surely are in no mood to endure quietly a claim by a rival sect to their last saint.

"There has been no rush to tell the truth about Bobby Kennedy," Beran declares, because "in his guise as the last great liberal, Bobby is a valuable commodity, a rare example of a liberal icon whose appeal remains undiminished today." However, the truth as Beran tells it is not as dramatic as he suggests.

He says, in his occasionally overheated way, that Augustine was a pagan before he was a saint, that Paul was a Jew before becoming a revolutionary Christian, that Luther was a priest before becoming a Protestant, and Kennedy . . . well, really. Beran acknowledges that as late as the beginning of 1965, Kennedy was "a most conventional statesman." What happened in his last three years to justify comparisons with the radical transformations of Augustine, Paul, and Luther? Not all that much, as measured either in words or in deeds.

Granted, particularly in his last campaign, the 1968 California primary contest with Hubert Humphrey and Eugene McCarthy, something—evolving convictions or short-term calculations or both—caused him to seem the least liberal of the three. And he had already been criticizing the welfare state as a blunt weapon against poverty and a dehumanizing instrument of patrician condescension toward the lower orders. But he simultaneously found fault with President Lyndon B. Johnson for not requesting funds for this and that portion of the welfare state more generously.

Still, about a month before the California primary, a headline in *The New York Times* announced, "Kennedy: Meet the Conservative." And California's governor, Ronald Reagan, genially said, "I get the feeling I've been writing some of his speeches." In the turmoil of the overlapping foreign and domestic crises of the mid-sixties, Kennedy did seem to become more than a runner to whom other people's batons had been passed. But even then his brief excursions into new ideological country consisted only of suggestive remarks and tentative actions, not sustained analyses and settled programs.

Beran is at his considerable best in tracing Kennedy's path to what Beran thinks was his disillusionment with a liberalism that had become "a curiously regressive phenomenon: though it ostensibly celebrated the Forgotten Man, it in fact trivialized and diminished him." That course was charted by Joseph Kennedy's cold-blooded and long-headed assessment of the revived patrician class, into which he was determined to insert his sons.

Beran believes that in late-nineteenth-century America, aristocracy "meant weakness; it meant effeminacy; it meant Henry James." But the first half of the twentieth century brought the "risorgimento of the well-to-do." With the sort of muscular assertion that makes Beran's book grip any argumentative reader, he says, "The revolt of the blue bloods against their consignment to an historical oblivion of poetry and country houses began on the day when the young Teddy Roosevelt, bullied 'almost beyond endurance' by two boys whom he had neither the strength nor the skill to subdue, decided to take up boxing and learn how to fight back." It was a straight line to the "aristocracy of action" and football on the Hyannis lawn.

This was, Beran says, "one of the more astonishing comebacks in the history of American political power. Thrown out by Jefferson at the beginning of the nineteenth century, the patricians returned to power at the beginning of the twentieth, and the second time they did not make the mistake of alienating the common man." But they did not respect him. "Franklin Roosevelt," Beran insists, "perfected the technique of enveloping the lower classes in a warm rhetorical bath of patrician solicitude." And: "The two Roosevelts made a great show of trying to help the Common Man, the Forgotten Man, the Average Man, but they never made any pretension to being, like Jackson and Lincoln, like Eisenhower and Reagan, common men themselves."

Beran contends that Bobby Kennedy was different, that he had (to use a term that was in vogue when he was) authenticity. Having had two brothers, a sister, and a brother-in-law die violently, he acquired a genuine identification with suffering, particularly that of what has come to be called the underclass. If so, liberal thinkers were slow to recognize his aptitude for empathy. When in 1964 he moved to New York (he lived in the same building as Truman Capote; try to imagine their small talk in the elevator) to run for the Senate against the moderate Republican incumbent, Kenneth Keating, such liberal authenticators as Archibald MacLeish, Richard Hofstadter, Barbara Tuchman, and the NAACP supported Keating. Kennedy won but ran more than a million votes behind President Johnson in the election.

And six months later he was saying, regarding poverty policy, "We have gone as far as goodwill and even good legislation will take us." He soon plunged, against the advice of the prematurely sobered, including Daniel Patrick Moynihan, into saving Brooklyn's Bedford-Stuyvesant section. It was to be done by—how anachronistic the phrase now seems—"urban renewal." But it was to be renewal from the bottom up, renewal by "participation" that would produce a true "community," which in turn would heal the souls of ghetto residents.

Kennedy did solicit capital and expertise from the traditional patrician sources. The key to his respectful liberalism was to be reliance on the untapped skills and spirit of the community. The problem was that if tapping this supposed local reservoir of virtues—this social capital of talents—were all that renewal required, the ghetto would have been basically healthy and would not have needed much renewing.

Still, this was a time when Lewis Mumford was testifying to Congress that "democracy, in any active sense, begins and ends in communities small enough for their members to meet face to face." The historians J. G. A. Pocock, Bernard Bailyn, and Gordon Wood were emphasizing the extent to which classical understandings of citizenship influenced the American Founders. Furthermore, Beran argues that by passing through the furnace of family tragedy, Kennedy had become both Greek and Emersonian. After his brother was murdered, Jacqueline Kennedy gave him a copy of *The Greek Way* by Edith Hamilton, and that deepened his thinking about the meaning of civic life. Also, reading Emerson fueled his interest in what Beran calls "the problem of the underconfident soul"—the conditions that cripple the growth of confidence, a prerequisite for success in an urban setting and in a world increasingly ruled either by impersonal market forces or by faceless bureaucracies.

If Beran reads Kennedy's career correctly, what was at least latent in his thinking was indeed a harbinger of today's problematic emphasis on therapeutic government's supposed duty to deliver "values" as well as the mail. That this ambitious agenda for government is central to today's conservatism (liberalism's version stresses "self-esteem" as a progressive aim of public policy) is among the paradoxes of contemporary politics.

Twenty-eight years would pass between Kennedy's death and substantial reform of the welfare state. When reform came, it involved repeal of a sixty-one-year-old entitlement (Aid to Families with Dependent Children) and the largest devolution of power from the federal government to the states since the end of Reconstruction. The aims of some state experiments now under way include the revitalization of intermediary institutions between individuals and government and a quickening sense of urban community. Beran dismisses "community" as political "snake oil," stressing that families are the incubators of successful citizens. But Kennedy was right: families cannot be severed from connection with communities, with their schools and churches and jobs and with their drug dealers, liquor, stores and gangs.

Beran's slender meditation on Kennedy's truncated life has an unusually high ratio of provocations per page. Some readers will angrily throw it across the room. But they will retrieve it and continue reading, avidly.

A New York Times *book review, May 24, 1998*

The Nutritiousness
of Pat Moynihan

When this Congress ends, so will one of the broadest and deepest public careers in American history. Daniel Patrick Moynihan—participant in John Kennedy's New Frontier, member of Lyndon Johnson's White House staff, Richard Nixon's domestic policy adviser, Gerald Ford's ambassador to India and the United Nations, four-term senator—will walk from the Senate and political life, leaving both better for his having been in them and leaving all who observe them bereft of the rare example of a public intellectual's life lived well—adventurously, bravely, and leavened by wit.

The intellectual polarities of his life have been belief in government's ameliorative powers—and in William Butler Yeats's deflation of expectations for politics:

> *Parnell came down the road, he said to a cheering man:*
> *'Ireland shall get her freedom and you still break stone.'*

Having served four presidents, Moynihan wrote that he did not remember ever having heard at a Cabinet meeting "a serious discussion of political ideas—one concerned with how men, rather than markets, behave." Regarding the complexities of behavior, Moynihan has stressed the importance of ethnicity—the Balkans; the Bronx, come to that. Moynihan knew how wrong Marx was in asserting the lost saliency of preindustrial factors, such as ethnicity and religion, in the modern age.

His gift for decorous disruptions was apparent early, in 1965, when, during an audience with Pope Paul VI, at a time when the Church was reconsidering its doctrine of the collective guilt of Jews for Christ's crucifixion, Moynihan, a Catholic, shattered protocol by addressing the pope: "Holy Father, we hope you will not forget our friends the Jews." Later, an unsettled member of the audience, the bishop of Chicago, said, "We need a drink." Moynihan said, "If they're going to behave like a medieval court, they must expect us to take an opportunity to petition him."

During his U.N. service he decided that U.S. foreign policy elites were "decent people, utterly unprepared for their work" because "they had only one idea and that was wrong." It was that the bad behavior of other nations was usually a reaction to America's worse behavior. He has been a liberal traditionalist, keeper of Woodrow Wilson's crusade for lawful rather than normless dealings among nations.

"Everyone," says Moynihan the social scientist, "is entitled to his own opinion but not his own facts." When in 1993 the Clinton administration's Goals 2000 asserted that by 2000 America's high school graduation rate would be 90 percent and American students would lead the world in mathematics and science achievements, Moynihan acidly compared these goals to the old Soviet grain production quotas. Of the projected 2000 outcome, he said, "That will not happen." It didn't.

Moynihan has written much while occupying the dark and bloody ground where social science and policy making intersect. Knowing that the two institutions that shape individuals most are the family and the state, he knows that when the former weakens, the latter strengthens. And family structure is "the principal conduit of class structure." Hence Moynihan's interest in government measures to strengthen families.

Moynihan understands that incantations praising minimalist government are America's "civic religion, avowed but not constraining." Government grows because of the ineluctable bargaining process among interest groups that favor government outlays that benefit them. And government grows because knowledge does, and knowledge often grows because of government.

Knowledge, says Moynihan, is a form of capital, much of it formed by government investment in education. And knowledge begets government. He says: Behold California's Imperial Valley, unchanged since "the receding of the Ice Age." Only God can make an artichoke, but government—specifically, the Bureau of Reclamation—made the valley a cornucopia. Time was, hospitals' biggest expense was clean linen. Then came technologies—diagnostic, therapeutic, pharmacological—that improved health, increased costs, and expanded government.

"Not long ago," Moynihan has written, "it could be agreed that politics was the business of who gets what, when, where, how. It is now more than that. It has become a process that also deliberately seeks to effect such outcomes as who *thinks* what, who *acts* when, who *lives* where, who *feels* how." Moynihan appreciates the pertinence of political philosopher Michael Oakeshott's cautionary words: "To try to do something which is inherently impossible is always a corrupting enterprise."

The fourteen-year-old Moynihan was shining shoes on Central Park West when he heard about Pearl Harbor. In the subsequent six decades he has been more conversant with, and more involved in, more of the nation's transforming controversies than anyone else. Who will do what he has done for the intellectual nutritiousness of public life? The nation is not apt to see his like again, never having seen it before him.

September 17, 2000

Patrick O'Brian's Sense and Sensibility

ABOARD THE HMS *SURPRISE*—Which is where hundreds of thousands of contented readers are once again.

A freshening Atlantic breeze has the ship's sails billowing. The deck is pitching, but agreeably. Stephen Maturin is anticipating a naturalist's delights at the next landfall. And Jack Aubrey, in command, is looking for excitement and advancement in the Royal Navy in the doldrums after the Napoleonic Wars.

It is difficult to describe to the uninitiated the *frisson* that Patrick O'Brian's readers feel when another installment in his Aubrey-Maturin novels appears. Not until he was fifty did William F. Buckley read *Moby-Dick*. Then he told friends: To think I might have died without having read it. That is *exactly* how O'Brian's readers feel about their voyage that began with *Master and Commander* in 1969 and now has its twentieth installment in the publication of *Blue at the Mizzen*.

O'Brian, living in the south of France, once disparaged himself as a "derivative" writer because he followed "most doggedly recorded actions" and "log books, dispatches, letters, memoirs and contemporary reports." He said he would "soon have originality thrust upon him" because he was "running short of history." But he became the greatest historical novelist of his era, creating a credible world—ashore as well as afloat—into which we can step without stumbling over anachronisms.

The Aubrey-Maturin novels (splendidly read by Patrick Tull for Recorded Books of Prince Frederick, Maryland) rank with the sequential novels of Anthony Trollope and Anthony Powell. And O'Brian is a literary cousin of Jane Austen (two of whose brothers were naval officers during the Napoleonic Wars). That is, his are novels of manners as well as of war and adventure, the manners of male friendship and of military settings.

Novels of manners are apt to be, as O'Brian's are, suffused with the conservative sensibility, because manners are accretions of practices rather than creations of reason. O'Brian writes of something being "worse than inhuman—contrary to custom." When Maturin, the intellectual, inveighs against "subordination," Jack says, "Subordination is in the natural order: there is subordination in Heaven—Thrones and Dominions take precedence over Powers and Principalities, Archangels and ordinary foremast angels; and so it is in the Navy. You have come to the wrong shop for anarchy, brother."

Actually, Maturin, the ship's surgeon, is an intellectual who becomes intensely appreciative of the deeply conservative, almost liturgical, rhythms of life aboard ship. The parallels between ship and society are clear: "The seaman's moral law may seem strange to landsmen, even whimsical at times; but as we all know, pure reason is not enough, and illogical as their system may be, it does enable them to conduct these enormously complex machines from point to point, in spite of the elements."

An O'Brian glossary of naval terms (futtock shrouds, fid-plates) has been published, as has a "gastronomic companion" of recipes of dishes (roly-poly, spotted dog) described in the novels, and an atlas and geographical guide to the novels. There also is a CD of the music Aubrey and Maturin—both are amateur musicians; they met at a concert—play from time to time.

Some of O'Brian's verisimilitude is a chilling reminder of the harshness of life two centuries ago: Maturin uses badgers or even "whole orphans for dissection when they were in good supply toward the end of winter." Sharks swarm where slave ships sail, feasting on jettisoned bodies. A sailor says Easter Islanders "are not an ill-natured crew" although "they ate one another more than was quite right. It makes you uneasy to be passed a man's hand." When Jack asks what a particular Turkish potentate had been hunting in the marshes, he is told, "Jews."

O'Brian's Aubrey-Maturin volumes actually constitute a single 6,443-page novel, one that should have been on those lists of the greatest novels of the twentieth century. Some list compilers probably decided that O'Brian was only—only!—a historical novelist. But as Paul Cézanne said, "Monet is only an eye, but what an eye!" Besides, O'Brian's themes—courage, honor, gentlemanliness—are oceanic.

A few weeks ago O'Brian said he was making headway on volume twenty-one. But the thirty-one-year voyage is over. *Blue at the Mizzen* refers to the blue pennant that a full admiral flew from his ship's mizzenmast. In volume twenty Jack Aubrey gets his blue. O'Brian sailed on, tacking into the winds of age until his old companion Jack reached his goal.

O'Brian died the other day in his eighty-sixth year, leaving a solid legacy of craftsmanship and proof of Chesterton's axiom that great men take up great space even when gone.

January 13, 2000

Holden Caulfield Turns Fifty

If you really want to hear about it, the first thing you'll probably want to know is where I was born, and what my lousy childhood was like, and how my parents were occupied and all before they had me, and all that David Copperfield kind of crap, but I don't feel like going into it, if you want to know the truth.

With those words, sixteen-year-old Holden Caulfield slouched into American life fifty years ago this month. He was feeling entitled to feel quite sorry for himself. His feelings fascinated him, and his creator, J. D. Salinger, thought readers should sympathize with them. By now many millions of them have. Holden was a new social type, which subsequently has become familiar: the American as whiner.

Anyone who doubts that the supposedly bland 1950s were pregnant with the undoubtedly stimulating 1960s should reread *The Catcher in the Rye*. Published in July 1951, it has sold more than 60 million copies worldwide and is considered a "classic," a designation usually reserved in America for a variant of Coca-Cola.

This mildly picaresque novel—reviewers then considered it risqué—recounts a boy's flight from prep school to an eventful weekend in New York. Like Ulysses he was a wanderer. And that exhausts Holden's resemblance to anyone heroic.

He found almost everyone—except children; this was Holden's class solidarity—and everything unworthy of him. By declaring reality a terrible disappointment, he helped teach America's youth how to pout, a talent refined by a Hollywood Holden, James Dean, in 1955 in *Rebel Without a Cause*. But at least the adolescents in *The Blackboard Jungle* (1955) were interestingly menacing. Holden's emotional range matched that of Katharine Hepburn in a Broadway performance about which one critic wrote, "She ran the whole gamut of emotions from A to B."

Holden was forever denouncing "phonys" and "phoniness," which put him squarely on the side of the advanced thinkers. Such thinkers were then understood, by the folks at the serious quarterlies, as people "alienated" by the shallowness of American society but bravely seeking "authenticity" and rather relishing the pleasure of despair. However, Holden's rebellion was somewhat, shall we say, unfocused, as was Marlon Brando's in the 1954 movie *The Wild One*, in which a local girl asks Brando, the leader of a motorcycle gang, "What are you rebelling against?" and he replies, "Whadayah got?"

Fears about the invisible shackles of social pressure in an opinion-worshiping democracy are as old as Alexis de Tocqueville's *Democracy in America*, and F. Scott Fitzgerald's *The Great Gatsby* (1925) subtly explored how the integrity of personality is problematic. But in the 1950s, worry about "conformity" became the conformity of the intellectuals, in novels such as *The Man in the Gray Flannel Suit* (1955) and sociology treatises with such telling titles as *The Organization Man* (1956) and *The Lonely Crowd* (1950).

Six years after Holden appeared as the Sympathetic Adolescent Misfit, Leonard Bernstein set *Romeo and Juliet* to music among sentimentalized youth gangs in *West Side Story*. Clearly, Holden the nonconformist—this nonconformity novel was a main selection of the Book-of-the-Month Club; think about that—was part of the herd of independent minds, happily "alienated" together.

Comparisons of Holden and Huck Finn are inevitable. Huck comes off better. Huck understood freedom in the American way, as the absence of social restraints, and did something about it by lighting out for the territories. Holden merely pioneered a new fashion statement with his red hunting cap: "I swung the old peak round to the back." In case you were wondering about the pedigree of that bit of contemporary infantilism.

Huck was American literature's first character to speak naturally. Holden, too, was a literary pioneer, inventing inarticulateness as a token of adolescent "sincerity." ("I shook my head. I shake my head quite a lot. 'Boy!' I said. I also say 'Boy!' quite a lot. Partly because I have a lousy vocabulary." Partly.) Sixties adolescents, who were Holden's siblings, punctuated utterances, often of un-knowable meaning, with "you know"; today's lace their locutions with swarms of "like."

The social ambiguities and hormonal turbulence associated with coming of age and the theme of tragically "sensitive" youth—Holden is too exquis-itely sensitive for friendship—have been the stuff of much fiction, some of it fine. However, critics, confusing self-absorption with sensitivity, invest Holden's banal discomfiture's with more meaning than they can bear and Byronic dash.

Byron was at least a youth "mad, bad, and dangerous to know." Holden was—is—just as limited and tiresome as his vocabulary.

July 1, 2001

Sara Jane Olson and Terrorism Chic

Radiating ripples from September 11 washed over a Los Angeles courtroom last week when an American pleaded guilty to terrorism. She was charged with attempting, twenty-six years ago, to kill Los Angeles police officers by at-taching pipe bombs to two patrol cars—bombs stuffed with heavy nails. Im-mediately after pleading guilty, she stepped outside the courtroom and said she was innocent but could not get a fair trial in the climate created by Sep-tember 11. Many "progressives" consider her a martyr.

Although neither the prosecution nor the defense requested it, a judge will hold a hearing this week to consider what, if anything, he can or should do about her disavowal of her plea. Her lawyer says "she meant she is not guilty of holding the bombs and planting them, but that she is guilty of aid-ing and abetting." If her plea stands, she can be sentenced to at least five years in prison, and perhaps much longer. However, if there is a trial it would use-fully reacquaint Americans with a radicalism that is still romanticized by some people. Kathleen Soliah, a.k.a. Sara Jane Olson, was raised in southern Cali-fornia comfort but embraced northern California radicalism in the early 1970s. In 1974 she achieved Berkeley stardom with a speech in that city's Ho Chi Minh Park eulogizing six members of the Symbionese Liberation Army who had been killed two weeks earlier in a shoot-out with police in South Central Los Angeles. Prosecutors say Soliah was seeking revenge for that when she conspired to place the bombs. Fortunately, the bombers were incompetent. When one bomb fell off a patrol car without detonating, an examination of all patrol cars revealed another bomb.

Soon after this, Soliah disappeared. By the late 1970s she was living as

Olson in Saint Paul, Minnesota, where she married a doctor, raised three daughters and was an activist liberal Democrat. Then, at 8:21 A.M. on June 16, 1999, near her home, police and FBI agents, acting on a phone tip following an episode of *America's Most Wanted* on the SLA and the Los Angeles bombing attempts, surrounded her white minivan. Ten days later, kindred spirits in her upper-middle-class neighborhood had raised $1 million for her bail.

Since then parts of her life have been something of a lark. She has given many talks to sympathizers about what she considers her persecution at the hands of what she calls "the shadowy" FBI and others. She has hosted "consciousness-raising" groups in her Los Angeles home. She has raised money selling a playful cookbook, *Serving Time: America's Most Wanted Recipes.* Until a judge suggested that it might appear to be an attempt at intimidation, her Web site contained the home addresses of the two men who were in the patrol car when the bomb fell off. One is still with the LAPD. The other, unnerved by the attempted murder, left the force.

The SLA first made big news in 1973 by assassinating Oakland's superintendent of education, an African-American. The SLA thought, mistakenly, that he wanted students to be required to show identification, which the SLA considered fascist. The SLA became briefly prominent when it kidnapped Patty Hearst. She soon said, "I've changed—grown. I've become conscious." She became an SLA "soldier" called Tania. After a nineteen-month hunt, Tania was arrested. When booked by the San Francisco police, she listed her occupation as "urban guerrilla."

Bank robber, too. In her memoir, *Every Secret Thing,* Hearst says that Soliah and two other SLA members conducted the robbery of a Carmichael, California, bank, during which a customer was killed. Olson denies being there and denies being a member of the SLA. Prosecutors say they have ballistic evidence that spent shells and bullets found at the Carmichael bank and in the dead customer's body match those found at an SLA hideout Soliah frequently visited. Prosecutors also say they have tapes of Hearst speaking to her family about the SLA and Soliah.

Olson's cookbook chapter on breads features a picture of her clutching $20 bills. (Get it? "Bread.") Prosecutors say this is a joking allusion to the Carmichael robbery, in which $20 bills were stolen. The customer killed during the robbery was a mother of four.

Olson is unconvincing when she says September 11 is the reason she now fears a trial. Although she says she wants a fair trial that post–September 11 America cannot provide, her trial would have begun six months ago if she had not successfully sought six delays. She pleaded guilty as soon as the judge said prosecutors could begin presenting the forty thousand pieces of physical evidence, which they say includes a 9mm pistol and ski mask she used in the

Carmichael robbery, and a map of Los Angeles with her fingerprints on it found in a car bought with the proceeds from the robbery.

Prosecutors say they have handwriting evidence that Olson ordered fuses two weeks before the bombs were attached to the two patrol cars. The *Los Angeles Times* reports that before her guilty plea, many of her Saint Paul supporters "had become increasingly uneasy" about her stalling tactics. In a chilly appraisal of Olson in the *Los Angeles Times Magazine,* Twila Decker says the word "contrite" does not seem to be in Olson's vocabulary.

Some of Olson's supporters opened an office over a Los Angeles clothing store called Closet Liberal. However, since September 11, "radical chic"—the romanticizing of political extremism (only the left-wing sort, of course)—seems especially repulsive. Soliah-Olson's story has many twists but one constant: She has had two identities but only one character, that of a familiar species of radical. She is dishonest, unrepentant, self-satisfied, self-dramatizing, self-pitying—she fancies herself a victim—and contemptuous of her country.

She is pleased to say of herself, "I'm still the same person I was then. I don't have any regrets." People can rise on the stepping-stones of their dead selves to higher things, but Soliah-Olson prefers not to.

November 12, 2001

On January 18, 2002, Olson was sentenced to 20 years in prison. The day before she was arrested for murdering a church volunteer during the 1975 bank robbery in Carmichael, California. She pled not guilty.

Daniel Johnson, Without Regrets

When Daniel Johnson, who is now twenty-three, was transferring from Wake Forest University to the University of North Carolina, he went to Chapel Hill to find an apartment. When he called his parents in Hickory, North Carolina—his father, Wallace, is the pastor of the First Presbyterian Church; his mother, Sallie, teaches history at Hickory High School—they asked him if he had found one. He said yes, and oh, by the way, I've joined the navy. From his hospital bed in Walter Reed Army Medical Center, he says he has no regrets about that decision.

After graduation, the commitment he made when he joined the Navy ROTC at UNC took him to Newport, Rhode Island, for six months at the surface warfare officers' school. On New Year's Eve 1998, he reported to his ship, the USS *Blue Ridge,* the flagship of the admiral commanding the Seventh Fleet. It was a good assignment for a young man attracted to the navy by a desire for travel: the Seventh Fleet operates from the international dateline to the east coast of Africa.

In his eighth month on board, on August 23, 1999, he was the safety observer at the aft mooring station as Korean tugs pulled the *Blue Ridge* into position to leave the harbor at Pusan. A tug was reeling in the messenger line, a rope about an inch and a half in diameter that is attached to the hawser, the big rope—about eight inches in diameter—that bears the weight in tugging and mooring. The tug was moving away and reeling unusually fast. Too fast.

What happened next happened very fast. The leg of Seaman Steven Wright, 21, from Pine Bluff, Arkansas, became tangled in a loop of the messenger line, which, under extreme tension from the tug, dragged Wright across the deck and pulled his leg into a chock, an oval opening about a foot long and eight inches wide through which ropes pass. The tremendous torque from the tug could have pulled Wright through the chock, ripping him apart.

"This part is a little bit fuzzy to me," says Johnson about what he did. "I tried to free him up." The official "summary of action" recommending the Navy and Marine Corps Medal says:

> *Immediately, without hesitation, and in the face of known risk to his own life, Ensign Johnson ran to the assistance of the entrapped line handler who was in imminent peril of losing the lower part of his leg. . . . None of the other seven personnel on scene attempted any similar act or endangered themselves to such a degree to come to the entangled Sailor's aid.*

Wright's life was saved because his leg was not. He was freed when the rope severed his leg (and four fingers above the knuckles). But before that happened, as Johnson struggled to help Wright, the violently jerking line entangled both of Johnson's legs, dragged him to the chock, and severed both limbs below the knee. He also lost a finger.

Why did he act as he did? He says, matter-of-factly, that officers are trained to be responsible for the well-being of their men, and besides, that's the way his parents—they are at his bedside this day, having made the seven-hour drive from Hickory for another stay with their son—raised him. He would rather talk about the prostheses that will soon be fitted to the stumps of his legs.

"They say that if I want to I can run a marathon. The only thing that will limit me is myself." He is thinking of going to medical school.

There is no recondite lesson to be learned from this episode. A good young man from a good family and a good community did something admirable. But in an age that thinks the phrase "good news" is an oxymoron, it is well to be reminded that the American population is leavened by a lot of people like the slender, unprepossessing young man propped up in bed on his elbows, unself-conscious about the neatly bandaged stumps of his legs.

And it is well to be reminded that in routine training and routine operations the men and women of the armed services are at risk, and have chosen to be. And that the armed forces know a thing or two about teaching honor and responsibility.

Johnson thinks there is more of him leaving the navy than entered it. "I developed a lot of self-confidence when I was doing my job. It's been a great experience. No regrets."

October 21, 1999

Meg Greenfield's Potent Measuredness

Meg Greenfield said that one thing she especially liked about her friend Daniel Bell, the distinguished sociologist, was that he was so smart he made her feel like a dumb blonde. Well, Bell is very intelligent, but not that intelligent. Nobody is, ever was, or could be.

Meg, who died at sixty-eight last Thursday of cancer, was not a blonde. She was very intelligent and, what is different and more important, she was wise. In a Washington chock full of clever ninnies from tony schools, Meg was the real article: a public intellectual. Time was, New York was the magnet that drew such people. Meg's 1961 move from Manhattan to Washington markedly increased the thoughtfulness of the nation's capital.

Indeed, discerning cultural historians will one day recognize that Meg's move was a significant episode in the making of modern Washington, D.C., and in the diminution of New York City as the center of the nation's political gravity. It was not so long ago, as eras in the lives of nations are reckoned, that Washington was physically, and in its mental makeup, a small town. As John Kennedy famously said, it was a place of Southern efficiency and northern charm.

Some say that Kennedy's glitter was decisive in the transformation of Washington into a great world capital. Some of us think the crucial ingredient in the transformation was the Greenfield Effect. It was the result of her potent measuredness, which by its gentle tug affected everyone in her orbit by making them more judicious.

I first read Meg when I was a high school student in Champaign, Illinois, and a reader of *The Reporter* magazine, for which Meg wrote. The magazine was edited by Max Ascoli, a European émigré who infused his publication with his liberalism and his anticommunism. That was a mixture that made Truman-Acheson liberalism heroic in the years when the United States put in place the policy of containment of communism. However, that mixture doomed *The Reporter* when the Vietnam War caused many liberals to embrace anti-anticommunism and become ex-subscribers.

Anyway, I remember reading Meg's report on some controversial welfare policies adopted by the town of Newburgh, New York. I have not the foggiest memory of the details—I vaguely recall that conservatives were enthralled and liberals were appalled by what Newburgh was doing. Meg was neither, and her essay caused, for me, an epiphany: this is what it looks like when judicious intelligence is brought to bear on complex questions of policy.

I first met Meg in May 1972, when she was deputy editor of *The Washington Post*'s editorial page—she would become editor of that page in 1979—and I was a thirty-year-old staffer for a U.S. senator. We both were invited to Kenyon College in Gambier, Ohio, to participate in yet another conference on the uneasy relationship between politicians and the press. (How long ago was 1972, measured in political time? Among the conference participants was Robert Novak, who was then considered, not without reason, a liberal.) During the course of the conference Meg turned to the person seated next to her and inquired, "Who is that smart aleck at the end of the table?"

She was told that I was soon to leave the senator's staff to become Washington editor of William F. Buckley's *National Review*. Before we all returned to Washington, she suggested that I submit some columns to the *Post*. Back then, liberalism was ascendant, not to say hegemonic, in Washington, and the *Post*'s editorial page was considered, especially by conservatives, as liberalism's gold standard. It is a measure of Meg's personal generosity and intellectual self-confidence that she often went out of her way to help people, such as me, with whom her political disagreements were many and occasionally robust.

For years Meg and I and columnist Charles Krauthammer regularly met on Saturdays for lunch and conversation with a guest, usually someone newsworthy. We met at a greasy spoon on upper Connecticut Avenue in Washington. The name, Chevy Chase Lounge, was decidedly more upscale than the place. Meg's favorite moment—how she savored such scenes from Washington's version of the human comedy—was when a guest, a senator once considered a presidential prospect, asked the waitress if the tuna was fresh. The waitress said, sure it was. She meant the can had just been opened.

Our little group, which Meg called The Tong, would chow down on tuna melts, french fries, and other things not recommended by the American Heart Association. One guest, Surgeon General C. Everett Koop, the nation's doctor, washed down a cheeseburger and fries with two martinis, bless his heart.

In such informal settings, the caliber of Meg's mind was revealed in her sparkling conversation. Her witty, mordant, and splendidly vinegary observations were informed by broad and eclectic reading. She never allowed her spirit to become, as, say, Henry Adams's did, curdled by long exposure to Washington's tawdry and pompous aspects. Washington often illustrates the cyclical theory of history—the theory that life is not one damn thing after another but the same damn thing over and over. Meg read a lot of history and saw a lot made. She knew that much of what Washington, in its incorrigible self-importance, thinks is important isn't. She also knew what was important, and why.

She never succumbed to the temptation of cynicism, which is Washington's foremost form of self-indulgence. Over the years she gathered around her table many cheerful, public-spirited friends in politics: Hubert Humphrey, Scoop Jackson, Mo Udall, Howard Baker, Pat Moynihan, and many, many more. In 1979 she asked a friend whom he favored for the 1980 Republican nomination. Howard Baker, he said. "Yes," Meg said, "he's funny." By funny she meant amusing, not peculiar, and her emphasis on humor was profound.

A truly humorous person has a lively sense of irony, which involves discerning, and not being disconcerted by, life's inevitable incongruities. That is why a sense of humor is crucial to keeping political people, and a political community, on an even keel. Democratic politics involves the businesslike, and usually amicable, splitting of differences that many ardent people consider unsplittable. This process works best when lubricated by humor.

Meg's flavorful irony was first served up to *Newsweek* readers in the issue dated June 24, 1974, which announced that Meg—a summa cum laude graduate of Smith College, a Fulbright scholar at Cambridge in England—was that week starting a column for the magazine. The notice quoted Meg: "I'll be writing about Washington life, which, contrary to widespread belief, does not exclude everything human." The "everything," with its delicate hint of drollery, was a Greenfieldian touch that readers would come to savor.

By June 1974 two years had passed since the Watergate break-in, two years of stonewalling that one of Richard Nixon's people called the "limited-hangout route." By June 1974 the transcripts of the Nixon tapes had been published. His presidency had about seven weeks remaining as Meg's first column, entitled "The Unlimited-Sanctimony Route," began: "It's not as if nobody told us. Shakespeare told us and Dickens told us and Mark Twain and Will Rogers and Sinclair Lewis told us." They told us to beware of people who are both self-righteous and unforgiving of others—"The brief and gruesome career of Mr. Agnew in national politics tells the story." Nixonians have filled the air with "moral bugle music" while making no connection between their own bad behavior and their condemnation of other, "lesser" people.

Meg, marveling at "the moral turnaround time" of Washington miscreants, imagined this bulletin: " 'St. Augustine will be autographing copies of his new book, *The Confessions,* at the Shoreham Hotel between 3 and 5 tomorrow; he also will be a guest on the *Today* show.'" The Nixon and Clinton administrations were the bookends of Meg's *Newsweek* years. She deserved better subjects, but *Newsweek* readers deserved her as a guide through the wreckage.

It is not easy anywhere, and least of all in Washington, to be, as Meg was, likable and logical. Intellectual rigor annoys people because it interferes with the pleasure they derive from allowing their wishes to be the fathers of their thoughts. That failing is common to humankind but is especially prevalent in a company town where the company's business is politics. In places where people make physical things—shoes, steel, bridges—the reality principle exerts some discipline: get things wrong, the shoes pinch, the steel buckles, the bridge falls down. There is rarely such swift, unambiguous refutation of political errors—foolish policies, dumb laws.

Which is why Meg should have been given Secret Service protection simply as testimony to her importance as Washington's one-woman early-warning system for detecting nonsense. Would that there were adequate protection against the disease that took Meg's life.

Longtime readers of *Newsweek's* back page know the toll that cancer has taken on journalism. Meg came to this page to replace her friend Stewart Alsop after he lost his long fight with cancer. She, like him, wrote right through the torments of the disease, which include treatments for it. Never, not once, was there evidence of diminished energy or flagging spirit.

For those of us who had, for too short a span, the pleasure—no, the delight—of her company, Washington will never again be quite as fun. *Newsweek* readers will feel that they have lost a friend who regularly dropped in for a deceptively casual chat that dispersed the fog that often envelops events. And all across the broad republic there are people who never read Meg but who nevertheless are beneficiaries of the wisdom she patiently, wryly, and on rare occasions indignantly injected into the nation's conversation.

Henry Adams said that fine teachers attain a kind of immortality because it is impossible to know when, or if, their influence stops. By her example, Meg taught the craft of political writing to many journalists, and she reassured millions of readers that tough-mindedness and civility are not incompatible in the nation's capital. Her influence radiates.

May 24, 1999

The Columnist at Sixty

When Harry Wright, star of the Cincinnati Red Stockings and then the Boston Red Stockings, pioneers of professional baseball, died in 1895, a floral arrangement at his funeral spelled out "Safe at Home." That delightful story would be more so, but for Wright's age. He was sixty.

Looking on the bright side, as conservatives are, for sound philosophic reasons, disinclined to do, I take comfort, of sorts, from the fact that by turning sixty I am freed from the fear of dying young. Unless sixty no longer counts as old. If so, that is, like blessings generally, a mixed one, because it extends one's eligibility for premature death. Life is like that, always supplying thorns with the roses.

Mrs. Alexander Hamilton, final survivor of the Founders' circle, died in Washington in 1854 in her ninety-seventh year. She had lived the entire life of the Republic. So had the slave interviewed in Virginia during the 1862 Peninsula Campaign, who recalled hearing cannonading at the Battle of Yorktown eighty-one years earlier. Someone who today is sixty has lived 26.6 percent of the nation's life. Being born May 4, 1941, I arrived in a year that ended badly, but I arrived eleven days before the beginning of Joe DiMaggio's fifty-six-game hitting streak. Life supplies roses amid the thorns.

Perhaps it is just the result of immersion in journalism, which is the opposite of literature, which is writing that deserves to be read twice. Perhaps it is a consequence of living in an obsessively political city, where last week's world-shaking events are forgotten, and epochal figures are forever rising without a trace. For whatever reason, being sixty in Washington sometimes feels like having had one year's experience sixty times.

However, age can confer a certain calm about the passing circus, a preference for understatement and for people with low emotional metabolisms. When a maid serving Arthur Wellesley (later the Duke of Wellington) drowned herself because of her unrequited love for a gardener, Wellesley expressed the hope that the remainder of the maids "will put up with the misfortunes of this world, & not destroy themselves." That's the spirit.

So is this. Mussolini, trying to impress a visitor, pointed to a buzzer on his desk and boasted, "All I have to do is press it and my army, navy, and air force go on instant alert." The visitor, Anthony Eden, supposedly murmured, "Awfully inconvenient if you just want a sandwich."

Three determinative events in this sixty-year-old's life were clustered in a few years about a third of the way here, between 1960 and 1964. Although the son of a professor of philosophy, until the summer before my junior year in college most of my reading was of the backs of baseball bubble gum cards.

Then I read Albert Camus's novel *The Stranger.* Since then, I have agreed with Logan Pearsall Smith: "People say that life is the thing, but I prefer reading."

Camus was catalytic because, back then, any undergraduate worth his weight in espresso and Gauloise cigarettes thought French intellectuals had hung the moon. The creed *du jour* was existentialism, the belief that life is absurd, so philosophy should be, too. A practicing existentialist marinated himself in foreign movies—make that *films*—ostensibly because they had the finest flavors of anomie, alienation, and despair but actually to savor, again and again, the sight of Jean Seberg in bed in *Breathless.*

In 1962 I saw the Berlin Wall, sufficient instruction in the stakes of politics. In 1964, having cast my first presidential vote, for Barry Goldwater, I heard election-night commentators happily declare the future irrelevance of conservatism, and I and many kindred spirits said, We'll just see about that. On May 31, 1967, this letter came to me at Princeton's graduate college:

Dear Mr. Will:

Just a line of thanks for your letter of May 18. Please know that I very much appreciate your good offer of help. My goal, however, is to solve the problems of California, and at the moment, this looks like a lifetime job.

Sincerely,
Ronald Reagan, Governor.

What turns out to be a lifetime job—very steady work—is conservatism's task of keeping government where it belongs, which is on a short constitutional leash, and politics in its place, which is at the margins of life. It has taken me sixty years to identify the three keys to a happy life: a flourishing family, hearty friends, and a strong bullpen. Actually, in my case, there is a fourth: the hope for Cubs baseball in late October. I shall be sixty-seven on the centennial of the Cubs' last World Series victory. Something to live for.

May 3, 2001

Frederick L. Will's Angle of Repose

NEWPORT BEACH, CALIFORNIA—Frederick L. Will, my father, recently died here. He was, as used to be said, well stricken in years, nearly eighty-nine of them, and suffered many of the afflictions that often accumulate in very elderly bodies. He was, it is safe to say, not sorry when the Dark Angel tapped him on his shoulder and said it was time to go.

In earlier ages, much was made of *ars moriendi,* the art of dying, of having "a good death." Nowadays, science often overwhelms that art. When death approaches the elderly on measured tread, they are apt to become tangled in the toils of modern medicine. Then the dying are pushed to the side of the stage as medicine becomes the leading actor in the drama. That is no condition to be in when the "summons comes to join the innumerable caravan."

Medicine is marvelous at helping fend off infections and diseases in bodies that, absent them, would thrive. However, medicine becomes problematic when it resists not the body's afflictions but the body itself—when the body is no longer impelled by an essential vitality and instead tries to subside.

In this downward turn of life's trajectory, the mind and body can be mysteriously complicit. Fred's life began to ebb when his wife, who survives him, disappeared into dementia, like a photograph left exposed to the sunlight. Fred could no longer bear to listen to music because it deepened his sadness, and he could no longer thrive.

Fred was a son of the middle border, and of a Lutheran minister who graduated from Gettysburg Seminary about forty years after the great battle. The minister served many marginal churches in Ohio, Pennsylvania, and Maryland, including one in Boonesboro, Maryland, hard by Sharpsburg, the hamlet on Antietam Creek that Robert E. Lee visited on September 17, 1862.

Lee and Luther were lasting influences. Fred's lifelong dignity and reticence, which did not desert him when he was dying, reflected Lee's model of American gentlemanliness. Fred's philosophic interest was quickened by witnessing pastor Will struggle to reconcile the ideas of grace and free will. After earning a Cornell Ph.D., Fred taught philosophy at the University of Illinois for thirty-nine years.

The U. of I. opened in Champaign-Urbana in 1868, six years after the federal government, during the presidency of a son of downstate Illinois, produced the Land Grant College Act, which began democratizing access to higher education. The U. of I. opened with three professors (not quite enough) and fifty students (about right).

Early in Fred's career he labored for nearly a decade completing a manuscript of a book that reached conclusions broadly congruent with the prevailing consensus among philosophers about his special interest, the problem of induction. Then one day, while standing at a blackboard, there suddenly came to his mind an episode from a Thackeray novel, which, after he reflected about it, suggested that he and the conventional wisdom since Hume were mistaken about induction. So he set aside the manuscript that was the fruit of his career until then, and began again. That unsung example of intellectual integrity is among Fred's finest works.

In Fred's last years he published a collection of his philosophic essays, and he died shortly after receiving, but when he was too ill to savor, the *Festschrift* published in his honor by some former students and colleagues. The essays and the essayists are radiating ripples from Fred's scholarship.

As he lay dying, we continued our lifelong playfulness of quizzing each other. What, I asked, was Special Order 191? The man who was a boy in Boonesboro remembered Lee's lost order that a Union soldier, on the way to Antietam, found wrapped around three cigars. One night when the nurse in the intensive care unit dimmed the lights, I asked, "Who said, 'The lamps are going out all over Europe; we shall not see them lit again in our lifetime'?" Barely audible through an oxygen mask, he said, "Easy. Lord Grey." Illness never dimmed Fred.

Joseph Epstein, the essayist, says that one of death's drawbacks is that it wipes out so much reading. Fred several times read Wallace Stegner's magnificent novel *Angle of Repose,* the protagonist of which is a retired professor. The title is a technical phrase used by mining engineers to describe the angle at which sliding dirt and debris come to rest. Stegner's protagonist, seeing the irresistible metaphor, calls the phrase "too good for dirt" and "descriptive of human as well as detrital rest."

Fred left life as he lived it, nobly composed, having reached his angle of repose.

April 2, 1998

Index